CONNECTING PEOPLE TO WORK:

WORKFORCE INTERMEDIARIES AND

SECTOR STRATEGIES

CONNECTING PEOPLE TO WORK:

WORKFORCE INTERMEDIARIES AND
SECTOR STRATEGIES

Edited by Maureen Conway and Robert P. Giloth

published by

THE AMERICAN ASSEMBLY
COLUMBIA UNIVERSITY

Sector-based workforce development is a strategy rooted in the context of regional economies and specific industries or occupational clusters within specific economies that is designed to improve the employment experience in ways that benefit both workers and employers. Its implementation requires a set of critical partners—workforce intermediaries, which bridge the needs of employers and workers. This book sets out how sector-based workforce development has evolved over thirty years, and while it focuses primarily on the significant work of the past ten years, it also charts where the field needs to go in the decades ahead.

This robust collection will inform public and private investments and policy decisions in the future and provide practitioners, policy makers, investors, researchers, as well as lay readers with thought-provoking readings about sector-based workforce development--its challenges, opportunities, and future directions.

Typeset in Adobe Garamond.

Designed by Mark Swindle

Printed by Createspace, an Amazon.com company.

Cover photographs: Rick Smith of Rick's Photography.

Contents

Acknowledgments

This book rests on the contributions of a terrific set of authors, and we are extremely grateful to them not only for their individual contributions but also for their thoughtful comments on other chapters and their collegial help in shaping the book as a whole. We are tremendously grateful to the Annie E. Casey Foundation for its generous support and Arin Gencer, Ryan Chao, Keri Libby, Sheryl Lewis, and Allison Gerber for their comments. We would also like to thank three anonymous reviewers for their comments and guidance.

We are grateful to Maya Goodwin of the Aspen Institute, who was invaluable in keeping track of the flow of chapters and coordinating communications among the authors and editors. Colleen Cunningham and Sinin Young, also of Aspen, provided patient support in managing the financial resources that supported this effort. We thank Tom Waldron of The Hatcher Group for his fine editorial work and good-natured guidance in working with the authors and moving the book forward. Thanks also to David Mortimer and Mark Leneker of The American Assembly who saw the book through the design, copy editing, and production process.

Finally, we would like to thank the broad field of local leaders of sector initiatives and workforce intermediaries—too many to name—whose work has been the source of learning that informs many of the chapters in this volume and continues to be an important means of connecting people to work. We hope this book offers them useful information, ideas, and inspiration as they continue to find innovative ways to help the economically struggling individuals they work with every day.

Maureen Conway and Robert P. Giloth

Dedication

This book is dedicated to four people who have made outstanding contributions to this field of practice.

Jack Litzenberg, who served as senior program officer at the Charles Stewart Mott Foundation for more than twenty years, was an early investor in sector strategies, supporting efforts to define the practice, build a community of field leaders, advance the knowledge and research base on which the field rests, and educate policy makers about the important contributions of sector initiatives. Jack died shortly before the publication of this book, but much of the work of this field would have not been possible without his vision, passion and consistent support of the many leaders in this field and their work.

Cindy Marano, who died in 2005, was the founding director of the National Network of Sector Partners (NNSP). Through national conferences, regional convenings, workshops, and tireless travel, visiting leaders of local sector initiatives, she built community within the field and brought the approach to national prominence.

Eric Parker, before his death in 2007, was the executive director of the Wisconsin Regional Training Partnership (WRTP), an important national model in this field, and also served as co-chair of the NNSP board. Eric's programmatic innovations and leadership in bringing a diverse set of stakeholders together to support the work of the WRTP have been an inspiration.

Bruce Herman played a number of important roles in the field before his death in 2012, including working as president of the Garment Industry Development Corporation in New York City, leading the AFL-CIO's Working for America Institute, heading the National Employment Law Project, and serving as deputy labor commissioner for workforce development for the state of New York. In all of these roles Bruce championed the principles of sector strategies, worked to strengthen workforce intermediaries, and promoted greater opportunity for the economically vulnerable.

Jack, Cindy, Eric, and Bruce brought enormous talent to their work and provided inspiration to us and many others. We gratefully dedicate this volume to them in honor of their important contributions to the critical task of connecting struggling Americans to work and brighter futures.

1

Introduction

Maureen Conway and Robert P. Giloth

This book is about sector-based workforce development over the past thirty years, with special attention to the progress made during the past ten. Indeed, the past decade has been a period of significant growth for the field of sector-based or sectoral workforce development, with a much greater number and variety of organizations engaged in the work. The sector-based approach to workforce development was the central point of conversation at the American Assembly, held in 2003, and the focus of the book that resulted from the convening, *Workforce Intermediaries for the Twenty-first Century*.[1] This volume expands on that earlier work and focuses on how the field of sectoral workforce development has developed since that time.

It is an important time to reflect on sector-based workforce development because of the policy and economic challenges facing the country, the field's past achievements, and the renewed efforts to improve the quality of jobs in low-wage sectors, such as home health care, retail, and food service. At the same time, community colleges and postsecondary credentials are gaining attention in public and philanthropic spheres in response to the increasing focus on "middle-skill" jobs and the concerns expressed among employers about the scarcity of appropriately skilled workers. In this environment, in which both the quality of skills that workers bring to the job and the likelihood that a job will support a middle-class livelihood are in doubt, the approaches pioneered by sector initiatives grow in importance.

The slow economic recovery has seen the loss of many skilled jobs, however, and an increase in the number of low-wage jobs, with persistently high rates of unemployment and a decline in overall labor-force participation. At the same time, international comparisons of adult skill levels indicate that the U.S. workforce has less of a competitive edge than it did a generation ago. Political stalemate, the business community's reluctance to invest in the human capital of all workers and especially low-skilled workers, and declining household incomes have led to scarce resources for skill development, as business, government (at all levels), and workers themselves are unable or unwilling to invest in relevant education and skills training. These currents make this an especially important time to reflect on the strengths of the sector approach as we think about ways to address these big challenges.

This introductory chapter provides background for a rich array of chapters exploring different aspects of sector-based workforce development, all aimed at charting what we have learned and where the field should be going in the decades ahead. The authors include academics and practitioners, providing multiple perspectives on the sector field. In this introductory chapter we briefly define sector-based workforce development and its relationship with workforce intermediaries and discuss some of the key features of the work. We then underscore the challenges for the sector workforce field going forward and provide a roadmap of the book's sections and chapters. Our concluding chapter summarizes the themes articulated in the chapters and underscores the challenges and opportunities ahead for the field of sector-based workforce development.

Our goal is to engage workforce practitioners, policy makers, investors, and researchers in a conversation about the sector field—its opportunities, challenges, and future directions.

What Is Sector-Based Workforce Development?

Sector-based workforce development — that is, organizing the training of workers in the context of an industry sector—is not a new concept. Its direct antecedents go back a century or more. The basic idea is the following: If policies and programs focus on a group of firms with similar products, processes, occupations, and locations, it will be easier and more efficient to get them organized to identify and address common business and employment needs. A similar logic has been applied to certain types of economic development, specifically the concept of "cluster development," made famous by Michael Porter, as well as to craft unions and their apprenticeship system, which harks back to the Middle Ages.

In this volume, however, we are most interested in the application of these concepts to meeting the needs of the poor and economically disadvantaged in

today's America. The vision of sectoral employment, with a focus on building
nomic opportunity, adopted the name "sector" in the 1990s after experimentar...
in the 1980s seemed to show promising results. The approach represented a depar-
ture in the thinking prevalent at the time about how to help the poor and minor-
ity communities connect to the workplace and succeed. Sector strategies recognize
the dynamic nature of regional economies and labor markets and seek to shape
change within that context. Recognizing that industries change in ways that shape
the quantity and quality of jobs available and influence how those jobs might or
might not be accessed by particular populations, sector initiatives develop a dy-
namic relationship with their targeted industry or occupational cluster and seek
to respond to expressed needs as well as to shape workforce opportunities in the
future. In developing relationships, expertise, and standing with public, private,
and philanthropic entities, sector initiatives look to expand opportunities for their
low-income constituency.

In an early description of the sector employment approach by the Aspen
Institute (supported by the Ford and Mott Foundations), sector strategies were
explicitly focused on poverty alleviation and connecting low-income populations
with better employment opportunities. Indeed, this defining publication was en-
titled *Jobs and the Urban Poor*, and it defined sector strategies as follows:

A sectoral initiative represents a distinct employment model that:

- Targets a particular occupation within an industry;

- Intervenes by becoming a valued actor in the industry that employs
  that occupation;

- Exists for the primary purpose of assisting low-income people to obtain
  decent employment; and

- Creates, over time, systemic change within that occupation's labor market. [2]

A number of alternative definitions have been offered since this publication
and have provided refinement or different emphasis. For example, it has been noted
that some targeted occupations are not contained within an industry, but across
multiple industries. In addition, some definitions describe community benefit as an
important goal, or focus less on benefiting low-income constituencies specifically.
In addition, the "systemic change" language has caused confusion, striking some as
overly ambitious or grandiose. Specific examples with descriptions of observed prac-
tices, however, have helped to clarify this element of the definition and make the
practice more accessible. Thus, while some descriptive language may vary, the gen-
eral idea of a sector strategy—focused on creating opportunity for workers, support-
ing strong industries, and addressing systemic issues—remains relatively constant.

Just as the language of the definition varies, so too do the specific practices of sector initiatives, which work within their industry and regional economic contexts. While these variations in implementation are part of the strength of the approach, the range of tactics and the variety of institutions that may be involved in an initiative make drawing a tight boundary around the field of sectoral employment development challenging. And this challenge has made it difficult to spread the sector approach consistently. One challenge is the breadth of the word "sector." Sector can mean manufacturing broadly or screw-machine businesses, food production or candy manufacturing in particular. Health care encompasses acute care, long-term care, ambulatory care, and behavioral health; a sector initiative may take a narrow occupational focus, working only with home health aides, for example, or working broadly with an institution and focusing on a range of occupations, ranging from patient care positions to dietary and administrative positions. In addition, the notion of a targeted sector can change. An initiative may begin by focusing on a narrow set of occupations or a small slice of an industry but expand over time as its depth of experience and relationships grows.

Sector initiatives have used a variety of criteria to choose an industry focus or set of occupations. Some have targeted industries that are characterized by low-quality jobs, such as home health care, home cleaning services, and restaurant work, often with a focus on how to improve job quality in these industries in which large numbers of the initiative's low-income constituency already work. More commonly, sectoral workforce development has targeted higher-wage industries, such as manufacturing, information technology, and the acute care segment of health care, and has worked to develop education programs and pathways that correspond to the needs of those industries and connect low-income populations to new job opportunities.

A second challenge is defining the set of activities that constitute a particular sector strategy. As noted above, some sort of human-capital development component is always a part of the work, but a sector strategy goes beyond training and placement and may include such activities as industry research, policy advocacy, business advising, case management and counseling, professional network development, and other work. Often a sector initiative may involve a number of different organizations, including public agencies, private nonprofits, educational institutions, industry associations, labor unions, and philanthropic entities, and these organizations may play different roles in different sector initiatives.

A related challenge is developing a systemic vision of the approach and attempting to create "systems change" to expand the scale of sector-focused work. We offer a framework of systems change below and identify the different systems that may be relevant. However, it is difficult to describe the activities that may be undertaken as part of systems change; it is also a challenge to evaluate the outcomes of such work in ways that are generally recognized by policy makers and others.

Sector Strategies and Workforce Intermediaries

The sectoral approach to workforce development is not a prescribed set of practices; rather, it is a strategy, a set of functions, and a guiding vision to achieve defined results. Its implementation requires an organizational home, resources, and dedicated staff, as well as a set of critical partners. This organizational home represents what we call a workforce intermediary, which can bridge the needs of employers and workers and broker resources and services to improve how workers and employers come together in their regional labor markets. This intermediary or partnership needs to build credibility with a range of stakeholders, most prominently employers, workers, job seekers, and the public and private investors that support the strategy.

The workforce intermediary need not perform all the specific tasks required of the strategy. For example, the workforce intermediary may or may not provide training and education services, it may or may not offer career counseling and case management, it may or may not conduct its own industry research. Given, however, that intermediaries need to build credibility with the three primary entities mentioned above, the workforce intermediary likely plays some role with all of these services, and often plays a lead role in at least one. Importantly, the workforce intermediary often articulates the strategy's goals, identifies a set of metrics to measure progress, and facilitates communication with partners and other stakeholders about progress and challenges.

A variety of institutions, including public agencies, nonprofits, educational organizations, or union apprenticeships, can organize the role of a workforce intermediary and serve as its home base. Factors that can influence how such an intermediary begins and operates include the particular industry sector that is targeted, the scope and breadth of regional civic organizations, the needs of the targeted worker population, and local leadership.

We acknowledge at the outset that there are other terms used to describe workforce intermediaries, including "workforce partnership," "industry partnership," and "sector-based partnership." Each calls slightly more attention to an aspect or dimension of the workforce intermediary role and practice. We also acknowledge that there is disagreement in the field about these definitions. For example, workforce intermediaries are part of a larger family of labor market intermediaries that includes staffing and professional organizations, nonprofits, educational entities, and employer associations. More broadly, the term "intermediary" is used in many fields, including workforce, to describe organizations that aggregate capital for purposes of investment and even systemic change.

Who Is Served by a Sector Strategy?

In determining who benefits from a sector strategy, there are two key questions to consider. The first is the degree to which the strategy is meant to serve the needs of employers or the needs of workers. The second is the degree to which the strategy strives to serve "harder-to-employ" populations.

With the first question, while helping low-income, low-skilled workers move ahead in the labor market was a founding principle of sector strategies, there was also a clear expectation that sector strategies would produce positive results for business and contribute to economic development goals. The sectoral approach explicitly linked the goals of economic development and business competitiveness with the mission of economic enfranchisement and creating access to opportunity for economically marginalized groups. So the idea of a sector strategy is that one can work toward economic development and economic inclusion at the same time.

In practice, however, the near-term interests of specific business owners and individual workers may not be aligned, and the degree to which an approach emphasizes the interests of business or workers has varied across initiatives. A variety of phrases are used to emphasize to a greater or lesser degree the idea that the approach makes sense from a business perspective. The phrases "demand-driven" and "dual-customer" emphasize the idea that the strategy should be designed around the needs of business customers or meet the needs of business customers as well as workers. To some degree, these are truly semantic differences, and indeed the same organization may use different language depending on the audience.

The best description of the spirit of the sector approach may be the customer-constituent frame. A sector workforce strategy is a people-focused strategy, generally designed to connect workers and job seekers to improved opportunities. The most commonly used measures of success assess the strategy's achievements in connecting workers to jobs. The strategy is meant to be well aligned with industry dynamics, but its true constituency is the worker or would-be worker. Supporting the success of industry is necessary for workers' employment and livelihood, so companies are the critical customers, but companies are truly good customers when their business success leads to the success of their employees. And just as companies often focus on those customers who are most profitable, sector initiatives focus on those companies that offer their worker constituency the greatest chance of success. A partnership that hews in practice to this frame of thought, regardless of the language they use to describe it, would, in effect, serve as a sector approach to workforce development.

The more difficult question: Which workers benefit? This question is not unrelated to the question of how much emphasis the strategy puts on serving business. To satisfy business customers, sector strategies are often pushed to work with

more job-ready workers or job seekers. On the other hand, public and philanthropic investors in sector strategies often tie their resources to assisting populations with employment barriers, such as the long-term unemployed, out-of-school
youth, low-income single mothers, and people who have been incarcerated. Sector
initiatives with multiple funding sources may be able to balance a funder-driven
push to choose one candidate over another based on criteria unrelated to the industry, focusing on the needs of the industry while also serving those who truly
need and can benefit from the service. And yet, when good job opportunities are
few, competition for jobs is fierce, and resources are limited, helping individuals
with barriers to employment develop sufficient skills to compete for high-wage
jobs becomes ever more challenging, and choices must be made about how many
barriers an individual sectoral training initiative can productively address. The language of "dual-customer," "demand-driven," and "win-win" solutions should not
lead one to overlook or underestimate the truly daunting challenge faced by many
sector leaders in navigating these difficult choices and constraints.

Sector Strategies and Systems Change

Sector strategies were explicitly defined to include "systems change" as a key
goal of their work. The workforce intermediary implementing a sector initiative is
an actor within a larger industry and regional labor market system with a number
of other actors with varying relationships with one another. Key partners in the
strategy, such as a funder collaborative, a policy-advocacy organization, a community organizer, or a trade association, may lead the systems-change strategy. A
partner organization may have an important set of institutional competencies or
relationships or may be in a better position to advance a controversial perspective
than the workforce intermediary.

The theory of system change is that if the workforce intermediary/agent can
find and move points of leverage within the system, then relationships of other
actors in the system may also be changed, with the result that opportunities for
disadvantaged workers improve, and that, as the system moves to this new pattern,
these improved outcomes can be sustained.

In order to try to describe systems change as practiced by sector initiatives
in more practical terms, the Aspen Institute conducted a series of interviews with
sector leaders, as well as a field survey about system-change activities. They found
three "systems" that were relevant to sector work and were areas in which sector
initiatives sought to promote change:

- industry practices that shape the way individuals are recruited, hired,
  trained, promoted, and compensated in the workplace;

- education and training infrastructure, including workforce investment boards, community-based training providers, community colleges, and apprenticeship programs; and

- public policy, including rules, regulations, and funding streams related to the workforce and education systems, as well as those that influence business practices.[3]

Also in the field survey, program leaders responded to specific questions about particular changes they hoped to effect in these systems and about their organizational strengths and limitations in achieving those goals.

Discussions of systems change, however, are often not precise in describing the system that is being targeted. To some degree this vagueness in language is intentional; changing the "system" often requires changing the behavior of another organization, often one that is important to the work of the sector initiative, such as an employer, a funder, or an education partner. While changing the operating practices or policies of these organizations may be an important goal of a sector initiative, saying so directly can be politically challenging when the "systems" are partners and funders. In addition, some systems changes, such as a strengthened public policy, may have been sought by a number of different organizations, and sector initiative leaders are often hesitant to claim credit for such outcomes.

Many argue that sector strategies are, in effect, work-around reforms to "siloed" systems focused on workforce development, education, human services, and economic development. Indeed, the positioning of sector initiatives, with both worker and industry constituents and with resources from—and relationships with—many of these separate public systems, generates the perspective to see where systems change is needed, and to engage other actors to help achieve it. This integrative role of sector strategies is essential, yet produces friction with many public systems.

Why Did Sector-Based Workforce Development Take Root?

It would be misleading to suggest that sector-based workforce development was simply an idea whose time had come in the 1990s and that, once articulated, was adopted quickly by all relevant stakeholders. In fact, it has faced a thirty-year uphill advocacy campaign—supported by training, institutional-capacity building, and leadership-development efforts—that continues today. In reality, it has been only partially adopted. We suggest that six key factors contributed to setting the stage for the gradual and piecemeal adoption of sector workforce strategies in this period: decreased support for skills training, information gaps, the skills gap, increased challenges facing vulnerable populations, a lack of adequate evidence, and the need for a field-building infrastructure.

Public and Private Shifts Away from Skills Training

The 1980s and 1990s witnessed dramatic changes in U.S. labor markets. Structural and global shifts away from manufacturing employment, leaner management, diminishing internal career ladders, declining unionization, adoption of new technologies, suburbanization of business, and new occupational skill requirements—all of these upset traditional business hiring and training patterns and institutions. As employers adopted lean staff structures and dismantled internal career ladders, internal investments in workforce training—particularly at the entry level—diminished. Firms began turning more and more to temporary-services agencies to fill their employment needs. Further, as large employers pushed cost-control measures down their supply chain, the ability of the smaller employers to invest in workforce training became more limited, with implications for large employers as well, who often draw talent from their supplier networks. At the same time, traditional vocational-training mechanisms had been dismantled in local educational systems, and public investment in training for the economically disadvantaged was largely seen as a discredited strategy and faced declining investment. As labor markets fragmented and institutions preparing workers declined, employers reported increased gaps in hard and soft skills. These were not just issues for the low-skilled and low-income; they affected a broader swathe of the labor force. New approaches were needed. The economic growth and tighter labor markets of the 1990s underscored these needs and provided an opportunity for low-income workers who gained skills to experience increased earnings.

Business-Information Gaps

The decline in unionization and the fragmentation of the labor market in general decreased channels of communication about workforce skills and challenges and increased reliance on third-party organizations to provide workers with occupational training. This increased reliance on third-party providers required employers to effectively articulate training needs to these external education and training organizations, which itself can be a challenge for small employers. Given employers' lack of understanding about how these organizations are funded and operated, on the one hand, and the inexperience of the education and training providers with the culture and operations of business, on the other, these communications were often incomplete, leaving frustration on all sides.

In this context, workforce development serving low-skilled, low income workers and job seekers faltered, because employers were not engaged sufficiently, especially in clarifying job and skill requirements. As a consequence, many training efforts failed by not training for real jobs or missing the mark in terms of what business needed for successful employees. One-by-one engagement with smaller employers imposed transaction costs for businesses that adopted leaner management approaches and that did not have available staff time to work with external providers. Similarly, the approach imposed inefficiencies for workforce service providers, which also found it costly to devote significant resources to the needs of an employer prepared to hire only one or two individuals. More broadly, the diverse and fragmented labor market required new bridging intermediaries to create the needed connections among workforce stakeholders. The sector approach provided a more efficient way to engage groups of employers with similar labor force needs, addressing some of these retail inefficiencies and also creating new information bridges between employers and their workforce and with education and training providers.

The Skills Gap

In the 1980s and 1990s, attention began to focus on the "skills gap" in the American workforce and its potential long-term negative economic consequences. At the same time, impending retirements in manufacturing and construction called attention to the looming and real difficulties employers faced in obtaining skilled workers. Certainly wages and benefits played a role in these perceived skill shortages, in that employers were often unwilling to pay higher wages in order to attract the skills they were seeking. And many question whether there really is insufficient skill within the current workforce to meet current employer demand or whether the vacancy challenge is more related to employer practices.[4] On the other hand, many point out that with technological change, demand for skills is likely to increase, and that investments in education have historically been an important part of the foundation that has contributed to the success of the American economy.[5] The sector approach provided one methodology for helping groups of firms build career pathways for new entrants as well as incumbent workers.

Continued Isolation of Vulnerable Groups

While labor markets tightened in the 1990s, it remained the case that unemployment among blacks was roughly twice the rate of whites, and this remains true today and holds across levels of educational attainment.[6] Other groups also face particular barriers in today's labor market, particularly in certain sectors. For example, women continue to struggle to gain jobs in male-dominated industries, such as construction, and the gender-based pay gap persists. This lack of access to higher-paying jobs is particularly problematic given the increasing importance of women's earnings to children's economic well-being over the past several decades. Sector initiatives continue to be motivated by issues of economic equity and often focus their efforts on these populations that continue to experience particularly large challenges in today's labor market.

Evidence

Sector workforce strategies emerged against the backdrop of the national evaluation of the Job Training Partnership Act (JTPA) in the early 1990s, which concluded that most JTPA-funded employment and training programs achieved relatively modest gains for adults and were by and large not effective for youth, with negative earnings results reported for young men. The study authors did note, however, that the investment in training was relatively modest on a per-participant basis, and thus the modest gains for adults were positive from a cost-benefit perspective.[7] There were some concerns that many control participants received employment and training services in other ways, that site selection did not result in a representative sample of programs and also could have potentially biased results, and that these issues likely had substantial influence on the results reported. Nevertheless, the results were conventionally interpreted as implying that training for the disadvantaged does not work, and Congress substantially cut resources for job training.

One bright spot was the Center for Employment Training (CET) in San Jose, California, which achieved remarkable results in several rigorous evaluation studies. There is some debate about whether CET was a sector-based effort, but it heavily involved groups of employers, crafted strong community connections, and adopted a variety of educational innovations. CET viewed "graduation" from the program as getting and keeping a job. Unfortunately, the national replication of CET by the U.S. Department of Labor showed few positive results for young workers. Sector-based workforce programs began with evidence in the 1990s related to the original CET evaluations but then faced ongoing skepticism about results until Public/Private Ventures' research in 2008 that showed strong employment and earnings effects achieved with the sector approach.

A Diverse Field

No one field of organizations led the adoption of sector workforce strategies. There were many strands, and this diversity was a source of strength and creativity for the spread of sector efforts. CET grew out of the Opportunity Industrial Centers (OICs) of the 1960s. In Chicago, such human-service groups as Jane Addams Hull-House and Chicago Commons experimented with sector strategies in the 1980s, working with businesses in the screw-machine industry and the auto supply chain. Union-led efforts like the Wisconsin Regional Training Partnership (WRTP) emerged after the 1989 recession, with a focus on manufacturing modernization and incumbent workers. Community-organizing coalitions like COPS/Metro, affiliates of the Industrial Areas Foundation, invented Project QUEST in San Antonio and later Capital IDEA in Austin. The Community Service Society in New York incubated Cooperative Home Care Associates in the South Bronx. The local chamber of commerce invented San Francisco Works in the 1990s in response to welfare reform.

A number of foundations supported sector strategies and helped build the field in these early years, notably the Ford, Charles Stewart Mott, MacArthur, and Annie E. Casey foundations. By the mid-1990s, there were at least twenty sector workforce intermediaries on the ground, yet this relatively small number held great promise and seemed to be producing distinctive outcomes. For the most part, the public workforce system—in the middle of experiencing its own redesign—was mostly uninvolved or excluded from the development of sector strategies, although the public system was an important investor in some of the early sector initiatives. Indeed, as agencies were transforming local workforce systems from the JTPA model to the new approach codified in the federal Workforce Investment Act (WIA), local leaders were unclear about whether a strategy that focused on a particular industry or cluster of businesses was an appropriate fit within this new system designed around a concept of universal service. Foundation funding provided these new sector intermediaries the space and resources to grow, but there was the nagging question of relevance for the public workforce system and whether these sector efforts were simply boutique experiments. Moreover, the "work first" approach embodied in the Temporary Assistance for Needy Families program and the WIA and the de-emphasis on skills training swept the country, which made sector workforce strategies a harder sell and more difficult to finance.

Growth in the Field of Sector-Based Workforce Development

Today the sector workforce field has greatly matured and built a partial infrastructure of policy, practice, and leadership. There is still a long way to go to have the sector approach fully adopted and implemented widely and faithfully in practice and policy. There are hundreds of sector partnerships, multiple states and localities have adopted the sector approach, national sector legislation is before Congress, funding mechanisms like the National Fund for Workforce Solutions are replicating the sector approach, strong evaluations have demonstrated the positive impacts of sector workforce strategies (see King, Chapter 11), and there is a resurgence of the sector approach for improving job quality. A diverse, vibrant field has been created over two decades.

Social investors are preoccupied more than ever with "scaling" the impact of promising approaches and using "collective impact" methods to align relevant stakeholders to achieve common results. In "New Pathways to Scale for Community Development Finance," Kirsten Moy and Greg Ratliff emphasize the need to develop "industries" at a certain stage of scaling innovations if these approaches are to grow on a larger basis. In other words, replication is insufficient in itself without broader infrastructure support. While there are some limitations in applying this scaling model to the sector workforce field, in that a natural heterogeneity of services and strategies will always remain in the field, the discussion of the development of an industry and the factors that can support its growth is nonetheless instructive. "Industry" here refers to an interrelated set of stakeholders and investors that cultivate human, intellectual, financial, and political capital on behalf of specific strategies like sectoral workforce development. What is created ultimately is a kind of "ecological system" that encourages growth through complementary and mutually reinforcing practices, policies, and investments. We use "system" advisedly here to describe the elements of the sector movement, realizing that public and private actors have not fully adopted the sector approach.

An industry or ecological system has emerged for sector-based workforce development. How did it arise, and what are its parts? Is it adequate? There was no overall guiding plan for the sector field, and the industry development occurred, for the most part, because of the investments of a small group of national foundations and an array of partners focused on technical assistance and policy change. To some degree these investments were coordinated; but they were also competitive at times, and sector entrepreneurs pursued their own specific interests.

We outline several of the most important component parts of this ecological system. This is not a complete list, but it gives a flavor of the range of investments and the investors and stakeholders involved.

Knowledge Development and Dissemination

The Aspen Institute published case studies of promising sector practices and organizations and worked with the now-closed evaluation firm Public/Private Ventures (P/PV) on a random assignment test of sector workforce development. The Rockefeller Foundation had been the lead funder in the CET evaluations in the early 1990s. Other foundations supported a range of other sector evaluations.

Practitioner Leadership

The National Network of Sector Partners arose in the late 1990s to bring together emerging sector leaders from around the country to exchange information and lessons and discuss advocacy. The National Skills Coalition also brought practitioners together for a policy focus at the federal and state levels. The Aspen Institute and P/PV started the Sector Skills Academy at the national level and built the Sector Skills Practicum in New York to cultivate and develop knowledge and leadership. These efforts have occasionally been adapted to fit the needs of other local areas as well. The Industrial Areas Foundation (IAF) spread the sector approach in the Southwest among its community-organizing networks, starting in Texas, with Project QUEST in San Antonio and then Capital IDEA in Austin, Project ARRI-BA in El Paso, and Valley Initiative for Development and Advancement (VIDA) in the Rio Grande Valley. The IAF affiliates have continued to expand this work in other communities in Texas, as well as in Arizona and Louisiana.

Leading Sectors

Over time, sector strategies developed the most traction in construction, health care, and manufacturing, for different reasons. But this focus led to specific initiatives and replication and policy attention at all levels of government. Representatives of businesses in these industries spoke frequently on behalf of the effectiveness of sector-based workforce development. The Great Recession and optimism about the clean-energy economy led to a short-term uptick in resources and focused attention on preparing individuals for green jobs and careers, but unfortunately the matching economic-development investment that would have stimulated the creation of these jobs did not materialize. The green-jobs initiatives boosted interest, but the paucity of jobs created in these sectors renewed skepticism about the long-run outcomes of workforce development.

Flexible Financing

A number of foundations supported individual sector models across the country. The Charles Stewart Mott Foundation has been an important supporter of Focus: HOPE, Cooperative Home Care Associates, Project QUEST, and many others, providing multi-year patient financing to these organizations as they develop their strategies and take root in their industries and communities. The Annie E. Casey Foundation's Jobs Initiative in the 1990s and 2000s was a concerted effort in six places over eight years to cultivate sector partnerships and investment models. At the local level, the Boston Foundation's work making three-year, flexible commitments to three sector initiatives, and organizing funders to consider longer-term time horizons in their fundraising, was a pathbreaking approach for a local foundation. These efforts led to early-stage planning for the National Fund for Workforce Solutions, a set of national and local funder collaboratives established to support sector-based workforce partnerships. Other efforts included the Robert Wood Johnson and Hitachi foundations' Jobs2Careers initiative, which focused on the health care sector.

Policy

A number of efforts sought to develop and spread sector policies. At the state level, Pennsylvania developed one of the most ambitious efforts to spread "industry partnerships" throughout the state. With support from the Mott Foundation, the National Governors Association launched the State Sector Skills Academy, which provided a forum for states to consider how their systems could better support the practice. Advocacy organizations such as the National Skills Coalition encouraged other states to adopt sector policies, including the creation of regional skills panels. At the local level, such cities as New York and Chicago supported sector-based one-stop entities and partnerships for career pathways. The National Skills Coalition became the federal advocate for including sector funding in the Workforce Investment Act and other federal legislation.

Technical Assistance

National and regional organizations took the lead in spreading the word about sector approaches and assisting state and local governments and leaders of local initiatives in adopting policies and practices that support sector strategies. These organizations included the Aspen Institute, P/PV, the National Network of Sector Partners and colleagues at the Insight Center, Jobs for the Future, Emerald Cities Collaborative, National Association of Manufacturers, and Corporation for a Skilled Workforce.

Public agencies also played an important role in the evolution of the ecological system of sector-based workforce development. Two major contributions are clear. First, the U.S. Department of Labor supported sector efforts on the ground through a variety of initiatives, including the Sectoral Employment Demonstration, the H-1B visa program, Health Careers, Pathways Out of Poverty, and Workforce Innovation in Regional Economic Development (WIRED). These funding streams were important for efforts on the ground, although their time-limited nature sometimes encouraged only short-term collaborations and results. Second, community colleges have played an increasing role as the educational partner for sector strategies, contributing a relatively stable infrastructure and accredited-education offerings that can substantially strengthen sector workforce initiatives. We are now seeing youth-oriented sector strategies that engage both K–12 systems and community colleges. These educational institution–based initiatives, however, continue to struggle to improve their labor-market connections and develop the level of flexibility needed to respond to a dynamic regional economy with changing skill needs.

About the Book

It is against this backdrop of accomplishments and challenges for the sector workforce field that we have assembled this book. Our hope is that, while updating *Workforce Intermediaries for the Twenty-First Century* (Giloth, 2004), this book also breaks new ground in addressing key issues related to the sector field overall, including job-quality improvement efforts, workforce-development capacity building, and career pathways. We hope as well that the book calls attention to challenges sector investors and practitioners must address if the sector field is to continue its growth in the coming decades.

The book is divided into five sections. The *Context and Strategy* section provides economic and historical background for the whole book. In Chapter 2, Paul Osterman reviews contemporary labor-market data, supply and demand factors, the changing employer role, and implications for workforce interventions. In Chapter 3, Maureen Conway provides a more in-depth look at the evolution of the sector field. In Chapter 4, Fred Dedrick analyzes the key components of industry or workforce partnerships and draws examples from the pathbreaking work in Pennsylvania in the 2000s. And in Chapter 5, Barbara Dyer, Robert P. Giloth, Richard Kazis, and Marlene Seltzer recount the history of the National Fund for Workforce Solutions.

The *Partnerships and Collaboratives* section includes five case studies of new and mature sector workforce approaches. In Chapter 6, Earl Buford and Laura Dresser recount the origin and accomplishments of the Wisconsin Regional Training Partnership (WRTP), one of the oldest and most respected workforce sector partnerships. Loh-Sze Leung, in Chapter 7, chronicles SkillWorks, the leading funder collaborative from Boston that invests in workforce partnerships and public policy. In Chapter 8, Marianne Krismer highlights the work of Cincinnati's Partners for a Competitive Workforce and one of its longtime workforce partnerships in the health care field. Denise Fairchild in Chapter 9 discusses the Emerald Cities Collaborative as a national network dedicated to connecting workforce partnerships to the emerging green economy. In Chapter 10, Saru Jayaraman shares the vision, history, accomplishments, and plans for the Restaurant Opportunities Centers United (ROC) and its efforts to improve low-wage jobs in the restaurant and food service industry.

The *Evaluation, Approaches, and Findings* section contains two chapters. Christopher King, in Chapter 11, reviews evaluation research about sector-based workforce development and related investments. Mark Popovich, in Chapter 12, summarizes the evaluation strategy and research findings for the National Fund for Workforce Solutions.

The *Institutions and Capacity* section contains three chapters. In Chapter 13, Sheila Maguire and Patricia Jenny address the neglected topic of capacity building in the workforce field, giving special attention to the multiple approaches attempted in New York City by the New York Workforce Funders Group. In Chapter 14, Evelyn Ganzglass, Marcie Foster, and Abigail Newcomer summarize various approaches for building sector-based career pathways with community colleges and how these efforts could be better connected to sector-based workforce development. In Chapter 15, Matt Helmer and Maureen Conway share their research about the construction apprenticeship system, pre-apprenticeships, and the challenges and opportunities for this type of sector partnership.

The *Policy, Financing, and Regional Change* section contains three chapters. In Chapter 16, Andy Van Kleunen assesses the opportunities for advancing sector workforce policies at the state and federal levels and the tensions between workforce innovation and system building. In Chapter 17, Orson Watson addresses the fundamental challenge of developing a sustainable financing model for sector and workforce partnerships. Chapter 18, by Chris Benner and Manuel Pastor, puts the experience of workforce intermediaries and funder collaboratives in the context of building the social networks and shared knowledge and values that can increase regional equity and economic competitiveness. In the concluding chapter, we summarize the critical themes of the book and call attention to key opportunities and challenges for the sector workforce field, both in the next years and in the coming decades.

What's Ahead for Sector Strategies?

Much has been accomplished in building the sector-based workforce field over the last decade. It is an ecological system and infrastructure with much strength, even at this stage of development. Yet there are major challenges for the field. Key philanthropic leaders have retired, and leading foundations have moved on to explore other workforce strategies. In the broader workforce field, new attention is focused on career pathways, reforming community colleges, youth unemployment, and sustainable employment for more vulnerable populations. A good question is whether there will be sufficient capital available to keep the sector infrastructure alive and vibrant. Neither employers nor the public sector has stepped up with the kind of support that many sector leaders thought they would once the sector approach was validated. In fact, federal financial resources for workforce development in general have diminished. While several states have adopted sector approaches, other states have cut funding, even though there have been good results. And we still haven't seen the passage of breakthrough federal legislation that would give a more sustainable foothold for sector strategies.

At the same time, some dilution of the sector workforce approach has occurred as it has become more popular. Some practitioners want to use the name without fully adopting the vision. It has become occupational training rather than deep engagement with multiple employers; career pathways to good jobs has given way to training for the first job; incumbent-worker training has grown, but sector training for people struggling to get into better jobs has languished, in part because of the slow growth in the economy; and the systems-change aspiration has tapered off as organizations compete for limited training dollars and job placements, hoping to keep their doors open. Some of this is a natural corollary of overall growth in the sector field. But there is reason to worry that dilution of the sector model will eventually show up in poor evaluation results that question the scalability of sector workforce strategies. This does not have to happen, but vigilance about implementation and accountability is required.

Sector workforce strategies have succeeded and built evidence, but there is still a large opportunity in the labor market. At the same time, a large, growing problem, underscored in our weak economic recovery, is the growth of poorly paying jobs in service industries like health care, food service, and retail. Training is not the answer, because career ladders do not exist in many cases. On the other hand, many workers require dramatic improvements in basic skills, and these workers find it increasingly difficult to maintain a firm attachment to the labor market at any level. Improving the quality of jobs—better wages, benefits, work schedules, and family-life balance—is required. These are sector-based and cross-sector advocacy issues. Is the sector field willing to take up these challenges? Is it even a relevant resource for upgrading job quality?

We hope this book of accomplishments, candid assessments, and challenges does justice to the remarkable efforts of sector practitioners, policy makers, researchers, and investors over the past two decades. The building of the sector workforce field has been a major undertaking that has occurred largely through bottom-up entrepreneurial energy and commitment. Yet we are now at one of those fundamental inflection points where we need to chart the future of the sector workforce field. We hope this book is a helpful contribution to that important effort and inspires the next generation of leaders to advance sector workforce practices and policies.

Notes

1. Robert P. Giloth, ed., *Workforce Intermediaries for the Twenty-First Century*, published in association with The American Assembly, Columbia University (Philadelphia: Temple University Press, 2004).

2. Peggy Clark and Steven L. Dawson, *Jobs and the Urban Poor: Privately Initiated Sectoral Strategies*, Aspen Institute, November 1995, p. v, http://institute.usworker.coop/sites/default/files/resources/001%201995_Clark%20and%20Dawson_Jobs%20for%20the%20Urban%20Poor.pdf.

3. For a discussion of the systems-change framework, see Maureen Conway, Steven L. Dawson, Amy Blair, and Linda Dworak-Muñoz, *Sector Strategies for Low-Income Workers: Lessons from the Field*, Aspen Institute, Summer 2007. For field survey results, see Maureen Conway, Amy Blair, and Allison Gerber, *Systems Change: A Survey of Program Activities*, Aspen Institute, March 2008.

4. See, for example, Peter Cappelli, *Why Good People Can't Get Jobs: The Skills Gap and What Companies Can Do About It* (Philadelphia: Wharton Digital Press, 2012).

5. See, for example, Claudia Goldin and Lawrence F. Katz, *The Race between Education and Technology* (Cambridge, MA: Belknap Press, 2008).

6. See, for example, U.S. Department of Labor, "The African-American Labor Force in the Recovery," February 29, 2012, http://www.dol.gov/_sec/media/reports/BlackLabor-Force/BlackLaborForce.pdf.

7. Larry L. Orr et al., *Does Training for the Disadvantaged Work? Evidence from the National JTPA Study* (Washington, DC: Urban Institute, 1996).

8. See, for example, James J. Heckman and Jeffrey A. Smith, "The Sensitivity of Experimental Impact Estimates: Evidence from the National JTPA Study," in *Youth Employment and Joblessness in Advanced Countries*, edited by David G. Blanchflower and Richard B. Freeman (Chicago: University of Chicago Press, January 2000), http://www.nber.org/chapters/c6810.pdf.

9. Gregory A. Ratliff and Kirsten S. Moy, "New Pathways to Scale for Community Development Finance," in *ProfitWise News and Views*, Federal Reserve Bank of Chicago, December 2004, http://www.chicagofed.org/digital_assets/publications/profitwise_news_and_views/2004/12_2004_pnv.pdf.

2

The Labor Market Context for Employment and Training Policy

Paul Osterman

The American labor market has long been an uncomfortable place for the majority of employees. Median wages are stagnant, insecurity is high, and the low-wage sector remains persistently large. Employers also face significant challenges, reflected in widespread complaints regarding skill shortages and the difficulty of attracting qualified and motivated employees. These concerns are mirrored in the national debate regarding the quality of education and the role of schools and other institutions in preparing people for work. Taken as a whole, the environment would seem ripe for a renewed national commitment to active labor-market policy, but this has not happened. The goal of this paper is to describe the labor-market context that is relevant for employment policy going forward.

The American Workforce: Trends and Challenges

The low-wage labor market has long been the central target for employment policy. The core observation is that far too many adults work in jobs that cannot support families. In the calculations that follow I limit myself to adults between the ages of twenty-five and sixty-four. Although there are young people who work to support their families many others are in casual jobs that are transitory and it would confuse the analysis to include youth in the analysis of wages. (Note that youth are discussed below.)

There is no official standard for what constitutes a low-wage job. A measure consistent with international usage would be wages that are less than two-thirds of the median, but this is not intuitive in a policy context. For this reason I work with the hourly wage needed to raise a full-time full-year worker (2,080 hours per year) above the poverty standard, but even here there is no accepted standard. Should we use a family of three or a family of four? Should we use the poverty line itself or, instead, a multiple of the line in light of the widely accepted view that the poverty threshold is well below a basic living standard based on a commonly accepted market basket? *Table 1* shows the percentage of adults whose hourly wages fall below alternative cutoffs.[1]

Table 1: Percentage of Adults Whose Hourly Wages Would Fail to Raise Them above the Specified Level If They Worked Full-Time and Full-Year, 2011

	Percentage of adults	Hourly Wage
Poverty line, family of three, including two children under 18	8.7	($8.71)
150% of poverty line, family of three, including two children under 18	30.8	(13.06)
Poverty line, family of four, including two children under 18	19.9	($10.96)
150% of poverty line, family of four, including two children under 18	44.6	($16.44)

Source: See endnote 1.

A reasonable compromise is to consider the wage necessary to lift a family of four above the poverty line (the 19.9 percent figure), and *Table 2* shows how this figure varies by demographic group.

Table 2: Percentages of Working Adults Below the Low-Wage Standard, 2011

Men	16.4%
Women	23.6%
Non-Hispanic Whites	14.8%
African Americans	28.1%
Hispanics	37.5%

Source: See endnote 1.

The incidence of low-wage work is disturbingly high. To make matters worse, a recent study published by the National Employment Law Project reported that low-wage jobs accounted for 21 percent of jobs lost during the Great Recession but 58 percent of jobs created since the downturn bottomed out.[2]

The fact that many Americans are employed in low-wage jobs would not be bothersome if there was substantial upward mobility. Such mobility certainly exists in some sectors of the low-wage job market. Think, for example, of young people in casual low-wage jobs—movie theater ushers, fast-food servers—who obtain better work as they age. The unfortunate fact is that there is considerable evidence that adults remain confined in low-wage jobs over the course of their working lives. [3]

Insecurity

A second significant trend confronting American workers is growing insecurity, a development intensified by the Great Recession but that also preceded it and will certainly continue after the recovery. The most recent data from the U.S. Census Displaced Worker Survey show that between January 2009 and December 2011, just over six million people were displaced from jobs they had held for three years or more. As of January 2012, only 56 percent of these dislocated workers had found new jobs.[4] For those who did find a new job, earnings loss for mature workers was roughly 20 percent.[5] Another indicator is that as of October 2012, there were more than four million Americans who had been unemployed for six months or more, and they constituted 40 percent of the entire unemployed population.

All this said, it is important to understand that insecurity in the job market is not simply the result of the recent recession. In 2008 Henry Farber summarized the evidence regarding job tenure as follows:[6]

> The overall pattern of results regarding mean job tenure and the incidence of long-term employment relationships suggests that there has been a substantial decline in long-term employment opportunities and a concomitant reduction in job security in the private sector.... I conclude that the nature of the private-sector employment relationship in the United States has changed substantially in ways that make jobs less secure and workers more mobile.

The Youth Labor Market

Youth employment has long been a central focus of employment policy, for good and less-than-good reasons. Common sense suggests that it is reasonable to intervene in a person's career as early as possible because the chances of success are seemingly better before an attitude of failure sets in. It is also politically easier to spend resources on youth, since they are more "innocent" of "bad behaviors" and hence less subject to blame-the-victim critiques of employment policy. Set against this are two concerns. First, even though youth unemployment is very high, the vast majority of youth settle into careers successfully as they age. Hence the target efficiency of early intervention is low. Second, while early intervention makes some intuitive sense, many young people may not be mature enough to take advantage of the intervention. The mixed results of youth-program evaluations support these concerns, as does the fact that while youth unemployment is high (24.4 percent for sixteen- to nineteen-year-olds in 2011), it does in fact fall as people age (14.6 percent for twenty- to twenty-four-year-olds and 7.9 percent for twenty-five- to fifty-four-year-olds).

However, it is also true that there is a subset of young people about whom we should be quite concerned. Often referred to as "disconnected youth," these are young people who are neither in school nor working. While some may be at the beach, or the equivalent, without doubt the group generally is in difficulty. Adding to the concern, the differences in racial and ethnic incidence are quite sharp. The patterns are apparent in *Table 3*. It is important to note that these data are drawn from the American Community Survey, which captures the circumstances of people in institutions like prisons, which is not the case with the more commonly utilized Current Population Survey.[7]

Table 3: Percentage of Disconnected Youths Ages 16 to 24, 2010

Whites		Blacks		Hispanic	
Men	Women	Men	Women	Men	Women
12.3%	11.1%	26.0%	19.0%	16.8%	20.2%

Source: Sarah Burd-Sharps and Kristen Lewis, "One in Seven: Ranking Youth Disconnection in the 25 Largest Metro Areas," Measure of America, Social Science Research Council. Note that disconnection is defined as neither being enrolled in school nor working full- or part-time. Individuals in institutions who are enrolled in educational programs are not counted as disconnected, nor are any members of the Armed Services. The underlying data are from the American Community Survey.

Roughly one in ten white youths are disconnected, but the numbers are dramatically higher, one might say shocking, for blacks and Latinos. Although some of these disconnected youths will land on their feet, the incidence is so high as to clearly constitute a fundamental challenge for educational and employment policy. The implication of these data would appear to be that scarce youth-policy resources are better focused on disconnected youth than on the more general, albeit politically popular, issue of summer youth employment and broadly targeted initiatives.

Table 4 sheds some light on the dynamics of disconnection since two factors are at work: whether or not the individual is in school and, for those not in school, whether the individual is able to obtain work. Looking across the first row, it is apparent that blacks stay in school nearly at the same rate as the age range as a whole (although black men are somewhat less likely to be enrolled), whereas Hispanics, particularly men, are out of school at a much higher rate. Regarding the out-of-school group, it is important to note the extremely low rate of employment among black men. Their employment situation is truly catastrophic.

Table 4: Dynamics of Disconnection

	All		Black		Hispanics	
	Men	*Women*	*Men*	*Women*	*Men*	*Women*
Percent enrolled	64.4%	58.6%	55.8%	62.3%	49.2%	57.4%
E/P* for those not enrolled	63.2%	60.3%	41.3%	49.5%	66.9%	52.5%

Source: See *Table 3.*   *E/P is the employment-to-population ratio.

Related to the concern about disconnection is the broader issue of trends in school attainment. This is important not only in the context of the youth labor market but also because it speaks to the skill level of the American labor force. If current trends persist, will new entrants have the skills necessary to do well in a modern economy? Unfortunately there are no nationally representative measures of skill attainment; the closest approximation is projected education level. *Table 5* shows the trends in high school and college completion among young cohorts. As is apparent, there has been a steady increase in educational attainment, and by 2012 more than 60 percent of young people had at least some post-secondary education. As we will shortly see, this matches comfortably with the projected skill requirements of jobs.

Table 5: Educational Attainment, 25- to 29-Year-Olds

	1971	*1991*	*2001*	*2012*
Completed high school	78%	85%	87%	90%
Some college but less than a four-year degree	17%	22%	30%	30%
Completed college	17%	23%	28%	33%

Source: Richard Fry and Kim Parker, "Record Shares of Young Adults Have Finished Both High School and College," Pew Research Center, November 5, 2012. The underlying data are from the Current Population Survey.

Although there are no direct measures of skill, one useful source is the Programme for International Student Assessment exams, the international tests of literacy, math, and science. The most recent available data are for fifteen-year-olds in 2009. These tests show that with respect to literacy and science, American scores are not statistically different from the Organization for Economic Cooperation and Development (OECD) average while for math U.S. scores fall slightly below that average. These patterns cast doubt on popular hysteria concerning the skills of young Americans.[8]

If the overall education and testing trends seem to be reasonably satisfactory, the same cannot be said when these data are disaggregated by race, ethnicity, or income. Doing so reveals substantial and troubling inequalities, as shown in *Table 6*.

Table 6: Differentials in Educational Attainment, 25-to -29 Year-Olds

	Non-Hispanic Whites			Blacks			Hispanics		
	1993*	2001	2011	1993	2001	2011	1993	2001	2011
Completed four years of high school or more	91.2%	93.4%	94.4%	82.8%	86.6%	87.7%	60.9%	62.4%	71.5%
College graduate or more	27.2%	33.7%	39.2%	13.2%	16.8%	19.6%	8.3%	10.5%	12.8%

Source: Current Population Survey Historical Time Series Tables, http://www.census.gov/hhes/socdemo/education/data/cps/historical/index.html, Table A-2.

*1993 is the first year in which consistent racial/ethnic information is available in the published data.

Making the problem worse is that the Current Population Survey, the source of these tables, understates racial differences because it does not include people in military barracks, prisons, and college dormitories. As we have already seen in the discussion of disconnection, this is an important consideration. In addition, the impact of family income on educational attainment has led to growing inequality. A recent study compared two cohorts: those born between 1961 and 1964 and those born between 1979 and 1982. For the low-income group, college completion increased by 4 percentage points across the cohorts; for the high-income group, it increased by 18 percentage points.[9]

One development that modestly improves this portrait concerns the growing importance of certificates. Certificates typically represent one-year courses of study in occupational fields and have a high rate of return in the job market. In some cases they are captured in the "some college" category of educational attainment, but in other instances they are not. This depends in part on how survey respondents interpret the question and in part on whether the certificates carry with them academic credit. Estimates are that 12 percent of the U.S. workforce holds a certificate, a figure higher than the 10 percent who hold an associate's degree. Whereas college attainment is biased toward non-Hispanic whites and people from upper-income families, the opposite is true of certificate holders.[10]

The Larger Context

Growth in the American labor force will slow considerably over the next decade. *Table 7* shows the projections of the Bureau of Labor Statistics for the entire workforce and for young people (which, of course, presages trends beyond the next decade).

Table 7: Change in the Size of the Labor Force

	Percentage Change 1990–2000	Percentage Change 2000–2010	Projected Percentage Change 2010–2020
Entire Labor Force	+13.3	+7.9	+6.8
16- to 24-Year-Olds	+0.1	−7.0	−12.4

Source: "Labor Force Projections to 2020: A More Slowly Growing Workforce," *Monthly Labor Review*, January 2012, Errata, www.bls.gov/opub/mlr/2012/01/errata.pdf.

Along with this slow growth, the labor market will be impacted by the coming wave of retirements. To get a sense of this, consider that the Bureau of Labor Statistics projects that net employment growth between 2010 and 2020 will be just over twenty million jobs, while replacement hiring will create more than thirty-three million job openings.[11] This will put considerable pressure on firms that will lose their most experienced employees, but it will also create opportunities for new entrants in the workforce as well as for people seeking to move up the job ladder.

While labor-force growth will slow, the composition of the workforce will change, although perhaps not as dramatically as popular discussion suggests. The percentage of the workforce that is African American, of Hispanic origin, Asian, or "other non-white" is expected to increase from 33.5 percent in 2010 to 39.2 percent in 2020.[12] Given the race-based differentials that we currently observe in earnings, educational attainment, and other outcomes, this trend clearly places an even greater premium on effective policy responses. In addition, while levels of immigration are expected to retreat from the peaks observed prior to the Great Recession, they will continue to be significant. While immigrants generally catch up to native-labor-market outcomes within a reasonable period of time, some groups do lag, and policy responses will be appropriate.[13]

The Demand Side

A useful first step toward understanding the demand side of the labor market is to simply examine where low-wage jobs are found. The middle column of the table below shows the industries where the bulk of low-wage workers (using the standard described above) are employed, and the righthand column shows the low-wage employment rate within each industry. The industries in the table account for 65 percent of all low-wage working adults.

Table 8: Industry Patterns, Low-Wage Adults, 2011

	Percentage of All Low-wage Adults Found in Industry	Low-wage Adult Rate Within Industry
Manufacturing	8.2	13.4
Retail	19.7	38.9
Professional Services	9.4	17.5
Educational Services	6.8	12.2
Health Care Services (except hospitals)	7.9	21.8
Food and Drinking Places	13.8	66.3

Source: See Note 1.

Not surprisingly, the two most important sources of low-wage jobs are retail work and food and drink; additionally, within these industries, the incidence of low-wage employment is high.

Skill Demands

The traditional goal of the employment and training system is to improve the skills of clients. The assumption is obviously that people in low-wage jobs lack the requisite productive capacity to move up in the job market. There is also a common view that employers' skill demands are increasing, which exacerbates skill deficits. A nuanced consideration of this situation is important. On the one hand, it is certainly true that skills are important and are often deficient. It is also the case that employer demands are growing. However, too often the skills argument is seen as the beginning and the end of the discussion about addressing the challenge of low-wage work, and other policies more directly aimed at improving opportunities in the labor market are overlooked.[14] The reality is that both perspectives are important, although this chapter focuses entirely on skill issues.

How are the skill demands of employers shifting, and are they accelerating beyond the reach of low-wage workers? A popular explanation is the polarization hypothesis.[15] The core of this argument is that what might be termed middle-skill jobs are being eliminated by information technology and that the bulk of future job growth will be at the two ends of the job spectrum: low-skill, low-wage work and very-high-skill, higher-wage work. If true, this "barbell" story carries a discouraging message, because it implies that there will be few opportunities for today's low-wage adults to get ahead and that any effective employment policy needs to focus on the long-term chances of young people.

The polarization story emerged as an explanation for the apparent failure of earlier models linking education to inequality. These models worked well in explaining the patterns in the 1980s, but beginning in the 1990s significant problems emerged. People with a high school degree or less held their own relative to the median wage, a reversal of the pattern in the 1980s when the bottom fell out of the high school labor market. In addition, the wages of those with only a college degree (as opposed to an advanced degree) stagnated.[16]

There is certainly some truth to the polarization description. In particular, service-sector jobs are growing as a proportion of the economy, although this does not prove the argument about computers. The demand for service occupations can grow for numerous reasons, such as the aging of the population and the changing demand for services.

This said, it is simply not the case that there will be few job openings for middle-skill work. According to projections by the Bureau of Labor Statistics, only 23 percent of all job openings projected between 2008 and 2018 will require a college degree or more.[17] Examples of good jobs that are attainable with less than a four-year degree include numerous health care technician jobs, skilled blue-collar positions, computer support jobs, truck drivers, and biotechnology technicians.

The continued importance of middle-skill jobs is also based on projected hiring to replace the retiring generation of baby boomers. The openings created by retirements will offer considerable middle-skill opportunities. For example, the net growth of production occupations by 2020 is projected to be only 356,000, yet replacement hiring will be 1,734,000. Recent research shows that the skills required by these production workers are at the community-college level, well within the range of most people.[18] These projections may be delayed by delayed retirements caused by the Great Recession, but they cannot be avoided.[19]

As just noted, the Bureau of Labor Statistics' projections of education and training requirements for jobs shows a very modest increase in demand for college-educated labor, which implies that the vast majority of jobs will be widely accessible. These projections have been criticized on the ground that even within occupations the Bureau classifies as not requiring post-secondary education there are large numbers of employees who in fact do have post-secondary education, and these people receive a positive rate of return for their education, suggesting that their skill and education levels are in fact productive and desired by employers. However, even when the Bureau's projections are modified the demand for middle-skill work remains strong. One estimate, which makes an adjustment to account for the issue just raised, is that by 2018, 35.5 percent of all jobs will require an associate's degree or some college while 31.5 percent will require a college degree. Good jobs will not be out of reach for most Americans.[20]

Direct evidence about skill trends (as opposed to occupational projections) comes from surveys and observations of firms. An example of survey-based evidence is the work of Michael Handel, who surveyed employees age 18 and older in two waves between 2004 and 2009. The survey asked concrete questions about skills and tasks at work and found a modest growth in skill demands but not any evidence of acceleration. Handel concludes: "The dominant impression from this portrait is that with some exceptions, the American workplace has not entered a radically new era but is likely in the process of a more gradual, long-term process of skill upgrading."[21] Osterman and Weaver (2013) surveyed a nationally representative sample of American manufacturers and also asked concrete questions about skill requirements. They found a modest growth in skill demands but nothing that put jobs out of reach of the vast majority of employees.[22]

A study conducted by Roberto Fernandez of technological change in a food-processing factory produced important observations.[23] The factory redesigned its production process to utilize continuous processing and control systems. Fernandez collected numerous direct measures of skill changes showing a modest, general increase in skill demands in the new jobs. However—and this is very important—the firm kept its old workforce and retrained them, despite the fact that average education attainment was below the twelfth-grade level. This example of how one employer embraced modern production technology but retained employees raises questions about the skill-shortage issue.

Not all ethnographic accounts are in agreement, but many do find the same pattern of steady but modest skill increases.[24] Combined with the survey-based research and the occupational projections, it seems fair to conclude that technology will not render it impossible for millions of workers to train for and aspire to middle-skill jobs.

Employer Practices

The past several decades have seen substantial shifts in the employment practices of employers. Although many of these developments do not bode well for the workforce, there have been positive trends. Many employers have implemented elements of so-called High-Performance Work Systems that entail more interesting, responsible, and varied work patterns.[25] In some industries, employees with high levels of human capital, such as in Silicon Valley, have been able to construct career patterns that give them more control over their working lives than is typical in traditional bureaucratic organizations.

Even so, many trends are adverse to employees. Those at risk are workers up and down the workplace hierarchy who cannot count on employment security and low-wage workers whose wages are under pressure, whose jobs are being outsourced, and who receive little training from their employers.

The trends in employment security are clear. We have already noted the large number of dislocated workers, as well as the same pattern in data on job tenure, which has fallen, especially for men. Firms simply face a more difficult competitive environment than in the past and are less able to provide stable employment commitments. Second, and independent of this, the attitude of firms toward their labor force has changed, for a variety of reasons. Pressures from financial markets push for cost reductions and a single-minded focus on profits. A focus on core competencies pushes firms to strip down their activities and shed labor. And new human-resource strategies, notably the use of temporary and contingent workers as well as part-time employees, leads to insecurity.[26]

Limited Training

It is well established that firms provide less training to frontline and less-educated employees. Training data are hard to find, but in a 2001 survey of employees, 19.8 percent of those with a high school degree or less reported receiving training, compared with 54.1 percent of those with a bachelor's degree or higher.[27] These practices may be reasonable, in that workers with low-skill jobs presumably need less training to do their work than do employees with more complex tasks, but the consequence is that it is difficult for lower-level employees to improve their circumstances.

In addition, firms have cut back on the amount of training they provide. As job tenure falls the time over which firms can amortize training investments is reduced hence the incentive to train falls. More generally, firms have dismantled traditional job ladders—internal labor markets—and are more willing to "buy" rather than "make" skill.[28] These patterns pose challenges not just for employees but also for training programs that seek to work with employers.

The paucity of training also reflects a state of mind—that some workers simply cannot learn and that improvements in the quality of their work or in the career trajectories are not feasible. Typical is the observation of an evaluation team that interviewed firms participating in activities organized by the National Association of Manufacturers aimed at helping them upgrade their production practices: "Employers knew they had problems of absenteeism, turnover, skill deficiencies, and low productivity but accepted them fatalistically as 'facts of life,' feeling that not much could be done about them."[29]

Another example of managerial skepticism emerged in a recent conversation with the head of a nursing home that was part of a chain. This leader worked with the Philadelphia 1199C union-management program (even though he was non-union) and by creating some career paths had reduced turnover of certified nursing assistants from 60 percent to 10 percent. Despite this success, he was unable to persuade his colleagues, the leaders of other nursing homes in the organization, to participate. He attributed this failure to inertia and to a lack of belief in training for this population of employees.[30]

In a study of a Massachusetts manufacturing program, a somewhat discouraging finding was that although employers expressed satisfaction with the training, they were explicit that this was in large part because it was costless. The firms did not continue making the training available when the subsidy ended.[31] A study of a Michigan subsidized on-the-job training program reached a similar conclusion.[32] The more positive finding in both examples was that as long as the training was subsidized employers were willing to let public programs through their doors, something that is not always easy to accomplish.

New Institutions

New labor market institutions are playing an increasingly important role in the job market. One key trend is the growth of temporary and contingent employment. This development is in reality a diverse set of arrangements spanning temporary-help agencies, in-house temporary pools, limited-term contracting, and independent contractors. There are no definitive data sources that offer confidence about numbers (Dey, Houseman, and Polivka, 2009), but all observers agree that the importance of these patterns has increased. A careful study of manufacturing found that in 2006 staffing industry jobs added 6 percent to manufacturing employment.[33] An important additional point is that measures of the stock of contingent jobs at a point in time is substantially less than the flow of people who experience these jobs over the course of a year. It is also worth noting that limited-term employment has extended to occupations that were previously shielded from the ebbs and flows of the market.

Conclusion

There is much to worry about in the American labor market. The large size and persistence of the low-wage sector is troubling, as is the increased level of insecurity up and down the job ladder. Racial and ethnic differentials are large. Firms are rewriting the employment contract in ways that are not favorable to employees. The high rate of disconnection among subgroups of young people is a disaster and cries out for a response.

The patterns and trends described in this chapter provide some clues for thinking about future directions of employment policy. One overarching point is the importance of not only improving skills but also encouraging employers to upgrade the quality of the work that they offer. This supply-and-demand-side orientation is important because even if skill levels could be upgraded across the board, too many low-quality jobs would persist and, absent efforts to improve these positions, a large number of adults would remain trapped in the low-wage labor market. There are a variety of approaches to working both sides of the labor market, ranging from modernized and better enforced employment standards to career-ladder programs. The good news is that recognition of the importance of working on both sides of the labor market is spreading rapidly in the field.

Shifts in what might be termed the institutional structure of the labor market pose challenges and opportunities. One example is that a growing number of firms require that new employees work as temps prior to being hired, and many firms are even turning to staffing firms as their main recruiting tool. Employment and training programs will now have to find a way to work with staffing firms rather than the eventual employer. The processes and, more important, the incentives of the staffing firms may be quite different from those to which the programs are accustomed. A second example is that many firms have reduced the resources they devote to internal training while, paradoxically, also requiring more from their employees in terms of attention to quality and customer service. This may create an opening for training programs to offer useful services to employers and hence connect to them more deeply than has been true in the past.

Trends in the labor market offer an opportunity for the employment and training system to broaden its reach and develop a new constituency in the employer community. First, and of crucial importance, due both to the trajectory of skill demand and to the coming wave of retirements, there will be middle-skill jobs to which many people can aspire. The metaphor of a barbell economy—that is, the polarization story—is exaggerated and does not preclude these opportunities.

These middle-skill jobs are attainable with community college degrees or certificates. As is well-known, community colleges enroll millions of young people and adults and are in many respects America's premier vocational-training system. However, at the same time that successful attainment of a degree or certificate carries with it good rates of return, far too many people wash out of community colleges before attaining these milestones. Furthermore, the multiple missions of community colleges sometimes can lead to less attention than desirable to the needs of the clients of the employment and training system. These challenges open the door to a potentially fruitful collaboration between the job-training and community college systems around issues of retention, remediation, and innovative approaches to serving hard-to-reach populations.

In the past, the job-training system narrowly defined its mission and constituency, and its weak level of political support and declining funding reflects this. But today, as we have seen, the need for an active training and placement policy extends well beyond the low-wage job market. Pervasive dislocation and insecurity provide the system with the challenge, but also the opportunity, to serve people who in the past would not have been seen as clients. The skill needs of employers create yet another potential constituency. All of this offers an opportunity to design programs and develop a political rhetoric that can broaden the reach and appeal of the system. Creative policy makers should turn themselves to this task.

Notes

1. The data on the low-wage workforce that follow are taken from the U.S. Bureau of Labor Statistics' Outgoing Rotation Groups (i.e., the Current Population Surveys of April and August), in which wage data are collected for that point in time. These wage data are considered to be more accurate than the wages calculated from the March Current Population Survey, which asks about earnings over the prior year and for which the wage has to be calculated by dividing annual earnings by annual hours worked, both of which are recalled with some error. In the calculations reported here, allocated wages are eliminated, as are wages that are reported below $1 an hour in 1979 dollars. For a discussion of processing these data, see Thomas Lemieux, "Increasing Residual Wage Inequality: Compositional Effects, Noisy Data, or Rising Demand for Skill?" *American Economic Review* 96, no. 3 (June 2006): 461–498. It also is worth noting that although in other contexts top-coding of wages is an issue, it does not affect our calculations, since we focus on the median.

2. National Employment Law Project report, "The Low-Wage Recovery and Growing Inequality," August 2012.

3. One study found that among low earners over six years starting in the early 1990s, a period of remarkable economic strength, only 27 percent raised their incomes enough to rise consistently above the poverty line for a family of four. See Harry Holzer, "Encouraging Job Advancement Among Low-Wage Workers: A New Approach," Brookings Institution Policy Brief No. 30, May 2004.

A more recent study looked at low earners in the years 1995 to 2001 and found that 6 percent of those working full-time and 18 percent of those working part-time in any year had dropped out of the labor force by the next year. Among those who did stay in the workforce, 40 percent experienced either a decrease or no change in their earnings. See Brett Theodos and Robert Bednarzik, "Earnings Mobility and Low-Wage Workers in the United States, *Monthly Labor Review*, July 2006. Using yet a third data source, this time tracking mobility from 2001 to 2003, researchers found that 44 percent of the employees at poverty wages in 2001 had no better wages in 2003 and an additional 22 percent were not even employed. See Pamela Loprest, Gregory Acs, Caroline Ratcliffe, and Katie Vinopal, "Who Are Low-Wage Workers?," Department of Health and Human Services ASPE Research Brief, February 2009, http://aspe.hhs.gov/hsp/09/lowwageworkers/rb.shtml.

The outcome of welfare reform points to a similar conclusion. Despite the strong economy of the 1990s, former welfare recipients were unable to escape the low-wage labor market. The results of an extensive study of the impact of welfare reform were summarized as follows: "Welfare reform—both state welfare waivers in the early 1990s and federal welfare reform in 1996—did not reduce the official U.S. poverty rates of women or children, we find. The big push from welfare to work also doesn't appear to have lifted more people out of deep poverty—defined as living below 50 percent of the U.S. federal poverty line." See "Five Questions for Signe-Mary McKernan and Caroline Ratcliffe," Urban Institute, http://www.urban.org/toolkit/fivequestions/Mckernan_Ratcliffe.cfm.

4. Bureau of Labor Statistics news release, "Worker Displacement: 2009–2011," August 24, 2012.

5. Till von Wachter, "Responding to Long-Term Unemployment," testimony before the Subcommittee on Income Security and Family Support of the Committee on Ways and Means, June 10, 2010.

6. Henry S. Farber, "Employment Insecurity: The Decline in Worker-Firm Attachment in the United States," Princeton University, Industrial Relations Section, Working Paper No. 530, July 1, 2008, p. 23, http://arks.princeton.edu/ark:/88435/dsp019k41zd50q.

7. Of the total of 5.8 million disconnected, 400,000 are in some form of institution.

8. See http://nces.ed.gov/surveys/pisa/pisa2009highlights_3.asp.

9. Martha J. Bailey and Susan M. Dynarski, "Gains and Gaps: Changing Inequality in U.S. College Entry and Completion," National Bureau of Economic Research, Working Paper No. 17633, December 2011.

10. Anthony P. Carnevale, Stephen J. Rose, and Andrew R. Hanson, "Certificates: Gateway to Gainful Employment and College Degrees," Georgetown University, Center for Education and the Workforce, June 5, 2012.

11. http://www.bls.gov/emp/ep_table_110.htm, http://www.bls.gov/emp/ep_table_102.htm.

12. Mitra Toosi, "Labor Force Projections to 2020: A More Slowly Growing Workforce," *Monthly Labor Review*, January 2012: 43–64.

13. Dowell Myers and John Pitkin, "Assimilation Tomorrow: How America's Immigrants Will Integrate by 2030," Center for American Progress report, November 2011.

14. For an extended discussion of the range of possible policies, see Paul Osterman and Beth Shulman, *Good Jobs America: Making Work Better for Everyone* (New York: Russell Sage, 2011).

15. For a discussion of the technology story, see David Autor, Frank Levy, and Richard Murnane, "The Skill Content of Recent Technological Change: An Empirical Investigation," *Quarterly Journal of Economics* 118 (November 2003): 1279–1333. For the application

of this story for explaining recent trends in wages, see David H. Autor, Lawrence F. Katz, and Melissa S. Kearney, "Trends in U.S. Wage Inequality: Revising the Revisionists," *The Review of Economics and Statistics*, May 2008, 90(2): 300–323. See also David Autor, "The Polarization of Job Opportunities in the U.S. Labor Market: Implications for Employment and Earnings," Center for America Progress, April 2010. For a critique of this literature, see Lawrence Mishel, John Schmitt, and Heidi Shierholz, "Assessing the Job Polarization Explanation of Growing Wage Inequality," Economic Policy Institute, Working Paper No. 295, January 11, 2013.

16. Among working adults in the Census ORG data between 2000 and 2009, the hourly wage of those with a college degree increased by a total of 0.3 percent, while the hourly wage of those with only a high school degree grew by 1.9 percent and those with a graduate degree by 2.7 percent.

17. Bureau of Labor Statistics, http://www.bls.gov/emp/ep_table_110.htm.

18. Paul Osterman and Andrew Weaver, "Skills and Skill Gaps in Manufacturing," in *Production in the Innovation Economy*, ed. R. Locke and R. Wellhausen (Cambridge, MA: MIT Press, 2014).

19. Bureau of Labor Statistics, http://www.bls.gov/emp/ep_table_110.htm, http://www.bls.gov/emp/ep_table_102.htm.

20. David Neumark, Hans Johnson, and Marisol Cuellar Mejia, "Future Skill Shortages in The U.S. Economy," National Bureau of Economic Research, Working Paper No. 17213, July 2011.

21. Michael J. Handel, "What Do People Do at Work? A Profile of U.S. Jobs from the Survey of Workplace Skills, Technology, and Management Practices (STAMP)," Northeastern University, June 2010, p. 34.

22. Osterman and Weaver, "Skills and Skill Gaps in Manufacturing."

23. Roberto M. Fernandez, "Skill-Biased Technological Change and Wage Inequality: Evidence from a Plant Retooling," *American Journal of Sociology* 107, no. 2 (September 2001): 273–320.

24. For example, see John P. Smith, "Tracking the Mathematics of Automobile Production: Are Schools Failing to Prepare Students for Work?" *American Journal of Educational Research,* Winter 1999: 835–878. Also see the account of the Honda Motor Company in Frank Levy and Richard Murnane, *Teaching the New Basic Skills* (New York: Free Press, 1996).

25. For a review of the evidence, see Paul Osterman, *Securing Prosperity, The American Labor Market: How It Has Changed and What to Do About It* (Princeton, NJ: Princeton University Press, 1999).

26. For a useful discussion of these issues, see David Weil, *The Fissured Workplace: Why Work Became So Bad for So Many and What Can Be Done to Improve It* (Cambridge: Harvard University Press, 2014).

27. Kelley S. Mikelson and Demetra Smith Nightingale, "Estimating Public and Private Expenditures on Occupational Training in the United States," Urban Institute, report for U.S. Department of Labor, Employment and Training Administration, December 2004.

28. See, for example, Matissa N. Hollister, "Does Firm Size Matter Anymore? The New Economy and Firm Size Wage Effects," *American Sociological Review* 69 (October 2004): 659–676; Peter Cappelli, *Why Good People Can't Get Jobs: The Skills Gap and What Companies Can Do About It* (Philadelphia: Wharton Digital Press, 2012).

29. Basil Whiting, "The Retention and Advancement Demonstration Project (RAD): A 'Win-Win' for Manufacturers and Their Workers at Entry- and Near Entry-Levels," Washington D.C. Center for Workforce Success, Manufacturing Institute, National Association of Manufacturers, August 2005.

30. See Osterman and Shulman, *Good Jobs America*.

31. FutureWorks, "Building Essential Skills through Training (BEST): Final Evaluation Report," Commonwealth Corporation, September 2004.

32. Harry Holzer, Richard Block, Marcus Cheatham, and Jack Knott, "Are Training Subsidies for Firms Effective: The Michigan Experience," *Industrial and Labor Relations Review* 46, no. 4 (July 1993).

33. Matthew Dey, Susan N. Houseman, and Anne E. Polivka, "Manufacturers' Outsourcing to Staffing Services," *ILR Review* 65(3) (July 2012): [533]–559.

3

A Brief History of Sectoral Strategies

Maureen Conway

Sector strategies have grown in prominence within the workforce community over the past decade. Recent research, legislative advocacy work, federal funding initiatives, state policy changes, and other efforts have worked toward supporting the adoption of sector strategies as an effective approach to workforce development. This chapter reviews some of the history of sector strategies and the varied efforts taken to build the sectoral field of practice. The chapter also touches on the accomplishments of the field in helping low-income workers and job seekers find opportunities, and offers ideas about how the principles of sector practice could be used to further expand economic opportunity for those who need it.

The Emergence of Sector Strategies

The strategy of focusing on sectors emerged in the late 1980s and early 1990s as local organizations sought new ways to better connect poor communities to productive opportunities in their regional economies. During a period of economic recovery that had nonetheless seen growing poverty, these organizations began looking for opportunities to link poverty alleviation and economic development and to identify and develop the assets of low-income communities as a basis for expanding the economic opportunities available to low-income individuals. The sector movement also was responding to changes in public-sector investments in education and training, issues of social equity and social exclusion, and current theories of economic development and economic competitiveness.

In essence, a sector approach identified a segment of the local or regional economy that had the potential to offer opportunities to low-income people and then developed a strategy that allowed that low-income constituency to find jobs in the sector, which supported both the employers in the sector and the low-income constituency. In its early days, this strategy took a number of forms. Some organizations worked to support clusters of entrepreneurs starting businesses in particular sectors, such as home care, food production, and building renovation. The strategy could include starting a business that offered training and outplacement opportunities. Greyston Bakery in New York followed this model in culinary occupations, as did Esperanza Unida in auto body repair in Milwaukee, and Asian Neighborhood Design in furniture manufacturing and building-trades skills in San Francisco. Some organizations invested in particular sectors of the economy to support business development in those sectors, with an eye toward creating accessible and family-sustaining jobs for local residents. Not all of these business-development efforts were successful over the long term, which is unsurprising, given the rate of success and long-term survival among business start-ups in general, but some of this work continues today. Over time, and particularly during the strong labor market of the 1990s, the sector strategy developed more of a focus on a workforce component, which seeks to facilitate the participation of a low-income constituency in a particular industry sector through a strategy that involves, at least in part, building the skills of that constituency through workforce development.[1] This sectoral workforce-development strategy is the primary focus of this chapter, and this book.

Sector-based workforce development is not new in the sense of organizing the training of workers in the context of an industry sector, and its direct antecedents go back a century or more. The basic idea is the following: If policies and programs focus attention on a like group of firms with similarities defined by products, processes, occupations, and locations, it will be easier and more efficient to get them organized to identify and address common business and employment needs. A similar logic has applied to certain types of economic and workforce development, specifically the concept of "cluster" economic development made famous by Michael Porter, as well as to craft unions and their apprenticeship system and even the guild system of the Middle Ages. In the time when sector strategies were emerging, however, unions and their apprenticeship systems were on the decline, and in many low-income communities unions had been seen as unsympathetic and unwelcoming to women and minorities. At the same time, vocational and technical schools had the reputation of being an inferior educational option to college-prep and college programs and were experiencing reductions in public investment. Thus sector employment programs were filling a growing void in practical and applied opportunities for development employment skills.

Sector initiatives were also often connected to social-justice movements, and the issues of race, gender, and geography shaped a number of early sector employment programs. The rate of labor force participation among women in the United States climbed dramatically in the 1970s and 1980s, but many found that women were often concentrated in lower-wage occupations and in general did not have earnings on par with their male counterparts. Several sector initiatives worked explicitly to advance women's opportunities and overcome the unique barriers they face in accessing economic opportunity. These initiatives often focused on jobs that would be considered nontraditional for women, and Oregon Tradeswomen, Inc. (see Helmer and Conway, Chapter 15) was founded with the mission of promoting economic self-sufficiency for women by creating access to employment opportunities in the building-trades sector and helping women build the skills and professional networks needed in those jobs.

A number of sector initiatives were in communities that had experienced disinvestment and economic isolation, including both poor rural communities and urban communities. One of the earliest sector initiatives was organized by the Mountain Association for Community Economic Development (MACED). Since 1979 it has focused on the forestry industry in the Appalachian region of Kentucky, working with local businesses and communities to improve forestry practices and forest-product businesses so that they could move up the value chain from a supplier of raw timber to a producer of high-value products. MACED worked to build skills in the forestry businesses and create connections to industry networks and economic opportunities, overcoming geographic isolation. A number of other sector initiatives focused on isolated urban communities, although many of these were communities of color and the issue of race was also prominent. For example, Focus: HOPE (mentioned below) was founded as a civil rights organization, following the civil rights riots of the 1960s, and focused on the issues faced by inner-city African American communities in Detroit. Its sector initiatives, begun in the 1980s, were a means to continue its work of expanding economic opportunity for these communities and overcoming the racism and economic exclusion that they often experienced.

While the issues of race, gender, and geographic isolation are less frequently discussed today as motivating factors for sectoral employment programs, they nonetheless remain important issues that many sector initiatives recognize as significant barriers in today's economy. For example, a 2012 report from the U.S. Bureau of Labor Statistics notes that the high rate of unemployment among blacks, which has been roughly twice that of whites for the past two decades, is not explained by differences in educational attainment, since the unemployment rate for blacks is close to double that of whites at every educational level.[2]

In addition, recent work on economic mobility has found substantial variability among cities and regions within the United States in the likelihood of low-income individuals moving up the economic ladder, highlighting the role of local systems in influencing access to economic opportunity.[3] (In Chapter 2, Paul Osterman provides more information about persistent challenges that women, minorities, and younger workers face in the labor market.)

Sector initiatives were also connected to ideas of economic development and community wealth generation, and they are often linked to cluster economic development strategies, popularized in the early 1990s by Michael Porter's work in particular. Cluster and sector strategies are often confused with each other but in practice are distinct, with the potential to be highly complementary. "Sector" is an employment concept, while "cluster" is an economic-development concept. In a sense, they mirror each other. A sector approach is an employment strategy that has economic ramifications; a cluster focus is an economic strategy that has employment ramifications. In a cluster strategy, the focus is on the business, and success is viewed in terms of new start-ups, business growth, and other measures of business success. In contrast, a sector strategy focuses on the worker and opportunities to improve his or her earning capacity, typically through a mix of skill building, social support, and professional networking services. A sector strategy can be designed to complement a cluster strategy by preparing workers for the jobs a cluster will create, developing networks to help create professional connections between workers and employers, and engaging to ensure that jobs are structured to deploy and reward skills at high levels, creating value in the community.

This approach has been taken, for example, in the biotechnology industry, a growing sector that has attracted the interest of many communities across the United States. These communities may offer biotechnology companies economic-development incentives, such as tax abatements, public infrastructure, and streamlined permitting, with the goal of encouraging the creation of a biotechnology "cluster" in the region, which would lead to new jobs, an increased tax base, and enhanced regional prosperity. Typically, the biotechnology companies will recruit nationally and even internationally to fill skilled positions and may even cast a broad net, in geographic terms, when recruiting for entry-level support or production positions. These recruiting practices can result in few job opportunities for current residents, reducing the economic development benefits for the community as a whole. A well-designed sector strategy, on the other hand, can benefit existing unemployed and underemployed residents, enhancing the economic-development value of the cluster effort.

In Baltimore, the BioTechnical Institute of Maryland, Inc. began with this purpose in mind. Founded in 1998 in response to the development of a city-sponsored biotechnology park in a low-income Baltimore neighborhood, the organization provides tuition-free pre-employment training to unemployed and underemployed residents of Baltimore City to prepare them for positions as entry-level workers in the biotechnology industry. Similarly, Skyline Community College in San Mateo, California, collaborated with a number of other agencies and leading biotechnology companies to create a biomanufacturing certificate program designed to open opportunities to area residents who might otherwise not find a pathway into this growing industry. The initial target population for this program, established in 2003, was baggage handlers who had lost their jobs in a wave of layoffs at nearby San Francisco Airport. Both initiatives helped eager workers develop new skills and secure high-quality jobs that supported the economic-development strategy of their region.

This vision of sectoral employment—with a focus on providing opportunities for skill building and the development of human capital and human potential, on overcoming social barriers and economic exclusion, and on building economic opportunity—adopted the name "sector" in the 1990s after experimentation in the 1980s seemed to show promising results, and represented a new wave of thinking about how to help the poor connect to economic opportunity.

Early Examples of Sector Strategies

Sector strategies started out by identifying a promising sector of their regional economy and developing a strategy that could improve access to economic opportunity for the low-income constituency they served. Strategies went beyond training and placement in a particular industry to include financing strategies to support job growth, entrepreneurship support and business development services, and direct creation of enterprises. In general, these organizations tied together the idea of developing strong, economically competitive businesses with the idea of economic opportunity and poverty alleviation, and were distinct from social-service approaches to addressing poverty that worked to improve the public provision of housing, food, or other basics to the poor.[4]

Sector work coalesced around jobs, rather than around entrepreneurship or asset development, as the key pathway out of poverty, and the area of sectoral employment development emerged as explicitly focused on connecting low-income people to employment. Among these sectoral employment development strategies, two schools of thought were prominent.

The first was the idea that low-income groups were often shut out of the best jobs in a community and that systemic barriers to these jobs needed to be addressed to open access to good jobs for low-income groups. Among the best of the early examples of this approach was Focus: HOPE in Detroit. Focus: HOPE founded its Machinist Training Institute in the 1980s to help low-income African Americans, primarily men initially, get high-paying skilled-machinist jobs, an occupation that was almost exclusively white at the time. The organization was founded as a civil rights and racial-equity organization after the riots in the 1960s, but up until that time, Focus: HOPE had not addressed job skills and employment issues, although it had fought workplace discrimination. The machinist occupation had barriers beyond outright discrimination, although that was an issue. The jobs required a set of skills that were not commonly found among Detroit's inner-city black men. Focus: HOPE leveraged the personal connections of its leadership to gain access to some of Detroit's most prominent employers, convincing these business leaders to hire their graduates and to encourage other companies to hire them as well. At the same time, Focus: HOPE carefully recruited, screened, and trained its first class of trainees, ensuring that they would succeed and build the organization's reputation so that they could continue this work. In addition, Focus: HOPE's leadership was very successful in attracting resources and raised money to build a state-of-the-art training center that impressed students, employers, and other visitors with its clear ambition and intention to be a long-term participant in the industry. Over time, and particularly in the wake of welfare reform in the 1990s, Focus: HOPE began reaching out to women, many of them single mothers, and helping them gain manufacturing jobs that were traditionally held by men. Focus: HOPE's training and industry connections led to substantial earnings gains for many low-income training participants; a study released in 2002 showed that participants' earnings were less than $10,000 annually before training and rose to more than $26,000 after. By addressing the barriers of education, professional connections, race, and gender, Focus: HOPE created pathways to better jobs in Detroit's manufacturing industry for populations who had previously been shut out.

The second branch of sectoral employment development strategies focused on poor-quality jobs and developed strategies that could change industry standards in a region and improve job pay and benefits. An example of this approach is Paraprofessional Healthcare Institute (PHI) and Cooperative Home Care Associates (CHCA) in the Bronx. CHCA is a worker-owned home health care agency in New York City. The homecare industry in New York City employs many low-income women, most of whom are racial or ethnic minorities and many of whom are immigrants. The founders of CHCA sought to develop a business that would improve the fortunes of home care workers. Homecare workers, typically women, have low hourly pay, few employment benefits, irregular hours, often long, unpaid commutes to patients' homes, and isolated working conditions in strangers' homes, where they provide care to elderly people and individuals with disabilities.

By forming a worker-owned cooperative, the founders of CHCA sought to both improve the economic return for workers and improve their ability to meet the challenges of the job. Shortly after CHCA began, PHI began as an affiliated non-profit. PHI designs and helps fund training for new and continuing workers at CHCA. Workers are offered a higher level of training than is required by the regulations that set the industry standard. In addition, they own shares of the company on a one-person, one-share basis, and innovations like a guaranteed minimum number of work hours for employees were instituted to improve the quality of the job, highlighting the value and dignity of the work and in turn improving quality of care for many disabled and elderly individuals.

CHCA developed a deep understanding of the homecare sector and used its position as an employer to both advocate for better policies and demonstrate the possibility of improved employer practices. One example of an improved practice related to the issues of commute times. Many homecare workers were often assigned patients who lived far from their homes but were not compensated for the time spent travelling. CHCA began developing business in the Bronx for its Bronx-based employees, but it also raised the issue of trying to match home care workers to nearby clients, a practice used in the nursing field but not for home care aides. By demonstrating that the practice of matching homecare aides to nearby patients was not only good for the aide but also good for care, since it reduced the likelihood that an aide would be late or not show up for an appointment, CHCA helped make a change in the industry that improved the quality of the aide's job. In the same vein, offering home care workers a guaranteed minimum number of hours gave them a predictable income level. It is important to note that while neither of these innovations raised the hourly wage, both had significant economic benefits for the home care workers.

As a separate but affiliated organization with CHCA, PHI took on an active role in policy issues, developed a suite of services offering coaching and consulting to businesses in the homecare and long-term care sectors, and continued its role developing and providing training. Because health care is such a regulated industry, with public policy often setting standards for reimbursement rates, staff requirements, and other elements, public policy plays a significant role in determining job quality in the industry, and PHI has been active in policy discussions. For example, in 2011, in close cooperation with SEIU 1199 (the health care union that has unionized tens of thousands of aides in New York and other states), PHI co-led a successful effort to achieve a mandated minimum wage of $10 per hour plus benefits in New York City and surrounding counties for all homecare aides paid with New York State Medicaid funding. This legislation raised the floor wage for more than 80,000 homecare aides by an average of $2 per hour over a three-year phase-in period that was completed in March of 2014-resulting in $250 million additional earnings annually for these workers, or an average of $3,000 per worker. In addition, employer-based benefits increased during that period by more than $2.50/hour. The total result is that, currently, home health aides receive $14.09/hour in wages and benefits, compared to approximately $9.25/hour in 2012. On a national level, PHI has been a leading advocate for revising the U.S. Department of Labor's Fair Labor Standards Act's "companionship exemption" so that homecare aides will be covered by federal minimum wage and overtime protections. In its work with employers—whether with its affiliated companies, which now include a cooperative in Philadelphia, Home Care Associates, and a managed-care organization, Independence Care System, or with unaffiliated nursing homes and other care providers—PHI focuses on improving the quality of the job to build a more stable and experienced workforce, which in turn improves the quality of care. It offers companies supervisory training and other services so they can better support the workforce they have, retain them longer, and achieve better customer care.

These two examples highlight the two schools of thought that have been prevalent in sector work. In short, these two schools of thought are often referred to as either promoting access to "good" jobs or making "bad" jobs better. They also highlight the differences and diversity of sector strategies. The industry, the particular population served, the institutions and policy environment of a region, the state of the regional economy, and a variety of other factors can shape a sector strategy, creating a diverse set of program offerings that share the sector term. Yet there are a set of strategic principles that guide the approach, and articulating these principles was the next step to building this field of practice.

Defining Sector Strategies

The ideas demonstrated by Focus: HOPE and CHCA, as well as other sector initiatives, began to get the attention of national philanthropic organizations in the early 1990s as an innovative approach to addressing challenges faced by low-income communities. In 1995, with funding from the Charles Stewart Mott Foundation and the Ford Foundation, both the Aspen Institute and Mt. Auburn Associates released publications to more clearly define what is meant by sectoral strategies and how these strategies can meet the employment need of low-income populations. Both papers were published under the title *Jobs and the Urban Poor*, the distinction being that the Aspen Institute researchers looked at privately initiated sector strategies, largely started by nonprofit organizations, while Mt. Auburn researchers investigated publicly initiated strategies.

This distinction is important if one considers the different resources and constraints faced by public agencies and private nonprofits, and indeed there was and continues to be a difference in how public and private-nonprofit entities frame and evaluate the benefits of sector strategies. In 1995 the Aspen Institute defined sectoral strategies as follows:

A sectoral initiative represents a distinct employment model that:

- Targets a particular occupation within an industry;

- Intervenes by becoming a valued actor in the industry that employs that occupation;

- Exists for the primary purpose of assisting low-income people to obtain decent employment; and

- Creates, over time, systemic change within that occupation's labor market.[6]

In this definition, the sector strategy was based on the premise that poverty alleviation can be linked to economic development, that human capital is important to the economy, and that the best way to address poverty is by helping poor people find productive employment. Certainly the idea of employment as a pathway out of poverty is not controversial and has been a hallmark of much of public policy over the last few decades. Welfare reform was based on the idea that work should be encouraged even among single mothers with child-care responsibilities; public housing has long included programs to help local residents find jobs; and the food stamp program includes funding for training, based on the idea that helping people earn a better living will allow them to buy their own food. A sector approach builds on the idea that the human capital embodied in poor populations is a resource that can further economic development and that to unlock that resource, systemic change in the labor market is needed.

In contrast to the findings of the Aspen Institute's research on privately initiated sector strategies, Mt. Auburn Associates found that publicly initiated sector strategies had a different guiding framework. Mt. Auburn looked at publicly operated or financed approaches in ten urban areas. While they didn't arrive at a specific definition, they did describe a number of common features of the strategy, which include developing clear goals that drive the choice of a sector, developing in-depth knowledge of the sector and its competitive dynamics, developing a strategy with a relatively long-term planning horizon, and including industry, government, labor, and other stakeholders in a collaborative process. A notable difference, however, is that the publicly initiated strategies did not have a primary purpose of advancing economic opportunity for those in need. In particular, the authors note:

[Publicly initiated] sector strategies have generally made expanding employment opportunities for the urban poor a relatively low priority (addressing urban poverty was not a stated goal of any of the case studies) and there are no intermediaries at the city level to represent the interests of low-income residents in a sector initiative.[7]

The authors caution that the tendency of sector strategies to be industry-driven can be a disadvantage in terms of their ability to advance opportunity for low-income residents, particularly given the lack of institutions to represent the interests of those citizens. The authors recommend:

The public sector needs to protect against programs being too industry-driven by ensuring [that] the interests of residents remain primary. While it is important to respond to the needs of businesses in the design and implementation of any sector strategy, the public sector needs to ensure that its primary mission remains the interests of residents. Helping business to remain competitive and promoting new job generating enterprises is a means to that end, not the end itself.[8]

While the early concept was rooted in the ideas and ideals of poverty alleviation, later definitions of sectoral employment development did not emphasize this aspect of the work. Instead, definitions moved to describe a strategy that was a generally good way of designing a labor market intervention and noting that it could be especially useful for low-income groups. For example, on their shared State Sector Strategies web site, the Corporation for a Skilled Workforce, the National Governors Association, and the National Network of Sector Partners describe the purpose of sector strategies as "…to address the workforce needs of employers, and the needs of workers for relevant training to advance into good jobs." They immediately note, however, that "Sector partnerships can be particularly effective for low-skilled and low-income workers."[9] This same shift in language can be observed in the definition the Aspen Institute offered in 2007, in which the sector strategy is described as one that is engaged in "typically on behalf of low-income individuals,"[10] but poverty alleviation is not included in the definition.

There are many reasons for this shift in the definitions away from an emphasis on poverty alleviation or targeting assistance to low-income populations. One view contributing to the shift is that the approach should emphasize the assets workers bring, rather than defining them by their deficits. The sector strategy is built on the concept of helping individuals build their assets through human-capital development and empowering individuals to take charge of their economic advancement, so there was a growing tendency to avoid language that emphasizes neediness and to favor language that puts greater emphasis on capacity and potential. A second contributing factor is that there was often some confusion about the right approach to defining a "low-income" population for purposes of the strategy, and which groups might "count" as disadvantaged. This could be particularly challenging for groups offering training to both new entrants and incumbent workers, seeking not only to help unemployed and low-income workers get into industries but also to promote advancement for current workers. If one is only willing to provide incumbent-worker training when workers are still officially poor, then the strategy would favor providing services to employers whose entry-level wages are very low. Thus a consistent, practical definition of what it means to target disadvantaged workers became a challenge. This conversation had the potential to derail a discussion of the strategy itself and thus encouraged a separation of the purpose of serving low-income groups from the description of the strategy itself. Another factor influencing the move away from poverty-alleviation goals had to do with marketing the strategy to business partners. A discussion of workers as low-income seemed, to many program leaders, to reduce the appeal of the strategy to business stakeholders, whose engagement was avidly sought. Finally, it is certainly the case that the term "poverty" is used less often across the policy spectrum and has acquired a taint among some members of the public and politicians, despite the fact that poverty is increasing. One can question whether this trend of avoiding a clear focus on low-income or poor populations has gone too far, inhibiting discussion of a large and growing problem in our society, but that is beyond the scope of this chapter. This broader trend, however, certainly influenced language and the articulation of goals and purpose in the sectoral workforce field, just as it did in many other areas of social service and human development.

Building the Sectoral Field of Practice

The early sector programs seemed to offer a new, market-oriented way to help address poverty and promote access to opportunity and had great appeal. The philosophy of the approach emphasized the assets of low-income populations and their ability to contribute to our economy if they were afforded the opportunity to fully develop those assets. In addition, several organizations that seemed to be operating with this spirit appeared to have noteworthy outcomes. National foundations made investments in several key areas to further the development of sector employment development as a field of practice. These investments supported research to build the evidence base and document effective practices; development of the infrastructure to support a field; investing in the capacity of individual leaders to create and manage complex strategies; articulating a policy agenda; and organizing regional funder networks to broaden the investment base and strategically focus investments. Taken together, these investments worked to build an approach into a field of practice. The fifth element is discussed in Chapter 5, which describes the evolution of the National Fund for Workforce Solutions and its affiliated local funder collaboratives, and the fourth is largely described in Chapter 16, which covers trends in workforce public policy. The other three are summarized below.

Building the Evidence Base

After arriving at a more or less agreed-upon definition of sector strategies, a better assessment of outcomes was needed to build the case for their effectiveness. The Mott Foundation, the Ford Foundation, and the Annie E. Casey Foundation supported the Aspen Institute's Economic Opportunities Program to conduct the Sectoral Employment Development Learning Project (SEDLP), starting in 1997, which documented the practices and outcomes of six well-established sector initiatives. Subsequently, the Charles Stewart Mott Foundation funded Public/Private Ventures (P/PV) in 1999 to undertake the Sectoral Employment Initiative, which sought to study the start-up and early-stage outcomes of newer sector initiatives. These early-stage evaluations offered detailed information on participants in sector initiatives and their experiences in the labor market before and after training. Both studies documented positive outcomes for workers.[11]

Results from these studies, which started to become available in 2000, were presented at a wide variety of national conferences and briefings, reaching a range of actors that included federal administration officials, congressional staffers, state policy makers, local practitioners, philanthropic leaders, and others. In a series of focus groups with state, local, and federal policy makers and other industry stakeholders, jointly sponsored by the Aspen Institute and the National Network of Sector Partners (NNSP) and led by a professional communications firm, early research findings were presented. Those who attended were surprised at the strong outcomes, as the view that "training doesn't work" was the common conception in the early 2000s. One factor observed to overcome skepticism about the findings was providing detailed information about the strategic approach and its connection with industry needs and the demands of the regional economy.

Program leaders were more likely to believe the outcomes but needed detailed information about practice. Early research and case studies provided information about how training strategies responded to specific industry needs, often addressing issues of workplace culture, technical skills, and basic academic skills in an integrated manner. A key element documented in early studies was the myriad ways sector initiatives sought to develop and maintain industry relationships. Many sector initiatives achieved this by engaging the industry in ways that went beyond employment training and placement, such as operating a business in the industry, conducting industry surveys on key issues, or becoming a hub of knowledge for specific issues. This broader engagement with industry was important for deepening relationships and maintaining connections, particularly at times when hiring demands were low. The wide variety of approaches to this level of industry engagement, however, meant that it was a difficult element to consistently describe or fit within the existing institutional capacities of employment-training organizations, and supporting these industry-engagement activities through regular funding streams proved challenging.

The early studies provided outcomes and information about practices that generated enthusiasm and support for expansion of sector strategies. Nonetheless, these studies were exploratory in nature and were designed for a young field of practice that had neither the scale nor the settled set of practices necessary for a more rigorous evaluation approach. After the American Assembly in 2003, however, it seemed that the field was ready for this higher level of scrutiny. With funding from the Mott Foundation, P/PV launched the Sectoral Employment Impact Study (SEIS) and began recruiting mature sectoral initiatives to participate in a rigorous study of participant outcomes using an experimental design. Given the long timeline of this type of research, the final report summarizing the findings of the study was not released until 2010. The outcomes were quite striking, with significant impacts on employment and earnings, and the study helped re-energize a focus on investing in this approach to workforce development.[12] (Christopher King offers more information on a range of evaluation research in Chapter 11.) The studies noted here garnered significant attention for their findings and played a key role in building evidence for the sectoral approach.

It is important to note, however, that the generalizability of the findings is often not well-defined, and this may limit the ability to replicate success. For example, during the SEIS research, one organization, the Wisconsin Regional Training Partnership, was observed doing less training in the manufacturing sector than was anticipated at the beginning of the study and more training in construction, in response to changes in the local economy. This ability to adjust to a changing local context is the response of a mature organization with an experienced staff and a deep set of connections in these sectors. Moreover, it demonstrates that the organization finds success not by implementing a defined service strategy consistently but by knowing when to deliver which service in response to what need. Indeed this sort of organizational capability and adaptability is difficult for many organizations to develop, and the lack of an understanding of and ability to replicate these qualities has impeded many efforts to replicate these complex strategies.[13] It is challenging to define the appropriate service strategy and set of activities that should be implemented in the absence of local context and an understanding of organizational capacity.

It is also important to note the limitations of current methods of assessing the outcomes of sectoral employment training efforts. The studies mentioned above all documented outcomes for the individuals who participated in a particular initiative, but they do not touch on employer outcomes or systems-change outcomes. Yet one of the key goals of sector work, as originally defined, was systems change; sector initiatives aim to create changes in the dynamics of how employees and employers come together for a particular occupational cluster in a particular regional labor market, such that even individuals who did not directly participate in the program might benefit and the overall competitiveness of the industry would be enhanced. The work of PHI and CHCA described above, in which they pushed for policies to raise industrywide wages or influenced changes in scheduling practice that affected workers not employed by CHCA, clearly benefited individuals who would not be counted as direct recipients of services from these organizations. Most evaluations of workforce-development programs, however, take the outcomes for individual workers as the unit of analysis, and thus the benefits from initiatives that create change industrywide will not be captured. Particularly in situations where the evaluation compares individuals who receive program services with those who do not, these efforts to create systemic change will be deemed unsuccessful, since the outcomes may be similar for both treatment and comparison groups. In approaches leveraging institutional change for the benefit of workers, the unit of analysis might more appropriately be thought of as industry practice, but isolating impacts on industry practice is not something that standard job training evaluations are designed to accomplish. It remains a challenge for researchers and the field to continue to describe this element of sector work, given the limitations of generally accepted evaluation techniques.

While there has been little progress in evaluating sector strategies' systems-change outcomes, there has been progress in measuring the outcomes of services for business. For example, in 2005 the Aspen Institute released a Business Value Assessment Toolkit, designed to help sector leaders identify the ways in which their services provided value to their business customers. In 2011, the Commonwealth Corporation released a practitioners' guide for measuring business impact, and in 2012 the National Fund for Workforce Solutions released a publication examining how to address the return to employers for investments in training of the frontline healthcare workforce.[16] These resources provide useful ideas to sectoral workforce practitioners seeking to deepen their engagement with their employer customers.

A number of initiatives have also found that they can develop compelling information for some employer partners using these measures. For the most part, however, the types of evaluations done to date would not meet the same standards of rigor that public investors often require when assessing whether a program is effective in creating positive outcomes for workers, but these efforts have been useful for operational management questions and for informing both business and workforce service providers' perspectives on the value of particular workforce-development efforts. Another limitation of these efforts to measure employer outcome is that they have limited relevance for initiatives that work with a number of small employers. In general, these measures of business outcomes are best benchmarked in a firm-specific way. For example, if the goal of training is to reduce turnover, then the relevant benchmark for a firm is the firm's turnover rate prior to the training initiative. An industry average or other external benchmark could be quite misleading, since the specific firm's turnover rate could be quite different from the industry average. Additionally, a small firm is unlikely to have enough employees or new hires from a training program to make an evaluation worthwhile. Even with large firms there can be challenges in accessing the full range of necessary information, since firms may not be comfortable sharing some information due to concerns about competitiveness or employee privacy. Notwithstanding all of that, efforts to measure business outcomes represent an advancement in this area and offer something to build on.

Developing the Infrastructure to Support a Field

In addition to building evidence, the sectoral employment efforts needed to engage local program leaders, connect sectoral employment leaders with one another, and spread the approach, which would contribute to building a field of practice. In the early days of sector work, many practitioners did not see themselves as engaged in a common endeavor. For example, a Chicago organization, which focused on building skills of workers and providing technical assistance and real estate services to small businesses to retain metal manufacturers and their jobs, did not immediately see that it had a strategic approach similar to that of an organization involved in community design and the development of low-income housing that trained and placed individuals in construction and related jobs. Despite their differences, as the sector initiative leaders had the opportunity to engage with each other, they saw that there were similar ideas about how to work within a sector, develop industry expertise and relationships, and find points of leverage on behalf of low-income groups.

The early research projects deeply engaged field leaders, and the approach's promise led to the founding of an association for the field. The National Network of Sector Partners (NNSP), established in 1999 as a national effort housed within what was then the National Economic Development and Law Center (today the Insight Center for Community Economic Development), worked to bring field leaders together, communicate the strategic elements of the approach to organizations interested in developing sector initiatives, and build awareness of the field nationally. NNSP hosted national and regional convenings, which emphasized peer learning but also included national and state policy makers, academics, business champions of the approach, and other stakeholders.

NNSP played a critical role in engaging the U.S. Department of Labor and encouraging the department to run the Sectoral Employment Demonstration in 2001. This effort was part of a larger effort within NNSP to reach beyond the traditional set of nonprofit and community-based organizations that had been engaged in sector work. The labor department demonstration, while not large by federal standards, provided funds to Workforce Investment Boards (WIBs) to plan and implement sector strategies, a key step that engaged the public system in such strategies. It was also one of the first efforts to fit sector strategies within a public-funding framework. These grants challenged the grantees to be specific about the businesses they would work with and about the needs of the worker population that would be served. Focusing on both was difficult, in part because that challenged the notion of universal service embedded in the Workforce Investment Act, and instead encouraged WIBs to design a strategy for a subset of businesses and a subset of workers looking for employment or for better employment, workers who had the potential to be a good fit for the industry if offered a well-designed mix of services. WIBs generally focused more on the business side of this equation. As noted in the demonstration evaluation:

> Because of the limited time frames and funding associated with the sectoral employment grants, many grantee organizations focused primarily on business and industry needs and then defaulted to working with a target population that could most easily be prepared to meet those needs. While these projects may have been quite useful to the workers involved, they were less likely to involve hard-to-serve populations. Such strategies are in contrast to those that initially focus equally on industry and selected target populations.[17]

As the trade association for the field, NNSP was a key part of the infrastructure that supported the growth of sector strategies over the past decade. As more organizations and more diverse types of organizations became engaged in sector strategies, however, the need for greater leadership-development opportunities became apparent.

Building the Next Generation of Leaders

One of the key elements of building the field of sector initiatives was to develop field leaders who would implement the strategy creatively in their own communities. Sector strategies need to be responsive to the dynamics of the industries they are working in, as well as to the needs of the working population and the community in which they operate. Given the many variables that shape a sector strategy, it is difficult to define one particular model or approach to implementation that field leaders should choose. As noted above, while most sector strategies include training, they may also include operating a business, conducting industry research, offering firms consulting services, engaging in policy advocacy, and other activities based on the needs of the industry sector and the targeted worker population. Effective implementation thus requires strong organizations and solid leaders who can articulate a vision to a range of stakeholders and work to achieve that vision.

After the American Assembly in 2003, the Aspen Institute, P/PV, and NNSP worked together with support of the Mott Foundation to design the national Sector Skills Academy to build the next generation of leaders to move the field forward. Housed within the Aspen Institute, the academy offered a leadership-development opportunity for individuals in the sector arena who were looking to deepen their strategy and build their skills to more effectively lead their organization's work. The structure of the academy was informed by a series of phone interviews with current leaders of sector initiatives, as well as research on the field, surveys of potential participants about their interests and needs, and a review of literature on leadership development.

To date, the academy has offered more than two hundred leaders an opportunity to improve skills specific to leading a sector initiative and to consider their personal role as leaders. Importantly, the academy has offered new spokespeople for the sector approach in many states and cities. While this work has been valuable for a number of individuals and has supported efforts in a number of regions and states, greater work on leadership development and capacity building is needed to support effective implementation. Sheila Maguire and Patricia Jenny offer a framework and further exploration of strategies for building organizational capacity in Chapter 13.

Uptake of Sector Strategies and Growth of the Field

As the sector strategy documented early wins, developed a set of champions, attracted increased support of public policy and philanthropic funding initiatives, and developed infrastructure to support field expansion, a wide variety of organizations sought to adopt the strategy. Given the complexity involved, concern grew about maintaining quality in this quickly growing field. Indeed, given the diversity of sector initiatives, defining practices that were essential to strong operations was a challenge. Further, the sector strategy grew within the larger arena of workforce development and employment training, which operates across an array of existing institutions, including community-based nonprofits, community colleges, and workforce investment boards. The path to scale for sector strategies was not to set up new sector-focused organizations but, rather, to infuse the strategy into existing institutional forms. This approach leveraged existing institutions and funding streams to reach scale more quickly. It was also somewhat constrained by the existing capacities and goals of these organizations, as well as the varied incentives and accountability structures associated with their funding streams. In response to some of these constraints, an approach that involved partnerships across institutional forms became much more common as different institutional types sought to leverage both different funding streams and different organizational capacities to implement a full complement of services in a sector strategy.

There is no question that the number of sector initiatives has grown over the past decade. Methods for counting specific initiatives can be a challenge, however, since sector initiatives may involve more than one institution, and an institution may have an important role in more than one sector initiative. Nonetheless, NNSP documented more than two hundred sector initiatives in 2003 but now estimates that they number more than a thousand and that number continues to grow.[18] While there has been continuing debate as to what precisely defines a sector initiative, it is certainly the case that a growing number of efforts would at least self-identify as such.

In addition, the variety of institutions leading a sector initiative has expanded from a concentration among community-based nonprofits in the early days to include WIBs, community colleges, labor-management partnerships, worker centers, and business associations. The institutional home for a sector strategy often shapes the way in which a sector initiative is adopted. For example, one community-based organization working in manufacturing adopted a strategy of offering manufacturing employers different levels and types of service depending on the quality of job they offered, since they saw influencing employer practice as an opportunity to improve economic outcomes for their job seekers. Within their tiered services model, the organization offered consulting to manufacturers with lower-quality jobs to help them improve the quality of job they are able to offer. That might include, for example, helping employers find a low-cost insurance provider or recommending improvements in operations that can reduce waste or improve safety. As these improvements take hold, the organization would then help identify workers and provide training services as needed. In contrast, a community college with a manufacturing strategy might focus on how students could get credit for existing skills or non-credit work and create pathways to help students improve their skills and obtain credentials or degrees more quickly. Both approaches offer training services to help workers succeed in manufacturing jobs, but the first takes advantage of opportunities to work with companies to improve human-resource and other practices, while the second focuses more on making improvements in the education system. Given that success for these organizations is defined differently, this difference in approach is not surprising. The organizations' chosen approaches were clearly shaped by their mission and goals and their existing institutional capacity.

Increasingly, sector strategies are described as partnerships, with two or more types of organizations combining to deliver a full complement of services and work toward a range of goals. One notable approach to this is partnerships involving community colleges. Community colleges have a relatively well-developed infrastructure and stable funding streams, and they can work with large numbers of students. In 2007 the Aspen Institute began a demonstration project, Courses to Employment, to examine the practices and outcomes of sectoral partnerships between community colleges and nonprofit organizations. These organizations worked together to provide education services, industry connection and navigation assistance, and social supports to individuals while they studied and made the transition to employment. These partnerships between an organization that measures success by student achievement and one that measures success through increased employment and wage gains appeared to help these initiatives support both goals in the interest of the student. In low-wage industries, worker centers have begun forming sector partnerships as they seek to provide services and advocacy to improve job quality and additional skills training to facilitate advancement. A good example is Restaurant Opportunities Centers United (ROC) (see Jayaraman, Chapter 10). While this organization engages in a variety of activities to improve wages and working conditions, it also forms partnerships with community colleges to facilitate skills acquisition and advancement for the workers it serves.

While community college partnerships have been important, partnerships with business organizations and unions have also played important roles. In Las Vegas, the Culinary Training Academy, a labor-management trust that provides entry-level and incumbent-worker training in the hospitality industry, has partnered with Nevada Partners, a community-based nonprofit that works with low-income and disadvantaged residents of North Las Vegas. Together these organizations created a pathway for many low-income residents to jobs paying a family-supporting wage in Las Vegas hotels. In Milwaukee, the Wisconsin Regional Training Partnership (see Buford and Dresser, Chapter 6) works closely with both the building trades unions and the Associated General Contractors, the trade association for the construction industry, as key partners in the work. The partners involved in sector work can vary from community to community, depending on interest, capacity, and needs of local organizations and the particular culture and policy environment of the region.

The range of sectors targeted by these initiatives continues to evolve. Health care has remained a strong and steady focus of many sector initiatives, as it is a major employment sector with a variety of employee-skill needs. Manufacturing and construction have always had a strong presence among sector initiatives, although the cyclical nature of these industries leads to growth and contraction in associated sector initiatives. Initiatives focused on sectors that have become more established, such as biotechnology, have themselves become more established. Sector initiatives targeting information-technology jobs, which often cross industries, evolve in response to changing needs and can vary widely in how they operate. Service industries, such as retail and hospitality, are also drawing more attention, as they are an important source of jobs in many communities.

Many growing service sectors, however, are generating jobs that pay low wages. Because of that, some workforce organizations, such as those funded through the Workforce Investment Act, have trouble placing people in jobs in these sectors, since the mandated wage threshold can be difficult to meet. Strategies led by worker centers in these sectors, however, often focus on addressing these job-quality issues and are engaging in interesting new sectoral initiatives in industries such as domestic work and day labor. Some of these worker centers, like ROC, have developed national networks of affiliates pursuing these strategies. These organizations have been playing a growing role in sector work over the past few years and may become leaders in revitalizing sector strategies targeting low-wage industries.

Conclusions and Future Directions

The sectoral approach has clearly influenced the practice of workforce development over the past decade or longer, encouraging a range of organizations to think strategically about the dynamics of their regional economy and the role their organization plays in that context. In particular, it has encouraged public, private, and nonprofit workforce organizations to consider how to build stronger relationships with employers in their communities and to better understand the dynamics of the workplace. The focus on a particular industry sector has offered a useful means for these organizations to engage more effectively with both workers and industry in their region.

The experience of sector strategies also offers a number of insights about building a field of practice. Philanthropic leaders made strategic investments in organizations engaged in innovative practices to keep pushing the edge of practice. In addition, investments in research, policy advocacy, and field-building institutions were important to developing credibility, resources, and a sense of identity for the field. Sector strategies have seen tremendous growth, and there is much to celebrate. As the field of sectoral employment development looks toward the future, however, there are a number of challenges that remain and new challenges to confront.

Clarity of Purpose

A critical challenge the field will have to address is how to define success. Sector strategies often have a range of goals. They may seek to improve the wages and working conditions of low-income people, improve the competitiveness and job-creation capacity of local employers, or support the delivery of improved health care or other services within a community. Sometimes these interests may work in concert, but sometimes they may come into conflict. How should sector leaders resolve these conflicts? Should some goals supersede others? Should the sector field have an overarching purpose and a set of values that can support sector leaders in navigating conflicts? While conflicts happen and priorities may need to be more clearly stated, sector initiatives will continue to have many goals. However, tracking progress to meet a range of goals is typically hard to accomplish. Developing indicators related to different goals could not only help track progress on multiple dimensions but also help identify conflicts among goals and provide a basis for discussion on how to resolve such issues. Clarifying and prioritizing goals and utilizing appropriate indicators of progress across goals will move the field forward.

Improving Evaluation Techniques

A related challenge is the role of evaluation and the need for a broader set of evaluation tools to assess the progress and contributions of sector strategies. For certain elements of sector work, generally accepted evaluation techniques work well, but for other elements, particularly those that relate to influencing institutional cultures or industry practice or systems-change efforts, we lack generally accepted tools for measuring progress. And yet the case study research and reports from the field would suggest that this work continues to be an important piece of a sector strategy. Determining how to describe the value of this work and ensuring rigor in doing so are challenges that needs attention.

Job Quality

The changing economy also creates new challenges. As described above, sectoral employment development originally targeted both career advancement and access to good jobs and worked to improve job quality. Over the past decade, the strategies focused on job quality have received less attention than those focused on creating pathways to higher-quality jobs. As the economy recovers from the Great Recession, however, many of these family-wage jobs have not been coming back, and instead we have higher numbers of low-wage jobs. This changing job mix is an acceleration of the long-term trend toward a service economy that the U.S. economy has been undergoing for some time. This economic challenge will require new strategies for engaging industry if sector strategies are to work toward positive outcomes for workers and businesses and contribute to strong communities and healthy regional economies. Worker centers that are creatively combining job training and skill development with strategies to empower workers and engage in policy advocacy offer an interesting approach to addressing the needs of workers in low-income sectors. Strategies that combine model businesses or entrepreneurship approaches with job training, such as that of CHCA and PHI, may work well in other regions and sectors. Microenterprise strategies in key sectors may also be valuable as the business trend toward contracting out more services continues. As workers today confront a job market in which a large number of jobs offer low wages and few benefits, and the path to family-wage jobs requires an ever greater number of qualifications, sector leaders need to think creatively about how to help workers across this labor-market spectrum. While skills training and education will continue to be important, sector leaders should be thinking about a broader range of labor-market efforts to make a difference in these fast-growing industries.

Notes

1. For more information on this landscape of early sector efforts, see Fred O'Regan and Maureen Conway, *From the Bottom Up: Toward a Strategy for Income and Employment Generation among the Disadvantaged*, Aspen Institute, March 1993, http://dev.aspenwsi.org/wordpress/wp-content/uploads/BottomUp.pdf.
2. U.S. Department of Labor, "The African-American Labor Force in the Recovery," February 29, 2012, p. 4, http://www.dol.gov/_sec/media/reports/BlackLaborForce/BlackLaborForce.pdf.
3. Raj Chetty, Nathaniel Hendren, Patrick Kline, Emmanuel Saez, and Nicholas Turner, Equality of Opportunity Project, http://www.equality-of-opportunity.org.
4. O'Regan and Conway, *From the Bottom Up*.
5. Lily Zandniapour and Maureen Conway, *Gaining Ground: The Labor Market Progress of Participants of Sectoral Employment Development Programs*, Aspen Institute, February 2002. p. 18.
6. Peggy Clark and Steven L. Dawson, *Jobs and the Urban Poor: Privately Initiated Sectoral Strategies*, Aspen Institute, November 1995, p. v, http://institute.usworker.coop/sites/default/files/resources/001%201995_Clark%20and%20Dawson_Jobs%20for%20the%20Urban%20Poor.pdf.
7. Beth Siegel and Peter Kwass, *Jobs and the Urban Poor: Publicly Initiated Sector Strategies*, Mt. Auburn Associates, November 1995, p. x, http://institute.usworker.coop/sites/default/files/resources/001%201995_Clark%20and%20Dawson_Jobs%20for%20the%20Urban%20Poor.pdf.
8. Ibid., p. xi.
9. Sector Strategies Web site FAQ, http://www.sectorstrategies.org/faq#What.
10. Maureen Conway et al., *Sector Strategies for Low-Income Workers: Lessons from the Field*, Aspen Institute, Summer 2007, p. 2.
11. Zandniapour and Conway, *Gaining Ground*; http://dev.aspenwsi.org/resource/sedlp3-gaining-ground; Anne Roder et al., *Targeting Industries, Training Workers and Improving Opportunities: The Final Report from the Sectoral Employment Initiative*, Public/Private

Ventures, 2008, http://www.sectorstrategies.org/sites/all/files/PVP%20Sectoral%20 Employment%20Inititive.pdf.

12. Sheila Maguire et al., *Tuning In to Local Labor Markets: Findings from the Sectoral Employment Impact Study*, Public/Private Ventures, July 2010, http://www.aspenwsi.org/ wordpress/wp-content/uploads/TuningIntoLocalLaborMarkets.pdf.

13. For a fuller discussion of some of these replication issues, see Robert P. Giloth, "Replicating Model Programs: A Fatal Attraction?" in Robert P. Giloth and Colin Austin, *Mistakes to Success: Learning and Adapting When Things Go Wrong* (Bloomington, IN: iUniverse, 2010).

14. Amy Blair, "How Does Business Benefit from Sectoral Workforce Development Services?" Aspen Institute Workforce Strategies Initiative Update 3 (September 2005), http:// dev.aspenwsi.org/wordpress/wp-content/uploads/05-021.pdf. Aspen Institute Workforce Strategies Initiative, Business Value Assessment Toolkit, October 2005, http:// www.aspenwsi.org/resource/bva-toolkit.

15. Lisa Soricone, Navjeet Singh, and Rebekah Lashman, *Measuring Business Impact: A Workforce Development Practitioner's Guide*, November 2011, http://www.commcorp. org/resources/documents/MBI_Guidebook_1215.pdf.

16. Randall Wilson and Robert Holm, *CareerSTAT: A Guide to Making the Case for Investing in the Frontline Hospital Workforce*, April 2012, http://nfwsolutions.org/sites/nfwsolutions.org/files/CareerSTATFINAL.pdf.

17. Nancy M. Pindus et al., *Evaluation of the Sectoral Employment Demonstration Program: Final Report*, June 2004, p. v, http://dev.aspenwsi.org/wordpress/wp-content/ uploads/04-OP06.pdf.

18. National Network of Sector Partners, "Sector Snapshot: A Profile of Sector Initiatives, 2010, Executive Summary," http://www.insightcced.org/uploads/publications/wd/Sector-Snapshots-ES.pdf.

19. Maureen Conway, Amy Blair, and Matt Helmer, *Courses to Employment: Partnering to Create Paths to Education and Careers*, 2012, www.aspeninstitute.org/sites/default/files/ content/docs/pubs/C2E.pdf.

20. For more on this topic, see Héctor Cordero-Guzmán, Pamela Izvănariu, and Victor Narro, "The Development of Sectoral Worker Center Networks," *Annals of the American Academy of Political and Social Science* 647, no. 1 (May 2013).

4

Industry Partnerships: Theory and Practice

Fred Dedrick

An explicit goal of most sector-based workforce advocates is to embed demand-driven strategies into workforce policy so that additional public resources can be dedicated and/or redirected to demand-driven models that benefit low-wage workers and employers. The recognition of the effectiveness of these strategies is now more widespread but still remains tangential to most federal workforce programs.

Among states, however, the interest in sector strategies is more pronounced. This probably developed through a growing appreciation of the success of local efforts and some rare state examples. It emerged from the work of Cindy Marano at the National Network of Sector Partnerships,[1] Eric Parker of the Wisconsin Regional Training Partnership (WRTP), and Project QUEST in San Antonio. There were also the Skills Panels of Washington State, the Boston Foundation's Skill-Works, and the Annie E. Casey Foundation's Jobs Initiative. These were supplemented by the compilation of sectoral case studies by the Aspen Institute[2] and various publications from Jobs for the Future (JFF).

In all of these examples, there was a clear focus on a deep engagement with a particular industry, such as health care, manufacturing, or construction. Commentators and researchers put a high value on a workforce intermediary that could bring that sector's employers and workers together to develop improved, more demand-driven training initiatives that addressed the needs of companies and mitigated the challenges faced by low-wage workers and job seekers. Some authors also noted that there was also a distinct entrepreneurial aspect that led to innovative practices as the sectoral efforts developed.

One of the largest public investments in sector workforce strategies was Pennsylvania's Industry Partnership program. The statewide effort was built on the practices, research, and learning from many of the aforementioned initiatives. From 2004 to 2010, Pennsylvania's commitment to this model added up to a nearly $100 million investment. It was initially seeded with Workforce Investment Act (WIA) discretionary funding; the Commonwealth then added substantial state resources ($20 million per year at one point), resulting in close to eighty industry partnerships involving more than six thousand businesses across a dozen sectors and eighty thousand trained workers. State administrative data provided evidence of a 6.6 percent wage gain within the first year for those who completed training.[3]

Pennsylvania built on the basic principles of the sector model but added some new conditions. It limited its initial grants to those industry partnerships—the term it used from the outset—investing only in an incumbent-worker strategy. This was a deliberate effort to engage more employers, many of whom were disappointed by or skeptical of the publicly funded workforce system as defined by WIA. Pennsylvania workforce officials reasoned that emphasizing the direct benefits to businesses or organizations from a more-highly skilled workforce would make them more willing to participate in the partnership.

Led by Scott Sheely, of the Lancaster Workforce Investment Board (WIB), many of the WIBs across the state sought out these state grants and eventually became the primary organizers of the industry partnerships. Chambers of commerce, community colleges, manufacturing extension programs, and economic-development organizations also participated in bringing sector-based projects together.

As the history of the National Fund for Workforce Solutions relates (see Dyer et al., Chapter 5), many states, regions, and organizations saw the value of this sectoral approach. The Center for Best Practices of the National Governors Association (NGA) highlighted the value of these workforce initiatives at meetings of state workforce liaisons and state WIB directors. NGA eventually sponsored a series of policy academies to spread the learning to other states about the value of sector-focused workforce development.[4]

The appeal was quite understandable. The strategy emphasized a deeper knowledge of a particular sector to generate a thorough understanding of the skills required by that industry so that education and training programs could be better designed and delivered. More important, because training was so closely tied to industry need, there was a lower likelihood of training people for jobs that didn't exist.

In 2007 the National Fund was formed by philanthropic leaders who had observed and studied these intermediary examples. They believed that improved career opportunities for low-wage workers and disadvantaged adults could be achieved through a deliberate strategy that worked closely with employers in a particular industry sector. They wanted to test this sectoral model to see if it would produce better outcomes than workforce-development programs with only a superficial understanding of industry skill needs.

These funders also sought to produce better outcomes for low-wage workers from the public "workforce system," which in the context of this chapter will represent the combination of publicly and privately funded workforce, training, and educational programs that seek to prepare workers and job seekers with skills to connect them to job opportunities and/or career advancement.

Over time the National Fund has learned to emphasize the need for an ongoing relationship, indeed a partnership, among employers and the intermediary. This evolved from an appreciation of a number of factors: increasingly complex methods of production, distribution, and service delivery; an excess of labor; declining public training resources; and an impersonal system of identifying or sorting qualified applicants.

This chapter explores the theory undergirding industry partnerships, developed statewide in Pennsylvania and now across the country by the National Fund. It provides examples from the application of these ideas and focuses on the value they add to today's workforce challenges. It proposes that industry, educators, philanthropy, and policy makers should view industry partnerships as an invaluable strategy leading to improved workforce and economic-development outcomes for workers, employers, and communities.

Theory

What Is an Industry Partnership?

The National Fund defines an industry partnership as a dynamic collaboration of a regional group of employers from a particular industry sector who convene regularly with training and education institutions to discuss their shared human-resource issues, exchange information about industry practices, and take specific actions to address workforce challenges.[5] Many partnerships also include representatives of organized labor, trade associations, workforce investment boards, and community colleges.

Although other concerns may be addressed, an industry partnership primarily focuses on workforce-related issues: recruiting skilled workers, training and advancing incumbent employees, improving staff supervision, replacing highly skilled retirees, team building, identifying appropriate credentials, language barriers, and leadership development. Larger companies may choose to discuss the trends of international competition, while small to medium-size firms may want a narrower focus. Sometimes the partnership may delve into the workforce implications of a new public policy (e.g., the mandate for electronic health records), consider new regulations like changes to federal workplace-safety standards, or review new food-safety requirements.

Who Organizes Industry Partnerships?

Most industry partnerships are developed by a workforce leaders with a strong desire to better understand and address a community's labor-market demand. It could be a workforce investment board, a regional funder collaborative, a community college, a United Way, or an economic-development organization. Each organizing entity has its particular motivations. Staff from well-run WIBs can bring companies or institutions, like hospitals, together to help guide their training investments. They know that the general representation of a variety of employers on a workforce board is no substitute for the information and relationships that result from a sectoral industry partnership.

In the case of the National Fund, a regional funder collaborative sponsors the organization of these partnerships. A group of funders, usually including a community foundation, a United Way, and a WIB, come together to prepare an initial strategy to address the lack of opportunity for low-income workers and the employer demand for higher-skilled labor. They pool funds and jointly decide to follow the industry-partnership model. Some collaboratives decide to include employers, educators, WIB staff, and economic-development officials to assist in developing a strategy with more collective impact.

The National Fund requires collaboratives to reach out to employers to develop strong relationships with their regional industries. It sees the importance of the partnership model in making more effective investments in training and education. It is acutely aware of the connection between high-quality human resources and economic development and sees industry partnerships as an essential step in developing a collective impact strategy.

Understanding Modern Industry

America's manufacturing facilities, distribution centers, health care institutions, and financial-services firms are highly complex organizations with both specialized skills and cross-industry occupations. Industries are in constant flux as global market forces, regulations, and technology require new products, greater security, and innovation. The Affordable Care Act is transforming health care delivery, changing the mix of clinical staff, and creating new occupations. Even the hospitality and retail sectors are demanding new skill sets that rely increasingly on information technology, customer-relationship techniques, and social media.

To invest well in developing talent, workforce-development initiatives need a thorough understanding of the regional economy, coupled with industry-specific knowledge. The diversity and dynamism of modern industry requires workforce professionals to analyze current business practices, occupational skill requirements, advanced technology, supply chains, regulations, markets, and customers. Wall Street investors, the business press, and the consulting world employ thousands of industry analysts to dig deep into particular industry sectors to uncover important trends and disruptive technologies. This knowledge can rarely be garnered from irregular one-on-one interactions, general industry surveys, or Bureau of Labor Statistics projections.

The size and diversity of the U.S. economy is a major impediment to making useful assumptions about the future demand for certain occupations. Analyzing one sector in a particular geographic region provides the opportunity to develop a level of industry comprehension that brings insight and understanding about that sector's current conditions and its future. Productive investments require a well-informed comprehension of regional labor-market demand and a good sense of how that demand will evolve over several years. This understanding can be generated through a concentrated focus on a community's key industry sectors.

During the period 2012 to 2013, the National Fund regional funder collaboratives supported ninety-six industry partnerships, primarily in health care (40 percent of all partnerships), construction (17 percent), and manufacturing (14 percent), but there were also active partnerships in energy, financial services, transportation and logistics, hospitality, biotechnology, marine trades, automotive repair, and information technology.[6]

Sector Focus

Sector specificity allows employers to have sufficient commonality of experience to help build cohesion of purpose. When there is so much to understand about each industry, special attention is critical. The Pennsylvania Department of Labor and Industry found that within just one industry, such as advanced manufacturing and materials, there was significant diversity of skill needs across food-production companies, metal fabricators, plastics manufacturers, and automobile-industry suppliers.

At the height of Pennsylvania's workforce investment activity, there were manufacturing-industry partnerships in powdered metals, rotorcraft, biotechnology, plastics, and food. Although there were common characteristics among these manufacturers, there were also important differences. The powdered-metals companies of north-central Pennsylvania were mostly small and specialized; the biotech companies of southeastern Pennsylvania were manufacturing carefully controlled batches of drugs for clinical trials; and the plastics companies were making anything from large playground jungle gyms to precision parts for the computer industry. Skill demands within the individual subsector varied from a need to upgrade machinist proficiencies to a need for trained biopharmaceutical researchers for managing clinical trials.

This diversity of training needs within manufacturing is also true in the partnerships supported by the National Fund. Regional differences and a wide variety of production practices from Mobile, Alabama to Cincinnati, Ohio, to San Francisco, California require a deep understanding of the geographic context and the supply chain. The automobile suppliers of Greenville, South Carolina, and Louisville, Kentucky, have many similarities but may differ from the aerospace industry's skill needs in Wichita, Kansas, and Seattle, Washington, or the food-manufacturing workforce demands of Wisconsin Rapids.

In some cases this may require that the employers design and implement the training themselves or seek out trade associations that have a track record for responding to new challenges common to the entire industry.

Selecting a Sector

Choosing a sector as a focus for workforce-development efforts will often begin with a labor-market analysis supplemented by an employer survey. The convener or organizer of the potential partnership may also take advantage of the business relationships of the intermediary organization sponsoring the work. Good labor-market research is essential but will rarely provide sufficient information to know whether organizing an industry partnership is possible or even advisable.

Whoever is tasked with reaching out to employers will need a combination of methods to make this determination: one-on-one meetings, group meetings, phone calls, and e-mails. The goal is to find individuals who, if brought into discussion with their peers, will see their workforce challenges as shared by others in their industry, including their competitors. This can take many weeks or months but will reward the partnership organizer with information that can lay the basis for a successful partnership.

Composition of the Partnership and the Role of Employers

Some partnerships may include other non-employer members, such as workforce-development professionals, educators, or community-based organizations. Labor-management training funds play the same role as an industry partnership and have the added value of resources contributed by both employers and workers available for specific investments in skill development.

However, the critical ingredient of an industry partnership is the sustained engagement and, in the best cases, the leadership of a group of employers. Depending on the sector, the typical employer representative could be anyone from the president of a small company to the vice president of human resources for a midsize firm to the local plant manager of a large conglomerate.

The most effective partnerships will include individuals who have a deep understanding of the day-to day workings of the company or institution. They will know how the work is organized, the prevalent technologies, the skills required, and the challenges of meeting management expectations. Ideally they will have the authority to make decisions to address particular challenges. Less effective are staff from community relations, public relations, or human resources, who are not fully informed about the actual work on the shop floor, the bedside, or other workplace settings. A partnership will want individuals who are close to or in direct contact with the firm or institution's workforce challenges. This allows the discussion among peers to be more detailed and nuanced, leading to greater opportunities for aggregated strategies.

Deciding on First Steps

Revealing consensus around an action step arises from a facilitated discussion, usually over a series of meetings. The partnership organizer uncovers the building blocks of this agreement during the process of pulling together the initial meeting. But the final decision on an initial action will require the opinions and ideas of each participant. A good facilitator will know in advance what each employer cares about and will ask the right questions to elicit these remarks. Ideally one of the employers will take on this role, but this may be too much to expect in the early stages.

One of the key differences between industry partnerships and other forms of workforce development is exactly this interaction among employers in the same industry. It is incredibly valuable to hear a variety of experienced managers discussing the key human-resource challenges of their industry. In many partnerships this interchange among peers is what brings employers back to the next meeting. They realize how much they can learn from one another and where their joint actions could yield benefits to the entire industry.

Data to Information to Intelligence

Few effective industry partnerships can be sustained solely through industry surveys, employer interviews, or focus groups, although these activities can be helpful, especially in the organizing phase, when there is a need to define a problem that is impacting the entire industry.[7]

A productive partnership relies on the face-to-face interactions of the sector-specific employers describing their workforce and business challenges in ways that bring new learning and insight to the conveners of the partnership. One can begin with survey data supplemented with information gathered through interviews with employers, but the real value of a partnership reveals itself through peer interaction as participants exchange opinions, share experiences, reveal challenges, discuss new technologies, and find common issues. This is where the partnership moves from data to information to intelligence.

The food-manufacturing partnership organized by Scott Sheely of the Lancaster WIB was built on solid analysis of secondary data sources and months of interviews and focus groups with Hershey Foods, Turkey Hill Dairy, Pepperidge Farm, and other firms. Scott brought these employers' representatives together, and they discovered that food safety was a common concern. Yet during the organizing phase they'd insisted they had little in common.

As various training initiatives were successfully implemented, the participants saw the potential of collaboration. Eventually they discovered their common competitive advantage in packaging technology, as every company had a strong interest in both the technology and the skilled workers necessary to reach higher productivity. None of this would have been possible without the convening process of an intermediary that brought them together to discover common interests and concerns. I participated in one of the early meetings and saw firsthand how seriously these employers worked to address challenges they shared. Meanwhile, Scott and the Lancaster WIB staff were gathering critical industry intelligence at each meeting, helping to develop new ideas and strategies for the partnership to consider.

This same process is being repeated throughout the National Fund partner communities. Insurance and financial-services managers in Des Moines have designed and developed the Financial Services Training Institute; forty Philadelphia-area manufacturers meet monthly to exchange ideas and strategies to address skill shortages and leadership training; and health care organizations in the Bradenton-Sarasota region of Florida work on common issues related to the implementation of the federal Affordable Care Act.

Communicating Industry Intelligence

A critical role for industry partnerships is to communicate to education and training providers the current skill needs of a group of employers important to a regional economy. Engaging these employers proactively is essential to uncovering business trends or disruptive technologies that could threaten the viability of a region's major industries. Although not every employer can relocate—such as hospitals and educational institutions—if a community cannot provide excellent talent to its most important industries, it hinders prospects for future growth.

It is challenging to organize the transfer of industry intelligence from the partnerships to the suppliers of education and training. Employers can be reluctant to discuss sensitive topics in front of non-industry members. In addition, there is sometimes a tendency for education and training providers to offer off-the-shelf solutions or sell their services before the employers have fully discussed their workforce challenges. This can lead employers to assume that someone has already developed the answer, so why bother continuing to meet.

Because every industry partnership develops and evolves in its own fashion, how it communicates industry intelligence about skills and career advancement will vary considerably. Employers need time to understand this role. They are cautious about sharing their human-resource needs in a semi-public environment.

Some partnerships move quickly to identify a particular occupational need, and with public or private resources, they initiate a relationship with a training provider or a community college. This is often accomplished through a Request for Proposal (RFP), where the partnership defines its requirements, allowing education and training providers to respond with their ideas for implementation. The RFP sends a signal about an industry's pressing needs and, in time, future employment opportunities in the community.

In other cases the partnership may take longer to find consensus around a particular course of action. The partners may conclude that they need a longer-term educational effort that involves more graduates from existing programs, adjustments to course curriculum, or an entirely new effort around a particular certificate program. Recently, health care organizations in one major city decided that the current education offerings were not producing graduates with the skills needed in today's hospital setting. They decided to rework the course offerings with the community college before investing in more training.

Impact on Workforce-Development Strategies

A major difference between an industry-partnership strategy and most other workforce-development approaches is the fundamental relationship with the employer. In an industry partnership the employer is seen not only as a customer to be served but also as a partner in creating a talent supply chain for the entire industry. This is a crucial distinction. It impacts four critical components in workforce development: improving skills, the hiring process, career advancement, and internal business practices.

Improving Skills

One of the primary goals of an industry partnership is to identify the appropriate investments in skills development that will benefit both employers and workers. Initially many employers choose to make investments in their current workforce, sometimes with grants provided by public and private sources. For small and medium-sized firms this can be a critical opportunity to upgrade workers' skills to take advantage of new technology or a surge of new orders. In a hospital setting these investments can form the basis of a comprehensive plan to create upward mobility for entry-level workers. At Boston Children's Hospital, Karen Schoch and her staff developed an entire program around investments in new skills, access to new tuition-reimbursement procedures, and team building. These reduced employee turnover, improved staff morale, and led to higher patient satisfaction.

Many employers initially concentrate on their own employees, because they are highly motivated to increase firm productivity, and the firms appreciate the new resources to help them achieve this goal. There are many advantages to beginning with incumbent-worker training. By offering resources that employers can apply to internal workforce challenges, partnerships gain an important insight into the industry's common problems. The intermediary's role is critical to finding an aggregated approach that meets the individual needs of each employer and upgrades an entire industry's workforce.

Many partnerships begin to coalesce as a group when they assume joint responsibility for choosing a training provider to address common challenges, such as inadequately trained supervisors, non-English-speaking staff, or the lack of appropriate curriculum at a local educational institution. By taking ownership of the process, they begin to understand the potential for additional joint action.

Another advantage is that some employers are exposed to training and career-advancement strategies they would not have considered. In a few cases these best practices lead to critical alterations in their own business practices. The Baltimore Alliance for Careers in Healthcare (BACH) had a major impact on other hospitals in the region as it shared its lessons from investing in programs for incumbent workers. This is similar to the impact of other hospital collaborations in Cincinnati and Boston.

The experience of the National Fund has shown that many employers are eager to learn how to better address concerns that range from high turnover to infection prevention to supervisory issues. This opens the door for the intermediary to provide strategies of how other firms addressed a particular issue. Seeing a peer's successful example can sometimes lead to changes in employer practices. This is especially effective if the new pratice is backed up by a business impact study (see the next section of this book).

The Hiring Process

Industry partnerships are valuable when employers are looking to hire new entry-level or middle-skilled workers. Too often the modern employer hiring system poses major barriers for these job applicants. Employers plow through thousands of resumes with little real understanding of what an educational credential or previous experience may mean from one candidate to another. Meanwhile job seekers submit hundreds of applications and receive little or no feedback.[8] A good industry partnership can eliminate this wasteful process by helping the industry better define credentialing and assessment systems. Once these are established, the community can create a series of stackable credentials and/or certificates that respond to the industry's definition. In exchange for creating this system of providing better-prepared candidates, the employers agree to provide interview and feedback opportunities. However, this process will break down if it does not guarantee some opportunity to those who are striving to meet employer expectations. Again, in a partnership-driven system both parties must offer value for the system to continue to serve both partners over time.

Career Advancement

If an industry partnership creates a well-developed system for identifying employer-supported credentials, opportunities for career advancement should logically follow. This is especially true if the partnership has assisted in the development of the internal career pathways. Monitoring how successful job applicants move up (or don't) into better-paying jobs is one method of evaluating how well the credential prepared the candidate for future success. If the investment provides a foundation for future success, education and training providers are likely to continue to invest, but if their graduates remain trapped in low-paying positions, it may be time for the partnership to review whether the credential is serving workers as well as it is serving the firm. Here again the industry partnership is critical to the development of internal career pathways with enlightened tuition-reimbursement practices, career coaching, or other opportunities to train and advance through the organization. Numerous partnerships have invested in assisting firms develop these pathways.

An industry-partnership strategy also helps in another area critical to career advancement: employer relationships. This is especially true in the case of investments in frontline workers already on staff. Since most incumbent-worker programs are developed with significant employer involvement, a relationship with management can be enormously helpful in analyzing barriers to advancement. If the partnership has developed good lines of communication, there may be opportunities for employers to see how changing their internal practices might lead to career advancement for valued workers.

For example, a number of hospitals have recognized that their current workforce is unaware of the variety of different occupations within the institution. To respond, some workforce partnerships have sponsored internal career coaches whose job it is to counsel incumbent workers on how their personal interests might align well with the human-capital needs of the organization. Johns Hopkins Hospital and BACH were early leaders in this effort. The hospital realized that despite its commitment to invest in the career advancement of its frontline workers, they were not academically prepared to take college-level courses and were unsure which courses would help them reach their career goals; it then invested resources to address both these issues. Many hospitals in the National Fund network have followed suit, some using grant funds to test the concept, with a commitment to keep the job and career coaches if they prove effective.

Business Practices

In most workforce-development programs there is little or no focus on improving workplace practices or generating greater investments by employers in the low-wage or middle-skilled workforce. Yet these changes could have a major impact on all the workers in the industry. Consider that according to the American Society for Training and Development,[9] private-sector firms invest approximately $150 billion in staff training and development. Unfortunately, it appears that most of this investment is spent on middle and upper management. If employers redirected 10 percent of this investment to their low-wage workers, it would have a profound impact.

However, as long as the relationship between the workforce system and the employer is one of service rather than partnership, this is not likely to change. Undoubtedly, service is very important, and most industry partnerships begin with good service to employer needs. Indeed, it would be counterproductive to begin the relationship with a skeptical employer by declaring that it must be prepared to change its internal practices. But it is important that there be an understanding that this is a partnership and therefore the benefits cannot flow only in one direction. A skillful partnership organizer will first build a mutually beneficial relationship while helping employers see that some of their human-resources challenges cannot be addressed through skill development alone. High turnover rates, low workforce morale, and absenteeism may be correlated to internal business practices that should be analyzed carefully and addressed proactively.

Lessons from the Field

Over the last ten years, a number of lessons have emerged from the implementation of sectoral partnerships in a wide variety of industries and regional economies. Among the most salient issues are those that follow.

Talented Staff

Talented and experienced industry-partnership organizers can make a big difference in the effectiveness of a partnership. Workforce-development organizations often hire individuals who are drawn to this work because of their desire to help people. They are predisposed to want to assist the unemployed, those on welfare, the working poor, a veteran, or someone recently released from the criminal justice system. However, most are unprepared to organize employers.

Good industry-partnership organizers, either individuals or organizations, are difficult to find and almost as difficult to train. They are as dedicated to helping people as any social worker but have come to the conclusion that to be most helpful to low-wage workers, it is essential to understand demand-side dynamics. They are unusually curious about how industries use, develop, and support human capital, and they build strong relationships through constant communication and responsiveness. They ask the right questions to draw out information about specific employer challenges and help articulate areas of common concern. They recognize that employers are volunteering their time and are constantly looking for opportunities to add value to that participation.

Entrepreneurial Spirit

Organizing a strong, productive, sustainable industry partnership is not for the faint of heart. Some employers are not interested; the economy takes a dive and hiring stops; resources run out; employer leaders get transferred; training providers don't produce.

Bringing a new initiative into existence in which the parties must voluntarily take many hours away from their primary responsibilities and invest in a radically different model can be daunting. Whereas industry partnerships have been successfully organized in health care, manufacturing, and construction, there are other sectors that present many challenges, including hospitality, food service, and information technology. Consequently the industry-partnership strategy should be approached with an entrepreneurial spirit, not as an ideology. Generating employer leadership can take a number of forms, and innovation will likely lead to new organizing strategies in the future.

The Power of Leverage

The availability of resources that had to be matched at the local level was a strong incentive for creating regional collaboratives. Local leaders pointed out that it was the offer of support from national philanthropic sources, as well as the opportunity to be recognized, that was a critical catalyst for bringing local funders together. The National Fund requirement for a four-to-one match was challenging, especially in rural communities, but it was somewhat mitigated by the ability to use "aligned" funding as part of the match. This type of support allowed entities that could not contribute funds directly to add their resources to the overall strategy.

A Talent Supply Chain

Most well-run companies will assiduously work to ensure that their material supply chain is reliably providing raw materials, components, and tools to their required specifications, at the right time and at the agreed-upon price. Yet many employers need to be reminded that providing skilled human capital requires similar diligence. In too many cases, industry leaders assume that the labor they need will suddenly appear or that they can have no substantial impact on the supply.

A well-organized industry partnership can change this dynamic by determining a set of credentials and qualifications that enable multiple education and training providers to deliver better-qualified applicants to the hiring process. Employers see the benefit of keeping training and education partners fully informed about their industry's requirements. Moreover, these education and training partners are highly motivated to satisfy the needs of industry. If they miss the mark too often, employers can remove them from the supply chain. Recommending a community college as a source of referral sends a strong signal about where good education, valued by employers, is being provided.

In the best cases, employers begin to appreciate the importance of extending the supply chain into junior high or even grade schools. They know this will require that more educators and parents understand their industry and the talent necessary to help it succeed. For example, the National Fund collaborative in Mobile, the Southwest Alabama Workforce Development Council (SAWDC), organizes an annual Worlds of Opportunity Career Expo for every eighth grader from eight counties. Employers from twelve different "worlds" (including aerospace, automotive technology, energy, health care, manufacturing, maritime, among others) set up booths, equipment, and products and give students the opportunity to weld, hammer, drive, examine, and mix. In 2012, 9,800 students, 1,000 teachers, counselors and parents, and 600 volunteers participated, along with 182 sponsors and exhibitors. Recently, adults seeking new career opportunities were invited as well.[10]

Proving the Value of Training

Employers want to know that their training investments are having a positive impact on their business. They see the benefit in developing a reasonably priced process to measure the cost and benefits of investments in technical and professional skills. Many hospitals are seeking to better document the business benefits of specific investments in certain types of education and training. Some of these hospitals have joined together to create CareerSTAT, an initiative of the National Fund and Jobs for the Future, and recently published "A Guide to Making the Case for Investing in the Frontline Hospital Workforce."[11] They are following up this initial effort with plans to develop a national recognition system that will highlight health care institutions that invest in frontline workers and measure the results. The implementation of the Affordable Care Act (ACA) will increase the need to better understand where specific skill upgrades can lead to better bottom-line outcomes.

The Health Careers Collaborative of Greater Cincinnati took business measurement to a new level with a return-on-investment (ROI) study that measured in dollars and cents the cost of all training investments and the business benefits of the outcomes, namely, lower turnover, higher productivity, etc.[12] (See Krismer, Chapter 8, for more on this initiative.) Philadelphia's JOIN collaborative completed a ROI study;[13] Workforce Central (Wisconsin Rapids) did an impact study with its manufacturing partnerships;[14] and CareerEDGE in Florida did a community-impact study. In addition, the Commonwealth Corporation of Massachusetts published a comprehensive and practical guide on how one could develop a business-measurement process.[15]

These studies are critical to generating additional investments in low-skilled, low-paid workers. They document the business benefits of training and improving skills, thereby protecting these investments from being vulnerable when companies are cutting back in lean economic times. More important, they encourage company executives to support participation in collaborative activities where staff can learn more about how others have successfully made these investments. Of course, measuring business impact is labor intensive and time consuming. It can rarely be undertaken without a strong and trusting relationship between the employers and the intermediary.

A major reason for needing this relationship is that some firms are understandably reluctant to reveal their productivity, injury or other key data to anyone outside the company; employers may also resist providing information on wages, retention rates, or internal training efforts. Other firms may discover they don't collect the relevant data, nor do they want to go to the expense of gathering it. Yet, when done correctly, this can lead to the institutionalization of a new approach to training investments that will positively impact hundreds of workers over time. Once a company proves to itself that these investments produce a better bottom line, they are more likely to invest their own resources and not rely on outside grants.

Connection to Economic Development

Going deep into a sector also can reveal opportunities for economic-development strategies. The aforementioned food-manufacturing partnership organized by the Lancaster WIB moved from food safety to supervision to industrial maintenance and mechatronics to packaging. As it progressed over a number of years, it organized a talent supply chain for this industry, called the Industrial Maintenance Training Center of Pennsylvania, that combined new programs at career and technical high schools, an advanced mechatronics associate's degree at Reading Area Community College, and a bachelor's degree in mechatronics and engineering technology at Purdue and Penn State Universities. This entity now works closely with the Center of Excellence in Packaging Technologies to address emerging packaging technology and the human capital that supports it.

Multiple Recruitment Efforts

Multiple-employer organizing efforts, whether for boards, advisory councils, or partnerships, can be frustrating. In extreme cases, employers simply say no to every request, and their industry knowledge (and perhaps their job opportunities) are lost. Each community must decide how to handle this problem, but there is a critical advantage when all education and training providers can benefit from the same well-organized partnership. Rationalizing disparate employer outreach initiatives can be an important role for the industry partnership.

Employer Leadership

The recent emergence of Business Leaders United (BLU) shows that a wide variety of employers are now ready to become more actively involved in promoting public policies that support the development of sector-based workforce development. BLU was organized by four organizations: the National Fund, the National Skills Coalition (NSC), Skills for America's Future, and Corporate Voices for Working Families. Each provided a group of employers committed to educating state and federal policy makers on how partnerships with industry are helping their companies or institutions upgrade the skills of their current workers as well as find better ways to identify skilled candidates for new openings. BLU has already presented its ideas and recommendations to Obama administration officials and members of Congress.

Challenges of the Industry-Partnership Model

Serving Individuals with Significant Barriers to Employment

One of the clear tensions within the industry-partnership model is the relationship between the employer partners and the organization providing candidates for hire. How does one supply the "best" candidate for the employer while not ignoring the many others who are just as eager to work but are insufficiently skilled or prepared to succeed? To maintain a good relationship requires not wasting the employer's time with individuals who do not fit the job qualifications. On the other hand, there is an important moral responsibility to provide all job seekers with the hope that with the right training they will eventually have job opportunities.

One useful strategy to address this challenge is for partnerships to be clear about the industry's skill requirements. Employers can define the specific credential, workforce-readiness certificate, or literacy level that will be used as a minimum standard. Once the standard is established, individuals can receive the necessary support that leads to the credential; most important, they now have a strong incentive for acquiring the credential. For example, once the credential is obtained, the firms in the partnership must provide these qualified individuals with special access to employment opportunities.

It is also important that the talent supply chain be constructed so that all communities have opportunities to reap benefits. No matter what the barrier, every job seeker should be able to recognize a pathway into the industry. This journey may be quite lengthy and involve major personal challenges, but it is critically important that community residents understand there is a system they can participate in.

The first step might be a computer class in a church basement that prepares individuals to take a WorkKeys test at the local One-Stop, or it could be a contextualized literacy program at Goodwill that builds reading levels through a focus on health care terminology, or it could be a bicycle-repair program at a homeless shelter. From there, individuals can be connected to occupational training programs with established employer relationships. Everyone should feel that he or she can connect in some way to the collective community strategy to build a talent-development system.

Finally, industry partnerships will need to consider opportunities for short-term on-the-job training for workers who have been prepared up to the industry's defined standard but lack experience. These "earn and learn" models need to be expanded to include more workers.

The Need for Patient Investments

It can take as long as five years for a region to develop two or three sectoral partnerships that are producing clear demand-side intelligence and engaging employers in the development of their talent supply chain. The intermediary organization will need adequate resources to pay for good staff over an extended period, supplemented by training resources for both incumbent workers and job seekers. Creating a talent supply chain that addresses the myriad needs of young adults with no job experience, older adults with antiquated skills, and the long-term unemployed with deteriorating resumes is a challenging task. Ten-year old SkillWorks in Boston is a good example of a high-quality workforce funder collaborative that has accomplished many of these outcomes (See Leung, Chapter 7, for a history of SkillWorks).

The most creative workforce collaboratives are responding by blending multiple sources to create a system that divides responsibilities but unifies around goals and a common way to measure outcomes. In these organizations, the leadership recognizes the importance of having resources from a wide variety of sources so that there are fewer funding "cliffs" that can bring progress to a halt.

Cincinnati's Partners for a Competitive Workforce, which includes three WIBs and covers parts of three states, is a good example of an organization that has continually challenged itself to bring in new partners and new resources. It has generated more than $25 million in pooled and aligned funding over its five-year span.[16]

Generating Employer Leadership

Unfortunately, the Pennsylvania experience and the subsequent work of the National Fund showed that it is possible to describe an entity as a sectoral workforce partnership without having much employer interaction or an ongoing conversation. Training and education providers, as well as some WIBs, were adept at developing surveys that generated initial industry information that allowed the intermediary to construct a sectoral-based training program. They referred to the employer as their customer and provided them with as many candidates as possible but had only a casual relationship with the business and even less of an understanding of industry trends, technology, or workplace practices.

Understandably, many communities have struggled with moving from a superficial engagement with employers to one with strong relationships and an ongoing dialogue. Successful partnerships are built slowly and carefully, with a commitment to seeking out many conversations with a variety of employers in the industry. It is fundamentally about asking the right questions, listening, and making connections. Finding an employer advocate for the creation of the partnership can be an enormous help. At that point the workforce leaders can invest in developing this "champion" and encourage this individual to recruit peers. In a number of National Fund communities, the collaborative has worked closely with an industry trade association that has bought into the strategy and sees the value of communicating its human-resource needs to a broader audience.

Recommendations

Employers

If employers want these demand-driven skill investments to continue, they will need to become more aggressive advocates for public and private investments. This leadership will require that they invest more of their own time and resources into the development of talent supply chains in their own communities. This means providing industry intelligence, partnering to reform education and training systems, and making changes to their own business practices, especially by investing a greater percentage of their training resources into low and middle-skilled workers.

Education

Community colleges will also need to be major advocates for industry partnerships, because of the partnerships' ability to define competencies, skills, and educational prerequisites. With multiple partnerships covering the major regional industries, educators can focus on developing certificates and credentials that respond to industry while leaving the organization and development of these partnerships to a dedicated intermediary.

Philanthropy

Philanthropy can be critically important by providing catalytic but patient investments to generate regional efforts to expand the industry-partnership model. Many communities are interested, but they need to be challenged and motivated to come together to create workforce-development strategies that either complement or confront the existing public system. Philanthropic resources are critical to leveraging local support and bringing communities together around a more collective approach to talent development. National philanthropy can add its imprimatur to regional efforts, thereby generating interest from local funders, workforce stakeholders, and elected officials.

Leadership Development

Additional resources are needed to develop the knowledge and capacity of experienced industry-partnership organizers and employer leaders. The Aspen Institute's highly regarded National Sector Skills Academy annually generates twenty-five graduates, but a new effort should focus on bringing together experienced intermediary and partnership organizers, particularly to take on the challenges of organizing new sectors, building better relationships with employers, and finding ways to develop talent supply chains. These experienced organizers need "case study fellowships" that encourage them to write about their experiences, especially through an analysis that captures the birth, evolution, and learning from particular industry partnerships.

Research and Evaluation

More targeted research is needed to identify what is working well or areas for improvement in industry partnerships. There is a critical need for better methods of evaluation, real-time feedback, and improved data collection. Capturing qualitative outcomes, such as changes in business practices or results of educational reforms, is a subject rich with possibility. As partnerships proliferate, producing this research could have a significant impact on public policy.

State Policy

Although an industry-partnership initiative generates most of its economic benefits within a regional economy, it can also be the foundation for a state's workforce-development strategy, as we have seen in Massachusetts, Pennsylvania, and Washington. Thousands of firms partnering in regional consortia tailored to their particular sector reveal an enormous amount of critically useful information. If communicated well, this industry voice can inform youth councils, chambers of commerce, career and technical high schools, literacy programs, and the general public—cutting through confusing supply-and-demand generalizations that protect inefficient status quo policies.

States should consider investing in industry partnerships, making them a cornerstone of a statewide workforce and economic-development strategy. It is difficult to imagine a more popular strategy for helping both business and labor: Both parties are engaged around their self-interests, and neither party can succeed without the success of the other. In addition, the potential for economic development is significant, as industry intelligence from multiple sectors provides insight into emerging threats to existing firms, as well as areas for potential growth.

Federal Policy

Requiring employer participation on regional workforce boards was an important step to elevate employers' voices, but now is the time to focus more closely on understanding and addressing industry needs. Federal policy should explicitly require the development of industry partnerships as a condition of receiving training funds. Since gubernatorial cooperation is critical to developing workforce partnerships on a large scale, states could be required to provide matching funds for the federal support. Current sector partnerships that meet the standards as described above should receive support to continue and/or scale up their work. All approved industry partnerships should be eligible to apply for local workforce investment funds directly from the federal and state governments.

Conclusion

The evolution of the U.S. economy over the ten years from 2003 to 2013, as it moved from low unemployment to deep recession and then into slow recovery, has challenged workforce intermediaries to quickly adjust to new demand and supply considerations. What remained consistent was the critical task of providing low-wage workers with the skills and opportunities to succeed in a dynamic economy with unrelenting technological change and sudden shifts in business strategies. To address this challenge, workforce intermediaries must have a deeper and more thorough understanding of their regional industries. They must be aware of each industry's competitive environment and be ready to respond proactively to challenges and opportunities. As important, they must also know the strengths and skill barriers of their community's workforce.

Intermediaries must generate closer relationships with employers so that they become a trusted source of talent. They need to bring new evidence about the positive business impact of intelligent training investments and persuade employers to provide their own resources for frontline workers. In addition, they should partner with employers to remove internal barriers to career advancement. Ultimately, because intermediaries can supply well-qualified workers as well as good ideas about how to support their retention and development, businesses may see a productive intermediary relationship as a competitive advantage.

Industry partnerships are a critical component of this strategy. They are the intermediary's intelligence-gathering arm and business-connection developer. Whether funded by regional collaboratives, WIBs, or economic-development entities, they concentrate on one sector to encourage relationships and generate expertise. They are especially important for the low-wage workforce, because they build bridges to employers with entry-level and middle-skill career opportunities.

However, some challenges to this model remain. Additional questions need to be answered on whether workers with significant employment barriers will receive the attention and resources they need to gain access to opportunities. Moreover, few evaluations have been completed that test the theories described in this chapter.[17]

Yet as the debate over the skills gap rages on, with employers bemoaning their inability to fill open positions and Congress continuing to cut training investments, industry partnerships stand out as a highly valued strategy. They bring employers and workers together, building community cohesion around a talent supply chain that serves to support economic development. They challenge employers to consider new investments and workplace-practices improvements. And they generate new investments from other community sources, providing additional program flexibility and the ability to innovate.

Undoubtedly, industry partnerships cannot respond to every issue of talent mismatch, but they can certainly be a foundational element of a much-improved workforce-development system that encompasses a wide variety of public and private educational and training initiatives. They could be especially beneficial if they can develop employer allies willing to join with workers, educators, and communities in promoting sector-focused workforce development.

Notes

1. I am grateful to the late Cindy Marano for providing scores of examples of sector initiatives from throughout the United States.
2. Case studies on Project QUEST (2001), Focus: HOPE (2000), and Jane Addams Resource Corp. (2000), Sectoral Employment Development Learning Project, Aspen Institute.
3. "Industry Partnerships in Pennsylvania," April 2009, www.paworkforce.state.pa.us.
4. National Governors Association, *State Sector Strategies: Regional Solutions to Worker and Employer Needs* (Washington, DC: NGA Center for Best Practices, 2006).
5. See the National Fund's publication "Workforce Partnership Guidance Tool," http://nfwsolutions.org/sites/nfwsolutions.org/files/publications/NFWS_workforce_guidance_tool_111110.pdf.
6. Leanne Giordono, Kendra Lodewick, and Stephen Michon, *The National Fund for Workforce Solutions: Data Brief 2013*, prepared by Program and Policy Insight, LLC, April 2013, www.nfwsolutions.org.
7. A good example is the excellent manufacturing study by Partners for a Competitive Workforce in Cincinnati that focused on a concentrated cluster of manufacturers in northern Kentucky; see http://www.competitiveworkforce.org.
8. Cappelli (2012).

9. ASTD, State of the Industry Report, 2012, www.astd.org. On the Web site ASTD indicates that this report shows that industry spent $87.5 billion internally on training, $21.9 billion for tuition reimbursement, and $46.9 billion on external services.

10. For more on the Worlds of Opportunity project, see www.worldsofopportunity.com. I attended this event in 2011.

11. See Wilson and Holm (2012), nfwsolutions.org/sites/nfwsolutions.org/files/Career-STATFINAL.pdf.

12. Joel Elervy and Christopher Spence, *Health Careers Collaborative of Greater Cincinnati: Return on Investment Report, 2011*, http://www.workforce-ks.com/Modules/ShowDocument.aspx?documentid=2154.

13. Elyssa Back, "ROI360: How Workforce Partnership Training Benefits Business, Workers & Community," Job Opportunity Investment Network, 2012, www.joincollaborative.org/wp-content/uploads/2012/03/JOIN_ROI_Without-Appendix.pdf.

14. Incourage Community Foundation, *Return on Investment Tools: A Companion to the Ultimate Source of Manufacturing Competitiveness, 2010*, http://nfwsolutions.org/sites/nfwsolutions.org/files/ROI%20brochure%20012512%20-%20plenary.pdf.

15. Soricone and Singh (2012).

16. Partnership for a Competitive Workforce, http://www.competitiveworkforce.com/Results.html.

17. A major exception to this statement is the Public/Private Ventures study completed in 2009. See Clymer (2009).

Bibliography

Conway, Maureen, Steven L. Dawson, Amy Blair, and Linda Dworak-Muñoz. 2007. *Sectoral Strategies for Low-Income Workers: Lessons from the Field*. Aspen Institute, Summer.

Blair, Amy, and Maureen Conway. 2011. "Results Driven: Using the Business Value Approach to Design and Assess Workforce Services." Aspen Institute Update 5 (May).

Cappelli, Peter. 2012. Why Good People Can't Get Jobs. Philadelphia: Wharton Digital Press.

Clymer, Carol, Maureen Conway, Joshua Freely, and Sheila Maguire. 2009. *Job Training That Works: Findings from the Sectoral Employment Impact Study*. Public/Private Ventures. May.

Giloth, Robert P., ed. 2004. *Workforce Intermediaries for the Twenty-first Century*. Published in association with the American Assembly, Columbia University. Philadelphia: Temple University Press.

National Governors Association. 2006. *State Sector Strategies: Regional Solutions to Worker and Employer Needs*. Washington, DC: NGA Center for Best Practices.

Soricone, Lisa, and Navjeet Singh. 2012. Measuring Business Impact: Lesson Learned from Workforce Development. Commonwealth Corporation.

Wilson, Randall, and Robert Holm. 2012. CareerSTAT: *A Guide to Making the Case for Investing in the Frontline Hospital Workforce*. National Fund for Workforce Solutions and Jobs for the Future. April.

5

Philanthropic Innovations for Workforce Impact: The National Fund for Workforce Solutions, 2003–2013

Barbara Dyer, Robert P. Giloth, Richard Kazis, and Marlene Seltzer

A t a gathering at the National Press Club in September 2007, leaders from the Annie E. Casey, Ford, and Hitachi foundations and the U.S. Department of Labor shared their vision of a nation dedicated to good jobs, skilled workers, and an adaptive, resilient workforce ecosystem. Those leaders launched the $50 million National Fund for Workforce Solutions with ambitions to engage one thousand employers, cultivate fifty thousand workers in good jobs with career-growth potential, and leverage more than $200 million in additional investments from local and regional co-investors.

At the time of this kickoff, unemployment rates were holding steady at below 5 percent. But troubling signs in the U.S. labor market had prompted the analysis that led to this new workforce approach. Mounting global competition had led to dramatic transformation in corporate organization, and whole industries moved offshore in search of cheaper labor. Many that remained flattened their organizations, relying increasingly on contingent workers and outsourcing significant functions that were once first-rung jobs on the career ladder. Technology had advanced to the point of automating the rote tasks that had been handled by people moving from entry-level jobs to middle-skill careers. Employers increasingly sought workers with a different profile, able to demonstrate good judgment, problem-solving, teamwork, and technological adeptness. For workers, employment had become more volatile, career ladders were steeper, frequently with rungs missing, and skills and credentials were increasingly important to attaining and holding a middle-class standard of living.

The founders of the National Fund sought to respond to the needs of a rapidly changing twenty-first-century economy by focusing on two groups: employers and employees. Employers determine whom to hire, whom to retain, and the quality of jobs in their firms. Moreover, they are the largest investors by far in the cultivation of worker skills. At the launch of the National Fund, the American Society for Training and Development (ASTD) estimated that employer investments in training totaled about $125 billion and growing. By comparison, the Employment and Training Administration programs of the U.S. Department of Labor today total less than $4 billion. National Fund founders saw the need to reposition workforce development for the new century. No longer would it be enough to fund and support a system that places workers in entry-level, often dead-end jobs, with incremental advancement based on seniority, as had been the approach of the traditional publicly funded workforce-development system for decades. Instead, the National Fund would measure success by credentials earned, wages gained, and career progress achieved. The new model would link a new emphasis on career advancement for workers and job seekers with a commitment to helping employers expand their access to potential employees who could contribute productively in an increasingly skill-intensive workplace.

The National Fund emerged from a workforce institutional environment that is deeply rooted in multiple public and private systems. It ranges from employer-sponsored training to public and private college-degree and certification programs. Within the federal government, it falls within several departments, including Labor, Education, Health and Human Services, Housing and Urban Development, and Commerce.

One of the important lessons from the workforce experiments in the 1990s and 2000s was that, while the workforce system is fragmented, strong local intermediaries can serve as bridges—or perhaps synapses—that enable key elements of the system to connect more effectively.[1] Within industry sectors, they allow employers to come together to define the suitable worker skills and training and then form partnerships for joint action. Within the broader system, they connect employers, employees, and the many players in the region, including public workforce systems, academic institutions, and community-based organizations. Within the community of investors, they help to align financial resources within a region and leverage national philanthropic and federal funds toward common purpose.

The initial goal of the National Fund was to form a community of funders with a common purpose first at the national level and then leveraged by similar collaborative and aligned funding at the regional and local level. An initial commitment of $15 million by the Annie E. Casey, Ford, Hitachi, and Harry and Jeanette Weinberg foundations primed the pump toward the goal of $50 million. By 2008 the National Fund's supporters had grown to include the John S. and James L. Knight and Prudential foundations, Microsoft, and the California Endowment.

Unlike many prior change efforts spawned by foundations and government policy makers, the National Fund focused on creating better results for employers and workers and overcoming system fragmentation rather than superimposing a programmatic model. As evaluation data now bear out, the sites with the greatest fidelity to the National Fund's design principles related to workforce partnerships and funder collaboratives are yielding the best results. At the National Fund's inception, its founders believed that creating new collaborative funding mechanisms in thirty to forty regions would serve as a model for reforming public workforce systems and attracting major business investments in career advancement and skill building.

In the year following the Press Club announcement, the Great Recession hit, and the nation's economy has been under enormous strain ever since. High unemployment exacerbated the troubling trends of wage and income stagnation and widening income inequality. Within the year following the launch of the National Fund, the perceptions of impending labor shortages dissolved, and addressing a cyclical recession and its attendant joblessness became the nation's focus. Throughout this period, the National Fund weathered the economic storms and its own developmental growing pains, remaining focused on solutions to the underlying structural issues. These achievements, however, were balanced by challenges. Initial buy-in for a joint approach among independent-minded national foundations, all worthy of their claims to seeding the ideas that shaped the National Fund, was not easy, and the years leading up to the launch were rich with experimentation.

This chapter[2] provides a detailed overview of the National Fund. The first section chronicles the workforce efforts that provided the grist for its creation. The second section highlights the work of the National Fund from start-up to the present and the challenges it has faced. The third section reviews lessons from the experience and implications for the workforce field, including a fresh look at long-term financing and policy strategies. The final section looks ahead at how the National Fund can expand its funding and influence.

We believe the story of the National Fund sheds light on two vexing questions in the workforce field and one big, long-term challenge. The first question is about replicating promising approaches at scale. The workforce field is littered with the replication failures of promising programs.[3] The National Fund's approach holds much promise for learning how to replicate more effectively. Second, the National Fund can shed light on application of the "collective impact" approach to workforce development, the mobilization of diverse investors around a common set of results, and the building of backbone organizations. In both cases, we need to take stock, as a field, of what has worked and not worked in bringing promising approaches to scale. Finally, although it is difficult to imagine major progress in the short run, the reinvention of the workforce system is moving up the agenda of "must do" public-policy challenges. The National Fund offers one important approach and provides many lessons from practice, not just theory, for linking workforce and economic development, industries and regions, and system building and public policy. We hope the discussion that follows helps deepen workforce policy conversations now under way.

An Emerging Focus on Sector-Based Workforce Development

The National Fund built from a foundation of knowledge and practice working with industry sectors—industries with common economic and workforce challenges and experiencing labor and skill shortages in specific occupations with career potential. The sector approach engages multiple employers with similar labor-force needs, is more efficient in designing and implementing workforce programs, and addresses industry-related human-resource and modernization challenges.

Sector workforce strategies differed dramatically from other workforce programs. First, they took a long time to grow, sometimes decades, and they resulted from entrepreneurial action or advocacy rather than simply growing out of the mandates of workforce legislation and policy. Second, these sector partnerships—or workforce intermediaries and partnerships, as they came to be called—were not programs, although they delivered concrete results, especially for workers and businesses. They were designed to be enduring civic structures that connect key partners for joint action toward common goals. Strategically, they focused on results related to skills and career advancement rather than the unwavering "work first" focus of models from the 1990s. In pursuing those results, sector efforts played important and frequently unrecognized roles as organizers, partnership builders, integrators of financing, information brokers, and policy advocates. Third, these partnerships involved multiple actors and were entrepreneurial, market-oriented, and frequently regional in scope.[4] Last, there was no one blueprint for these partnerships and intermediaries, and their center of gravity or point of origin included community organizing, business, unions, community colleges, and nonprofit human-service organizations. Unfortunately, a relatively small number of workforce partnerships formed during this period (see Conway, Chapter 3).

The February 2003 American Assembly, a nonpartisan deliberative convening strategy, considered and made recommendations about how to grow and strengthen workforce partnerships though advocacy, policy, and philanthropic investment. The recommendations called for business to invest more intentionally in industry-focused workforce development to address the long-term economic competiveness of the U.S. economy. More specific recommendations in *Keeping America in Business: Advancing Workers, Businesses, and Economic Growth*[5] focused on enhancing the capacity, learning, and financing of workforce intermediaries and building a more powerful constituency for advocacy and action on behalf of these recommendations. In particular, the financing recommendation referenced the example of the Living Cities community-development funding collaborative as a potential model for aggregating venture funds for supporting and spreading investment in workforce intermediaries. The resource materials for the American Assembly became a published collection, *Workforce Intermediaries for the Twenty-first Century*[6], and included a chapter on the lessons from community development for the start-up and financing support of workforce intermediaries, namely a dedicated fund in support of their replication.[7]

The American Assembly convening coincided with foundations in Boston creating a new mechanism for raising and coordinating financial resources to support workforce partnerships and workforce policy advocacy. The initiative that came to be named SkillWorks formed in 2003, resulting from eighteen months of planning under the leadership of the Boston Foundation, the Annie E. Casey Foundation, and other local and national foundations. Thirteen foundations assembled $14 million over five years to invest in sector-based workforce partnerships and a statewide advocacy agenda (see Leung, Chapter 7).[8] Philanthropy collaboratives like SkillWorks were not a new invention, but Boston broke new ground in collaborative grant making. Local and national funders complemented one another—much as they did when the Local Initiatives Support Corporation (LISC) was created for the community-development field in the 1970s. Moreover, SkillWorks demonstrated the convening power of local philanthropy and the important knowledge and influence roles of foundation program officers and leaders in their communities.[9]

SkillWorks demonstrated that local capital aggregation in support of workforce intermediaries and partnerships should build on local assets, capacities, and opportunities, not follow one blueprint model. Not all communities, for example, have strong community foundations or prior experiences with funder collaboratives. Some communities do not even have a strong foundation sector. Finally,

public workforce agencies in some communities welcome the organized investment of philanthropy in workforce to complement their efforts, while public
agencies in other communities find collaboration of this kind challenging. The
common experience for all communities, however, was the present and looming
skills gap. And this is why SkillWorks inspired other communities and local foundations to emulate their funder collaboration in support of career advancement.

Creating the National Fund for Workforce Solutions

Four years after the American Assembly, foundation leaders and partners created the National Fund, weaving together the promising practices of workforce
partnerships and local funding collaboratives.[10] This remarkable philanthropic in-
vention facilitated the spread of these promising approaches across the country
and informed policy debates even as the economy collapsed with the recession.
The path to the formation and growth of the National Fund, however, was not
easy under these conditions. It took advantage of local employment pressures, new
evidence about the effectiveness of sector-based workforce approaches, and new
federal initiatives to expand evidence-based practices.

The National Fund became a major presence in the national workforce field
during four overlapping phases. The first phase was a period of prototyping, feasibility testing, and planning next steps. The second phase involved the formal
start-up and launch of the National Fund, choosing an implementation partner,
launching several cohorts of new sites, fundraising, learning conferences, and
working on policy. The third phase required the consolidation and improvement
of National Fund management, competition for federal Social Innovation Fund
resources, and expansion in up to thirty-two sites. A fourth phase, described in the
next section, is still very much a work in process and involves the strategic positioning and sustainability of the National Fund.

Demonstration and Feasibility

The American Assembly, while inspiring, did not lay out a blueprint for next
steps. The Annie E. Casey, Ford, and Rockefeller foundations, with their partner
Jobs for the Future (JFF), took several steps together. They started a $2 million
demonstration, Investing in Workforce Intermediaries, with a handful of sites
focused on building and funding workforce partnerships. Casey and Rockefeller
funded the direct site efforts.[11] The Ford Foundation invested in identifying new
financing options for workforce partnerships and supporting a feasibility study for
a national venture fund to support workforce intermediaries. Finally, the funders

supported several follow-up conferences and more in-depth conversations with stakeholders about next steps.

The small cohort of demonstration sites chosen showed a diversity of approaches even within a common framework.[12] SkillWorks, at the center of the group, was already supported by multiyear grants from Casey and Rockefeller. It served as a model for other communities to visit and learn about workforce partnerships and funding collaboratives and to examine which approaches worked to bring local funders together. Choosing sites for this demonstration entailed sites taking up the approach on their own initiative and a targeted request for proposals for interested sites.[13]

Workforce partnerships presented two basic financing challenges for local communities. First, career advancement for workers required additional financial resources, public and private, to support short- and long-term skills training and certification, for both new and incumbent workers. A basic role for workforce partnerships was integrating disparate financial resources, but this was a time-consuming task, and available funds did not meet their overall growth requirements. New, dedicated resources were needed for career advancement. Second, workforce partnerships entailed specific new and ongoing costs for industry organizing that most public funding sources could not or would not support. Sectoral strategies are predicated on having a deep and ongoing knowledge of specific industries, leading to the co-design of workforce-related interventions. This organizing requires resources and the hiring of staff with substantial knowledge of and experience in specific industries.

Exploring financing options to support career advancement for low-skilled workers, a key goal of workforce partnerships, produced a compilation of six promising ideas: program-related investments, unemployment-insurance trust funds, bond financing, food stamp employment and training, lifelong-learning accounts, and venture funds. In 2006 JFF convened a conference of demonstration sites and other key stakeholders to discuss these ideas, where they were working, and how they could be adopted and spread.[14]

The Ford Foundation commissioned a feasibility study for a national funding collaborative in support of regional collaboratives and workforce partnerships. The study overwhelmingly endorsed the idea of a national fund dedicated to supporting local funder collaboratives that would in turn catalyze and invest in workforce partnerships. Armed with positive results from the feasibility study, an event was convened at the Ford Foundation in May 2006 to begin the fundraising process.[15]

Start-up and Launch

Feasibility studies do not always translate into immediate success at the levels projected, and that was certainly the case with the new national fund. Progress accelerated when the Hitachi Foundation joined as a founding member, bringing staff and leadership, as well as financial resources and a deep interest in the employer role in workforce development. The next several years involved foundation leaders reaching consensus, lots of fundraising, creating the institution, choosing partners, adding new sites, and a "soft" launch in Washington, D.C., in September 2007, with a more formal launch at the spring 2008 meeting of the Council on Foundations.

Funders confronted two big decisions at the outset: an institutional structure and home for the fund; and a name. Funders wisely chose not to start a new organization from scratch but to partner with an existing organization that brought credibility and possibly even some fundraising cachet, as it was becoming clear that fundraising assistance was needed. Ultimately, funders chose JFF to operate the fund as the implementation partner and chose the Council on Foundations as a leadership partner to cultivate funding opportunities and introduce the fund to other philanthropies. As to the name, after many torturous discussions, funders agreed on the National Fund for Workforce Solutions, a name that said simply what the fund was about.

Several more cohorts of sites joined over the next several years through a targeted process that required proposals and site visits. Sites entered the targeted pool through referrals and funder recommendations. The National Fund added a few additional sites in California because of its regional partnership with the California Endowment and a targeted request for proposals for rural sites.

Limited national funding produced a national evaluation that required sites to provide aggregate data on job seekers, workers, and employers once a year. This streamlined evaluation approach reduced the burden on sites and cost less, but it precluded longitudinal tracking of individuals and employers. This would eventually become a knowledge-building limitation, given the importance of telling the National Fund story with good data. However, the evaluation did provide implementation feedback to the funders and raised key questions about defining effective workforce partnerships, funding collaboratives, career-development outcomes, and employer benefits. (See Popovich, Chapter 12, on National Fund evaluation.)

Maturing and Scaling

The National Fund start-up and launch coincided with the beginning of the Obama administration and the onset of the Great Recession. Early on, the fund's leaders briefed the U.S. Department of Labor on its approach in hopes of obtaining new federal investment similar to that obtained early on by Living Cities from the U.S. Department of Housing and Urban Development. Federal funding was appealing as private fundraising was slower than expected, and the economic downturn made raising philanthropic dollars more difficult. The administration, however, curtailed the use of sole-source contracts at the time and put all investments through a competitive-bidding process. But the National Fund did play an important role in crafting the purpose language informing the American Recovery and Reinvestment Act stimulus bill, emphasizing the role of sectoral workforce development and workforce partnerships.

By 2010, seven years after the American Assembly, the National Fund had become a significant player in the national workforce world through its promotion of regional collaboratives and sector-based workforce partnerships. Funder collaboratives across the country formed to take advantage of their communities' unique circumstances. For example, collaboratives coalesced around the initiative of the United Way and community colleges in Des Moines, state-led industry partnerships in Pennsylvania, and funder interests in community colleges in Seattle. The National Fund became recognized as a unique, large-scale, national funding collaborative and received the Distinguished Grantmaking Award for Collaboration from the Council on Foundations at its 2010 annual meeting in Denver. At the same time, the release of the Public/Private Ventures (P/PV) evaluation of sector strategies in 2009, a rigorous random assignment evaluation of three workforce partnerships, provided additional strong evidence about the power of sector partnerships for low-income job-seekers and workers.[16]

But major challenges lay ahead. Implementation was inconsistent, and basic definitions varied from site to site; only a few funders were involved early; and the initiative required increased fundraising to expand and deepen investments in the most promising sites. The first step in meeting these challenges was to hire a full-time director and consolidate staffing and management within JFF. The National Fund was able to hire an experienced workforce leader from Pennsylvania who had recently managed the country's most ambitious state-led industry-partnership program and had also been active in federal policy advocacy. His first priorities were to develop consistent definitions of workforce partnerships and funding collaboratives, deploy the most effective site coaches to help build local capacity, and align partners for the most effective policy advocacy.

In particular, the new director paid special attention to the critical role of employers in workforce partnerships. Too often, the workforce field merely pays lip service to the notion of employer engagement. Yet practitioners knew that the dual-customer approach required more than rhetoric and that deep employer engagement improved results. So more attention was given to the role of employers and the supports they required, their "ownership" of workforce partnerships, the more accurate measurement of employer benefits and return on investment, and eventually their increased role in policy advocacy efforts at the state and federal levels. In fact, in 2011 at a meeting of the Clinton Global Initiative, the National Fund became a founding partner in the formation of Business Leaders United, a consortium created to bring mostly small and medium-sized employers into workforce-development policy discussions at home and in Washington, D.C.

Although the National Fund did not receive direct, sole-source federal investment, it did compete for and obtain two major federal investments. The first was part of the Recovery Act's Pathways Out of Poverty initiative and focused on training for the green economy. JFF worked with five National Fund sites to apply for and implement this federal grant, while several other workforce partnerships connected to the National Fund obtained individual grants. The more direct federal investment in the National Fund flowed from the Social Innovation Fund (SIF), which aims to support the replication of evidence-based programs. The National Fund was perfectly suited to apply, given its local and national funding structure, its reliance on evidence, its capacity to serve as an intermediary, and its strong engagement with funders. The National Fund applied for funds to support two tiers of sites: a set of existing, more mature sites that wanted to invest more deeply in specific workforce partnerships and a cohort of eight new sites, many of which were in the South, that wanted to build funding collaboratives. SIF funding required the National Fund to develop a more rigorous evaluation plan and raise matching funds. The new evaluation would enable more accurate and long-term tracking of individual and partnership outcomes. This would make up for the limitations of the National Fund's existing evaluation and make a better case to the federal government about the efficacy of workforce partnerships. The National Fund won a second round of SIF funding in 2012 and an additional grant in 2013. The fund and its local partnerships are well positioned to compete for future federal investment.

National Fund Challenges

The ongoing and future challenges for the National Fund can be grouped into three broad clusters.[17] Much has been learned about addressing these challenges.

The first, not surprisingly, has to do with making sure National Fund investments and activities respond to the needs of two core constituencies: employers and workers and job seekers. This is a long-standing tension within all workforce efforts targeting lower-skilled and lower-income individuals: how to structure a win-win strategy—a balanced "dual-customer" approach—that serves the interests of both sides of the labor market and is sustainable over time. National Fund sites have developed varied approaches for getting the balance right in different labor market contexts, with different levels of success.

A second set of challenges relates to the third core constituency of the National Fund model: the philanthropic community. The long-term future of the National Fund depends on being able to secure and sustain the support of private and public funders for workforce partnerships and regional collaborative structures, as well as for other activities, including research and advocacy that can expand the National Fund's impact.

The National Fund's start-up years have yielded lessons on how to influence education and training systems, particularly a region's workforce boards and community colleges. Some sites have made significant progress in connecting with and influencing these institutions, and there is much to be learned from their efforts. However, given the entrepreneurial, primarily "outsider" nature of the National Fund's workforce partnerships and funder collaboratives, leaders at both the local and national levels need to be realistic about the possibility of generating changes in these established systems—and strategic about presenting the National Fund's value proposition in ways that engage mainstream institutions on their own terms. These strategies will have to combine high-quality local implementation and partnering with advocacy for targeted state and federal policy changes that can alter the context within which local partnerships take root and operate.

Serving Labor Market Needs of Employers and Low-Income Individuals

The steady, significant increase in the number of individuals and employers served in National Fund sites validates its core dual-customer principles. Workforce partnerships funded by the National Fund exceeded the goal of engaging 2,000 employers in 2010 and by the end of 2012 had served more than 4,064 employers. By 2012 the 101 National Fund partnerships in thirty-two communities had served more than forty thousand individuals, making it likely that the goal of serving fifty thousand would be reached by the end of 2013. The dual focus on career advancement for low-income individuals and deep engagement of employers has clearly kept both groups motivated to use National Fund services.[18] By no means is this the scale of impact needed by workers and employers, but the National Fund's footprint is large enough for model refinement, evidence building, and advocacy.

According to National Fund director Fred Dedrick, the commitment to work closely with employers became both the distinguishing characteristic of the fund's approach and the key to its success. This kind of deep engagement creates, in Dedrick's view, a "shared value relationship" with specific employers who come to feel like partners, not just customers. If the workforce partnership is responsive and delivers, employers keep coming back. Over time, they may become more willing to entertain changes to their business practices that can help low-income workers advance. In a number of sites, for example, after becoming involved with the National Fund, employers decided to switch from tuition reimbursement to tuition advancement for their incumbent workers. In another, trust between the National Fund site and a local hospital led to a study of why the hospital was having such a difficult time retaining medical assistants. The assessment concluded that the institution was paying wages far below those of its competitors. The hospital raised wages by about a dollar an hour, and the retention problem eased. As Dedrick notes, while difficult, working with employers to change their behavior and policies can have a huge payoff: "When an employer changes its hiring or training practices, the benefit accrues not just to current employees but to future employees as well, over time."

The most effective workforce partnerships have had active and sustained employer engagement, according to the most recent National Fund evaluation. Employer involvement and roles have varied across sites. Several partnerships are employer-formed and employer-led, such as the Health Careers Collaborative of Greater Cincinnati (see Krismer, Chapter 8). These typically serve firms' incumbent workers rather than new job seekers. Other workforce partnerships, like JumpStart in Baltimore or Boston's Healthcare Training Institute, are run by community-based organizations that respond to employer needs and interests. In these communities, employers do not formally run the partnership but are active in participant selection, program design, and program support. A third variant is the labor-management partnership, like the Wisconsin Regional Training Partnership's construction initiative. In this model, labor unions bring employers to the table; employer involvement is usually negotiated, substantial, and long-term (see Buford and Dresser, Chapter 6).

There is an inherent tension between the dual-customer approach and creating opportunities for job seekers with significant barriers to employment, including very low basic skills, criminal records, mental health problems, and unstable family environments. In the dual-customer model, employers find value when they efficiently gain access to workers who can succeed in the jobs they are trying to fill and/or when they are able to effectively advance incumbent-worker skills.

Workers find value when they find good-quality jobs with opportunities for advancement and/or when they can refine their skills and advance their careers.

Highly effective workforce partnerships add value that employers and workers appreciate. They do this by providing effective supports and preparation for job candidates, sophisticated screening and assessment procedures to ensure a good fit between the candidate and the industry, basic and technical skill development to meet employer standards, and ongoing support for workers who find jobs. In these cases, workforce partnerships compensate for broken employer hiring systems and lower hiring costs. Some sites have also focused on incumbent workers by offering advancement training that helps to move people up and open the door to hiring new workers.

The National Fund has amply demonstrated that employers do not see "low income" per se as a barrier to hiring and advancement, so long as a candidate has the right skills and motivation. Some National Fund partnerships have chosen to prioritize services to individuals with many serious barriers to employment, only to be frustrated that employers are not receptive. Or, in instances where they can place these job seekers, they are frustrated by firms that do not offer wage and benefit gains, invest in employee education, or provide a safe place to work. High turnover and discouraged workers are too often the results.

While sector-based partnerships are a means to build new standards of quality regarding workplaces, workers, and the employment system, they are not well tailored to the toughest to employ. The National Fund experience has tested and defined the boundaries along the lower-skill end of the jobs continuum. To reach the toughest to employ might require starting the pipeline to employment with social enterprises that offer quality entry-level jobs and training for those facing significant barriers and create explicit links and pathways to National Fund sector partnerships for career advancement.

Sustaining Funder Investment and Will

The National Fund has been a remarkably successful mechanism for focusing significant resources on workforce development. Since 2008 it has leveraged $200 million in matching funds from 432 funders of local collaboratives and partnerships. This is a major accomplishment.[19] Many funders who had never supported workforce development joined local investor collaboratives. And the National Fund created an approach at the national and local levels that was very different from typical past practice, which was characterized by every funder investing as its board and staff saw fit, diffusing investment impact and making it more difficult to expand successful innovations. The National Fund has changed the landscape of workforce philanthropic investment.

But will the enthusiasm, commitment, and investment be sustained? Or will key funders reach a "sustainability cliff"? There are many more needs in any given community than philanthropic funders can meet. After a few years funders frequently feel pressure from their board or leadership—and from past and potential grantees as well—to change grant-making priorities and to address and invest in other needs. Funders that made a significant initial five-year commitment to the National Fund might be reluctant to reinvest or to do so at a similar level. It is encouraging that, at this juncture, most of the national funders in the National Fund are staying the course and new investors are joining.

One lesson the National Fund's sites have learned, or relearned, is that the systemic change it is seeding takes a long time and that some funders and sources of capital are more patient investors than others. To commit to helping individuals without high school diplomas advance to post-secondary credentials and ultimately degrees is to commit to a very long process. One National Fund grantee, for example, has launched a program to move low-skill adult workers into and through college-degree programs. They estimate that by the end of 2014 they will have supported the advancement of eighty workers into college-degree programs and will have fifty more in a pre-college pipeline. Funders in the grantee's city have invested in the National Fund site and in this provider for five years. Will they stick with it for several more years? Or will the pressure to reallocate resources to new purposes and goals win out? Communities will answer this question in different ways. Fortunately, in the current economy, jobs and economic mobility remain at center stage across the United States.

There are strategies the National Fund can pursue to encourage funders to stay the course and to attract new investors. Being more specific about the return on investment for local funders may help some sites to sustain their investment. Others may be willing to keep investing if they understand the scaling-up strategy and timeline for reaching more individuals. Still others might continue to invest if their fund investments will promote activities in addition to workforce partnerships, such as research and a learning agenda, policy and advocacy, or field building and communications.

Influencing the Delivery Models of Mainstream Education and Training Institutions

From the outset, National Fund investors agreed that success in achieving its goals at any significant scale would require systemic change in employer practices, public policy, and the practices of key institutions in the local education and training system, particularly workforce boards and community colleges. Progress on spurring changes in employer practices has been widespread: Close to half the local collaboratives reported an increase in employer investment in frontline hiring and training as a result of the National Fund's work, and a further 30 percent reported some other type of change.[20] On public policy, progress has been more uneven. Many collaboratives did not engage in campaigns to influence public policy, some because of inhospitable policy environments, others because they were still building their program infrastructure. The few sites that did target public-policy changes—including SkillWorks in Boston and the statewide Pennsylvania Fund for Workforce Solutions—had notable success channeling public resources to local workforce partnerships and preventing cuts to workforce development as the recession deepened.

Many National Fund sites have worked to engage local Workforce Investment Boards (WIBs) and community colleges. Three-quarters of all collaboratives reported some change in institutional practices, mostly in curricula, program design, and leveraging of funds.[21] Local collaboratives typically prioritized bringing workforce boards and colleges, as well as community-based organizations and adult-education providers, into partnerships offering structured career paths in particular sectors. Where successful, linkages among these institutions were strengthened and rationalized. Resources for sectoral training and services often increased.

Some local sites were able to leverage important changes in workforce-board practice and policy; in some cases, workforce systems became more responsive to employers. Progress tended to be more common and deeper among more mature collaboratives with broader reach, more effective employer leadership, and a clearer understanding of effective leverage points. Perhaps the most impressive was the creation in Cincinnati of the tri-state Partners for a Competitive Workforce, which organized the region's four workforce boards to formalize a ten-year-old partnership to coordinate workforce services for employers.

The variation in local progress reflects what had been an early tension around strategy among the National Fund's initial philanthropic investors and strategists. Should its purpose be to lay the groundwork for an alternative workforce system—one focused on career advancement for individuals and effective service to employers? Or should sites help rejuvenate and reinvent the existing system and the public funding streams critical to sustaining workforce services over time? The National Fund was slow to specify a consistent answer, and variation among sites proliferated. (As the National Fund evolved, it did take a stand on this issue, promoting local National Fund entities not as an alternative to the workforce system but as partners able to add significant value and critics committed to driving toward more effective local solutions.)

The relationship of National Fund sites to their local community colleges has also been complex and varied (see Ganzglass et al., Chapter 14). Individuals receiving partnership services at the fund's sites have earned more than eighteen thousand credentials, about half of which were workplace-readiness certificates. The second-largest group of credentials earned in 2010 was industry-recognized occupational skills certifications (37 percent, most commonly in health care), and very few participants (fewer than 2 percent) earned an associate's or bachelor's degree.[23] The priority for most local sites has been career advancement through better employment outcomes. The target population for the National Fund will struggle in college without "on-ramp" programs that help them make the transition into for-credit programs.

Community colleges are large, complex institutions, driven primarily by enrollments in credit programs and, increasingly, by measurable outcomes grounded in the granting of credentials. National Fund sites' efforts to build strong win-win relationships with local community colleges have been uneven. For sites to influence their local colleges, they must be more explicit about the value proposition for those institutions, given their many competing priorities and concerns. However, even if they are more strategic in approaching their local colleges, energetic and creative local collaboratives and workforce partnerships may not find the local community colleges sufficiently motivated and responsive to the proposed partnership.

Some sites, including San Francisco, have made relationships with community colleges central to their strategy for workforce partnerships and career advancement. This approach may become more attractive to community colleges as state and federal policies shift toward greater emphasis on employment and earnings outcomes. As one local collaborative leader put it, "If and when employment outcomes become more important in state community college funding and accountability systems or in federal financial aid policies, the National Fund can bring to local colleges something quite valuable: employers and the potential for improved outcomes on employment measures."

A few National Fund leaders feel that local sites will find willing partners among community colleges that are pursuing innovations to improve outcomes for nontraditional students, such as loosening the constraints of the traditional semester structure, giving more credit for prior learning, and making career-focused programs look and feel more like work than like traditional college. This may be true, but it underscores the reality that partnerships between National Fund sites and community colleges will have to be targeted, will probably start off small, and will have to evolve over time as the institutions come to understand one another's interests better. Local collaboratives and workforce partnerships will have to identify and try to align with the broad reform strategies that colleges are being pressed to implement by their public funders and their customers, including stronger accountability for results that require persistence, completion of credentials, and labor-market outcomes. They will have to be careful as they work hard to find common ground with colleges, stay focused on their key constituencies, and keep employer interests and needs front and center.

In both cases—the workforce system's WIBs and one-stop centers and local community colleges—the National Fund has found its entrepreneurial, intermediary role and approach to be both a benefit and an obstacle to influencing mainstream institutional behavior. The fund's commitment to creating new, vibrant partnerships at the local level enables it to be nimble and entrepreneurial and seize opportunities that might otherwise be missed. But sector partnerships are a kind of reform response to the gaps in the local career-advancement system. As such, they can be seen as challenging to the more established workforce system and its legacy emphasis on new employees and entry-level placements. From the community-college perspective, the National Fund's size and its target population of nontraditional adults can be seen as bringing insufficient leverage to such a large institution.

It may be that the growth of the movement to create career pathways to and through the community college can be an "insider" complement to the National Fund's more "outsider" approach. If the two can be aligned effectively at the local level, the result could be greater interest from colleges and from the workforce system, too, given the growing commitment of the federal departments of Labor and Education to career pathways as an advancement strategy (see Ganzglass et al., Chapter 14).

Given how difficult it is for the National Fund partnerships and collaboratives to effect significant change in the mainstream workforce institutions—both WIBs and one-stop centers and community colleges—the fund's local and national public-policy efforts are critically important. As SkillWorks and a few other sites have shown, coordinated public-policy campaigns can help change the incentives facing mainstream institutions in ways that make them more receptive to career pathways and sectoral strategies. Performance-based funding systems, metrics based on labor-market outcomes in addition to educational outcomes, and incentives for employer engagement are a few of the policy and advocacy targets that can help the National Fund's local efforts become more embedded in the mainstream workforce institutions of their region and state.

Next Generation: Toward Expanded Funding and Influence

As the evaluations of local and national efforts funded by the National Fund demonstrate, there has been significant progress in the first five years. New partnerships and collaboratives have formed in cities and regions across the nation. Large numbers of participants have enrolled in and completed training and earned credentials through local partnership efforts. Significant resources have been focused on building robust partnerships and training programs. And all of this has taken place during a deep recession and slow recovery, a particularly challenging time to engage employers in investing in their workforce, particularly their lower-skilled and lower-income workers.

At the same time, there is much more to be accomplished, and many questions about strategy, design, and implementation still need better answers. To continue to attract resources and support from existing and new investors for the next generation of work, the National Fund and local sites will need to demonstrate growing influence and progress and also generate new knowledge and lessons from the progress and challenges to date.

The next section explores what the National Fund should do over the next five years to have greater impact and influence locally and nationally.

Local Collaboratives

To achieve maximum impact and sustainability, local funder collaboratives should consider broadening their governance and "ownership" of local strategic planning—from a funders-only group to one that represents the key stakeholders in the career-advancement system. These could include employers in particular industries, education and training institutions in the region, and political leaders. Cincinnati, where a freestanding collaborative is aligning with the United Way to increase sustainability over time, is a good example. There is a lot to learn from the first communities where National Fund collaboratives are evolving into broader collective-impact organizations, particularly about how to keep funders deeply engaged as other stakeholders begin to exercise greater influence. There are, however, potential downsides to this approach that must be considered, such as competing with WIBs, diluting sector workforce investments, and moving too quickly to a broader coalition before achieving results. Collective-impact approaches in the workforce field are challenged by a lack of agreement on defining challenges and outcomes, multiple and divergent target populations, fragmentation of workforce institutions and systems, and different perspectives on the role of the private sector.

Workforce Partnerships and Intermediaries

There has been a healthy debate within the National Fund on the priorities for the next phase of its evolution: Should the goal be to expand and improve outcomes among existing partnerships, or are more partnerships and new sites still needed?

To attract new funders, it is likely that expansion of both sites and partnerships within sites will be needed, so that momentum continues and spreads. The National Fund's leadership sees the strategic need to add about three new communities a year for the next five years, until collaboratives exist in forty-five communities, urban and rural, serving a hundred thousand people during that period. Any expansion effort must be undertaken strategically—in terms of the occupations or industries targeted, the new communities approached, and the ways in which employers, WIBs, and community colleges are engaged. Moreover, as has already begun to occur, expansion will have to be balanced by decisions to pull back from sites where performance is below acceptable benchmarks.

Whatever the outcome of this debate, there is a clear need for sharper definition and specification of the essential roles workforce partnerships should play in the regional economy—and how partnerships that target employers in a single sector can take on the broader intermediary role that many within the National Fund community see as critical to long-term sustainability and value. The National Fund must help define the specific and tangible contribution of sector partnerships to regional economic competitiveness. In all of these efforts, deepening the various roles of employers is critical.

In the coming years, the National Fund's partnerships will also have to continue its efforts to influence the core practices of workforce-development institutions, community colleges, and employers as they relate to low-wage workers' career advancement. The National Fund's leadership recognizes this and has committed to making systems-change efforts the top priority of local workforce partnerships nationally, including the commitment to influencing changes in low-wage-worker training and employment practices in one hundred workplaces.

State and National Advocacy

During the first five years, investors wanted to influence national policy, and the National Fund was able to inject its principles into workforce legislation and influence the priorities of federal grant solicitations. However, because of the intense political gridlock in Washington, initial progress stagnated. The National Fund's leadership made a strategic decision to target advocacy work in a few states rather than at the federal level, leading to a relative decline in the fund's visibility in Washington debates. In the coming years, new strategies will be needed to aggregate voices from different National Fund sites and make them more influential on career advancement and employer engagement issues and policies.

The ultimate success of the National Fund will be assessed in terms of changes in regional economies and labor markets, as evidenced by both individual progress in employment and earnings and employer satisfaction with and reliance on the local fund partnerships for quality workers. This embedding of National Fund efforts in regional approaches will require advocacy and policy change at both federal and state levels—a dual approach to policy innovation that recognizes the growing significance of state action while reaffirming the importance of federal legislative and executive branch policy changes that can promote regional strategies supporting employer engagement and effective sectoral and career pathways initiatives. The National Fund has turned to the National Skills Coalition and the Business Leaders United partnership to expand its capacity to advocate for state and federal policies that support a movement for career advancement through employer-led partnerships. Given its wealth of on-the-ground knowledge and relationships, the National Fund will need to continue to develop, update, and pursue policy targets at both the state and the national level, in conjunction with its advocacy partners (see Van Kleunen, Chapter 16).

At the federal level, the reauthorizations of the Workforce Investment Act, the Perkins Vocational and Technical Education Act, and the Higher Education Opportunity Act in the coming years present opportunities for reinforcing National Fund principles and priorities, perhaps institutionalizing the regional partnership strategy for strengthening career pathways, and strengthening incentives for employers to support frontline-worker training and credentialing. So, too, do competitive innovation funds administered by the Departments of Labor, Education, and Health and Human Services and other federal agencies, as well as interagency federal efforts to align career-pathways support. At the state level, National Fund priorities can be integrated into economic development, workforce development, and higher-education policies. At all levels, the policy agenda will have to address financing models for growing and sustaining the local partnerships and their workforce activities. This will require creative thinking about how to support private-public partnerships and specification of incentives that can keep pushing the key employment and education systems to reorient resources toward career advancement and the pipeline to middle-skill jobs that are so critical to most regional economies.

The role of employers—and their national, state, and regional organizations—in an expanded National Fund advocacy effort is key but remains challenging. The National Fund sites have done a good job engaging business in workforce partnerships and in governance roles at the local level. There are certainly many employers of low-skilled workers in varied industries and of varied size and well-being that offer good jobs and opportunities for low-skilled employees. The National Fund has many such companies in its network and is poised to help many others move toward developing better training advancement ladders and improving job quality.

However, much more work is needed if National Fund employers and their organizations are to take on significantly expanded advocacy roles in support of career-advancement policies. There are several obstacles to employer advocacy for the fund's approach, at both local and national levels. Employers have public policy priorities that trump human capital, including tax policy and regulatory relief. Moreover, employers often have other human-capital advocacy targets besides training of low-skilled employees, such as immigration policy or technology policy. And in a slack labor market, employers can have varied sources for identifying qualified workers, minimizing a sense of urgency, except in certain occupations.

The National Fund can and should strengthen its case to employers for the quantifiable value of its services. Demonstrating a clear return on investment to employers—in terms of worker quality and productivity, reduced turnover, and hiring costs—might keep participating employers engaged, bring in new firms, and increase their willingness to invest resources and time to support and promote the fund's services. The CareerSTAT Return on Investment pilot, among National Fund health care sites, is a case in point, energizing employers and laying the groundwork for sustainability. However, it will remain a stretch for many employers to engage in advocacy for workforce and career-advancement policy innovation. Local and national leaders of the National Fund should be circumspect and realistic about the role that participating employers are likely to play in the advocacy arena, even those who are quite supportive of the National Fund.

Flexibility in Implementation of the National Fund Model

During the next five years, fidelity to the initial National Fund model might have to take a backseat to greater flexibility that can sustain investor and employer engagement and increase the fund's influence and impact. As one consultant to the fund put it, the need in the coming years is for continuous improvement and adapting the current model to local conditions and opportunities.

During the recession, collaboratives and sites that persisted and had strong outcomes were those where the leadership was entrepreneurial and agile. Some sites shifted quickly from training individuals for new jobs in growing manufacturing or aerospace firms to training for incumbent workers to make them more productive so they could keep their jobs or move to others in the firm. Other sites adapted by changing the industries they worked with and the kinds of services they provided. The importance of this kind of opportunistic flexibility to respond to changing economic and fiscal realities should not be underestimated—even though it runs somewhat contrary to the fund's initial insistence on fidelity to the original model.

Knowledge Development and Dissemination

Many of the original and current investors in the National Fund see the next five years as a period for gleaning lessons while continuing to grow. From interviews with local and national leaders of the fund, three areas for additional knowledge development and dissemination rise to the fore.

One clear lesson is that we need to know more about the specifics of local implementation if outcomes are to continue to improve. Career-advancement pathways vary from one industry to another, and different population groups fare better with certain learning programs and supports. These variations need to be better understood so that a clearer picture emerges of what kinds of approaches work for such groups as immigrants, service workers, or the formerly incarcerated and how we should create career "ladders" and pathways in fields ranging from health care to manufacturing and construction. This analysis can help local sites set appropriate expectations and seize opportunities effectively.

A second topic for research and learning that is critical to long-term sustainability of National Fund sites—and funder engagement—is the quality and cost-effectiveness of local implementation. Several services have emerged across local sites as important for implementation success. The first include coaching of job seekers and trainees, the provision of wraparound support services, and employer engagement and services. Across the sites, questions of how to deliver these services in cost-efficient ways are an area of great interest. The second challenge is cultivating and training an entrepreneurial leadership that can organize workforce partnerships and broader groups of workforce stakeholders.

Finally, thoughtful research and analysis are needed on the local structures emerging and evolving across the sites. How far should the workforce partnerships and local funder collaboratives go toward becoming regional labor-market intermediaries that undertake not just training but brokering across industries and service-delivery systems and other functions played by more mature organizations like SkillWorks and the Wisconsin Regional Training Partnership? The fund's national evaluators argue that partnerships and collaboratives that have expanded to play a community-wide integrative role—organizing employers, workforce boards, education providers, and others, aligning resources across the region, and setting clear goals—are making tremendous progress in systems change. But they also note that it takes a long time for sites to build trust, identify their niche, and reach organizational maturity. What can the National Fund do to encourage and accelerate this process? This is perhaps the most important design and implementation challenge facing the National Fund's sites as they move into the next phase of work. Understanding the pros and cons of different models and options as they have played out in the past five years could help accelerate the specification of sustainable models for the National Fund's local sites.

Conclusion

America's economy and indeed its social fabric rely on our ability to ensure decent work now and in the future and to cultivate skilled employees ready and able to work. If we fail to address the structural challenges that have contributed to wage and income stagnation and anemic economic growth, we as a society will lose our ability to imagine and build a better future. Instead of being daunted by this challenge, we must meet it with confidence in our people and institutions. It is reassuring that those who have toiled in the field to restore the dignity of workers, enhance the efficacy of work, and support business prosperity have achieved some notable success.

Across more than thirty communities from Boston to San Diego, Seattle to Sarasota, the National Fund for Workforce Solutions has built a strong network of committed funders, employers, and professional staff who have developed productive, inclusive regional workforce collaboratives. This community-based infrastructure is actively directing the investment of scores of millions of dollars into the training and advancement of tens of thousands of low-wage workers through more than one hundred workforce partnerships. Progress in growing and institutionalizing such efforts is always slower, more uneven, and more fragile than both investors and practitioners would like. Moreover, each step forward raises new and often complex questions about future opportunities, challenges, and resources. However, the reach and progress of the National Fund and its sites are impressive. The National Fund's first five years provide a solid platform and much to build upon as the nation strives for increased economic prosperity and more effective and efficient regional workforce development.

Notes

1. Hebert (2010).
2. Thanks to Fred Dedrick, executive director of the National Fund for Workforce Solutions, and John Padilla, formerly of the Annie E. Casey Foundation and former chair of the National Fund, for their comments and suggestions on this chapter.
3. Giloth (2010).
4. Giloth (2004); Jobs for the Future (2004).
5. American Assembly (2003).
6. Giloth (2004).
7. Walker and Foster-Bey (2004).
8. Scott (2007).
9. Several of this volume's authors played a role in the formation of SkillWorks. The Annie E. Casey Foundation was an early funder, and Jobs for the Future provided technical assistance.

10. Waldron (2008).

11. Jobs for the Future (2005).

12. Scott (2007).

13. Jobs for the Future (2005).

14. Prince (2005).

15. Ford Foundation (2006).

16. Clymer et al. (2009).

17. The section on National Fund lessons is based on published evaluation materials and a set of interviews with national staff and partners, evaluators, and local National Fund leaders.

18. Baran et al. (2012).

19. Ibid.

20. Baran et al. (2012a).

21. Ibid.

22. Baran et al. (2012).

Bibliography

American Assembly. 2003. *Keeping America in Business: Advancing Workers, Businesses, and Economic Growth*. Summary of the 102nd American Assembly. New York: Columbia University.

Baran, Barbara, Stephen Michon, Suzanne Teegarden, Lianne Giordono, and Kendra Lodewick. 2012. *Implementing the National Fund for Workforce Solutions: Data Brief for the Fourth National Evaluation Report*. Boston: National Fund for Workforce Solutions.

———. 2012a. *National Fund Principles: Collaborative and Partnership Achievements: Fourth Annual National Evaluation Report*. Boston: National Fund for Workforce Solutions.

Clymer, Carol, Maureen Conway, Joshua Freely, and Sheila Maguire. 2009. *Job Training That Works; Findings from the Sectoral Employment Impact Study*. Philadelphia: Public/Private Ventures. May.

Ford Foundation. 2006. *Towards a National Fund for Workforce Partnerships, Briefing Materials and Case Statement*. New York: Ford Foundation.

Giloth, Robert P., ed. 2004. *Workforce Intermediaries for the Twenty-First Century*. Published in association with American Assembly, Columbia University. Philadelphia: Temple University Press.

———. 2010. "Replicating Model Programs: A Fatal Attraction?" In Robert P. Giloth and Colin Austin, *Mistakes to Success: Learning and Adapting When Things Go Wrong*. Bloomington, IN: Universe Press, pp. 17–34.

Hebert, Scott. 2010. *Changing Systems Is Like Moving a Mountain*. Baltimore: The Annie E. Casey Foundation.

Jobs for the Future. 2005. *Investing in Workforce Intermediaries, A Project of the Annie E. Casey, Rockefeller, and Ford Foundations*. Boston: Jobs for the Future.

———. 2004. *Workforce Intermediaries and Their Roles in Promoting Advancement*. Boston: Jobs for the Future.

Prince, Heath, ed. 2007. *Financing Workforce Intermediaries: Working Papers.* Boston: National Fund for Workforce Solutions.

Scott, Geri. 2006. *Funder Collaboratives: A Philanthropic Strategy for Supporting Workforce Intermediaries.* Boston: Jobs for the Future.

Waldron, Tom. 2008. *The National Fund for Workforce Solutions: A History of Collaboration.* Baltimore: The Annie E. Casey Foundation.

Walker, Chris, and John Foster-Bey. 2004. "Community Development Intermediation and Its Lessons for the Workforce Field." In Giloth (2004), pp. 336–366.

6

The Wisconsin Regional Training Partnership: The Evolution of an Intermediary, the Shifting Target of Twenty-first Century Manufacturing, and the Continuing Relevance of Unions in Labor Markets

Earl Buford and Laura Dresser

The Wisconsin Regional Training Partnership (WRTP) is one of the nation's premier workforce intermediaries and unique among its peers for the central and driving role of labor unions in the project. Rigorous evaluation of participant outcomes has proven the WRTP's significant and positive effects on earnings. The organization has weathered the ups and downs of the Milwaukee regional economy for more than two decades. Its survival has required flexibility and innovation in its approach to sectors, employers, and funders. This chapter charts the evolution of the project and the emerging challenges of staying relevant in the aftermath of the Great Recession. The chapter also emphasizes the core and unchanging principles of the WRTP: commitment to shared priorities of labor and management, pursuit of solutions to industry needs, and building solutions that work not only for firms and future workers but the current workforce as well. These principles help the WRTP stand out, even as it continues to evolve to find new ways to stay relevant to its mission.

Introduction

The WRTP, established in the early 1990s and still thriving today, can reasonably be called the nation's premier labor-led workforce intermediary. Evolving from roots in manufacturing, the WRTP has proven through rigorous evaluation and ongoing sustainability that intermediaries can build lasting solutions to problems that riddle firms, workers, communities, and our labor market. The model is both flexible and evolving in many ways while being unique and firmly committed to specific principles that are uncommon in the field of workforce intermediaries. Perhaps the most important principle of the WRTP is the organizational and programmatic focus on joint labor-management leadership of all initiatives.

Joint labor-management leadership of the organization is foundational. These labor and management leaders are not looking to the WRTP as community service or as a means to connect with a few employees; they are creating an organization that can build the solutions their industry needs, that can go out and secure public and private resources to respond to those needs, and that can advocate with public systems for the sorts of policy changes that will help solve those problems. From this perspective, the WRTP is much more than any single project it works on. It is not just a way to train and connect central-city workers to entry-level jobs, though it does that well. It is an industry voice and an industry-driven generator of solutions, the collective site where shared problems can be identified and solutions promoted and pursued.

This labor-management focus generates a number of benefits for the organization and for the community. Most obviously, the WRTP is connected to some of the best-quality jobs in the regional labor market in terms of wages and benefits. Too often, programs respond to or are designed in response to the needs of employers with much lower-quality jobs (and higher turnover, which generates a consistent need to hire). Additionally, the WRTP reaches more consistently to all jobs within the firm. Its focus reaches past the entry level directly to development of mentors and attendance policies, on to incumbent-worker training issues and even to questions of modernization of process and technology. That reach provides a more dynamic mix for program development and provides the project with a stronger understanding of a firm's internal dynamics, not just the hiring process from the outside. In these ways, the unique labor foundation of the project pays off for workers and the community.

It also is clear that this independence and industry focus can have downsides. The WRTP has never been a creature of the workforce-training system in the region. As such, it must constantly develop and redevelop relationships with partners and funders. The organization has proved sustainable but does not have a steady and reliable institutional funding base that carries it through the ups and downs of a fluctuating economy. At times organizations that have funded or otherwise worked with the WRTP change priorities or direction and end the relationship. The cost of being very much outside the public workforce system (both the state's technical colleges and workforce boards) is the ongoing work of staying connected to and supported by that system, even as the WRTP seeks reform and improvement of public partners. A navigable tension, to be sure, but one that requires nearly constant attention to ensure that projects with partners will work and that funding can be secured.

One defining feature of the WRTP, then, is its capacity to evolve in terms of project, program, and industry in response to ever-changing economic and political climates. But the other key feature is its anchor of stability: the core value of the centrality of labor-management partnership and worker voice. The WRTP builds success by building a program on the interests and strength of the independent voice of working people in an industry. This constant foundational focus provides the WRTP with stability and core value, even as its work has evolved dramatically over time. And these values will support that work for the decades to come.

Roots of the WRTP

In the early 1990s, manufacturing leaders in Milwaukee from both labor and management knew they had problems. The WRTP was their answer.

Like other cities across the Midwest, Milwaukee was devastated by the "Rust Belt recession" of the early 1980s and the massive flight of manufacturing firms over the subsequent decade. In the 1980s Milwaukee lost fully a third of its traditional industrial base. These losses accelerated both union decline statewide and poverty growth in the city itself.

In the early 1990s manufacturing firms began emerging from the prolonged slump. Unions and firms realized that things had changed and that sustainability of the sector would require new approaches to training. Especially in light of firms' abandonment of apprenticeship programs in the 1980s and changing production to more cellular and modularized systems, the need for new means of training was evident to all. Employers were open to a constructive discussion about training problems and ways to fill the skill deficits that seemed to be emerging. Labor leaders also wanted to be much more involved in process and production issues than in the past, from firm restructuring to modernization and human-capital formation.

Eventually the Center on Wisconsin Strategy (COWS), a think-and-do tank at the University of Wisconsin–Madison, formally facilitated the emerging manufacturing conversation. With research in hand on labor and management perspectives on industry challenges, training, and modernization needs, and clarity on what the shared concerns actually were, leaders agreed to a partnership approach covering multiple firms and aspiring to extend the influence in support of training and a stronger sector even beyond the boundaries of the original members. The WRTP is the partnership born of those discussions.

Over the past two decades, the WRTP has provided a place where employers and unions identify common problems and best practices, develop pilot projects to solve them, and implement those projects. The issues have changed over time, and at different times in the organization's history its work with any industry falls into roughly three categories of work.

First—and this was especially true in the early days of the manufacturing partnership—the WRTP helps strengthen training systems for incumbent workers. It worked with the region's leading firms to build and support joint labor-management training committees inside those firms. These committees identified skill needs; established training centers; and developed curriculum and systems to identify, train, and support mentors and trainers and thus brought new and directly relevant training to thousands of workers in the region's firms. Workplace education centers provided training that ran the gamut of skill needs, providing everything from advanced computer numerical control (CNC) and other machine skills to process and communication skills so relevant in increasingly team-based production systems and also basic skills at the high school level and lower for adults (including work toward a GED). The workplace training centers were managed and overseen by joint labor-management committees, which developed policies, training content, and operations norms for the centers. These committees also developed a cadre of peer advisors who served as outreach agents for the training centers, informing co-workers of the opportunities at the center. The project from the very start, then, was about building labor-management consensus on and capacity for training inside the firm.

At the same time, labor and management leadership also identified the need for industry modernization and improvement of production processes. The atmosphere of cooperation between labor and management on training issues was a critical support as the difficult work of renegotiating contracts with changing job titles was under way. Eventually the WRTP even housed labor specialists who, working with funding from the state's Manufacturing Extension Partnership, reached out to labor in union firms and helped facilitate conversations around process and productivity enhancements in the context of work reorganization. Again, this work was in service of industry competitiveness and took part mostly inside member firms.

In the late 1990s, this infrastructure provided a foundation as the region's manufacturing industry began to expand. The WRTP was perfectly positioned to develop future workforce programs and customized skills-training programs that met industry needs and connected disadvantaged workers to union jobs in the regional economy. At that time, the WRTP developed an entry-level curriculum for manufacturing jobs (thus standardizing a project when firms were used to customization). Disadvantaged workers from the central city were provided short-term training and guaranteed employment at the end of successful completion of training. The program was a success, connecting more than fourteen hundred Milwaukeeans with good jobs.

Those entry-level trainings were core to the Milwaukee Jobs Initiative (MJI) and its success in the late 1990s:

- From 1997 to 2002, 1,405 MJI participants were placed in **full-time jobs at an average starting wage of $10.55 per hour**. Generally, this provided an average hourly gain of more than $2 over the participants' prior jobs.

- The overwhelming majority of placed participants were **people of color**: 68 percent were African American, 20 percent Latino, and 2 percent American Indian.

- MJI improved the well-being of the **children** (at least 1,687) living in households of MJI-placed participants.

- All MJI jobs offered access to **family health benefits**; only 35 percent of participants had received health benefits at their previous jobs.

- Of all MJI placements, **73 percent were still working after a year, with 41 percent at the same or a better wage**, a significant accomplishment given the challenges associated with retaining entry-level workers, such as educational deficits and lack of work experience.

In addressing the future workforce need, the WRTP played a unique and essential role: as honest broker bringing manufacturing opportunities to the local workforce-development system. The WRTP used these opportunities to help direct public resources to jobs that really mattered in the region while also securing enhanced job quality for the central-city workers it served. Over the late 1990s it brought together the different actors in that system to leverage their unique strengths while seeking to reduce the (prevalent) redundancy in the system. So, for example, employers and unions have the job openings and best understand skill requirements, community organizations are good at recruiting workers and offering support services, and technical colleges have the training expertise. Rather than each group trying to do everything on its own (and inevitably failing), the WRTP's goal is to help develop a well-coordinated and efficient system of recruiting, training, and placing workers. The logic is simple: Train workers for specific jobs that already exist. But this level of coordination doesn't happen on its own. It requires an intermediary, such as the WRTP, with strong ties in all the respective communities.

It is this work connecting central-city residents to regional union jobs that has been rigorously evaluated. Entry-level training for and connections to jobs has a strong positive effect on employment and earnings of participants in the WRTP's programs. These positive results have contributed to the evaluation of sector strategies and their success as a whole. In some ways also, WRTP programs stand out, even in the field of sector strategies.

In fact, the efforts of WRTP/BIG STEP (see page 121) were lauded in a recent two-year study conducted by Public/Private Ventures on sector employment strategies.[1] The study found that participants in "sector-focused programs" like WRTP/BIG STEP earned 18.3 percent more than individuals who did not receive such program support. Participants in sector-focused programs, the study noted, were also more likely to work, and to work more consistently, in the second year. Moreover, when compared with individuals unaffiliated with programs like WRTP/BIG STEP, these participants also earned more. Sector-focused training-program participants were significantly more likely to work in jobs that offered benefits, too.

The Need to Evolve

The WRTP relies on strong relationships with employers and union leaders in order to secure better outcomes for workers inside firms and a means of access to those firms for Milwaukee's central-city residents. This is widely understood but implies a level of flexibility and dynamism that is often hard to develop in an intermediary. Markets are moving targets; supply and demand are in constant flux. The mix of relevant intermediary services—their capacity to provide answers to firms while delivering on social priorities—is less a project than a process. This is not simply a puzzle with one solution; it is a dynamic market where solutions must be developed, re-forged, analyzed, and improved.

In the following section we talk about key stages of evolution of the WRTP as a project. These are critical changes made in response to industry need that shifted the services and program of the WRTP. Each evolution was needed to maintain the relevance and enhance the organization's sustainability. Any intermediary project will be required to respond and to change over time. This program flexibility and responsiveness challenge the projects themselves but also should challenge funders and policy makers to consider how to build flexible funding streams, including sustainable sources of funding for infrastructure that supports all partnership work.

From Ladders inside the Firm to Access to New Jobs in the Mid-1990s

Our description of the WRTP's roots and history hints at the first real evolution in the program. The WRTP was born out of internal labor-management dialogue and a program that focused on building the capacity for labor-management partnerships within firms to take on and support training in the region's manufacturing sector. The hallmarks of this early work—labor-management committees on training, the development of dozens of workplace training centers jointly managed by those committees, the development of a cadre of shop-floor trainers and peer advisors to increase the skills of the manufacturing workforce—were internal to firms. Information flowed through the network, perhaps especially through union leadership, and one training center was established to serve multiple firms, but the WRTP work in the early period was largely within firms. And that work put more skills in the reach of incumbent workers. The project enhanced the level of training and skills in the region's manufacturing industry by dramatically extending the number of firms that were building strong internal training systems.

By the second half of the 1990s, these firms actually began hiring again, some of them for the first time in well over a decade. The WRTP was in a perfect position to move into the work of helping solve this entry-level worker need for the industry. And they could do it in a way that would more firmly connect disadvantaged workers to these family-supporting manufacturing jobs.

Given low unemployment rates across the country, many projects started around this time, and many developed programs very similar to the WRTP: Work with firms to identify skills needed for job openings, connect with training providers to develop courses to build those skills, work with community groups to identify and support candidates, and facilitate the connection to and support from the public system to pay for the customized training. Somewhat uniquely, the WRTP model included employer screening at the front end as well, so successful completion of the program guaranteed being hired. But the work of the early 1990s provided a unique platform for the WRTP's entry-level manufacturing work. The WRTP already knew the entry-level and more advanced jobs at these worksites. Firms had established training systems for current workers, and workforce leaders already had been trained as trainers and peer mentors.

Even the entry-level work evolved in important ways in manufacturing. As this area of work geared up, the WRTP partnered with firms to develop customized training programs. The process was slow, requiring technical-college curriculum development and funding approval by the workforce board, plus a recruitment process with local community organizations. Each step in the process could break down for idiosyncratic reasons in ways that often seemed random and always took astonishing amounts of time. The first class, from the agreement with the firm to hire and train on the system to the actual graduation and employment of the class, took more than ten months. Over the course of the next five years, however, systems were established and became standardized. Perhaps most impressive, the WRTP showed firms that they generated roughly the same training curricula, and using this knowledge, the organization gained the support of member firms to simply employ an entry-level manufacturing skills training package (ELMS). The WRTP had customized its way to a regional entry-level skill standard.

Not only did the delivery of customized training evolve across the late 1990s; the WRTP also began to develop other new program areas to support entry-level workers. Building on its connections with peer advisors inside firms, the WRTP developed a network of mentors to assist in the orientation, retention, and acclimation of new entry-level workers inside firms. This work involved training for the mentors as well as explicit connecting at the worksite for the central-city residents who were just making their first steps into manufacturing. Given that many of these firms had not hired in years and that the incumbent workforce was often much older, whiter, and more male than the entry-level workers coming in from WRTP training programs, the gaps between long-term and new workers were substantial. Entering manufacturing has never been easy, and secrets of survival, conveyed by an uncle or other relative, could make all the difference for a worker just making it to his or her second day on the job. The mentor networks helped promote a less family-based flow of support and information from long-term workers to newer ones.

Further, the WRTP also realized that attendance policies and other practices at many firms had become outdated and stood as a barrier to retention of good workers. So it began working with firms and unions to review attendance and discipline policies and to make changes that helped modernize them. Those changes also helped with retaining the entry-level workers who came in through training programs. (It is worth noting that the WRTP has the intent and capacity to work with a firm on attendance policies for all employees, not just for their "participants." This approach of embracing the entire workforce and making systematic policy change stands in contrast to more caseworker style, individualized work to keep workers in firms. Clearly, that work is needed as well. But the WRTP also was able to take on the policies of retention more broadly, and that is critical, too.)

This evolution to training entry-level workers was required by the industry; the most pressing need in the late 1990s was not workplace skill development (though much of that work continued) but filling jobs and retaining the newly trained entry-level workers. The change in work required the organization to develop new services and skills and to seek and secure new funding sources. The WRTP did this both because industry needed it and thanks to resources invested by the Annie E. Casey Foundation in the region's Jobs Initiative. The effect was to open opportunity to disadvantaged workers, though this was not the original reason behind the project and partnership.

Into New Sectors and a Formal Partnership with BIG STEP

Another evolution of the project has been to expand the sectors of concern. Each time the WRTP has expanded its work, it has engaged a steering committee of labor and management leaders in the relevant sector to direct the work so the model is the same even as sectors expand. Over the late 1990s, as the WRTP's manufacturing work absorbed much of the partnership's time, new projects emerged. The industrial model was so successful that the U.S. Department of Labor granted WRTP an implementation grant in 2000 to expand to additional sectors, including construction. A short-lived hospitality partnership floundered and eventually ended, but projects with health care and utilities were established and provided training and other services to their respective sectors over time.

In the construction sector, the WRTP did not develop a new line of work; instead, it formed a partnership with BIG STEP 2001. In 1976 BIG STEP was formed by the building trades, contractor associations, and community organizations in order to connect more women, minorities, and younger workers with the skilled trades. The project provides support for workers as they navigate the complexity of entry into and progression up through apprenticeship. It provides basic-skills and other training in order to get potential apprentices ready for tests and for the hard work of getting connected to the work sites/training hours they need. The merger was aided by the similar leadership structures of both organizations. BIG STEP's board of directors, made up of building-trades and contractor-association representatives, serves as the construction steering committee for the building-trade and apprenticeship relationships for the WRTP. Connection to industry information and leadership is foundational to both organizations.

The merger gave the organization the breadth of program it needed for further growth. In 2005, with support from Wisconsin governor Jim Doyle, WRTP/BIG STEP developed a new concept for the organization. The Center of Excellence for Skilled Trades and Industries (COE) was launched that year to address growing demands for skill in both construction and manufacturing. In 2006, with the acquisition of a thirty-thousand-square-foot building, the COE became the home of WRTP/BIG STEP, a training center for business and industry and a one-stop point of access for Milwaukee residents seeking information and access to jobs and advancement in construction and manufacturing.

The sectoral evolution of the WRTP has been a process of innovation, program development, and, in some cases, the need to close projects for lack of relevant initiatives and funding for them. This, too, is a story of industry-led work.

At times a sector may have no work or projects that need to be developed by an intermediary. Sometimes the low quality of the jobs and/or the low barriers to getting into the jobs make a training strategy at the entry level irrelevant to the real needs of workers and firms. When you have high-wage jobs with specific and identifiable skills needed and, even better, an internal training system for workers once they are connected to the firm, you have a real asset. But when the entry-level job is one that might be obtained just by applying off the street, developing a training program is substantially less interesting to prospective workers and a substantially greater risk to the investment. So, again, the opportunity and the project both evolve. But also, the WRTP is willing to end a project when the need disappears or when the strategies the organization can deploy are not essential to solving the sector's problems.

The Changing Route into Manufacturing Jobs

Nothing makes the need for evolution clearer than economic collapse. The 2001 recession ushered in a brutal decade for manufacturing in the United States as the industry and its workforce contracted, restructured, fell again in 2007, and revived in 2010, permanently changed. The WRTP saw many of the firms that had hired workers through its entry-level manufacturing work shed those workers and in some cases even shut down entirely. Further, the stress and decline of the collapse eliminated long-standing infrastructure, diminished human-resource leadership, and undermined labor-management relations as well.

Despite of the decline and difficulty, in the new decade (around 2011) firms began to hire. They again turned once more to the WRTP for support, recruitment, and entry-level training. It is not as simple, however, as just dusting off the entry-level manufacturing skills curriculum and setting up classes, though that has occured. The WRTP has always been, in some ways, an alternative and a competitor to the other sources of new workers in manufacturing, most obviously staffing-service firms. So the WRTP is still a resource to firms in hiring but, given changes in internal training and human resources at firms and in strategies and practices by staffing-service firms, the WRTP has been seriously challenged to develop new models for the new manufacturing expansion. Working together, COWS and the WRTP have conducted exploratory research regarding these changes that raises some serious issues for the WRTP to tackle in the next phase of its development.

The first challenge is the spread of staffing services in the union sector in Milwaukee. Direct competition exists at almost every worksite for the WRTP's entry-level recruitment and training services. Importantly, staffing-service firms are chosen not only for recruitment but also for their methods of assessment and screening. In the late 1990s the WRTP had a strong community-based network for recruitment of workers. Working with employers, the WRTP would screen individuals to participate in training programs. Computer screening tools have replaced much of that sort of screening, but the WRTP is wary of the unintended impact of those tools. Additionally, and important for worker retention and advancement, firms' internal training systems (workplace education centers) have been significantly reduced.

During the late 1990s the WRTP's in-depth firm and industry knowledge enabled the manufacturing partnership to outcompete alternatives on recruitment. Today, however, firm reliance on computer assessments presents a challenge. While WRTP's industry knowledge means its personal assessment systems may actually be more effective, firms have become increasingly reliant on the "black box," technical solution of assessment. And though the "black box" of assessment deployed by staffing-service firms may leave out many qualified and quality workers (the anecdotes on this are many, and shocking), the standards and the screening it offers (in the context of large applicant pools) often prove attractive.

The WRTP is able to continue to provide entry-level services for firms, but the context is much more challenging than it was in the late 1990s. The new types of screening systems are one challenge. Another is that the WRTP model relied on not only its connections but also the internal training capacity and workforce organization that helped secure retention and skill development for workers connected to regional manufacturing jobs. With the context changed, the model is challenged and evolving.

2012: Despite Challenges, a Good Year in Manufacturing Programs

As Milwaukee's manufacturers began hiring in 2012, the WRTP began connecting workers to the new opportunities. Its work developed stronger connections between community and area manufacturers in spite of the challenges in the environment. To meet the demands, and with support from the city's Manufacturing Partnership initiative, headed by Mayor Tom Barrett, WRTP/BIG STEP implemented two strategies to meet industry demand and connect individuals to employment. The first was direct placement of unemployed qualified individuals at area manufacturing firms. The second was pre-employment occupational skills training tied to career pathways and connected to employment upon completion.

For direct placement, WRTP/BIG STEP developed strategies to help employers improve and enhance their ability to identify, hire, and retain a qualified and productive workforce. Direct-hire services include recruitment, applicant pre-screening, assessment, and job matching. Several employers—including SPX Transformer Solutions, Harley-Davidson, HB Performance Systems, Oilgear, and HellermannTyton—utilized direct-hire assistance to meet multiple openings.

WRTP/BIG STEP also developed and ran customized skills-training classes in partnership with area manufacturers in the course of the project-funding period and conducted outreach and recruitment to identify and place individuals into employment with more than twenty manufacturers throughout the region. In 2012 WRTP/BIG STEP designed and operated six entry-level manufacturing skills (ELMS) training programs in conjunction with manufacturing partners committed to training and developing their entry-level workforce. The ELMS training program is a flexible and customized response to the occupation- and production-specific needs of the individual manufacturers and provides a direct link between graduates and employment. Notably, the project was built on the experience of the partnership between Milwaukee Gear, WRTP/BIG STEP, and the Milwaukee Area Workforce Investment Board and directly on the foundation of the ELMS programs developed in the late 1990s in response to manufacturing's previous hiring boom. ELMS training programs were developed and operated with GE Energy, HB Performance Systems, Trace-A-Matic, and Herker Industries in conjunction with labor partnerships. All participants were trained in the ELMS curriculum with a CNC-machining focus. ELMS is standard industry-designed essential-skills training that integrates a combination of occupation-based, hands-on training—as needed to ensure that new workers have the basic safety skills and knowledge needed to gain employment with a particular employer—with exposure and connection to career pathways and advancement opportunities in the industry.

In these two streams of work in manufacturing, WRTP/BIG STEP worked with 109 employers throughout the region and facilitated 284 employment placements at an average starting wage of $17.80 per hour. Of those placed, 63 percent were racial minorities. Women accounted for 7 percent of placements in nontraditional occupations.

Beneath the Evolving Projects, Core Principles Define Focus and Direct Evolution

The nature of intermediary work does require extraordinary flexibility and capacity to find opportunity and to shift as industry needs change. The unique work of the WRTP also is guided by a fundamental commitment to develop projects that respond to industry needs by working with both labor and management leadership.

It is worth examining this principle and its importance to the unique work of the WRTP.

Industry Needs Defined by Labor and Management

As indicated by the description above, the WRTP has always begun projects with steering teams of labor and management in key industries in the Milwaukee region. This puts industry at the very front of the project. Industry—not the public workforce system and not a primary concern with specific populations of need—drives the project. This is an advantage in many ways: Programs are responding to real needs, and firms are "bought in" from the start. But it can be a disadvantage as well. For one thing, this model does not necessarily square with any funding stream. Further, a project driven by employer demand still is heavily dependent on the responsiveness and interest of public systems. Changes in public workforce system leadership, indifferent trainers, and overtaxed caseworkers can stifle any WRTP project, and the organization rarely has direct leverage over these partners. Even so, the WRTP always has been committed to working on the industry needs first and lining up the resources in response, which is essential to the project's success.

Beyond this industry drive, however, it is critical also to note the central role of labor unions in the project. From the outset, unions have been essential in determining the shape and activities of the partnership. First and foremost, labor leadership secures and protects the interests of workers in all these projects. But further, the involvement of labor is often essential to and overlooked in the development and implementation of projects as well. Sustained worker support of and input on training systems or the selection of new workers can make dramatic differences in terms of the actual shop-floor functioning of projects. Employers trying to change production and service-delivery systems have quickly learned that knowledge from the floor is critical to the process, helping identify what should be improved, whether the new technologies and machines are working, safety issues, and what training should actually look like. Similarly, the participation of older workers in bringing new workers into the fold—through mentoring and on-the-job training—has turned out to be one of the hallmarks of the WRTP.

The benefits of inclusion and leadership of labor in the WRTP should be clearly spelled out. First, by including labor unions in the design and organization of the industry partnership, the project naturally puts its arms around some of the region's best opportunities. Union status is one way to secure a connection to the better-paid opportunities in manufacturing. That fact alone should make public systems interested in connecting more systematically with labor and management when developing projects. Too often public systems become demand-driven by responding to the squeakiest wheel—the region's worst employers with highest turnover and associated high levels of hiring—rather than building systems that cultivate relationships with and solve problems of their better employers. The WRTP, by working with to union firms, secures access to better jobs that are desperately needed.

Further, with union representation, projects can be developed with workers' voices at the table. This can, in many ways, determine the success of a project. Too often human resource departments are the key contact for public systems within firms. Their view is generally focused more on hiring criteria than actually doing work. Ask a supervisor and a co-worker, and a job previously described as "unskilled" is quickly understood to require very specific skills and capacities. This is perhaps best understood through a story. In one distribution center managers noticed that boxes were consistently being routed incorrectly. They assumed a basic literacy problem and developed, over months, a significant and critical investment in workers' basic literacy skills. But the problem persisted; boxes were still regularly sent to the wrong bay. Finally the firm consulted with the workers, who, when asked, pointed out that the routing slips were badly designed and very hard to read. The firm redesigned the slips, and the problem was solved. As in this story, the actual experience of workers is overlooked, often to the detriment of the firm. Workers in and supervisors of entry-level jobs have a much more detailed understanding of required skills than do human resource managers. But all too often it is the hiring unit that is working with trainers to develop curriculum. With labor and workers at the core the project, the WRTP has been able to build better programming.

Additionally, union representation at the worksite generally means that the internal system of advancement is established and understood by workers and the firm. In projects without union reach, the internal working of the firm is distant and generally opaque from the perspective of project design. So again, the union helps make the worksite and all workers in it the universe of concern, rather than simply the folks who are connected through a specific stream of funding and program design. And with unions at the table, all jobs within a firm are the subject of interest, not just entry-level positions. By leveraging training initiatives or contract changes or joint labor-management strategies for work organization, the project is supporting all workers.

Finally, union reach also secures information on industry trends that is much more difficult to secure in a non-represented environment. Business agents and other staff at labor unions often know exactly what is going on in multiple shops in a region. With a handful of interviews, the WRTP can gather information about dozens of manufacturing firms employing thousands of workers in the region. This information helps develop and direct programming and makes industry trends clear. This is another way in which the insight and reach of labor has been leveraged to support and promote the project.

Conclusion

Since its inception twenty years ago, the WRTP/BIG STEP has been an innovator. Its mission has been defined by commitment to employers, workers, and the community. It has achieved significant success, especially in good economic times, and, equally impressive, it has survived in an ever-changing and often challenging economic and funding landscape.

A few things from the first two decades seem clear. First, the position of the WRTP/BIG STEP is unique, because the labor and management leadership of the initiative is entirely outside the traditional workforce funding, education, and training systems in the city. This is and always has been both an asset and a challenge. The organization's success in both program development and policy reform are directly the result of the labor and management leadership of its work. As detailed above, being part of the industry, and driven by industry needs and concerns, is essential to every step in its process, from identifying opportunity to designing programs and connecting current and future workers with the skills they need. And the capacity to advocate for stronger policy for industries also is directly attributable to the labor and management leaders, who provide a broad reach in the political spectrum. Being part of the industry is what has made the WRTP so strong over the last two decades.

Being so closely tied to industry also has downsides. The primacy of labor-management leadership necessarily distances the organization from public and private systems of education and training and funding for disadvantaged workers. That distance can create room for misunderstanding. This is not an impossible problem to overcome, but it is a consistent requirement of the WRTP/BIG STEP. The organization is constantly working to build relationships and understanding with the leaders of the public systems. When those leaders change, the relationship needs to be re-established. And this is true from the leadership and policy level down to the frontline-staff level. The WRTP/BIG STEP is not always easy to understand or connect with when your focus is directed to securing the best outcomes for disadvantaged workers. So there is a significant and ongoing need for relationship building, explanation, and connection. And at times the relationship comes under stress or even ends for reasons beyond the WRTP/BIG STEP's control. When funder priorities exclude manufacturing, for example, or as the stress of reduced resources shifts partners to focus on internal issues, the WRTP/BIG STEP, and its significant resources, are removed from discussions. Clearly, advocacy and the evidence of good impact provide a route for moving the WRTP back into the conversation, the WRTP/BIG STEP do not control the conversation and must only respond to it.

Another observation is that this work of intermediation—translating need and opportunity from industry to the resources to meet it—is essential and ongoing. It is very difficult to fund. The WRTP/BIG STEP excels because of its strong industry connections, and it is in touch with workers and managers in both good and bad economic times. It is also focused on industry and its needs. However, workforce funding is tied, generally, to projects—meaning that the intermediation is fundable only when firms are hiring. The WRTP/BIG STEP has stepped outside workforce-development funding streams to secure the ongoing stability and staffing it needs to be an industry intermediary, not just a developer of entry-level projects when firms are hiring. The tension is there. WRTP/BIG STEP wants strong demand-side connections from its public workforce funding, but it does not have the means of funding ongoing connections to specific industries. The field of intermediation clearly needs a better private and public answer to the question of ongoing convening and fieldwork in the future.

Finally, going forward, workers' voices need to be more central to the development and theory of workforce intermediaries. Already at the WRTP/BIG STEP and in other labor-led training initiatives, workers have a more significant role in the training. Experience suggests that this worker role makes essential contributions to the training. These projects, found in sectors from construction to health care and supported by diverse sources from privately negotiated training funds to public training dollars, are not even always considered part of the field and practice of workforce intermediaries. Their increasing inclusion in the discussion can enhance practice inside union settings and across the field.

Equally important, the field needs to grapple with a means of engaging workers in non-union settings. This is a challenge in numerous ways, but engagement of workers and inclusion of their voices makes critical, meaningful contributions to WRTP/BIG STEP's work. Over the next twenty years it is hoped that the field grapples with creative approaches to expand workers' voice and contributions to the project.

Notes

1. Sheila Maguire, Joshua Freely, Carol Clymer, Maureen Conway, and Deena Schwartz, *Tuning In to Local Labor Markets: Findings from the Sectoral Employment Impact Study*, Public/Private Ventures, July 2010, pp. ii–v, http://www.aspenwsi.org/wordpress/wp-content/uploads/TuningIntoLocalLaborMarkets.pdf.

7

A Brief History of SkillWorks: Partners for a Productive Workforce

Loh-Sze Leung

This case study provides a history of SkillWorks: Partners for a Productive Workforce, one of the longest-standing workforce funder collaboratives in the country. Officially launched in 2003 by the Boston Foundation, the City of Boston, and a number of other public and philanthropic partners, the initiative had nineteen funders as of mid-2013 and had raised nearly $24 million in support of workforce-training partnerships, capacity building, and policy-advocacy efforts in the Commonwealth of Massachusetts. Along the way, SkillWorks evolved to meet changing economic circumstances, employer needs, and funder interests and is now recognized as a go-to resource for workforce development and a noteworthy example of public-private partnership.

Introduction

In 2000 a group of Boston-area foundations and government officials were invited by the Boston Foundation to a workforce-development meeting to discuss two important questions: What could the philanthropic community do to support dwindling federal investment in workforce training, and how could the workforce system be more responsive to employers, meeting their needs for a skilled workforce, while also helping workers attain economic self-sufficiency?

This initial gathering led to a series of convenings, funded in part by a planning grant from the Annie E. Casey Foundation, to help funders better understand and analyze the publicly funded workforce system and how they might work together to improve it. The funders discovered that their combined investments in workforce training were greater than the Workforce Investment Act (WIA) funds available to train Boston residents, and they were "energized by the conviction that their joint investment could achieve real change in the system."[1] This knowledge, in addition to a rich history in Boston of funder collaboration around issues ranging from homelessness to out-of-school time, kept funders working together over the next two years to complete a lengthy research and design process for a workforce development systems change initiative.[2]

SkillWorks: Partners for a Productive Workforce[3] was launched in 2003 as an ambitious $14 million, five-year initiative aimed at improving the way workforce training services were delivered to businesses and job seekers.

SkillWorks launched Phase II of the initiative in 2009 with a goal of continuing the initiative by raising and investing $10 million over the five years, from 2009 through 2013. After a strategic-planning process was completed in the winter of 2013, SkillWorks funders approved a plan to launch a third five-year phase of the initiative, from 2014 through 2018.

SkillWorks's Goals, Principles, and Theory of Change, 2003–2013

SkillWorks's funders established two primary goals from the beginning:

- Help low- and moderate-income individuals attain family-supporting jobs, and

- Help businesses find and retain skilled employees.

They also established six core principles to guide the design of the initiative:

- Advancement to economic self-sufficiency: Workforce development should help low-skilled individuals—both employed and unemployed—get the skills they need to earn enough to support their families.

- Dual customers: The workforce-development system should serve both individuals and employers.

- A continuum of career-ladder services: Individuals should be able to access education and training at the right point, given their skill level and career stage.

- Workforce partnerships: Workforce systems are complex. Diverse entities must be organized and coordinated to meet customers' needs.

- Sectoral organization of services: Certain sectors and occupations have labor or skill needs that provide the best opportunities for low-skilled workers to move up. These sectors and occupations also require common services from the workforce system.

- Systems change: Funding training programs is not enough. For Skill-Works, success would mean seeing the sector-partnership model and the five principles above, as well as lessons learned from the initiative's work, integrated into the workforce-development system to benefit more employers and job seekers and leverage more public and private funding.

To achieve the large-scale, sustainable improvements to the workforce-development system the funders envisioned, SkillWorks invested in three interrelated strategies, each of which was to include systems-change elements and approaches. (See *Table 1* for an overview of SkillWorks's investments.)

- Workforce partnerships: These would aggregate employer needs, organize resources, and provide or broker career-advancement services for low-income adults and disengaged youth. The partnerships' activities would also influence and change employer policies and practices and improve the access of entry-level workers to advancement opportunities. Finally, the partnerships would identify practices that affect the success of the workforce-development system in meeting needs of low- and moderate-income individuals as well as employers. These practices would inform SkillWorks's advocacy as well as build the expertise and capacity of the workforce-development field. In Phases I and II, SkillWorks supported a total of fifteen sector partnerships spread across seven industry sectors.[4] (See *Table 3* for a list of sector partnerships.)

- Capacity building: These efforts would build the infrastructure for, strengthen alliances within, and enhance the knowledge of workforce partnerships and other workforce-development providers. Capacity-building activities were aimed at helping staff better manage partnerships, implement promising practices, develop new programs and services, and advocate for policies and practices to improve services to employers and low-skilled workers. Capacity-building services would also build the expertise of the workforce system and encourage the adoption of improved practices.

- Public-policy advocacy: These efforts would raise the visibility of the workforce-development system in Massachusetts and its critical role in helping workers and employers; sustain and increase state funding for the workforce development system; and identify opportunities to improve services for workers and employers. Advocacy for the adoption and funding of successful workforce strategies and programs would be informed by SkillWorks's capacity-building and workforce-partnership investments.

Table 1: SkillWorks's Investments in Phases I and II

	Phase I 5-Year Total (2003–2008)	Phase II 5-Year Total (2009–2013)
Workforce Partnerships	$7.1 million (50%)	$5.4 million (55%)
Public-Policy Advocacy	$1.5 million (11%)	$1.3 million (13%)
Capacity Building	$2.6 million (18%)	$465,000 (5%)
Data and Evaluation	$650,000 (5%)	$770,000 (8%)
Initiative Management	$2.2 million (16%)	$1.9 million (19%)
Total	**$14.1 million**	**$9.8 million**

The SkillWorks Funders Group: A Mutual Investment Model

Public and private funders agreed to pool their investments in a "mutual fund" held at the Boston Foundation, which also served as fiscal agent for the initiative, chaired the SkillWorks Funders Group, and housed the initiative's staff. This fund provided large, blended public-private grants to service providers. The merging of funds was also meant to reduce the burden on grantees for fiscal and participant tracking.

With some exceptions, each SkillWorks investor made a financial pledge to the overall initiative to be allocated as needed to grants, research, management, evaluation, and other activities.[5] All investors were invited to join the SkillWorks Funders Group, which approved spending plans and grant awards and therefore helped maintain accountability. Each funder had one vote in the Funders Group, regardless of the size of its investment.

A number of standing committees were formed to oversee SkillWorks investments. An executive committee comprising the chairs of each subcommittee, the co-chairs of the SkillWorks Funders Group, and SkillWorks's executive director ensured ongoing leadership for and oversight of the initiative. (See *Table 2* for a list of SkillWorks funders in Phases I and II.)

Table 2: SkillWorks Funders in Phases I and II

Phase I (2003–2008)	Phase II (2009–2013)
The Annie E. Casey Foundation Bank of America Charitable Gift Fund and Frank W. and Carl S. Adams Memorial Fund, Bank of America, N.A., Trustee Boston 2004 The Boston Foundation City of Boston's Neighborhood Jobs Trust The Clowes Fund, Inc. Commonwealth of Massachusetts The Hyams Foundation The Jessie B. Cox Charitable Trust The John Merck Fund The Paul and Phyllis Fireman Foundation The Robert Wood Johnson Foundation The Rockefeller Foundation State Street Foundation United Way of Massachusetts Bay and Merrimack Valley The William Randolph Hearst Foundation	A. C. Ratshesky Foundation The Barr Foundation BNY Mellon The Boston Foundation Chorus Foundation City of Boston's Neighborhood Jobs Trust The Clowes Fund, Inc. Commonwealth of Massachusetts The Garfield Foundation The Hyams Foundation Mabel Louise Riley Foundation Microsoft Corporation National Fund for Workforce Solutions Nellie Mae Education Foundation Perpetual Trust for Charitable Giving, Bank of America, N.A., Trustee State Street Foundation Surdna Foundation United Way of Massachusetts Bay and Merrimack Valley U.S. Department of Labor Green Jobs Innovation Fund, through Jobs for the Future

SkillWorks's Accomplishments

SkillWorks's commitment to workforce development and its investments of $24 million over ten years have resulted in an extensive record of accomplishments and lessons learned.[6] Some of the highlights follow.

Workforce Partnerships

In Phase I, nearly 3,000 job seekers and incumbent workers received skills training, with the goal of gaining employment or advancing along career pathways toward self-sufficiency. During Phase II, the initiative served more than 1,700 participants as of June 2013, with two added emphases: on strengthening pathways to post-secondary education, training, and credential attainment for low-skilled

adults, and on better connecting the workforce-development system to Massachusetts's community colleges and other postsecondary institutions. In total, Skill-
Works's partnerships served more than 4,500 individuals and engaged more than
eighty employers in its workforce-development partnerships from 2003 through
mid-2013. More than 1,300 individuals have earned wage gains; nearly 1,000
have been placed in jobs; nearly 1,000 have attained credentials (mostly in Phase
II); and more than 500 have earned promotions.[7]

Capacity Building

SkillWorks has strengthened workforce-development providers and partnerships in the city of Boston and beyond. As a result of SkillWorks's technical-assistance investments, one grantee started and then sustained a highly successful
bridge-to-college program; a number of grantees added more robust retention and
follow-up services; and relationships among grantees were strengthened, allowing for more peer learning and resource sharing. SkillWorks sought to influence
a broader network of workforce providers through workshops and resources on
topics including the following: coaching for college and career; measuring business and participant impact; integrating financial capability with career coaching;
using labor-market information; working with community colleges; public-policy
advocacy; and program sustainability. SkillWorks's technical-assistance tools on
topics like succession/staff transition planning for workforce partnerships, tuition
advancement, and college navigation and coaching were also broadly disseminated
and well received.

Policy Advocacy

Phase II advocacy efforts by SkillWorks and a grantee, the Workforce Solutions Group, resulted in the inclusion in the 2012 Economic Development
and Jobs Bill of $5 million to fund the Workforce Competitiveness Trust Fund
(WCTF). The WCTF was initially established with SkillWorks's advocacy and
support in 2006, during Phase I. In 2012 advocates worked with legislative leaders
to establish the Community College Workforce Development Fund, which will
receive up to $47 million in the next few years from casino licensing fees. On the
employer front, SkillWorks partnerships have successfully worked with a number
of businesses to change their tuition-reimbursement, training-participation, and
compensation policies. In total, SkillWorks's advocacy efforts have helped leverage
an additional $60 million in public investment in workforce training in the Com-
monwealth of Massachusetts.

What SkillWorks's funders and partners have learned is as important as the
specific accomplishments. A continued focus on evaluation, learning, and dissemination has helped the initiative hone its strategies and next steps. The following

sections in this chapter provide a summary of these lessons for participant advancement, employer engagement, public-policy advocacy, and funder engagement. SkillWorks's evaluation reports describe many of these lessons in greater detail.[8]

Creating Pathways to Advancement for Participants

Phase I Approach and Learning

When SkillWorks issued its first requests for proposals for workforce partnerships in 2003, it sought to make three- to five-year investments in industry-sector and/or occupational partnerships that offered multiple points of entry to education and skills training leading to career-oriented first jobs and advancement opportunities. (See *Figure 3* for a list of SkillWorks's partnerships and industries.)

Table 3: Workforce Partnerships (Phases I and II)

	Phase I	Phase II
Health Care	• Partners in Career and Workforce Development	• Healthcare Training Institute
	• Boston Healthcare and Research Training Institute	• Emergency Medical Careers Partnership
	• Community Health Worker Initiative of Boston	
Hospitality	• Hotel Career Center	• Hotel Training Center
Financial Services		• Year Up Financial Services Partnership
Building Services	• Building Services Career Path Project	
Automotive	• Partnership for Automotive Career Education	• Partnership for Automotive Career Education*
Energy		• Chinatown Green Collar Career Pathway Project*
		• Energy Efficiency Technician Apprenticeship Program*
Construction		• Youthbuild Green Construction*
Manufacturing		• GreenSTREAM*

*Denotes partnership was part of SkillWorks's Green Jobs Initiative.

SkillWorks funders expected to see these investments lead to accelerated wage gains and promotions for significant numbers of low-skilled workers each year, in addition to placement of a significant number of participants into entry-level, career-ladder jobs.

Phase I job placement was strong, at 78 percent of training completers. Despite strong placement, however, advancement of incumbent workers was lower than expected. Only 14 percent of Phase I incumbent workers obtained promotions over the five years, while 39 percent received wage gains and just ninety were documented as having obtained credentials. (See *Table 5* for a summary of participant progress in Phases I and II.)[9] The initiative learned a number of valuable lessons about the difficulty of achieving career advancement, including the importance of credentials in many of Boston's industries, the time and cost required to obtain these credentials, and the difficulties of balancing low-wage work with education and family. These and other lessons are summarized below:

Economic conditions can impact opportunity.

Especially in the early years of Phase I, a Massachusetts economy still recovering from the technology bust of the early 2000s contributed to slower advancement for SkillWorks's target population. Funders need to account for economic context when designing and measuring career-advancement programs.

Sector characteristics affect advancement pathways.

Advancement within the health care industry often requires credential attainment, and SkillWorks's investments in postsecondary education in Phase I were not as robust or focused as they could have been. In addition, credential attainment for low-skilled adults is almost by definition a long-term proposition. Most low-income adults require basic-skills remediation and other preparation for college. When they do enroll, they often must choose part-time programs that allow them to work and care for families but that also extend the time to completion. The cost of postsecondary education is another barrier; many participants could not afford tuition, books, materials, transportation, and child care, even with tuition assistance or financial aid when it was available.

Other barriers to advancement included seniority-based systems in some industries that meant a worker might have to leave a highly preferable work schedule in order to take a promotion that would leave him or her at the bottom rung of the next job classification. In some cases, participants were reluctant to apply for promotions because added workplace duties or changes in schedule would interfere with family responsibilities.

New graduates of pre-employment programs may not be ready for immediate advancement.
SkillWorks funders assumed that there would be a direct connection between the initiative's job placement (pre-employment) training programs and its advancement (incumbent worker) programs and that participants hired through SkillWorks-funded programs would go right into further education and training. In practice, most participants needed time to settle into their new positions before thinking about the next step. This lengthened the time needed to realize the initiative's advancement goals; it also changed the target population in some partnerships, as they realized they would have to recruit and work with a different set of "seasoned" incumbent workers more ready to advance.

Quality of teaching and coaching matters.
SkillWorks's Phase I evaluation report on incumbent-worker advancement emphasized the importance of high-quality teaching to keep participants engaged and on track to advancement and described a correlation between those who were promoted and those who had access to ongoing coaching. Unfortunately, while SkillWorks provided some resources for training in this area, the initiative had not identified the area as a primary investment focus in Phase I and therefore did not build in enough technical assistance for assessment or measurement of effective coaching and instructional quality.

Phase II Approach and Learning

As SkillWorks developed Phase II, funders made a key decision to emphasize postsecondary credential attainment and to better connect basic-skills training to credentialing and postsecondary pathways. This decision was influenced by lessons learned from Phase I as well as a growing body of research showing the important role of credentials in metro Boston's high-education, high-skill labor market. From 2008 to 2010, more than 40 percent of the working-age population had a bachelor's degree or higher and in ten out of seventeen major industries more than 40 percent of the employees had a bachelor's degree or higher.[10] While recognizing the challenges of tackling such a long-term advancement pathway, SkillWorks funders were convinced that the initiative's investments should try to build these pathways for low-skilled adults to attain credentials in order to ensure that they would be able to compete in the Boston labor market.

Therefore, SkillWorks also had to get better at tracking progress toward advancement; building bridges and interim steps to credentials; strengthening connections between adult basic education, workforce training, and college; working more closely with community colleges; and strengthening the initiative's focus on coaching. SkillWorks emphasized this shift through its capacity-building and technical-assistance offerings to build knowledge and capacity within the workforce field. (See *Table 4* for a summary of changes in partnership investments between Phase I and Phase II.)

Table 4: New Components SkillWorks Added in Phase II to Strengthen Post-secondary Pathways for Adults

Issue/Concern	SkillWorks Approach
Workforce providers needed more information about best practices and innovation in creating efficient/accelerated pathways to post-secondary credentials for adults.	• Workshop and technical assistance for Phase II applicants after RFP was released in 2008; SkillWorks brought in experts and examples from around the country.
Not many strong college-workforce partnerships in the Boston area.	• Post-secondary education partner strongly recommended in Phase II Partnership RFP.
Some partnerships needed help strengthening basic-education pieces and tying into a larger post-secondary pipeline.	• Required some partnerships to strengthen these pieces by adding partners and services as condition of funding.
Coaching was important, but coaches were often isolated and overtaxed. Coaches needed additional resources, especially in terms of building relationships with and knowledge about community colleges and post-secondary pathways.	• As part of capacity building, funded a peer-learning network of coaches that included all SkillWorks grantees as well as some non-grantees. Became a forum of sharing best practices, troubleshooting, and developing resources. • Funded a college-navigator position at the area's largest and most popular community college to help SkillWorks participants and programs better navigate the college system and access resources.
SkillWorks had little information about and no system to track progress or interim benchmarks toward advancement at the individual level, including post-secondary credential attainment and promotions. Phase I partnerships reported aggregate data only.	• Building from an existing state data platform for sector strategies, SkillWorks began collecting participant-level data on participation, progress, and advancement, including participant progress toward an ultimate career or educational goal.

| Participant advancement and economic self-sufficiency are impacted by many other factors outside of educational pathways or access to training. | • SkillWorks allowed partnerships to use funds to address emergency child care, transportation, utility, or even housing needs.

• SkillWorks's college navigator was given a pool of funds to address emergent needs and help keep participants progressing toward credential completion.

• SkillWorks added a financial-capability pilot in 2012 to better train coaches and integrate asset building with workforce-development services. |

Phase II investments in post-secondary education pathways have paid off for SkillWorks and its participants. As of June 2013, with six months left in Phase II, enrollment in post-secondary programs had increased more than fourfold and credential attainment nearly tenfold in raw numbers over Phase I, despite a smaller number of participants overall. In addition, the promotion rate for incumbent workers increased by 75 percent (from 14 percent to 25 percent), and the wage-gain rate increased by more than half (from 39 percent to 61 percent).

Table 5: Participant Progress (Phases I and II)

	Phase I	*Phase II* *(as of 6/30/13)*	*Total* *Phases I & II*
Participants Enrolled	965 pre-employment 2,134 incumbents	866 pre-employment 757 incumbents 94 college navigation only	1,831 pre-employment 2,891 incumbents 94 college navigation only
Participants Completing Training	840 pre-employment N/A incumbents	606 pre-employment 452 incumbents	1,446 pre-employment N/A
Participants Attaining Credential	90 4% credential-attainment rate	877 54% credential-attainment rate	967 total
Participants Placed in Job	527 78% training completers	451 74% training completers	978 total
Participants Attaining Wage Gain	841 39% of incumbents	485 incumbent/57% 87 pre-emploment/10%	1,413 total
Participants Attaining Promotion	269 14% of incumbents	192 incumbents/25% 43 pre-employment/10%	504 total
Participants Enrolling in Post-secondary Education	81 3% of all participants	394 22% of all participants	475 total

SkillWorks's investment in college navigation, which started in mid-2011 with support from the Social Innovation Fund and the National Fund for Workforce Solutions, was particularly gratifying. Investing in college navigation increased the initiative's "on the ground" knowledge of and direct access to college information and resources, while helping the initiative and each of its partners become more knowledgeable about and more connected to the college. The feedback from students in the first year of implementation was overwhelmingly positive, emphasizing the navigator's "depth of knowledge and ability to answer questions ... and [her] relationships with [college] employees and her hands-on work advocating for them." The college navigator has been called a "godsend" for her ability to almost miraculously get things done and to help working adults feel comfortable on campus.[11]

Of the students the navigator has worked with for more than one year, the year-to-year retention rate in college is approximately 80 percent. This compares with a fall-to-fall retention rate of first-time, part-time degree-seeking students in Massachusetts community colleges of 42.9 percent.[12]

SkillWorks's task in 2013 and beyond is to institutionalize the knowledge and pathways that have been built so non-SkillWorks participants as well as future cohorts of adult learners and workforce programs can benefit from what the initiative has learned.[13] Already the initiative has created a Coaching for College and Careers Toolkit; held numerous trainings around the state; and convened an ongoing peer-learning group for coaches both within and outside of the SkillWorks network to share practices, strategies, and lessons learned. SkillWorks is also working with college navigators who were hired by the community colleges with U.S. Department of Labor funding in 2012–13 and helping to inform their work with adult students.

Lessons Learned and Questions for Further Exploration

Advancement pathways vary.

Pathways vary by sector, by employers within a sector, and by individual. They vary in terms of length of time, what's required (credentials, experience), how far apart the steps are, and whether the paths are more like a ladder or a lattice. More and more workers seeking advancement first move to another firm or make lateral moves to pick up new skills. In some cases, as SkillWorks has experienced, incumbent-training participants' goal is to gain skills or credentials that are now required if they want to keep their current job, and advancement in this case may mean getting the credential and maintaining employment, not moving to a new job. In addition, some participants may be held back from advancing because of the way their work is affected by seniority or other work rules.

Funders need to be open to a more flexible definition of advancement.
The variation in advancement pathways has implications for how programs and funders define and measure advancement and what expectations should be around the length of that pathway. It is critical to examine the assumptions underlying any career-advancement program, to gain an understanding not just of the different steps and pathways that are possible but of how actual employees advance, how long it typically takes, and any policies or programs to support them in getting to the next step.

Funders should think through, together with grantees, a system to better capture advancement in different forms, including but not limited to promotions, wage gains, lateral moves, increases in responsibility and skill, retention, and improvements in job quality or work conditions.

Coaching is critical.
Effective coaches work with employers to help workers better understand career pathways within a chosen industry and their options for advancement. They also understand how to help participants navigate the education and training systems successfully. SkillWorks's research showed that individuals who accessed ongoing coaching in Phase I attained higher wage and promotion outcomes.[14] An avenue of increasing interest is documenting the practices and qualities of the most effective coaches, as well as best practices in how organizations and partnerships support and retain them. Two questions merit further work and research. First, coaching is expensive because it is highly labor intensive, often delivered one-on-one. Are there effective ways to scale it up while maintaining quality and outcomes? A second, related question is how the workforce-development sector, including community colleges, can find the resources to support coaching over the long term and better document its value and return on investment?

Expect, and prepare for, the unexpected.
Partnerships should do as much as they can to ensure participant readiness for training, placement, and advancement through detailed assessment, orientations, screening processes, and job readiness. Inevitably family crises, unexpected health issues, child care emergencies, housing challenges, and other issues will arise. Family needs can easily derail a worker's career-advancement plan.[15] To support success, funders can allow for and indeed plan for supportive-services dollars in a partnership budget, including an emergency-assistance fund flexible enough to deal with needs ranging from transit passes to rent or utility payments. Partnerships and employers can also help participants build assets and can develop partnerships with a variety of local service providers that may be able to help meet—and head off—emergent needs before they derail progress.

Use funding to leverage change.

Company policies and the managers who implement them make a huge difference in terms of career advancement. Building or expanding a workforce partnership is an opportunity to seek change and build champions within particular companies or within a sector. Release time, tuition advancement, scheduling flexibility, and on-site classes make it possible for participants to make greater education and career gains. Grant dollars for training can often provide leverage to make these changes in employer policy possible.

As part of its SkillWorks grant, Partners HealthCare developed an internal recognition program for "Workforce Champions," managers who hired from the Partners pre-employment program or provided opportunities for their direct reports to participate in education and training. This recognition created a supportive atmosphere and opened many doors for entry-level workers at Partners to advance. An entrepreneurial manager within Boston Children's Hospital, another SkillWorks employer, leveraged grant funding to help institute a limited tuition-advancement program, on-site pre-college and college classes, and wage gains for certain successful training participants. Funders should support and seek out these and other types of employer investments in making decisions about funding workforce partnerships.

Meeting Employer Needs for Skilled Workers

SkillWorks originally funded workforce partnerships to convene training providers, employers, and other relevant partners. The partnerships would engage employers and work to meet their needs for skilled workers through training incumbent workers and new hires to fill critical positions. As individual employees made progress, partnerships would move toward systems-change activities, making a case for sustaining this work beyond the SkillWorks grant, as well as working with employers to identify opportunities to change policies and practice to benefit larger numbers of their entry-level workforce.

The practical implementation of this model varied from the original concept. Where SkillWorks worked with large businesses with hundreds or even thousands of employees, workforce partnerships touched a very small percentage of their total workforce, which might span several states or countries. These employers looked to SkillWorks-funded partnerships to help meet a specific set of workforce needs, particularly at the entry level, as one strategy among many to address their talent and training needs.

In working with small employers, SkillWorks partnerships faced other challenges. Each employer might have only one or two openings per year at a particular level or skill set, as well as limited advancement opportunities, restricting the partnerships' impact and ability to work intensively with each employer. Despite these limitations, SkillWorks found that training partnerships and funders played important roles in convening and working with employers, in meeting some critical hiring and advancement needs, and in catalyzing systems changes.

SkillWorks's requirement that partnerships convene two or more employers was important for a few different reasons. This approach ensured that outcomes were not dependent solely on the success of one company. This also allowed partnerships to have a broader perspective about the industry sector's needs and to design programs that might meet the needs of a cross-section of the industry. It also provided opportunities for employers to learn from one another. A few examples from the Phase II SkillWorks partnerships:

- Hospitals that met quarterly as part of the Healthcare Training Institute, collaborating on and adopting one another's training courses and policies, including a tuition-advancement policy piloted by one hospital that spurred others to explore similar models.

- Financial-services employers working together to develop mentorship programs for entry-level employees.

- Hotels agreeing to jointly develop programs and strategies to engage more African Americans in Boston's hospitality industry.

SkillWorks investments provided an impetus for employers to use grant funds to pilot innovative, untested ideas and then leverage institutional funds to sustain successful activities after the end of grant funding. For example, Partners Health-Care and Brigham and Women's Hospital both decided to sustain the most successful programs piloted with SkillWorks funding after the grant period ended. In SkillWorks's Building Services Career Path Project, Service Employees International Union (SEIU) Local 615 used SkillWorks funding to establish union member and employer buy-in to the value of training. The partnership then worked to sustain training investments through the renegotiation of the master contract in 2007 to include a new employer-funded Education and Training Trust that would provide training opportunities for employees and meet employer needs for a more skilled workforce.

In SkillWorks's green-jobs work, the funder collaborative convened employers directly rather than relying on a workforce partnership. This was due to the newness of the industry sector and the lack of an obvious, strong intermediary. In this role, SkillWorks helped employers communicate their workforce and training needs and manage the multiple requests they were receiving from community-based organizations seeking partners for grants. SkillWorks also proved to be the neutral convener needed for a sensitive conversation among training providers and employers about employment of ex-offenders and people with records in Massachusetts's Criminal Offender Record Information (CORI) system.

Lessons Learned

Employer engagement varies.

Employers have many reasons for participating in workforce partnerships, and their engagement in the partnership will vary by sector, experience with workforce development, and size of the company. It's important for the partnership to identify the employers' motivations and expectations early on and to utilize different engagement models to keep partners at the table.

Engaging at all levels of an organization is key to success.

With some exceptions, employers generally need to have a certain level of internal infrastructure in place (such as human-resource personnel) to participate in the leadership of a workforce partnership. Regardless of the size or structure of the employer, however, SkillWorks's experience showed it was important to engage and obtain buy-in from all levels of the organization, including the chief executive, department heads, and frontline supervisors, who often had different interests and perspectives on career advancement and how it would affect the organization's day-to-day operations. The chief executive and/or department heads were critical to provide leadership and vision, but the frontline supervisors' support or lack thereof could make or break the implementation of training and advancement strategies.

Peer-to-peer learning is powerful.

Just as peer-to-peer learning networks were critical for workforce-partnership staff, the employer advisory groups convened by SkillWorks partnerships provided a safe space for employers to learn from one another, share ideas, and identify opportunities to take best practices back to their own organizations. Partnerships that leveraged these opportunities made the most progress in helping employers see the value in staying at the table to meet their workforce needs.

Use funding to leverage change.

Workforce partnerships and funders can influence change within employer institutions and sectors. The flexible funding, as well as the leadership and visibility provided by the participation of the pubic and philanthropic funders in a workforce-funding collaborative, provides a golden opportunity for motivated employers to pilot or expand career-advancement initiatives. Often an effort piloted with support from the funder collaborative can be sustained. The funder collaborative can also play an active role in helping employers and workforce partnerships plan for sustainability by building this expectation into requests for proposals and by providing technical assistance and resources for sustainability planning.

The funder collaborative can convene employers in a different way than workforce partnerships can. Many employers valued SkillWorks as a neutral convener and an honest broker that could bring parties together without taking sides or promoting a particular organization or set of services. Employers found Skill-Works to be an important source of information, best practices, and technical assistance, in addition to catalytic funding. These functions of the funder collaborative were essential for helping employers identify and act on systems-change opportunities, enhance advancement opportunities for lower-skill workers, build partnerships with community-based organizations and community colleges, and engage in policy advocacy on behalf of workforce training.

Creating Systems Change through Policy Advocacy

Policy advocacy has been a key component of SkillWorks's theory of change from the beginning. Funders recognized that scale and sustainability of impact could be realized only by linking the initiative's efforts to and influencing the publicly funded workforce system in Massachusetts. The idea was to use the learning from the on-the-ground work of SkillWorks's partnerships to inform the initiative's advocacy and systems-change agenda. In reality, advocacy and partnership investments started concurrently, so at the beginning it was too early to glean lessons learned for advocacy. And since SkillWorks chose to take a bottom-up approach to setting the advocacy agenda, much of SkillWorks's advocacy was not systems change focused at all but, rather, aimed at increasing state funding for the existing workforce system, with a few notable exceptions. Advocating for more resources to support adult basic education and workforce training had many allies and few downsides.

SkillWorks, its funders, and its policy-advocacy grantee, the Workforce Solutions Group (WSG), were successful early, helping to win a $6 million appropriation in the 2004 state economic-stimulus bill in support of the BEST III state sectoral-workforce initiative.

In 2006 SkillWorks and WSG led another push for the inclusion of workforce funding in an economic-stimulus bill. The coalition's efforts reflected a growing capacity for advocacy. SkillWorks even sponsored a community forum on workforce-training issues, held just as the economic-stimulus bill was being considered and attended by all of the state's gubernatorial candidates. The bill passed by the legislature included an additional $24.5 million in state funds for workforce development and language that raised the state's cap on accessing federal workforce-training funds under the Food Stamp Employment and Training Program (now called SNAP-ET). The 2006 bill[16] included:

- $11 million to establish a Workforce Competitiveness Trust Fund (WCTF) to provide job training in high-demand occupations

- $3 million in additional funds for Adult Basic Education and English for Speakers of Other Languages (ESOL)

- $2 million in additional funds for One-Stop Career Centers

- $3 million in additional funds for School-to-Career Connecting Activities, to link in-school youth to employment opportunities

- $1.5 million for the Educational Rewards Grant Program, which established the only source of state grant aid to low-income students attending school less than half-time and pursuing credentials or degrees in high demand or critical fields

- $4 million for the STEM Pipeline Program, in support of science, technology, engineering, and math education

- The creation of a Workforce Accountability Taskforce, which was mandated to produce a report to the legislature each year on the performance outcomes of the workforce-development system

- The extension of the Workforce Training Fund for incumbent-worker training to 2010

While primarily about funding, the bill nevertheless contained a number of systems-change pieces. The WCTF was the first permanent state budget line item in support of sectoral training programs.[17] The Educational Rewards Grant Program built on the work of an earlier state initiative,[18] which recommended improving the connection of working adults to post-secondary education and skills valued by employers. The Workforce Accountability Taskforce sought to make the workforce system and its outcomes more transparent.

Over the next few years, as the economy and state budget suffered, WSG's primary legislative agenda was to stave off budget cuts to workforce programs. At the same time (2009–2011), SkillWorks also added a job-creation component to its legislative agenda, advocating for job creation through public works, infrastructure improvements, and youth employment programs. SkillWorks and WSG participated in the state Jobs Creation Commission and on the advisory committee for the state's Economic Development Policy and Strategic Plan. All along the way, however, the funders cautioned against getting too deeply involved in job creation, mostly because this was not SkillWorks's area of expertise and others were much more credible advocates in this area.

As the state's economy started to recover in 2010, SkillWorks saw an opportunity to get back to systems-change work around workforce development and to raise the visibility of the workforce system as a solution to helping unemployed and underemployed people access jobs in a changing economy. In partnership with the National Skills Coalition, WSG, and many partners from the workforce, business, labor, community, and education sectors, SkillWorks launched the Skills2Compete-Massachusetts campaign in July 2010 with the release of the Massachusetts's Forgotten Middle-Skill Jobs report. The message, focused on a skills gap during a time of high unemployment, resonated with policy makers, business leaders, funders, and the general public, and the report received a lot of attention, including from legislators. In September of 2010, building from the successful campaign launch and report release, SkillWorks sponsored its second gubernatorial-candidates forum on jobs and the economy. The forum and report raised the profile of middle-skill jobs and injected the issue of how to better prepare people for these jobs into the Massachusetts governor's race.

After the election, SkillWorks and WSG capitalized on relationships developed with legislators and administration officials over years of consistent advocacy to file the Middle-Skills Solutions Act (S921/H2713) in the 2011–12 legislative session.[19] The act sought to recapitalize the WCTF, essentially unfunded since 2009, and create Regional Skills Academies that would align the adult-education, workforce-training, and community-college systems to better meet worker and employer needs. SkillWorks was finally at a point where the legislation could be built on the experiences of SkillWorks's training partnerships, participants, and employers and recommended improvements that would make pathways to credential attainment more clear and accessible, especially for working adults. Skill-Works and WSG organized a large coalition in support of the legislation, including many business partners and training providers from across the state.

Though the legislation was championed by key state senators and representatives, was co-sponsored by more than fifty members of the state legislature, and was reported favorably out of committee, it did not pass as a stand-alone bill. Undeterred, SkillWorks, WSG, and their legislative champions continued to seek alternative ways to incorporate the language into other vehicles, such as the state budget or a jobs bill that many parties hoped would be considered before the end of the session in July 2012. With legislative champions taking the lead, language was finally incorporated into the Economic Development and Jobs Bill (H4352), providing $5 million for the WCTF to build pathways to middle-skill jobs. The bill was passed by the legislature and signed into law by Governor Deval Patrick in August 2012. Additionally, up to $12 million per year from gaming license fees was designated for a sector-oriented Community College Workforce Development Fund, incorporating WCTF elements suggested by SkillWorks and WSG.

Lessons Learned

SkillWorks's work on the Middle-Skill Solutions Act and its leadership of the Skills2Compete-Massachusetts campaign represented a culmination of many years of relationship building, advocacy, and communications work to raise the visibility of workforce development, especially with legislators and policy makers. The campaign engaged SkillWorks's partners in advocacy in ways that demonstrated the power of the collaborative. The campaign also reflected an evolving dynamic between SkillWorks and WSG in implementing SkillWorks's advocacy agenda, as the collaborative itself took on a more proactive, visible role at the State House.

The long history and evolution of SkillWorks's advocacy component led to some lessons learned.

Cultivate relationships.

Cultivate relationships with state leadership at multiple levels and within executive agencies as well as the legislature.[20] This was important in a state like Massachusetts, where the legislature is powerful, especially in the budget process. It was also critical to be in sync with executive agencies and ultimately the governor's priorities. Timely, open communication with both the administration and the legislature were critical to getting middle-skill priorities included in the final version of the 2012 jobs bill and in the FY14 budget.

Be opportunistic and flexible.

Respond quickly to address opportunities as well as crises.[21] SkillWorks was not tied to a rigid policy agenda and was able to adapt as the political environment changed. This proved critical at many points, including staying relevant during lean budget years and being able to quickly frame workforce development as an economic-development and jobs issue when the state was considering economic stimulus to spur faster recovery.

Balance efforts on both increasing resources and changing policy or systems.[22]

A focus on increasing resources builds a big tent and allows many organizations to come to the table. Getting into the specifics of policy change usually narrows the coalition. SkillWorks's years of experience and credibility with budget advocacy made it easier to transition to systems-change work with greater support.

Funders have an important and powerful voice.

SkillWorks's ability to meet with legislators and policy makers as a "co-investor" that could share lessons learned added credibility to the recommendations and asks being presented. The collaborative also makes it easier for funders to participate in the political process. In SkillWorks's case, the director was able to represent the funder voice at legislative meetings and hearings that individual funders might not have had the time or ability to participate in. The director was also able to assess when individual philanthropic leaders' voices would be most important and reserve them for those meetings.

It takes time and investment to sustain both funding and change.

SkillWorks invested $2.8 million over ten years in advocacy, funding a core coalition of partners over the ten years of Phases I and II. This support resulted in a high level of commitment and engagement in advocacy, as well as the ability to build and sustain relationships over time. Even so, wins can be fragile and fleeting, and constant partnership building, along with legislative and budget vigilance, is necessary to protect gains from disappearing over time.

Advocacy is not systems change, and systems change is not advocacy.

Advocacy is a valuable tool for driving systems change forward, but it is not a substitute for it. In the early years of SkillWorks, it was easy to refer to the public-policy advocacy as the initiative's systems-change work. In reality, SkillWorks was engaged in a lot of budget advocacy, which, while important, was not systems change. Conflating advocacy with systems change also had the unintended consequence of downplaying the systems-change opportunities and work that could happen through the workforce partnership and capacity-building components or even through the funders group itself.

The Workforce-Development Funder Collaborative: Roles and Lessons Learned

Key Features

One of SkillWorks's signature elements and indeed one of its most significant accomplishments has been creating and sustaining its Funders Group. While the idea of a funder collaborative is hardly new, several features of the SkillWorks Funders Group are worth highlighting.

Strong Anchor Institution with a Broad Base of Support

The commitment of the Boston Foundation, a major philanthropic and civic institution with robust investments in workforce training, and the vision of its president and CEO, Paul Grogan, enabled the initiative to attract local and national support right from the beginning. Guidance from key staff, including Angel Bermudez, senior director of grant making, and Jill Griffin, senior director of programs, then gave the initiative the capacity to pool funds, as well as to manage

and report on them over time. As important, the broad base of support from local philanthropic institutions allowed SkillWorks to grow, to establish a learning
community, and to maintain momentum for the initiative over time.

Public-Private Partnership

One of the initiative's earliest and most significant partners was the City
of Boston, which made a commitment to SkillWorks equal to that of the Boston Foundation for the first five years. The city's active participation and Mayor
Thomas M. Menino's leadership were critical in facilitating a greater connection
to and knowledge of the public workforce system and policies, as well as the many
nonprofit workforce providers that partner with the city to deliver services and
training.

SkillWorks's connection to the Boston Private Industry Council (PIC),
the city's workforce board, has evolved over time. Federal workforce funds flow
through the City of Boston even as the workforce board charters the career centers. The city also manages a key funding resource for workforce programs, the
Neighborhood Jobs Trust. The trust—funded through linkage fees large-scale developers must pay to ensure that the city has a means to invest in its residents as
well as its buildings—was the source of funding for SkillWorks. Therefore, all parties really saw the city as SkillWorks's connection to the public workforce system.

Even so, the PIC has played a few key roles in the initiative. Early in Phase
I, the PIC provided technical assistance to the initiative's grantees under contract
to SkillWorks. Then, in Phase II, as both the PIC and SkillWorks took a more
active interest in post-secondary education pathways for adults, SkillWorks once
again contracted with the PIC to implement the initiative's college-navigation
work, and the PIC invited SkillWorks's director to join its Workforce Development Committee, overseeing workforce investments in the city.

Over time, the initiative also built strong relationships with Massachusetts'
workforce agencies and departments, including Commonwealth Corporation and
the Executive Office of Labor and Workforce Development, first as a grantee and
later as a funding and advocacy partner.

Local-National Partnership

From the Annie E. Casey Foundation's support of the initiative's initial planning stages to the multi-year operating support of the National Fund for Workforce Solutions, SkillWorks has been fortunate to have significant support from
national foundations in addition to local institutions. While the majority of Skill-
Works's funding came from local sources, national funders played an important
role in connecting SkillWorks to a larger community of practice, providing credibility as well as visibility and opening doors to leadership and funding opportunities. The National Fund for Workforce Solutions was especially important in fa-

cilitating peer learning and best-practice sharing, leveraging funding, and creating a sense of scale and movement attractive to local funders through the legitimacy and heft of its national funding partners. (See Dyer et al., Chapter 5, for a history of the National Fund.)

Pooled Funding and Mutual Support

The SkillWorks funder collaborative was formed to "provide a flexible source of support for innovative workforce development programming over an extended period."[23] As one of SkillWorks's early evaluation reports stated, the initiative's ability to bring together various foundations and public funders to invest in a pooled fund to address workforce issues was an innovative feature at the time.[24] SkillWorks's governance model of "one funder, one vote" has also been critical to maintaining the initiative's collaborative nature, leveling the playing field among funders and building buy-in.

Staff Leadership

Collaboratives cannot function for a long period of time, at this level, without consistent staff leadership. SkillWorks's funders initially relied on a consultant-staffing model. As the initiative grew, however, the funders realized they needed a full-time staff director to consistently organize materials and convenings, manage relationships, and oversee the work. A director was hired in 2005 to serve as the single point of contact for the collaborative's grantees, funders, and consultants and to keep them moving in the same direction and toward the same goals.

Roles and Lessons

As the initiative has evolved, the roles, functions, and outcomes of the collaborative have been much broader, and the lessons learned much richer than those gained from simply pooling grant funds. These are described below.

Funder Collaborative as Learning Community

As SkillWorks funders became comfortable with grant making and the day-to-day operations of the initiative, the Funders Group evolved into more of a learning community. Its meetings, especially in Phase II, were often used less as a management tool and more as a means of educating collaborative members about workforce-system issues at the local, state, and federal levels.[25]

This approach has engaged the public sector and the philanthropic community in a common learning process. Many of these meetings have included Skill-Works funders as well as funders outside of the SkillWorks initiative and grantees. One outcome has been a growing level of understanding among funders in the philanthropic community about the structure, operations, and funding of the public workforce system at the local, state, and federal levels.

SkillWorks has provided a forum for funders to build relationships with one another and to share information about funding for workforce programs and initiatives outside of SkillWorks. This has led to increased coordination around a broader universe of workforce-related activities, including communication between meetings about issues with common grantees, policy matters, or other concerns and areas of interest.

Funder Collaborative as Change Agent

SkillWorks has been a leading voice advocating for job seekers, adult learners, and low-skilled, low-to-moderate-income workers and an agenda setter for workforce issues in Massachusetts.

The leadership of the funders through participation in SkillWorks has raised the profile of workforce-development challenges and best practices. The collective voice of the funders has added weight to conversations with legislators, community colleges, employers, and community-based organizations and often opened the door to increased investments and systems change.

SkillWorks played a leadership role in the inclusion of workforce components in each of the economic-stimulus bills, in sponsoring gubernatorial forums on jobs and opportunity, and in surfacing and addressing the challenges faced by adult learners in community college through the Skills2Compete-Massachusetts campaign.

In addition, SkillWorks influenced the Commissioner of Higher Education's increased focus on system alignment and stackable, transferable credits as part of the Vision Project to improve outcomes of public higher education in Massachusetts.[26]

Another example of the funder collaborative's ability to incentivize change has been SkillWorks's Phase II grant to Year Up to have the organization offer career-advancement services, as well as job placement support. The grant has led to changes in Year Up's organizational structure, in its core curriculum, and in the national Year Up model to focus more on long-term labor-market retention, career advancement, and post-secondary education.

Funder Collaborative as Convener and Intermediary

While SkillWorks has been a significant grant maker in workforce development, the collaborative has also played an important role as convener and intermediary. One example of this work was the SkillWorks Green Jobs Initiative during Phase II. As SkillWorks convened employers, funders, and training providers interested in green jobs, it moved from newcomer to the field to a credible leader and sector intermediary statewide.[27] SkillWorks also used the Funders Group to convene groups ranging from national evaluators of workforce initiatives, capacity-building providers, employers, and service providers. This has led to conversations about common areas of interest in evaluation of career-advancement initiatives, greater coordination in capacity building for workforce programs, and more efficient utilization of resources among service providers.

Conclusion: Charting the Future of SkillWorks

As of December 2013, SkillWorks has invested in workforce programs and systems change for ten years. During this time, it has become a nationally recognized workforce-development intermediary and funder collaborative known for its work in Massachusetts as well as its influence on other workforce-funding collaboratives around the country. Its three-pronged strategy of industry-sector workforce partnerships, capacity building, and policy advocacy has changed the landscape of workforce development in significant ways, increasing funding for and pushing the effectiveness of the workforce-development system.

SkillWorks funders undertook a comprehensive strategic-planning process during the latter half of 2012 to consider exactly this question in light of successes, challenges, and lessons learned.

The following value proposition for SkillWorks Phase III (2014–2018) emerged from this process:

SkillWorks leverages its leadership position and collaborative model to convene business, labor, education, and civic leaders and catalyze change through innovative investments, adoption of best practices, and advocacy.

After spending ten years building this leadership position and collaborative, SkillWorks funders took a step back to examine the continuing need for the initiative and heard convincingly from stakeholders that there was still a role for Skill-Works to play, especially in pushing for systems change and innovation in the workforce-development system.

SkillWorks funders also received feedback from stakeholders about the value of flexible philanthropic funding in helping incentivize change and innovation, which all agreed would be necessary to achieve the funders' Phase III goal of **improving the workforce system's effectiveness and efficiency, resulting in significantly improved economic outcomes for job and skill seekers, with a priority focus on those in Greater Boston who are low-income and low-skilled.**

Phase III investments will make the following impacts:

- Help more individuals progress faster toward family-sustaining wages.
- Help more employers find and retain skilled workers.

- Enable more funders, policy makers, and practitioners to sustain effective practices.

As SkillWorks moves into Phase III, future investments will be guided by the principles of systems change, innovation, and opportunity to address a key gap in the workforce system.

In working to implement programs and strategies that adhere to these principles and help realize these impacts, the SkillWorks funder collaborative will continue to leverage its convening, learning, and change-agent roles to lead to greater scale and sustainability of efficient and effective pipelines that connect workers to employers and help advance them toward economic independence. (See *Table 6* for a summary of how SkillWorks Phase III builds upon and changes from Phase II.)

Table 6: How SkillWorks Phase III Builds Upon Phase II

	SkillWorks Phase II (2009–2013)	SkillWorks Phase III (2014–2018)
Training/ Program Investments	• Large, multiyear general-support grants for workforce partnerships in key sectors with pre-employment and incumbent-worker services • Focus on pathways to post-secondary education and training • Focus on Greater Boston residents and businesses	• Smaller, programmatic grants, possibly multiyear, that support innovative strategies addressing specific points along workforce pipeline • Continued focus on transitions and pathways to postsecondary education/training and middle-skill jobs • New emphasis on addressing barriers to employment and training for underserved populations • Continued focus on Greater Boston residents and businesses

Capacity Building	• Primary focus on providing one-to-one technical assistance to grantees
	
	• Secondary focus on building capacity of workforce-development field
		• Primary focus on documenting and sharing lessons learned to build field.
		
		• Develop a regional "SkillWorks network" of providers supporting workforce development that:
		
		  * agree to adopt core best practices and receive recognition for so doing
		
		  * participate in capacity building, professional development, and technical assistance
		
		  * form peer groups to share and pilot new, effective practices
		
		• Leverage technology to increase reach of SkillWorks learnings
		
		• Convene employers to better understand and meet needs, to promote the adoption of best practices, and to promote greater system alignment

Public Policy	• Relied on one coalition that represented SkillWorks's policy interests • Broad focus on advocating for workforce funding and some systems change • Increased leadership by collaborative staff in Phase II	• Support multiple avenues for organizing in workforce development, including sustained advocacy capacity • Increased focus on systems change, especially to better connect skilled workers to employers and help them advance, and to increase access to training and jobs for harder-to-serve individuals • Greater involvement of collaborative funders and staff in advocacy • More proactive and strategic in supporting specific campaigns aligned with SkillWorks's goals

Funder Collaborative	• Pooled funding only • Decision making led by funders only, with support from initiative staff and consultants • Collaborative provides learning opportunities for funders and partnerships	• Pooled *and* aligned funding, with greater focus on aligning philanthropic and public resources • Decision making led by funders, with additional leadership provided by aligned funders and employers and support from initiative staff and consultants • Increased focus on building resources for and knowledge and capacity of workforce funders and other leaders

Final Thoughts

The public-private funder collaborative occupies a unique place in the universe of workforce development and has the potential to make important contributions to the field in terms of service delivery, employer organizing, resource development, public policy, and ultimately systems change. While the SkillWorks collaborative is highly structured, with pooled funding, staff, and formal committees, as well as evaluation and other consultant capacity, the structure of the collaborative seems to be less important than the relationships developed both within the collaborative and outside of it, with employers, policy makers, educators, community-based organizations, and others.

Even so, the importance of consistent leadership and commitment of the funders over time cannot be overstated, especially given the trend of public disinvestment in the workforce system that we have seen in the first part of the twenty-first century. In fact, we have seen that a creative and persistent funder collaborative can help reverse this trend at the local, regional, and state levels.

For too long, we have allowed the workforce-development system to be defined by its perceived and real challenges. The funder collaborative can help change the narrative. The collaborative should be able to articulate a vision of success and then honestly acknowledge strengths as well as areas for improvement. It must work with all parts of the public-workforce system even as it pushes for improvements and change. The collaborative's abilities to leverage, align, and invest public and private resources in training; elevate the visibility of the workforce-development sector; demonstrate effectiveness; develop a broad-based coalition; and advocate from the position of co-investor will be keys to its success.

While a collaborative like SkillWorks may not be able to change the national conversation about how and why we support workforce training, we have seen at least a glimpse of how we might work to shape and change the local and state level conversation.

The work of economic advancement and systems change needs vision and is not accomplished overnight. The structure and guidance of a relatively stable collaborative can buffer some of the inevitable changes in public and philanthropic funding priorities and initiatives. A funder collaborative's ability to lead, coordinate and provide resources, and enhance visibility can help communities adopt a forward-looking, ambitious set of priorities for workforce training, education, and systems change.

Notes

1. Scott (2007), p. 15.
2. Scott and Rubin (2004), Scott (2007a), and Scott (2007b) are additional resources that cover the history of SkillWorks very well.
3. SkillWorks was launched as the Boston Workforce Development Initiative; the name was changed in 2004.
4. These partnerships included both large investments in established industries and smaller, exploratory training partnerships in the emerging green-jobs economy.
5. No public-sector funds could be used for public-policy advocacy, to prevent any appearance of conflict of interest; a few funders applied their pledges to specific components of the initiative.
6. SkillWorks Phase I ran from 2003 to 2008; over $14 million was invested in workforce partnerships, capacity building, and public-policy advocacy. Phase II ran from 2009 to 2013; nearly $10 million was invested in the three strategies, primarily with a different set of grantees.
7. All figures as of June 30, 2013. Enrollment numbers are unduplicated. Outcome numbers count unduplicated participants within each category (wage gain, placement, credential attainment), but some participants may be included in more than one outcome category—if, for example, they have attained a job placement *as well as* a credential. Only a small number of pre-employment participants were placed in jobs and then earned wage gains or promotions over the course of their involvement with SkillWorks. Therefore the placement metric and the advancement metrics (wage gains and promotions) are generally counting different populations and are unduplicated.
8. SkillWorks's evaluation reports can be accessed online at http://www.skill-works.org/resources-evaluation-reports.php.
9. It is likely that some of these numbers were underreported in Phase I, given the nature of data collection and participant tracking, which was reported by grantees only in the aggregate and not at the participant level. The initiative thus did not have precise participant-level data across all partnerships.
10. Clifford (2012), pp. 14, 28.
11. Winey (2012a), pp. 8, 9.
12. Massachusetts Board of Higher Education, p. 12.
13. Ibid., pp. 12–14.

14. Ibid., p. 9.
15. Scott (2007b), p. 26.
16. The text of the bill can be found online at http://www.malegislature.gov/Laws/Session-Laws/Acts/2006/Chapter123.
17. The WCTF was modeled on the earlier BEST and BayStateWorks initiatives.
18. The Reach Higher Initiative.
19. The text of the bill can be found online at https://malegislature.gov/Bills/187/Senate/S921.
20. Siegel et al. (2009), p. 9.
21. Ibid., p. 9.
22. Ibid.
23. Ibid.
24. Hebert and Siegel (2005), p. 30.
25. Siegel (2011), pp. 3–4.
26. Ibid., p. 5.
27. Winey (2012b), p. 16.

Bibliography

Clifford, Robert. 2012. *Labor Market Trends in the Boston/Metro North Region*. Boston: Commonwealth Corporation and New England Public Policy Center of the Federal Reserve Bank of Boston.

Hebert, Scott, and Beth Siegel. 2005. *Baseline Report of the SkillWorks Initiative*. Boston: Abt Associates and Mt. Auburn Associates.

Massachusetts Board of Higher Education. 2007. Final Report from the Task Force on Retention and Completion Rates at the Community Colleges. Boston.

Minzner, Amy, Glen Schneider, Joshua Vaughn, Beth Siegel, and Devon Winey. 2009. *SkillWorks Incumbent Worker Pathways: A Qualitative Investigation*. Boston: Abt Associates and Mt. Auburn Associates.

Scott, Geri. 2007a. *Funder Collaboratives: A Philanthropic Strategy for Supporting Workforce Intermediaries*. Boston: Jobs for the Future.

———. 2007b. *Working Toward Reinvention: SkillWorks at Three*. Boston: Jobs for the Future.

——— and Jerry Rubin. 2004. *Reinventing Workforce Development: Lessons from Boston's Community Approach*. Boston: Jobs for the Future.

Siegel, Beth. 2011. *SkillWorks Systems Change—Phase II Year 2*. Boston: Mt. Auburn Associates.

———, Devon Winey, Amy Minzer, Glen Schneider, and Joshua Vaughn. 2009. *The Public Policy Component of SkillWorks*. Boston: Mt. Auburn Associates and Abt Associates.

Winey, Devon. 2012a. *College Navigator Report*. Boston: Mt. Auburn Associates.

———. 2012b. *SkillWorks Green Collar Career Pathways Initiative Year 3 Annual Evaluation*. Boston: Mt. Auburn Associates.

8

Health Careers Collaborative of Greater Cincinnati: Partners for a Competitive Workforce and Healthcare Sector

Marianne Krismer

The Health Careers Collaborative of Greater Cincinnati (HCC), founded in 2003 as a comprehensive regional workforce partnership, has become a national model for effective systemic change and innovation in workforce development. The collaborative has made significant progress in five main areas and continues to work to meet challenges related to economic issues and implementation of the Affordable Care Act. This chapter describes the collaborative's formation, highlights its accomplishments, and looks at challenges ahead.

Planning and Launch: 2003–2005

Founding Managing Partners

In 2003 Greater Cincinnati as well as the nation faced workforce shortages in nursing and several allied health fields. Healthcare systems were offering sign-on bonuses and incentives for new graduates, who would pick and choose employment based on the "best deal." Employees would often demonstrate no loyalty to the new employer and would, for example, leave after the one- to two-year commitment for a signing bonus to obtain more money or better shifts. Employers reported staff leaving for positions at competitors offering as little as fifty cents more per hour. Continually hiring and orienting new employees cost money but also

...ted in a lack of continuity of delivery of services for the employers. It was in this chaotic environment that the Health Professions Academy was founded, later to be known as the Health Careers Collaborative of Greater Cincinnati.

The four founding member institutions of what would become the Health Careers Collaborative of Greater Cincinnati were the Health Alliance of Greater Cincinnati (now UC Health), Cincinnati Children's Hospital Medical Center, Cincinnati State Technical and Community College, and Great Oaks Career Campuses. The two hospital systems constituted the largest healthcare employers in the region, employing more than twenty-five thousand. The educational organizations trained the most entry-level health practitioners in the area, including nursing assistants, health unit coordinators, registered nurses, respiratory therapists, and other essential healthcare workers.

Initial conversations were focused on how to create a career pathway so that loyal, low-wage incumbent workers could get training to move into key jobs and provide a seamless entryway to employment for the unemployed.

At the same time, the KnowledgeWorks Foundation, a social enterprise organization focused on improving student readiness for college and careers, offered a planning grant to this fledgling collaborative. It focused on getting the community colleges, career technology centers, employers, and regional workforce investment boards to come together to solve employment and training issues within their communities. The four founding members met with a KnowledgeWorks consultant to explore possibilities and decided that the grant could provide the foundational structure and operational guidelines needed to form the collaborative.

HCC Foundational Framework

The planning grant was awarded to Great Oaks as fiscal agent. With the assistance of a KnowledgeWorks consultant, the team met to develop a full proposal, which laid out its intention to plan a new organization that would enable workforce and education entities to work together to overcome existing challenges and prepare to meet future needs. The collaborative was one of six statewide workforce/education collaboratives that were awarded full planning and implementation grants. Three of the six were awarded to healthcare initiatives.

A local consultant was assigned by KnowledgeWorks to facilitate and provide ongoing resources and support in the collaborative's formation. The collaborative had several intense sessions identifying its purpose, guiding principles, and implementation model. Local meetings occurred weekly, and statewide meetings of all six grantees were held two to three times each year from 2003 to 2006 in Columbus, Ohio. The Columbus meetings included state workforce leaders and were structured to share common issues and progress. These sessions were extremely valuable in providing professional development from workforce innovators while also sharing promising practices among the peer networks and providing insight into similar issues and alternative solutions. While relationships between employers and workforce entities varied across the state, these meetings promoted open discussion of promising practices and how training needs could be captured and adapted to the college system while still meeting the specific needs of regional employers.

The first order of business for HCC was to identify additional partners. Invitations were made to the Southwest Ohio Regional Workforce Investment Board and the Greater Cincinnati Health Council, the region's hospital association. The first order of business was to define the overarching and compelling reason for assembling the collaborative. The founding members and partners narrowed it down to three interrelated and complementary purposes that continue to drive HCC to this day.

1. *Increase access to health care careers for underutilized labor pools, including low-wage incumbent workers and unemployed or underemployed workers within the community.*

HCC recognized a major opportunity to help the 60 percent of the workforce that was low-wage or entry-level move up to higher-skilled positions within the organizations. Many of these individuals were loyal and hardworking but, due to life circumstances and generational poverty, had never had an opportunity for advancement. More important, entry-level employees were not taking advantage of the education benefit provided by all of the employers.

Several barriers kept these employees from accessing tuition-assistance programs. One, the up-front tuition requirement was a barrier for most employees, as they did not have resources to pay tuition costs on entry-level salaries. Two, none of the tuition policies allowed for funding of developmental education, which more than 85 percent of the participants needed. Three, these students indicated that they did not view themselves as healthcare professionals. Their families had served in roles as nursing assistants, transporters, and housekeepers for generations, and that was how they saw themselves. And four, there was no evidence of employer encouragement or support prior to the implementation of the incumbent-worker program.

2. *Alleviate regional health care workforce shortages.*

The collaborative believed that it could help improve skills and opportunities for the targeted employees and that they could move into higher-level positions if they were provided support and encouragement. It was further noted that by promoting internally, the "job hopping" and relative costs related to orientation and continued hiring of new employees would be reduced, thus increasing return on investment. Human-resource staff reported being extremely frustrated with the high number of vacancies, which numbered in the hundreds for each of their organizations. In some cases, employers were forced to seek nursing staff from outside the country, which came with a high price for relocation and visa costs, not to mention complexity. When sufficient staff could not be recruited, the facilities were often forced to close down hospital wings or reduce services, which hurt profitability. Healthcare facilities were often short-staffed, and employee morale suffered. Clearly, the crisis had hit a peak, and future projections identified that it would only get worse.

3. *Increase the diversity of the healthcare workforce in Greater Cincinnati.*

As in other urban environments, Cincinnati had a disproportionate balance of minorities in entry-level and low-wage positions compared with the higher-wage professional positions. By working with this population and providing training opportunities, the collaborative believed it could help bring more diversity to the healthcare workforce.

Guiding Principles

The founding partners spent a great deal of time discussing the issues and agreed to solidify the vision and mission in guiding principles, which are listed below. They remain in place today, and they are routinely reviewed during annual planning sessions. The principles are broad enough to allow them to conform to the healthcare system changes being implemented with the Affordable Care Act.

- Focus on job and educational advancement for low-income adults while also meeting employer needs.

- Map advancement pathways and opportunities in job sectors of importance to the region.

- Build on existing state-supported initiatives, such as the Higher Skills Partnerships, Workforce Investment Act, and One-Stop Career Centers.

- Commit to systemic change within and across institutions and not just implementation of unsustainable demonstration projects.

Implementation

To solidify their relationship, the presidents and CEOs of the four managing partners developed a memorandum of understanding. Each partner agreed to contribute $100,000 to complete the remodeling of a training facility within walking distance of the largest population of workers. Additional funds from a Department of Labor Community College Job Training Grant provided for furnishings. In 2005 the partnership's name was changed from the Health Professions Academy to Health Careers Collaborative of Greater Cincinnati to better reflect the mission.

It was clear from the beginning that although the Southwest Regional Workforce Investment Board was at the table, the collaborative also needed to consider recruiting community-based partners that could assist with recruitment and support for entry-level and unemployed workers. The collaborative recruited Mercy Connections (now Mercy Neighborhood Ministries) to provide GED courses, basic-skills training, and access to social support services. Dress for Success–Cincinnati was brought in to provide referrals, career counseling, and assistance with job readiness in the pathways curriculum. The Greater Cincinnati Health Council (GCHC) provided important data, as well as access to its members, who represent all health care systems in the greater Cincinnati region. Three of the four founding partners provided leadership on GCHC committees, which gave them regular opportunities to share the vision and work of the collaborative; that helped lead to the recruitment of additional collaborative members.

In addition to the KnowledgeWorks grant (approximately $130,000), the United Way of Greater Cincinnati provided funding for education and support for unemployed job seekers. (This grant was for approximately $250,000; it varies annually, depending upon funds available, but has remained a high priority.) This grant provides important funding for training for nurses' aides, patient-care assistants, and health-unit coordinators. Cincinnati State received some funds from this grant to provide advising support for students as they continued on the career pathway.

Cincinnati State received a $1.5 million Community-Based Job Training Grant from the Department of Labor, which supported an additional cohort for nursing training and the expansion of labs and faculty. It also provided funds to purchase equipment for the new shared HCC classrooms, which enabled nursing, science, and other courses to be taught at the HCC site, which was within walking distance for most of our incumbent workers and accessible by bus for others.

In 2005 a cohort of students seeking associate's degrees in nursing was recruited, followed by one for allied health professions. The students recruited held a variety of entry-level and lower-skilled positions within the Health Alliance and Cincinnati Children's Hospital. The collaborative found that 95 percent of the students needed developmental education, which was offered as a component of the pathway. Later it was offered as a preselection requirement, as time to master the information varied greatly among the participants. All prerequisite courses, general education, and curricular courses were offered to the entire cohort, which proved to support retention and persistence.

As HCC was beginning to generate results for job seekers and incumbent workers, other stakeholders across the community took notice. In 2008 the City of Cincinnati and the Cincinnati USA Regional Chamber of Commerce both launched regional economic-development planning processes that highlighted the two-pronged workforce challenge the community was facing: Employers were demanding a higher-skilled workforce, yet far too many residents lacked the skills and preparation required.

Civic and business leaders made the case that businesses cannot compete if they cannot find qualified workers. Residents cannot get family-sustaining jobs unless they further develop their skills to match the needs of employers. Moreover, workforce-development efforts at the time were too fragmented, did not respond adequately to employer needs, and insufficiently focused on career advancement.

The opportunity for HCC to join the National Fund for Workforce Solutions was a catalyst in bringing the philanthropic community to respond to the challenge. The Greater Cincinnati Foundation, the region's largest community foundation, brought together philanthropic, business, workforce, education, and economic-development leaders to create the Greater Cincinnati Workforce Network (GCWN). Now renamed Partners for a Competitive Workforce, this regional public-private partnership seeks to align workforce training with employer needs in priority sectors to help low-income adults attain good jobs while helping businesses access skilled workers. HCC provided the "proof of concept" for GCWN in how to do workforce development differently. This initiative was driven by employers, organized around an in-demand industry, and focused on long-term career development. When GCWN was launched, with support from the National Fund and local funders, its core strategy was to invest in the expansion and operations of HCC while catalyzing similar employer-driven workforce partnerships in new industries, including advanced manufacturing, construction, and, most recently, information technology.

GCWN's investment allowed HCC to bring on an executive director to expand the partnership to serve more employers and workers. TriHealth, a health care system with eight thousand employees and two hospitals, joined in 2008, and Mercy Health, a regional healthcare system with five hospitals and several long-term and outpatient facilities, joined in 2010.

An opportunity presented itself to apply for another U.S. Department of Labor grant on behalf of HCC in 2010. The American Recovery and Reinvestment Act grant was a perfect fit to support HCC's efforts to expand, with Cincinnati State as the lead. Each of the partners was to receive funds to support their individual contributions to the overall expansion. Miami University of Ohio was recruited to provide, along with Cincinnati State, a new health information-technology pathway that would seamlessly transition students from certificates to bachelor's of science degrees and more advanced work. Job coaches were embedded in each hospital system, academic advisors and support personnel were provided for educational and community-based programs, and funds for all partners were included to pay for equipment, travel, and innovations. The four job coaches embedded within the hospital systems, the academic advisors at Cincinnati State and Great Oaks, and community-based support staff created a synergistic team supporting student success.

The team now meets formally on a monthly basis to review current cohort progress, discuss program needs, recommend policy and procedure changes to the pathway process, and identify issues that need to be resolved. Employer coaches represent their healthcare constituents by identifying incumbent workers who are a good fit for certificate or degree cohorts, working with underskilled workers to provide bridge support, and referring staff with significant academic needs to community-based partners for assessments and basic-skills training.

College advisors help students navigate the education pathway and overcome barriers to success in direct consultation with the job coaches and community-based partners. The community-based partners work with entry-level and high-risk individuals to help prepare them for the workforce. Mercy Neighborhood Ministries, for example, offers a program called Building Foundations for Life. It provides training in basic workforce readiness and personal development in a twelve-week program and uses assessment tools to guide the participant. After completing this rigorous program, the graduate is offered the opportunity to earn a training credential through the Home Health Aide certification program. Upon successful completion of the eighty-hour program, the graduate either is considered for employment by an HCC partner or may be offered a position with another health care agency.

When the Recovery Act grant ended in June 2013, HCC had exceeded its outcome goals and was identified as a best practice by the U.S. Department of Labor Education and Training Administration. The table below shows the final HCC outcome measures for the Recovery Act grant.

*Table 1: Health Careers Collaborative of Greater Cincinnati
U.S. Department of Labor ARRA Grant Final Outcomes*
January 1, 2010–June 30, 2013

Outcome Measure	Goal	Participants Actual #	Percentage of Outcome Goal
Referrals for service/education	750	2,115	282%
Participants who complete degree/ certificate program	650	1,371	211%
Participants who complete credential	650	1,553	239%
Participants placed into unsubsidized health care employment	600	811	135%
Participants who retained employment for two quarters	525	252	48%

As HCC has continued to evolve and mature, additional partners have joined. Gateway Community and Technical College in Northern Kentucky joined and provides complementary pathway programs for the northern Kentucky market. The changes to the healthcare industry brought on by health care reform and the Affordable Care Act will require a focus on home health care and long-term care organizations. With less care being delivered in acute-care hospitals and more in long-term, ambulatory, and home settings, the collaborative must adapt. A significant change occurred in 2012 when Mercy Neighborhood Ministries took over the Council on Aging of Southwest Ohio's training program for homecare aides. Mercy added basic workplace-skill development to the curriculum and integrated an assessment tool to better help this low-skilled, chronically unemployed population take the first step in a health-career pathway.

Success Story

HCC has helped many residents of the Cincinnati region build their credentials and move into better-paying jobs. Here is one person's story.

In 2008 J.S. was a loyal employee who had worked several years as a transporter at Cincinnati Children's Hospital. She was industrious and hardworking, which resulted in her being promoted to team leader. However, she had a dream to become a nurse. It seemed totally out of reach for her until she heard about the Health Careers Collaborative program. When she applied for her employer's support to enter the HCC cohort program, she wrote:

My interest in participating in the HCC is to better myself, not only for myself, but for my family as well. My expectations of this program are that it will help me to achieve an otherwise unattainable goal. I believe this program will help me succeed in graduating with an associate's degree, without taking away financially from my four children. I am a trustworthy, hardworking, determined woman. I am a loving and caring mother, and I believe these qualities will be the basis of success in this program for me. Through this program I will be able to get the help needed to educate myself, to set a good example for my children and to eventually help others. I am so excited to even have an opportunity of this nature available to me. Thank you.

J.S. graduated with an associate's degree in nursing in June 2012. She graduated with four other students from Cincinnati Children's Hospital. Immediately upon her graduation, the department that she was working in as a team leader in patient transport offered her a position as a registered nurse. She started her new position in October 2012 and nearly doubled her salary.

Growth and Sustainability: 2012 to the Present

Initial conversations within HCC focused on career pathways for loyal, low-wage incumbent workers and providing a pathway to entry-level employment for the unemployed. In ten years of operation, HCC has continuously refined that model and expanded to include additional employers, education providers, and community-based partners to meet the needs of the region's healthcare workforce. Sustainability of the collaborative has been a topic of constant consideration since early inception. HCC to date has been able to secure grants to support an executive director, advisors, and job coaches. Each of the partners has been working to identify ways to continue funding of positions and programs as budgets tighten within organizations in an unsure economy.

Generating and documenting a strong return on investment is a critical step. In 2011 the New Growth Group completed a study of HCC's return on investment, using UC Health data. The analysis documented a 12 percent return on investment for the incumbent training program, generated through recruitment-cost savings, and a net benefit of $2.6 million for the entry-level certificate-training program due to lower turnover and reduced recruitment costs. The return-on-investment findings can be viewed on the HCC website: www.healthcareerscollaborative.com.

More recent data from HCC's employer partners is promising. Data from Cincinnati Children's Hospital demonstrates an increase in participants' wage rates. TriHealth noted in its 2012 return-on-investment study that participation in HCC had lowered the turnover rate for all participants, improved employee satisfaction, increased employee diversity, and led to higher pay.

An ongoing challenge is ensuring that HCC can respond to the shifting and diverse needs of the region's healthcare employers; recent needs included highly skilled researchers and neurodiagnostic technicians. While these are real employment needs, HCC may not have the capacity to address them. All partners are working in a landscape of diminishing resources, increased requests for services, and the need to keep quality high. HCC provides a collaborative infrastructure to tackle shared problems.

In HCC's recent planning meeting, future challenges emerged: managing diverse employer needs, developing financial sustainability, building buy-in to change dated practices to meet new models, and working within the confines of the Affordable Care Act and new cost models for employers, educators, Workforce Investment Boards, and community-based organizations. As it has gained experience, HCC has become a bit less idealistic and more realistic as it faces the daunting task of working collaboratively. However, partners remain committed to addressing future health care workforce challenges collaboratively.

HCC's Promising Practices

Employer Leadership and Policy Change

HCC has been employer-led from its inception, and employers provide the formal leadership and set the stage for the career-pathway process to meet their projected demand for qualified workers. HCC employers have made significant policy changes to facilitate the career advancement of their incumbent employees, such as pre-paying tuition and covering developmental-education tuition costs. In fact, these changes in tuition policy became a requirement for employers to join HCC, which is driving substantive systems change.

Commitment to Demand-Driven Career Pathways

In the early development of the HCC partnership, its focus on developing connected sequences of coursework and stackable credentials into a coherent healthcare pathway was groundbreaking. Over time, because employers were deeply engaged and meeting on a monthly basis, HCC was able to understand and respond to the shifting labor-market need for training for different occupations. That led to the additions of occupational-therapy, medical-laboratory, and orthopedic pathways, in addition to the original nursing pathway. Most recently the model was able to accommodate emerging and new pathways, such as health information and orthopedic technicians. These were real-time labor-market adjustments between supply-side education and community-based partners and demand-side employers.

For example, when the emergence of electronic medical records created a demand for trained employees, HCC worked collaboratively with three education providers—Cincinnati State, Miami University, and Northern Kentucky University—as well as information technology leaders from health care and developed an articulated pathway to guide participants through the steps to obtain, in order, a certificate, an associate's degree, a bachelor's degree, and a master's degree. The employers provided expertise, validated the curriculum, and identified career opportunities for each of the points along the pathway, which is helping to address employment needs within the region.

Robust Partnerships

HCC's success depends on deep partnerships between employers, educators, community organizations, and workforce partners. Employers, for example, changed their policies to give incumbent workers more flexibility to pursue education and training. There is also financial support, including prepaid tuition funding, for all courses, including necessary preparation courses. The workforce investment board provides students with access and funding for entry-level and degree programs. Community-based partners provide support for learners at all levels. Educators identify funding to develop new cohort models, core curriculum, and stackable credentials and train advisors to provide intensive support that leads to certificate and degree completion.

Cohort Model

As the targeted population typically has low training-completion rates, HCC intentionally created a cohort model to allow groups of participants to move together through all levels of training, from certificate to associate's degrees. Cohorts are recruited at the hospital locations via open houses, e-mails, publications, and word of mouth. When candidates express interest, job coaches verify their eligibility and work with the college academic advisors to select the cohort. To date, cohorts of twenty-four students have been selected every six months in either nursing or allied health tracks. Each of the four hospital systems sends applicants based on need for positions and candidates' qualifications. The cohorts are mixed with students representing all employer partners. Anecdotal evidence from the partners confirms that the students also find the cohort model helpful as it provides peer-based support and interpersonal connections.

There are many challenges to establishing a cohort model, namely the inevitable ebb and flow of the number and availability of spots within certain health care pathways. For example, there has recently been an increased need for medical laboratory technicians; however, the incumbent workers choosing this pathway are insufficient to fill the spaces available, while nursing has more candidates than openings. Also, due to the multiple life challenges these entry-level workers face, many drop out of training for periods of time and then must be included in subsequent cohorts. Also, the amount of time and energy expended by the employer staff is much greater in this population of low-skilled individuals, who generally have not experienced previous academic success. Although community colleges have had intermittent grants and funding to support high-risk students, efforts are inconsistent and often not sustainable. The cohort model has had ten years of success largely because it is a true partnership between the education providers and the employer.

The result of this collaboration has been retention rates that far exceed those of the general community college population, with an average 61 percent completion rate for cohort students. The National Center for Education Statistics reported a national average community college completion rate of 21 percent.[1] The associate's degree programs are offered a maximum of three days each week in late afternoon and early evening to accommodate full-time work schedules. Nursing students take all courses as a cohort, and allied health participants take prerequisites and general education as a cohort until they enter technical courses, when they become assimilated with traditional students. Intensive advising practices continue for all participants until completion and job placement. Although the goal is to graduate students with associate's degrees within three and a half years of enrollment, some students require a longer time to complete coursework. Data indicate that many of these individuals ultimately receive credentials.

Cohort models are labor intensive and not the best solution for all incumbent workers and employers. Support systems for incumbent workers who do not elect a cohort are also in place, with job coaches and student-success counselors monitoring them as they navigate traditional education pathways.

Leveraging Resources

HCC's ability to leverage three large-scale grants, as well as local and national funds ranging from the KnowledgeWorks Foundation and United Way to the National Fund for Workforce Solutions and U.S. Department of Labor grants, has proven critical to support and expand the work. The vision and commitment of the partners was evident as they developed the proposals for each of these grants and consistently achieved successful outcomes. This attention to high-level performance based on commitment to foundational principles and collaboration, rather than competition, has continually paid off as new grant opportunities have emerged.

The bottom line is that HCC is delivering results for workers, employers, and the community. Since 2008 it has trained more than 3,700 job seekers and incumbent workers, with 88 percent completing training and more than 3,800 credentials earned; 88 percent obtained employment, and 81 percent retained employment after twelve months. Moreover, HCC has delivered bottom-line benefits to employers through lower turnover and reduced recruitment costs. Finally, HCC has provided a model for how to build employer-driven career pathways that is now being adapted into other industries in the Greater Cincinnati region and across the country.

Final Insights

The process of developing a highly functional collaborative that brings together employers, community-based organizations, and education and workforce agencies is complicated and requires a high level of commitment and trust. Initial discussions made it clear that although all were focused on developing a highly skilled regional workforce, each had different perspectives as to why this was important and how organizations could and should contribute. An early mantra was "Check your egos at the door." This proved to be an important reminder as creating a "collaborative" with a central focus required agreement on the vision and mission based on the collective needs of the workforce community. All had to compromise and adapt. Finally, there were very few non-negotiable items as HCC was formed and implemented, and this remains true now as it works to maintain its sustainability.

At present the collaborative is fairly homogenous, with healthcare employers representing large traditional hospital systems. Recent attempts at recruiting the long-term care and home health care employers has had limited success. However, the collaborative recognizes that their interests must also be represented. Because many long-term and home health care providers are small and many are proprietary, their interests are different from those of the traditional hospital employers. Upward mobility of employees is limited, and providing up-front tuition funding is difficult, as these benefits are rarely offered in the industry.

HCC understands that it must adapt to the changing healthcare market and may have to provide alternate opportunities and pathways for new employer participants. Educational institutions can provide stackable credentials for entry-level employees that allow them to be hired by long-term care and home health care agencies. By creatively working with hiring managers at these facilities, institutions can develop education pathways that are appropriate for their organizations and provide skill development and training for employees.

For example, a home health aide could receive training at a Mercy Neighborhood Ministries program and then be hired by a home-aide employer for entry-level duties at a rate of $9 per hour. This employee could continue with nurse's-aide training from Great Oaks, Cincinnati State, or Gateway Community College and then be promoted to a home health nursing assistant position at $11 per hour. This credit could then be applied to a practical nursing program at Cincinnati State. Those who earn the LPN credential could move into a position paying $21 per hour. All of this could happen with no investment from the employer, with education expenses instead covered through federal financial aid. Employers would, however, need to be flexible with scheduling to allow employees to take classes.

Achieving a strong return on employers' investment is very important, and the collaborative is working to document that. Such studies validate the importance of investing in frontline workers as vigorously as employers have traditionally supported their professional staff. Since this population has a history of rapid turnover and performance issues, there needs to be consistent support, evaluation, and monitoring of the investment to decrease costs related to training and turnover and increase the quality of service.

HCC leadership has found that having staff for the collaborative is extremely important to assure continuity and accountability. Its leadership is composed of busy people with other responsibilities. The work of the collaborative could easily be set aside if there was no one to direct the day-to-day activities. The group has an executive director, who began working part-time in 2008 and became full-time in 2013. Also, to move forward and continue to significantly benefit the region, recruiting organizational decision makers is critical. Although HCC currently has individuals in leadership capacities, executive leadership is limited. To remove institutional barriers, inclusion of these decision makers is crucial. Efforts are underway to recruit more executive leaders to the HCC executive board.

Appendix

Partners' Roles

Each HCC partner has unique roles that have evolved over time. The next table highlights some key responsibilities for each of the partner types.

Table 2: Partners' Roles

Healthcare Employers	Education Partners
• Focus on employment outcomes • Chair the executive team • Participate in the development and funding of a training facility • Identify training and hiring needs • Offer tuition advancement, including covering developmental education • Provide job coach to support employees • Recruit students/employees • Provide preceptors and clinical experiences for students • Provide educators and guest speakers • Assist with marketing plan and design sustainability plan • Make accommodations to help the students achieve success	• Pre-enrollment assessment • Contextualized remediation for academic preparation • Provide specialized pathway advisors • Innovative pathway curriculum development, including core curriculum • Financial support for classrooms and staffing • Stackable credentials
Community-Based Partners	Workforce Investment Board
• Support entry-level pathway assessment and preparation, including use of the WorkKeys® assessments leading to the National Career Readiness Certificate, as well as the assessments for fit and soft skills • Support students in pathway programs, mitigating financial and other social-service challenges to support student success • Offer access to public benefits and work supports through the Benefit Bank • Identify entry-level employment needs along with employer providers	• The Southwest Ohio Regional Workforce Investment Board has provided leadership and tuition support for pathway students. More than $1 million in WIA training funds has supported unemployed job seekers entering the career pathway over the past five years. • In 2012 HCC classrooms, offices, and computer assessment labs were relocated to the Super Jobs One Stop Center. Great Oaks co-located its Health Professions Pathways programs, and Cincinnati State implemented a Pathway to Employment Center, partially funded with Department of Labor grant funds to support a new comprehensive pathway for students from preliminary assessment and career exploration through credential attainment and employment.

Table 3: Major HCC Investments since 2004

Private Grant Support	U.S. Department of Labor— Cincinnati State Lead College
• KnowledgeWorks Foundation: Funding used for formation • United Way: Funding unemployed workers for entry-level health credential • Partners for a Competitive Workforce—National Fund for Workforce Solutions: Funding for administrative support	• Community-Based Job Training Grant: Capacity building, student support—$1.5 million • Employment and Training Administration ARRA Grant: Expansion of partner initiatives—$4.9 million • Trade Adjustment Administration Community College Career Training Grant: Funded national expansion of health-career pathways, community-based partnerships—$19.6 million

Author's Note

In preparing this chapter, the author acknowledges the assistance of HCC executive director Sharron DiMario and Ross Meyer, vice president of community impact, United Way of Greater Cincinnati.

Notes

1. Mark Schneider and Lu Michelle Yin, "Completion Matters: The High Cost of Low Community College Graduation Rates," Education Outlook, no. 2, April 2012, American Enterprise Institute for Public Policy Research.

9

Emerald Cities Collaborative: Case Study of a High-Road Sector Initiative

Denise G. Fairchild

This chapter presents a case study of Emerald Cities Collaborative (ECC), a national workforce intermediary committed to linking disadvantaged populations to careers in the emerging green-building sector. This case study offers a specific example of the important and complex role workforce intermediaries play in creating high-quality job opportunities for their constituents.

Sector employment strategies generally are recognized for preparing disadvantaged populations for existing middle-skill jobs in vital sectors of the regional economy. However, the changing nature of work toward "low road" pathways demands we pay equal attention to shaping the sectors themselves to produce higher-quality employment opportunities. The fact is that "demand side" factors serve as formidable barriers to quality employment. Some of the structural challenges include industry and employer hiring practices, wage and benefit structures, the absence of occupational ladders, and opportunities for continuing education. Sectors throughout the U.S. economy are undergoing dramatic structural changes that, without concerted efforts to reverse trends, will undermine the employment prospects of disadvantaged workers.

The construction industry is one such sector trending toward diminishing job quality. Over the next decades, substantial numbers of construction jobs are expected to be created, given the major investments in the growing green-building and infrastructure sector. ECC creates job opportunities for low-income populations in this emerging green-building sector and tackles fundamental issues of job quality and job access. This entails transforming both the construction industry and job opportunities and hiring practices within union apprenticeship programs. Through apprenticeships with the building and construction trade unions, ECC connects participants to quality training, decent wages and benefits, and long-term career opportunities. ECC's model, however, goes beyond traditional work-force preparation and placement. The organization uses a collaborative, sector-based strategy to re-engineer both the demand-side and the supply side of the construction (and utility) industry.

This case study is laid out in five sections: ECC'S organizational background and "high road" sector development strategy; labor market analyses of the green-building sector; ECC's operating model and strategy; demonstration project outcomes and lessons learned; and recommendations for transforming existing and emerging economic sectors to adopt high-road policies and practices.

ECC's Organizational Background

Emerald Cities Collaborative is a national 501(c)(3) organization comprising an unprecedented network of business, labor, and community organizations; civil rights and social justice advocates; development intermediaries; and research and technical-assistance providers committed to sustainable development in metropolitan areas across the United States.[1] The collaborative came together in 2009 around an integrated strategy to green our cities, build our communities, and strengthen our democracy.

With the support of nine national foundations,[2] ECC was formally incorporated as a national nonprofit sustainable-development intermediary in 2010. As an intermediary, ECC members leverage their assets to develop both the demand side and the supply side of the emerging sustainability sector, with an initial focus on energy as it relates to the utility and green-building sector. Demand-side (job creation) support services include financing, policy, and project development. Supply-side (workforce) strategies include training and certifications, infrastructure-development assistance, and local-hire planning services. A five-year business plan was developed and a high-road sector demonstration project was launched in ten metropolitan regions: Atlanta, Cleveland, Los Angeles, Milwaukee, New York, Oakland, Portland, Providence, San Francisco, and Seattle. The specific goal and objectives follow.

High-Road Goal

ECC pushes for the rapid, scaled, and deep greening of the nation's cities and metropolitan economies and infrastructure using a high-road strategy. This strategy focuses on "triple-E" outcomes: "environmental" sustainability; "economic" opportunities for family-supporting wages, careers, and business opportunities; and "equity" inclusion of disadvantaged populations in this emerging clean economy.

ECC's mission, therefore, is as much about transactions that produce "green jobs" and reduce carbon emissions as it is about fundamental changes in how the American economy and society works, especially for disadvantaged workers. It seeks to fundamentally change the behavior of the energy industry, the building and construction industry, the education and training systems, as well as ordinary Americans. The ECC brand requires a commitment to a low-fossil-fuel economy, conservation of nonrenewable natural resources, and restructuring of the inequities in America's social and economic relationships and the related policies and practices. Together, these changes are intended to create a market that creates the jobs and a workforce pipeline that works for all.

High-Road Objectives

Clean-energy retrofits of institutional, commercial, and multifamily properties, achieving at minimum 20 percent carbon reduction.

- All targeted building retrofits generating family-supporting jobs and careers.

- At least 20 percent to 30 percent of jobs targeted for disadvantaged populations.

- At least 10 percent of business and contracting opportunities established for small, minority-owned, and women-owned businesses.

- Significant inclusion of communities of color participating in all aspects of the clean-energy economy, including policy, planning, and implementation.

ECC's Green-Building Initiative: Sizing Up the Market

ECC focuses on jobs in the construction industry with a specific focus on the opportunities and challenges in the emerging green-building sector.

Green-Jobs Opportunities

ECC was formed to take advantage of the growing job market involved with rebuilding and greening America's physical infrastructure to bring disadvantaged populations into the economic mainstream. Numerous indicators of growth, as well as challenges, in construction informed ECC's sector strategy. This included infrastructure needs, investments trends, job-creation studies, and policy initiatives.

Specifically, in 2013 the American Society of Civil Engineers (ASCE) Report Card for America's Infrastructure gave it a cumulative grade of D+ across sixteen categories. The infrastructure most in disrepair and at risk of failure included energy, drinking water and wastewater, levees and inland waterways, transit and roads, aviation, and schools.[3] It was estimated that a total of $2.75 trillion of infrastructure investment is needed between 2013 and 2020 to upgrade all infrastructure to achieve a B grade. With $1.66 trillion in funding available, we still face a $1.1 trillion gap.[4]

Despite the magnitude of the problem and the requisite investments, the cost of failing to act and, conversely, the potential return on investments are even greater. A growing infrastructure movement evidences this recognition. In 2013, for example, there were thirty-two state infrastructure banks to finance critical projects (albeit mainly in transportation), up from six in 2007.[5] Since 2007 a series of bipartisan congressional proposals to create a national infrastructure bank have advanced, with varying levels of success, to create jobs and to keep the U.S. economy strong.[6]

Moreover, within construction, the efficiency/renewable energy subsector was particularly defined as the "sweet spot" for immediate job creation.[7] The demand in this emerging sector was huge. ASCE rated the U.S. energy infrastructure D+ and identified $629 billion in expected funding and a $107 billion gap needed for a B upgrade by 2020. Energy-efficient buildings, a modernized power grid, renewable power, and public transportation not only addressed multiple national problems (climate change, energy security, and infrastructure crises) but also were considered labor-intensive job generators. A plethora of studies staked out the job prospects. Apollo Alliance identified 21.5 jobs in energy efficiency per $1 million of investments. U.S. Metro Economies' 2008 study projected 4.2 million U.S. jobs between 2008 and 2038 by increasing renewable use and implementing energy-efficiency measures.[8] Another study projected two million jobs based on spending $100 billion in public funds in a "green recovery program."[9] And in 2008 President Obama anticipated five million jobs based on $150 billion in stimulus funds in clean energy.[10]

A number of factors put the market opportunities in clean energy on a gradual but continuous ascent. First are the diminishing supplies of fossil fuel and the inevitable higher cost of energy that will stretch the shrinking budgets of governments, businesses, and households. Venture capital continues to fuel research and development in alternative-energy technologies. Local and state regulations—such as energy disclosure laws, new building codes, and carbon-reduction targets—and new no-cost installment-type financing mechanisms, such as on-bill and Commercial PACE (Property Assessed Clean Energy) financing, are designed to spur the market to respond to a different energy future. Extreme weather conditions precipitated by climate change and the importance of U.S. energy security also are among the important drivers of a clean-energy economy.

Green-Jobs Challenges

To convert these investment and policy trends into job opportunities for disadvantaged workers, three challenges must be addressed: job creation, job quality, and job access.

Job Creation/Demand Generation

Clean-energy jobs require a clean-energy market. The more demand for energy efficiency and renewable energy, the more work there is to be had. Clean energy, however, is best characterized as an emerging sector in the U.S. economy. Like all emerging sector strategies, therefore, its full potential requires building demand and, in the case of the energy sector, radically transforming it from fossil fuel to alternative energy. The core components of market transformation include (1) policies—carrots and sticks—at the national, state, and local levels to drive demand, (2) affordable and accessible market-based financing for consumers (the market), and (3) a reliable service-delivery system to get products and services to markets.

The fact that the clean-energy sector had none of the aforementioned prerequisites for a vibrant job market put Emerald Cities in the demand-generation business to deliver the green-jobs promise. Despite $80 billion in U.S. stimulus funds in 2009, the job promise in the energy-efficiency sector did not fully materialize. This led many workforce practitioners and funders to abandon the sector. Several factors caused the false start:

1. Concentration on the single-family residential market, a difficult, low-volume market with career-limited job opportunities.

2. Focus on single-measure retrofits, for example, lighting or insulation, versus whole-building, deep retrofits that produce more jobs (and more carbon reduction).

3. The lack of market-based, affordable energy-efficiency financing to sustain the effort past government-stimulus funding.

4. The absence of policies—carrots or sticks—to drive demand for energy-efficient buildings.

5. Real estate and credit crises that made it hard to keep a building, much less retrofit it.

ECC's sector-development strategy, therefore, included advancing policies, financing options, and project-development services to build local energy markets.

Job Quality

Notwithstanding clean energy's rocky start, enough forces are converging to suggest that a clean-energy economy is inevitable. The more critical question is less about the potential size of the labor market or how fast it will happen, and more about the quality and character of the emerging labor market.

Fifty-seven percent of the clean-energy jobs are in the construction field. Energy auditors, solar installers, weatherization technicians, plumbers, insulators, glazers, electricians, and laborers work within the traditional building and construction trades. They become "green jobs" only in that the skills, technology, processes, and materials produce positive environmental outcomes—less energy consumption, reduction in greenhouse-gas emissions, etc. Similarly, most operations jobs in the utility sector are construction related—lineman, operating engineers, etc. Jobs in the green economy, therefore, substantially depend upon "mining" the construction industry.

Construction is a sizeable and relatively enduring sector of the U.S. economy. But not all construction jobs are good jobs. In fact, most are not. The industry is notorious for its low-road conditions: low wages, off-the-books pay, no benefits, seasonal work, difficult and unprotected working conditions, and limited skills training and career advancements. While union construction offers a high-road option, providing family-wage careers and viable working conditions for its members, union labor agreements are increasingly hard-won battles and are especially challenging in right-to-work states.

The construction jobs in the clean-energy sector, therefore, are similarly challenged with respect to the different entry points that produce qualitatively different job outcomes. The first, and most common, is through industry certifications and/or community college career and technical education programs. Skills certificates—including those related to the Building Performance Institute or the Home Energy Rating System—or academic certificates and degrees are important measures of basic competencies in the energy field. They also improve access to entry-level positions. But these certifications and college programs have been challenged by their failure to put people to work or pay family wages or offer long-term career prospects. A prime example of the challenge relates to the $50 million federal investment in weatherizing single-family homes during President Obama's first term. Clearly, it was successful in weatherizing a million homes, with significant impact on energy consumption, carbon emission, and job creation. Yet when the money was gone, so were the jobs. This story mirrored, to a lesser degree, the renewable-energy business, where training preceded market demand. The credibility gap in the green-jobs movement was, in no small measure, due to these careerless jobs programs.

Union construction-training programs help mitigate the challenges inherent in stand-alone training programs. Not only do they offer the benefits of paid on-the-job training and career development, but with a construction trade (as opposed to an energy certification), they position and support training participants (apprentices) for a full range of construction jobs beyond the energy subsector.

Job Access

The pathway into the clean economy and high-quality construction careers is neither clear nor easy, particularly for low-income communities of color. Obtaining a union apprenticeship in the construction trade is an especially formidable undertaking. While the benefits are huge—on-the-job skills training, mentoring, paid learning, and high-wage construction careers—so are the barriers. Chief among these are (1) a legacy of exclusion, (2) the lack of networks into and knowledge about the trades, (3) fragmented and disconnected workforce pipelines, (4) lack of basic academic and job-readiness skills, (5) lack of mentors/support systems, and (6) lack of jobs, especially union jobs.

ECC: The High-Road Solution

ECC operates within this exciting but complex green-building economy by pursuing the transformation of a substantial sector of the economy—construction—from low road to high road by channeling investments in the emerging clean-energy industry to operate differently. ECC assumes nontraditional roles as a workforce-development intermediary, including organizing, project development and financing, policy development, and workforce-systems development.

ECC's Operating Model

The three core elements of ECC's operating model correspond to its triple bottom line: civic infrastructure development, demand generation, and workforce development.

A Strong Civic Infrastructure (Equity)

Broad-based coalitions were organized to build a unified voice and maximum inclusion in the build-out of a clean-energy economy. These coalitions essentially function as market intermediaries in the clean-energy sector. Labor, community, business, and government stakeholders—at the national level and in each region—work collaboratively to advance a high-road clean-energy agenda. This multi-stakeholder structure differs from traditional workforce intermediaries in at least one fundamental way: It is organized for power.

The unique and complementary capacities of the collaborative members include political, financial, social, intellectual, and institutional assets and experiences that are compelling enough to (1) influence national and local policy and decision makers, (2) deliver financing options to the market, (3) identify and implement project opportunities, and (4) prepare residents with diverse needs and capacities for the emerging opportunities. The assets of national collaborative members, for example, include one million energy-inefficient affordable and public housing units; $10 billion in pension funds committed to high-road infrastructure projects; 1,500 construction training facilities funded by $1 billion in annual private-sector revenues; an extensive community-based training network and pre-apprenticeship curricula; a portable national certification program developed and approved by fifteen construction trades; high-level legislative, legal, and research capacities; and broad-based access to people and institutions.

Local collaboratives bring similar assets to this sector-development work. Perhaps their most important value, however, has been the mission-driven, "honest broker" role that they bring into the local marketplace. These local multi-stakeholder coalitions are able to open doors and make deals happen. No matter where the market opportunities exist—with city hall, school boards, commercial property owners—when labor, community, and business speak with one voice, there is greater access, interest in listening, and participation in the vision.

ECC's core task is to knit together these assets to produce outcomes that green our cities, build our communities, and promote equity. A variety of capacity-building tools are used to facilitate the effective functioning of these market intermediaries:

- Project-based high-road development training programs to build local political and social capital for clean energy.

- Planning grants to build a collaborative strategy and work programs.

- Operating grants to pay for local staff to keep the collaborative process authentic and well-functioning.

- Technical-assistance grants to "move the market," providing the technical know-how to identify, finance, and implement clean-energy projects.

Demand Generation (Environment)

This component focuses on building the clean-energy market through project development, new financing structures, and policy development. ECC's development role is extraordinary for a workforce intermediary but not entirely unique. It combines the tradition of a small number of others that push for workforce policies with those that provide job-producing services that also earn revenue that sustain the core workforce mission.

Specifically, ECC is directly engaged in **project development** to move the market and to demonstrate the value of high-road projects. The focus is on large-scale projects that can produce the greatest impact on carbon reduction and job creation. ECC's sweet spot has been its partnership with anchor institutions that share its mission, such as local government, K–12 schools, community colleges, hospitals, and affordable and public housing owners. ECC facilitates technical assistance to get the projects done, including structuring financing, project planning, and energy audits, along with workforce monitoring and compliance services. For these development services, ECC receives a "developers/origination/management fee" that is paid out of the project budget.

Finally, market demand is stimulated using **policy levers**. ECC collaborates with national and local partners to stimulate energy efficiency in the commercial market. This includes improved building codes, local disclosure ordinances, and point-of-sale transactions that require sellers to identify for buyers the energy-consumption rates of their buildings. Over time, real estate value will be influenced by energy uses.

In addition to influencing the commercial market, ECC affiliates advocate for Community Benefit Agreements—citywide commitments to local hiring and procurement—to channel public investments into high-road projects. A broad-based coalition in Portland, Oregon, for example, won a citywide community benefit agreement for all public-works investments. The immediate result was a $100 million sewer/wastewater treatment project that will not only produce high-wage job opportunities but also guarantee that 20 percent of apprenticeship slots go to disadvantaged individuals. Moreover, 1 percent to 1.5 percent of this public investment is set aside for workforce-development support services for these target communities.

Workforce Development (High-Road Economy)

The promotion of high-road jobs and business opportunities with standards and procedures for job quality and access is realized through four sets of tools: project labor agreements; community workforce agreements; pre-apprenticeship and registered apprenticeship training, and an integrated workforce system.

1. Project Labor Agreements. These are the single most important tool to ensure job quality in construction and on clean-energy projects. Collaborative members advocate for and otherwise propose "full value" as opposed to "low cost" public investments on all infrastructure projects. These agreements specify wage standards, journey-apprenticeship ratios, performance guarantees, and other important factors to ensure not only high-quality workmanship but also a quality work experience.

2. Community Workforce Agreements (CWAs). These are legally binding documents (as opposed to best efforts) used to specify local hire and
contracting commitments for ECC's high-road projects. The CWAs are
integrated into the Project Labor Agreements. This ensures that joint
labor-community advocacy efforts for union contracting produce mutually beneficial work opportunities.

3. The Multi-Craft Core Curriculum (MC3). This is a national pre-apprenticeship certification program approved by the AFL-CIO's Building and
Trades Construction Department that is used to create a pathway for
community residents into the union apprenticeship programs. Community-based training organizations that have developed a working relationship with their local building-trades council are trained on the use of the
curriculum. The curriculum exposes participants to the various trades, the
history and unique set of norms of the construction trade unions, as well
as the challenges particularly related to race and gender.

MC3 is the centerpiece of ECC's programmatic efforts to break down the silos that left a legacy of exclusion, mutual misunderstanding, and mistrust. The
Building and Construction Trades Department requires that the curriculum be
delivered by community-based training organizations in partnership with their local building-trades councils. This mandate engages building trades in the education, training, and mentoring of ECC's target populations. The national building
trades standing committee on apprenticeship has recommended that local joint
apprenticeship committees give weight to completion of the Core Curriculum by
providing expedited consideration for applicants to apprenticeship programs and,
where appropriate, as in our Providence, Rhode Island program, direct entry and
advanced credit to students who successfully complete the 120-hour curriculum.

4. Integrated Workforce System. Building a "system of access" into these apprenticeship programs holds great promise for rebuilding the middle class,
preserving the skilled-crafts profession, forming a new generation of construction workers from demographically diverse communities, and building specialized knowledge and skills in the emerging green-construction
industry. These outcomes, however, require ECC's high-road brand and
comprehensive sector-development strategy. This is achieved by building
a workforce collaborative in each site that assembles the essential elements
of a stellar workforce program: (1) intake and assessment, (2) soft skills
and basic skills training, (3) effective technical pre-apprenticeship training, (4) bridge programs into and after apprenticeship placement, and (5)
case management and support services.

ECC: What Has It Accomplished?

This section outlines ECC's accomplishments within the start-up phase of its business model. The first three years saw ECC launch and test its innovative program model, to good outcomes. ECC's local coalitions are realizing success harnessing investments, developing high-road projects, and placing their constituents into registered apprenticeships and jobs. The early outcomes include the following.

Equity: Civic Engagement around High-Road Commitments

- Signed threshold agreements in nine out of ten markets, representing major buy-in for high-road clean-energy projects from mayors and local elected officials, labor, business, and community.
- A national multi-stakeholder collaborative.
- Nine local coalitions with paid staff and functioning committees.
- Providing forty hours of training on a quarterly basis to sustain and build local capacity in clean energy.

Environment: Demand for High-Road Clean-Energy Projects

Signed project-level agreements/resolutions with building owners representing approximately $250 million in high-road clean-energy projects in development and $200 million of potential projects, including:

- Two community college systems, representing thirteen campuses.
- Three county government resolutions and high-road partnership agreements, including Cleveland/Cuyahoga County, Los Angeles, and Milwaukee.
- One city government retrofit project, in Providence.
- Twenty-five hundred affordable-housing units.
- Commercial-project workforce partnerships in Atlanta and Seattle, representing fifty million square feet of project opportunities.
- Energy-efficiency pilot project with the California Public Utilities Commission, which demonstrates the economic outcomes of high-road energy-efficiency investments.
- Community-benefit agreements with community workforce standards in Portland, Oregon, and Atlanta. Portland's high-road agreement also garnered commitment to allocate between 1 percent and 1.5 percent of each project (e.g., a $100 million water-treatment facility) to support workforce-development services.

Economy: Jobs and Business Development

- Strengthened the jobs pipeline of disadvantaged workers into construction apprenticeship programs through the implementation of the Building and Construction Trades Department training program for community-based training providers.

- Trained fifty community-based training providers in the use of the Building and Construction Trades Department's MC3 curriculum.

- Successfully negotiated community workforce agreements on two projects currently in construction: Seattle Steam Project (downtown commercial) and Mission Housing project in San Francisco.

- Established a Minority Contractors Green Building Training Program in partnership with Citi Community Development Corp.

ECC: What Have We Learned?

Much can be said about the state of the clean-energy economy and the construction industry and what it takes to link disadvantaged communities to these particular sectors. The focus of the lessons offered here, however, is on general recommendations that can be applied to workforce intermediaries across other sectors of the economy. *Table 1* identifies the lessons learned and offers suggestions for expanding an advocacy-based sector-development program for traditional workforce-development intermediaries.

The twenty-first-century challenges of workforce intermediaries directly mirror those found within the larger economy. We are witnessing the rapid growth of new industries, technologies, and skill requirements and the simultaneous trending-down of job quality and working conditions within both new and pre-existing markets. Only two responses are possible: acquiesce or engage. The welfare of our constituents depends on the latter pathway. We need to harness the trends in the new economy and ensure that they take the high road with family wages, benefits, career options, and working conditions.

This is not laissez-faire work. It means aggressively working the demand and labor supply of our target markets. If we become job creators, we are in the strongest position to define the terms and conditions of work. We can shape the hiring practices, salaries, and working conditions. This requires taking on nontraditional roles beyond workforce preparation and placement—through organizing, legislative advocacy, project development, financing, and technical assistance.

The question, of course, is how to do this when constrained by traditional sources of revenue and capacity. Transforming and building labor markets requires expanded roles and staffing capacity for workforce intermediaries. Keys to success include (1) an active and committed coalition of labor, community, business, and government to undertake and invest in high-road policies and programs; (2) a flexible network of resource consultants committed to the workforce mission; (3) a revenue model grounded in market-based services; and (4) the use of high-road tools—registered apprenticeships, responsible contracting policies, and community-benefit agreements.

Of course, the most important element is an organizational commitment to changing not just the capacity of our constituents to work but the larger structural conditions within the labor market to make work pay. For ECC, attracting today's generation into construction jobs means reshaping the industry so that it pays well, is safer, and provides better job security and supports. And in more dramatic terms, stemming global climate change demands a concerted effort to attract a large number of these new workers to replace our aging construction workforce. Accordingly, the demand-side advocacy and negotiations are critical parts of the workforce intermediaries' job in forging opportunities for disadvantaged populations.

Table 1: ECC Lessons Learned and Recommendations

Subject Area	Lessons Learned/Issues	Recommendations
Transforming Markets	The public messaging and programming for the adoption of high-road policies and practices—family wages, careers, and benefits—are largely absent. America is failing in its commitment to rebuild the middle class.	Workforce intermediaries need to support—directly or indirectly—organizing and advocacy efforts for high-road jobs.
	Changing the status quo requires a power base, broad-based buy-in, and a large and compelling vision of change (as opposed to a narrow focus on jobs).	Establish broad-based coalitions to provide the social, political, and intellectual capital needed for long-term market transformation.
	Policy development is vital to market development and market transformation.	

Subject Area	Leesons Learned/Issues	Recommendations
Building Demand	Investment in emerging sectors places workforce intermediaries in a value-added role as market leaders. It offers unique opportunities to shape the labor market to fit the needs of constituents.	Workforce intermediaries should develop expertise, as well as products and services, to not just access existing market opportunities but proactively grow them.
	Independent nonprofit, mission-driven, market-based intermediaries of multiple stakeholders serve as honest brokers of high-road projects for like-minded mission-oriented customers.	
	Doing it all—policy, financing, and project development—is neither possible nor necessary.	Broaden capacities to include a network of subject-matter experts (paid or volunteer) with specific knowledge and services: vendors, consultants, financial specialists.
	Nontraditional sources of revenue can be realized when market-based services are provided to industry.	Find a value-added role in your target sector to produce revenue to support these broader workforce strategies.

Subject Area	Lessons Learned/Issues	Recommendations
Workforce Development	Tools that promote labor and community standards (e.g., family wages, local hire and procurement requirements) provide the best return on workforce investments. Collective-bargaining agreements and community workforce agreements are being contested on legal grounds, especially in right-to-work states.	Connect with registered apprenticeship programs as first-order priority. Encourage public-purpose decision makers to pursue high-value vs. low-cost economic-development strategies. Participate in labor-community partnerships to protect the rights of workers.
	Large contractors will more readily embrace local hire, procurement, and wage standards if they are included in the projects' specifications.	Actively engage the employer community in high-road structures.
	Small, minority- and women-owned contractors require capacity building and working capital to meet higher wage standards, equipment and leases to be competitive in the high-road building retrofit market.	

Notes

1. ECC members include AFL-CIO, Alliance for an Energy Efficient Economy, Bronze Investments, Building and Construction Trades Department, Building Owners and Managers Association, Center on Wisconsin Strategy, Corps Network, Council of Large Public Housing Authorities, Enterprise Community Partners, Green for All, IBEW, Institute for Market Transformation, LIUNA, Local Initiatives Support Corporation, MIT Co-Lab, National Association of Energy Services Companies, National Association of Minority Contractors, NeighborWorks, Partnership for Working Families, PolicyLink, United Association of Plumbers and Pipefitters, UPAT, U.S. Green Building Council, and YouthBuild.

2. ECC's inaugural funders were the Annie E. Casey Foundation, Atlantic Philanthropies, the Joyce Foundation, the Kendeda Fund, the Kresge Foundation, Living Cities, the Rockefeller Foundation, The Nathan Cummings Foundation, and the Surdna Foundation.

3. ASCE, 2013 Infrastructure Report Card, http://www.infrastructurereportcard.org.

4. ASCE, "Failure to Act: The Impact of Current Infrastructure Investment on America's Economic Future," January 2013, http://www.asce.org/failuretoact.

5. Council of State Governments, Capitol Research.

6. Deutsche Bank Group, "Economic Stimulus: The Case for 'Green' Infrastructure, Energy Security and 'Green' Jobs," November 2008; Abby Phillip, "'Infrastructure Bank' Gains Steam," Politico 44, March 15, 2011, http://www.politico.com/politico44/perm/0311/banking_on_bank_b47de358-f285-4cf2-ad8b-25ed5da4493b.html.

7. Ibid.

8. United States Conference of Mayors, "U.S. Metro Economies: Current and Potential Green Jobs in the U.S. Economy," October 2008.

9. Robert Pollin, Heidi Garrett-Peltier, James Heintz, and Helen Scherber, "Green Recovery: A Program to Create Good Jobs & Start Building a Low-Carbon Economy," Political Economy Research Institute, 2008.

10. Barack Obama, Energy and Economic Policies, 2008, http://energy.gov/sites/prod/files/edg/media/Obama_New_Energy_0804.pdf.

10

Restaurant Opportunities Centers United: Serving the Service Sector

Saru Jayaraman

The Restaurant Opportunities Centers United (ROC) is the only national restaurant-sector partnership helping low-wage workers advance to livable-wage jobs in the industry. Founded after 9/11 by World Trade Center survivors, ROC has grown into a national restaurant sector initiative with thirteen thousand restaurant worker members and one hundred employer partners in thirty-two cities nationwide. ROC has trained more than five thousand low-wage workers to advance to livable-wage jobs in the industry; opened two worker-owned restaurants, called COLORS; promoted ROC's one hundred employer partners to conscientious consumers; published approximately twenty reports based on more than five thousand surveys of restaurant workers nationwide; and more.

The ROC experience provides significant lessons about the possibilities of intervening in large and growing low-wage sectors and of combining efforts that move workers to livable-wage jobs while simultaneously advancing job quality for all workers in a sector. In this way, this chapter describes a gap in the current workforce-development system that overlooks the persistent low-wage work sectors, which, as described in Chapter 2, typify the reality of the present labor market. In particular, the chapter illustrates the ways in which ROC has tackled both career-ladder and job-quality issues in one of the fastest-growing sectors of the economy, the restaurant sector.

The Restaurant Industry: Not Living Up to Its Potential

More than 50 percent of Americans eat out at a restaurant at least once per week, and 20 percent eat out two or more times per week[1], supporting the restaurant industry's continued growth in the midst of the recent economic crises.[2] In fact, *the restaurant industry is one of America's two largest private-sector employers, with more than ten million employees nationwide.[3] Census data show that in regions across America, the restaurant industry and service sector clearly represent an increasingly important aspect of the economy. These jobs are rapidly replacing declining manufacturing jobs and potentially providing livable-wage jobs and career ladders.* The National Restaurant Association's 2012 industry forecast projected that total industry sales would reach a record high of $635 billion, a 3.5 percent increase over 2011, and that one in ten American workers would work in the industry.[4]

Unfortunately, despite its growth and potential, the restaurant industry provides largely poverty-wage jobs with little access to benefits, pervasive noncompliance with employment laws, and little or no opportunities for career advancement. In 2010, seven of the ten lowest-paid occupations were all restaurant occupations (see *Table 1*).[5] The median hourly wage for restaurant workers in 2010 was $9.02,[6] meaning that over half of these workers earned less than the wage of $10.75 that a family of four needs to remain out of poverty.[7]

Indeed, people who earn the minimum wage or less are highly concentrated in the restaurant industry. Thirty-nine percent of all workers making minimum wage or less are in the restaurant industry. Of all workers earning below the minimum wage, almost half (49 percent) are restaurant workers.[9] *A major cause of low wages in the industry is the fact that the minimum wage for workers who earn tips has remained stuck at $2.13 per hour for the last twenty-one years, thanks to the influence of the National Restaurant Association.*

Table 1: OES, National Cross-Industry Estimates: Ten Lowest-Paid Occupations, 2010

Occupational Code	Occupational Title	Hourly Median Wage ($)
35-3021	Combined Food Preparation and Serving Workers, Including Fast Food	8.63
35-2011	Cooks, Fast Food	8.70
39-3011	Gaming Dealers	8.70
35-9021	Dishwashers	8.73
35-9011	Dining Room and Cafeteria Attendants and Bartender Helpers	8.75

39-5093	Shampooers	8.78
35-3031	Waiters and Waitresses	8.81
35-3022	Counter Attendants, Cafeteria, Food Concession, and Coffee Shop	8.83
35-9031	Hosts and Hostesses, Restaurant, Lounge, and Coffee Shop	8.87
39-3091	Amusement and Recreation Attendants	8.87

Source: Restaurant Opportunities Centers United, *Serving While Sick: High Risks and Low Benefits for the Nation's Restaurant Workforce, and Their Impact on the Consumer*, 2010.

Low wages tell only part of the story; workers also lack access to benefits and face pervasive noncompliance with employment regulations. Ninety percent of restaurant workers surveyed nationwide by ROC reported not having access to paid sick days. Similarly, 90 percent reported no health benefits through their employer. Under such conditions, it is not surprising that two-thirds of workers surveyed (66.6 percent) reported cooking, preparing, and/or serving food while sick.[9] Workers also reported a pervasive noncompliance with employment regulations, including nonpayment of wages and misappropriation of tips.

Extensive research conducted by ROC on the industry has demonstrated that, unbeknownst to many, there are some livable-wage jobs in the industry. *Waiters in fine-dining restaurants can earn between $50,000 and $100,000 annually. In fact, we estimate that about 20 percent of jobs in the industry pay livable wages. Unfortunately, immigrants, workers of color, and women often are not able to access these livable-wage jobs because of discrimination, lack of training, and lack of social networks to assist advancement.* Through several matched-pair audit-testing studies described in further detail below, ROC found that white workers had twice the chance of a person of color obtaining a livable-wage job in the industry, and that workers of color are concentrated in the industry's lowest-paid jobs. Workers also reported discriminatory hiring, promotion, and disciplinary practices.[10]

The segregation of women in lower-paid fine-dining occupations was borne out in research conducted in New York City, where ROC canvassed forty-five Manhattan fine-dining restaurants in 2007. As shown in *Figure 1*, the results were consistent with our findings that women are underrepresented in the highest-paid positions, such as bartenders, managers, maître d's, sommeliers, and captains. Men held 67 percent of observed highest-paying front-of-the-house positions, while women held only 32 percent. Men held 79 percent of observed front-of-the-house management positions, while women held only 21 percent.[11]

Figure 1: Gender in Front-of-House Restaurants

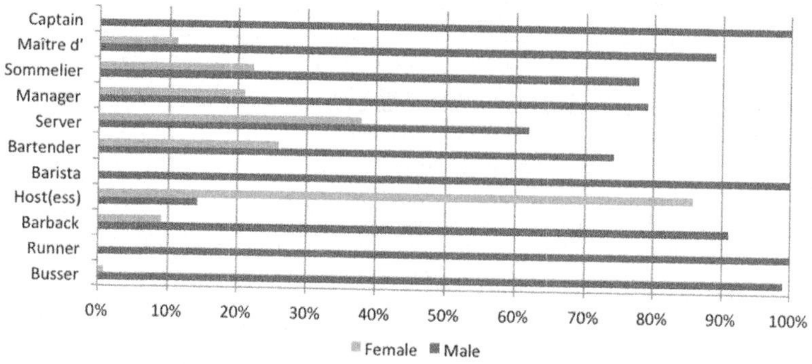

Captain
Maître d'
Sommelier
Manager
Server
Bartender
Barista
Host(ess)
Barback
Runner
Busser

0%   10%   20%   30%   40%   50%   60%   70%   80%   90%   100%

■ Female ■ Male

Source: Canvassing of Manhattan fine-dining establishments. Restaurant Opportunities Centers, *Tipped Over the Edge*, 2012

This observation of forty-five Manhattan dining rooms further suggests that the more elite the establishment, the fewer women occupy the highest-paying front-of-the-house positions. American Community Survey data from 2005 to 2009 confirm this observation. During this period, only about 10 percent of front-of-the-house workers in Manhattan restaurants were paid $40,500 or more. However, the front-of- the-house workers earning more than $40,500 per year were more than twice as likely to be male.[12]

Occupational segregation by race resulted in a $3.53 wage gap between white restaurant workers and workers of color in the eight regions, with the median hourly wage of all white workers surveyed in the eight localities being $13.07 and that of workers of color being $9.54.[13] The gap between white and black workers in particular exceeded $4, with black workers earning a median hourly wage of $9. Immigrants and workers of color in the restaurant industry suffer from poverty wages, lack of benefits, and—ironically as food-service workers—lack of access to affordable and healthy food to support their families.

Figure 2: Median Wage by Race

Source: Restaurant Opportunities Centers United, *Blacks In the Restaurant Industry*, 2012.

The root cause of this pay gap is racial segregation by segment and position. Wages vary greatly between the three broad segments of the industry: quick serve, family style, and fine dining. They also vary within restaurants between positions in the back of the house and those in the front of the house, as well as between top-tier positions, such as servers and bartenders, and lower-tier positions, such as bussers, runners, and barbacks. Whites disproportionately work in the highest-paid positions in the highest-paid segments, while blacks disproportionately work in low-wage positions and in low-wage segments. *Figure 3* shows the results of extensive survey research that found that 58 percent of black restaurant workers are employed in the lowest-paid segment, quick serve, while only 26.6 percent of white restaurant workers work in quick serve.[14]

Figure 3: Segment Distribution by Race

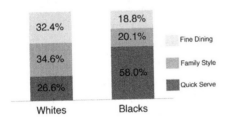

Source: Restaurant Opportunities Centers United, *Blacks In the Restaurant Industry*, 2012.

Survey research also found that the highest-paid positions, fine-dining servers and bartenders, were disproportionately held by white workers. Fine-dining bartenders were more than three times more likely to be white than black, and fine-dining servers were almost four times more likely to be white.[15] Moreover, canvassing forty-five randomly chosen fine-dining restaurants in Manhattan found that the highest-paid positions were held almost exclusively by white workers, while the lowest-paid positions were held almost exclusively by people of color (see *Figure 4*).[16]

Our research shows that, due to lack of mobility, while many workers stay in the industry throughout their lifetimes, they move from establishment to establishment seeking better wages and working conditions. It is for this reason that ROC constructed a comprehensive workforce-development model that includes training and placement, employer engagement, and higher-education opportunities for these low-wage workers, creating career ladders in an industry where such ladders formerly have been obscured. This model is uniquely housed within an organization that is simultaneously working to lift standards for workers industrywide.

Figure 4: Fine Dining Segregation by Position

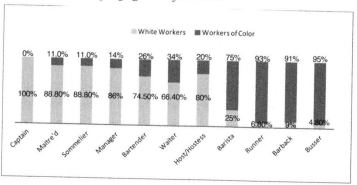

Source: Restaurant Opportunities Center of New York, The Great Service Divide, 2009.

Over the past decade, ROC has created clear career ladders for these marginalized groups. While there are other localized workforce-development programs that offer workers entry into the restaurant industry, most programs focus solely on gaining entry-level employment. To fully realize the potential of the industry and adequately address the reality that many workers will stay in the industry throughout their careers, ROC offers the only free and easily-accessible national workforce-development program designed to give restaurant workers concrete steps to advance to livable-wage positions in the industry.

ROC'ing the Industry

Initially founded after September 11, 2001, to provide support to restaurant workers displaced as a result of the World Trade Center tragedy, ROC has grown into a national restaurant workers' organization with close to thirteen thousand members in thirty-two cities across nineteen states. Members include low-income restaurant workers, most of whom are people of color and many of whom are immigrants. ROC has fully staffed affiliates in New York City, Boston, Chicago, Detroit, New Orleans, Philadelphia, Houston, Los Angeles, Washington, D.C., Miami, Seattle and the San Francisco Bay area. Within each of these localities, ROC affiliates build memberships comprising local-area restaurant workers.

Understanding the size of the industry and the depth of challenges workers face, ROC created a three-pronged model to improve worker conditions and increase opportunities for advancement for low-wage workers. The three prongs are (1) providing legal support to workers facing exploitation and creating consequences for employers who take the "low road" to profitability; (2) promoting the "high road" to profitability through extensive employer partnerships, workforce development, and cooperative restaurant development that encourages entrepreneurship; and (3) conducting industry research and worker-led policy work to lift conditions industrywide. This model is unique in that it engages and addresses the needs of all three industry stakeholders: workers, employers, and consumers. It also is effective because it helps workers advance along a career path while simultaneously working to improve wages and working conditions—addressing job quality and equity—industrywide. This chapter focuses on the second and third prongs of ROC's model, since they are most relevant to the traditional sectoral model of "building the ladder" and "raising the floor."

Using this three-pronged model, ROC has accomplished much, including the following:

- Opening two worker-owned restaurants, COLORS, and in them creating the COLORS Hospitality Opportunities for Workers (CHOW) Institute. Through CHOW, ROC has trained more than five thousand low-wage workers to advance to livable-wage jobs in the industry.

- Winning fifteen workplace-justice campaigns against large, high-profile corporations, totaling more than $8 million in stolen tips and wages and discrimination payments.

- Publishing more than two dozen reports on the industry in partnership with academics around the country, based on more than five thousand surveys of restaurant workers, three hundred employer interviews, and three hundred worker interviews.

- Organizing an alternative national restuarant association called RAISE (Restaurants Advancing Industry Standards in Employment) comprised of 100 responsible employers around the nation to promote the high road to profitability and provide an alternative voice to the National Restaurant Association (NRA), the powerful lobby for employers that has tried to stifle nearly all policy changes that would improve conditions for restaurant workers.

- Playing a leading role in educating decision makers about the need to raise the minimum wage for tipped workers in New York State and educating city council members about the need for a tip-protection policy in Philadelphia.

- Waging a policy campaign to educate decision makers about the need to raise the federal minimum wage for tipped workers, currently $2.13. The 2012 minimum-wage bill introduced in Congress represented the first time in twenty years that congressional leadership introduced a bill with a significant increase for tipped workers.

- Launching a consumer-education campaign that includes an annual Diner's Guide, a bestselling book, *Behind the Kitchen Door*, short films, a full-length feature film, and interactive social media tools to educate and engage consumers to support this work.

Promoting the High Road to Restaurant Profitability

Organizing Those Who Take the High Road

For the last decade, ROC has organized responsible restaurant owners into an alternative national restuarant association, both to guide the CHOW Institute and hire graduates and to work with ROC to promote the high road to profitability in the industry. ROC currently has about one hundred employer partners, ranging from celebrity chefs to owners of very small restaurants. These employers have testified with us in local and state legislatures and in Congress about the need to improve employment standards and the benefits derived from doing so. In each local ROC affiliate, organizers continue deepening relationships with restaurant-owner partners, training them on their legal obligations and providing support and technical assistance as necessary to help them operate more responsible, ethical workplaces.

Not surprisingly, the industry suffers from particularly high rates of employee turnover. As mentioned earlier, our research shows that, due to lack of mobility, many workers move from establishment to establishment seeking better wages and working conditions and opportunities for advancement. At the same time, high-road employers—restaurant owners who are committed to paying their workers a living wage, providing comprehensive benefits, and advancing workers equitably regardless of race and gender—complain about the lack of trained and experienced candidates. *With funding from the Ford and Rockefeller foundations, ROC partnered with Cornell University to complete a two-part study that both qualitatively and quantitatively examined the relationship between a restaurant's employment practices and its profitability. The study involved 1,100 phone survey interviews with employers nationwide. These surveys determined the relationship between employers' practices (wages, benefits, business policies, etc.) and employee turnover and productivity, and the real cost of turnover for restaurant operators. We found that an employer can cut her turnover almost in half through "high road" employment practices. ROC is working with "high road" restaurant employer partners to conduct educational seminars and other events for restuarant employers nationwide, to help them see the benefits of sustainable working conditions. In these ways, ROC is directly engaging employers to improve job quality industrywide.*

Creating New Career Ladders in the High Road

Understanding that the difference in earnings between the front and back of the house can mean the difference between poverty and sustainability for an immigrant family, ROC set out to develop formalized career ladders in this informal industry and to help immigrants and workers of color advance along these ladders. ROC first organized forty immigrant workers to open their own worker-owned restaurant, COLORS, in 2006. ROC then developed COLORS to serve as a venue in which workers could obtain hands-on restaurant training and experience in a guided environment. ROC now has opened a second COLORS restaurant in Detroit and is opening additional restaurants in Washington, D.C., and New Orleans.

At COLORS and in partner restaurants around the country, ROC provides much-needed customer service, culinary, and front-of-house advanced training through the COLORS CHOW Institute, placing workers in high-end, living-wage jobs. COLORS and CHOW provide thousands of workers in the industry the opportunity to obtain a standardized certificate in advanced restaurant skills that is increasingly recognized by employers across the country as the sign of a highly trained candidate.

ROC's workforce-development model provides low-wage workers with restaurant-specific English skills and customer service, wine, and serving skills in order to obtain living-wage jobs in the industry. Each of ROC's twelve fully-staffed local affiliates runs multiple eight-week training sessions and then works with graduates to further strengthen their soft skills and prospects for job placement. Through relationships with responsible employers and by providing workers with comprehensive training and confidence building, ROC has been able to help bussers and runners obtain positions as waiters in fine-dining restaurants, where they can earn living wages, sometimes earning up to $50,000 to $100,000 per year. ROC also has helped fast-food workers obtain their first fine-dining front-of-house positions. As tracked in its national database, ROC has trained more than five thousand workers nationwide over the last several years, placing 75 percent in living-wage jobs or helping workers advance to higher-paid positions. ROC also has worked to track the six- and twelve-month retention rates of these workers and provide ongoing support as needed. Workers who participate in the CHOW Institute and/or become worker-owners in COLORS restaurants in New York and Detroit have experienced wage increases between 100 percent and 300 percent.

Thanks to the Ford Foundation, over the last year ROC was able to develop a formal partnership with Kingsborough Community College (KCC) in New York City to provide participants with college credit for their CHOW training. This program has been replicated in Detroit, so that CHOW graduates also receive articulated credit at Macomb Community College and Henry Ford Community College, and is being replicated in Miami, Philadelphia, and Los Angeles as well. ROC has worked with Professor Jonathan Deutsch of Drexel University to formalize ROC's nationally standardized curriculum and gain its endorsement by employers and industry professionals to increase its credibility and cachet within the industry. ROC also is finalizing a new nationally standardized job placement and tracking software system to ensure uniformity across ROC sites and increase success rates and documentation.

One of the unique aspects of ROC's training programs is that they are worker-led. ROC hires the most experienced restaurant-worker members and trains them to use the national CHOW curriculum. As part of every fine-dining server or bartender class, ROC integrates political education, teaching workers about their rights on the job, policies that impact them, such as immigration, minimum wage, and health care, and the state of the restaurant industry.

CHOW intentionally addresses occupational segregation by race. Having conducted the research to understand that the wage gap arises from both segregation by position and segregation by segment, ROC seeks out and trains not only those workers who have not been able to advance in a fine-dining restaurant, say, from a busser to a waiter, but also those who have not been able to approach fine-dining restaurants at all. This includes everyone from youth working in fast-food restaurants to formerly incarcerated adults. ROC has been able to help all these different types of individuals obtain livable-wage jobs in fine-dining restaurants.

CHOW's central challenge is its capacity to grow. It is housed in COLORS restaurants and in employer partners' restaurants in cities without a COLORS. In those latter cities, the training program's ability to serve more workers is limited by the amount of time for which these restaurants are able to provide their space. While the demand from workers is overwhelming—a posting for a CHOW class on craigslist can generate three hundred responses in an eight-hour period—CHOW simply is not able to meet that demand, given its staff capacity and the time and space available for training.

Even with limited capacity, however, CHOW has produced outstanding results for ROC, including the fact that it is the most popular recruitment tool for new workers that exists. It is also a wonderful leadership-building tool, since graduates and member instructors go on to lead ROC's policy campaigns and even serve on its board of directors in various localities and at the national level.

One example of this outstanding development is Sekou Luke. Sekou was the only African American male server in the Fireman Hospitality Group, the company that owned all of the restaurants surrounding Lincoln Center and Carnegie Hall in midtown Manhattan. Sekou joined a campaign led by ROC against discrimination and tip misappropriation at the restaurant company and ended up leading the campaign to a victory that included a $4 million settlement and a new promotions policy to promote workers of color and women. Sekou became more involved with ROC in New York and ended up becoming an instructor at CHOW and even drafted portions of the CHOW curriculum. He trained literally hundreds of low-wage workers of color to advance to server positions and also educated them on their rights and ways in which they could become more engaged in ROC. Sekou himself ended up serving on both the local and national board of directors and was ultimately hired by KCC as a lecturer to teach their Dining Room Management course. Sekou is one of the many people who helped to create CHOW and mold it into the effective program it is today.

Addressing Job Quality Industrywide

Over the last decade, ROC has conducted extensive research on the restaurant industry, publishing more than two dozen reports on a plethora of issues. In every locality in which it has an affiliate, it has conducted a participatory research study of the local restaurant industry. These local industry studies, called *Behind the Kitchen Door* are always the most comprehensive studies of a local industry and include government data analysis, more than five hundred surveys of restaurant workers conducted by workers themselves, thirty to forty employer interviews, and thirty worker interviews. These studies serve as the foundation for all other work in the region, informing training programs, launching ROC's local policy campaigns, and introducing the organization to workers and employers who join the local ROC affiliate as members.

In some localities and at the national level, these participatory research studies have led to further inquiry into particular issues, such as worker health and consumer impacts. ROC has conducted extensive government-funded research on issues of health and safety in the restaurant industry, as well as studies on the impact of the lack of benefits, such as health care access and paid sick days, on both workers and consumers.

In several localities, ROC also has conducted a second study focused on occupational segregation and discrimination called "The Great Service Divide." Working with the nation's foremost employment-discrimination research experts, ROC conducts "matched pairs" audit-testing studies in which pairs of people—one white applicant and one person of color, men and women—apply for livable-wage waitstaff and bartending positions in fine-dining restaurants. ROC conducts these studies to document discrimination and examine the barriers these workers face in advancing up the ladder. In New York, a white applicant had twice the chance of obtaining one of these livable-wage jobs than an applicant of color, even when the applicant of color had a better resume. Other research has focused on the particular impact of discrimination in the industry on women and African Americans.

To directly confront such discrimination, ROC has engaged in and won campaigns against exploitation and discrimination in fifteen high-profile restaurant companies, helping them change their practices and promote workers of color and women. For example, in one instance several Latino and Bangladeshi bussers approached us from one of New York's few four-star restaurants, complaining that they had been passed over for promotions by less-qualified white workers. These white workers were quickly promoted to waitstaff and bartending positions, earning almost five times as much as the Bangladeshi and Latino bussers who had trained them. After filing litigation and engaging in a public campaign, ROC was able to move the company to promote several of these bussers to waitstaff positions, create a new promotions policy monitored by the Equal Employment Opportunities Commission, and provide raises to the bussers. In this instance, the employer's agreement to inform bussers and other lower-paid staff about opportunities to apply for new waitstaff positions was a major step forward, since previously the company had simply hired white workers from outside the restaurant as waitstaff rather than providing the opportunity for workers to advance from within.

All of this research has been the basis for ROC's local, state, and federal policy advocacy. The research has demonstrated that two priority issues for restaurant workers are the low wages and the lack of benefits, such as paid sick days. To this end, ROC has been working to raise the federal minimum wage for tipped workers—still stuck at $2.13 per hour—as well as the minimum wage for all workers, currently $7.25 per hour, and to advance legislation to guarantee these workers paid sick days in almost every locality in which ROC has an affiliate. ROC's research has shown that these two issues—low wages and lack of benefits—impact not only workers but also hurt consumers and even employers, who suffer from one of the highest turnover rates of any industry.

For this reason, ROC has launched a multiyear consumer-engagement campaign to build public support for these policy goals and to engage consumers in encouraging more employers to take the high road to profitability. Despite the recent recession, consumers of different classes and ethnicities still are going out to eat in record numbers. Diners remain an important yet untapped constituency in our movement. In observing the success of consumer engagement in moving the industry to provide locally sourced, organic, and healthier menu items, especially after the release of pivotal books, such as Eric Schlosser's *Fast Food Nation* and Michael Pollan's *The Omnivore's Dilemma*, we realize that there has been a cultural shift in how we think about our food. Accessible cultural tools, such as guides, books, and movies, could help propel diners not only to demand more sustainable, organic, and healthy food but also to demand that their server has an economically sustainable job with good benefits and an equal opportunity to advance.

Thus ROC, in partnership with the Applied Research Center and Louverture Films, has launched a multiyear consumer-engagement campaign that includes (1) a National Diners' Guide that includes the minimum-wage, paid-sick-days, and internal-promotions practices of the 150 most popular restaurants in America, and those of ROC's responsible-restaurant partners; (2) a book called *Behind the Kitchen Door* (Cornell University, 2013), profiling specific workers' stories and experiences in the industry; (3) short films profiling workers across the food-chain system; (4) a full-length feature film; (5) an interactive web site platform—thewelcometable.net—that allows consumers to engage both online and offline in support of policy change for restaurant workers; and (6) educational and outreach materials to accompany these pieces. Together, these pieces will create a narrative to share with a wider and wider audience of consumers, encouraging them to push more employers to take the high road and improve job quality in the industry. *Behind the Kitchen Door*, released in February 2013, kicked off the consumer-engagement campaign and has become a national best seller.

Important Lessons for the World of Work

ROC's model provides several lessons for the workforce-development sector. First, the nation's largest and fastest-growing employment sectors simply cannot be ignored; as other sectors decline, these are the jobs that most workers in America are taking. Not all workers will be able to be trained and placed in health care and high-tech industries, typically the favorite sectors of the workforce-development world. This is especially true as restaurant and retail sectors continue to grow during economic crises.

Second, within the restaurant sector, there are definitely livable-wage jobs available, along with a potential career path. Workers take great pride in hospitality, but the industry needs professionalization in the form of genuine career paths that help workers build a career while supporting their families.

Third, and perhaps most important, in shifting to a new focus on the largest and fastest-growing sectors, it becomes essential to address issues of job quality and equity alongside pathways for advancement. Racial discrimination must be squarely confronted and addressed. However, even if these barriers were removed and all of these workers were provided training, ten million restaurant workers will never fit into the two million livable-wage jobs in the industry. It is for this reason that ROC helps workers advance to livable-wage jobs while simultaneously engaging in policy work to lift wages and benefits industrywide.

Health care jobs were not always good jobs. Unions and other worker associations struggled for decades to create higher-quality jobs and real career pathways in the health care sector. The time has come to turn our attention to the sectors most workers in the U.S. economy are entering and similarly intervene to create real pathways to more good jobs. If we do not, our current workforce-development system will soon be focused on a negligible portion of the U.S. workforce.

Notes

1. Rasmussen Reports (2011) describes the national increase in food consumption outside the home.
2. U.S. Bureau of Labor Statistics (2011).
3. Restaurant Opportunities Centers United analysis of Bureau of Labor Statistics, Occupational Employment Statistics, 2010. 2010 OES for Food Preparation and Serving Related Occupations (350000) NAICS 722 employees, plus 35-0000 occupations in such industries as amusement parks, spectator sports, and gambling. This method excludes Food Preparation and Serving Related Occupations in such institutions as prisons and schools.
4. National Restaurant Association (2012), pp. 2–7, 41–46.
5. Bureau of Labor Statistics, Occupational Employment Statistics (2010).
6. Ibid.
7. Hereafter, unless otherwise stated, "poverty line" or "poverty wage" refers to the income below which a family of four falls into poverty as defined by 2011 HHS Poverty Guidelines. *Federal Register* 76, No. 13, January 20, 2011: 36737–8. A poverty wage of $10.75 assumes full-time, year-round work.
8. Bureau of Labor Statistics, Characteristics of Minimum Wage Workers, 2010, Table 4, Employed wage and salary workers paid hourly rates with earnings at or below the prevailing federal minimum wage by major occupation group, 2010 annual averages, food preparation and serving related occupations.
9. Restaurant Opportunities Centers United, *Serving While Sick*, (2010), pp. 11–13.
10. Ibid. *Behind the Kitchen Door: The Hidden Reality of Philadelphia's Thriving Restaurant Industry*, (2012).
11. Ibid., *Tipped Over the Edge*, (2012), p. 19.
12. NWLC calculations of ACS, 2005–2009. Steven Ruggles, J. Trent Alexander, Katie Genadek, Ronald Goeken, Matthew B. Schroeder, and Matthew Sobek, *Integrated Public Use Microdata* Series: Version 5.0 [Machine-readable database] (Minneapolis: University of Minnesota, 2010).
13. Restaurant Opportunities Centers United (2012), pp. 2–4.
14. Ibid.
15. Ibid.
16. Restaurant Opportunities Center of New York (2009), pp. 1–4.

Bibliography

U.S. Bureau of Labor Statistics. Occupational Employment Statistics, National Cross-Industry Estimates. May 2011. Sorted by median hourly wage for all Standard Occupational Classifications. Accessed January 16, 2011. bls.gov/pub/special.requests/oes/oesm11nat.zip.

———. Quarterly Census of Employment and Wages Data, NAICS 722 Food Services and Drinking Places. 2001–2010.

National Restaurant Association. *2012 Restaurant Industry Forecast.* 2012.

Rasmussen Reports. National Survey of 1,000 Adults. July 21–22, 2011.

Restaurant Opportunities Center of New York. *The Great Service Divide: Occupational Segregation and Inequality in the New York City Restaurant Industry.* 2009.

Restaurant Opportunities Centers United. Blacks in Restaurant Industry. 2012.

———. National survey data set. 2012.

———. *Serving While Sick: High Risks and Low Benefits for the Nation's Restaurant Workforce, and Their Impact on the Consumer.* 2010.

———. *Tipped Over the Edge: Gender Inequality in the Nation's Restaurant Industry.* 2012.

11

Sectoral Workforce and Related Strategies: What We Know … and What We Need to Know

Christopher King

Workforce development programs have traditionally focused largely on the supply side of the labor market, striving to ensure that job seekers linked up with jobs that were a good match for their skills and aptitudes, and that sufficient numbers of them were trained with the requisite skills for the positions employers were posting. While employers were rightfully seen as the source of jobs and career opportunities, if programs reached out to them, it was primarily to determine how many new workers they might need, what their entry requirements were, what type of training new hires might need to qualify, and whom they should contact for job referrals.

Several decades ago, federal policy sought to involve employers and the private sector more directly in planning and oversight committees, starting with changes to the Comprehensive Employment and Training Act in 1977 and the Job Training Partnership Act of 1982. In the 1980s and early 1990s, all of this began to change in substantive ways. Policy makers and program administrators at all levels began to focus more on real employer "engagement" and to create mechanisms for targeting training and placement efforts more on high-demand occupations and industries. Eventually, this evolutionary process yielded what are now referred to broadly as sectoral strategies. These strategies can encompass both career-pathway and bridge programs and often work through or closely with workforce intermediaries, organizations that mediate between job seekers, employers, and service providers and strive to improve working conditions on the demand side of the market.

The family of strategies to help low-income, low-skilled individuals succeed in the labor market and to help employers meet their needs for workers with the right mix of skills began to emerge in the 1980s and 1990s. Initially, such initiatives began to respond to the needs of key industry groups in various sectors and low-skilled populations seeking better jobs and advancement opportunities in them. Over time, as it became clear that such responses would require far more structured offerings, especially including programs at community and technical colleges, sectoral strategies began to evolve into broader career-pathway approaches involving provider institutions as well as employers. Finally, given the desire to address the particular needs of job seekers pursuing sectoral and career-pathway opportunities, many of whom had basic skills deficits that impeded their progress in for-credit as well as non-credit course sequences, so-called bridge programs were developed. Some of these programs, such as Integrated Basic Education Skills and Training (I-BEST), are now seen as national models for helping low-skilled adults contextually build basic *and* occupational skills at the same time and move along career pathways into the workforce sectors they are pursuing.

In this chapter, I summarize the findings of evaluations and studies of sectoral, career-pathway, and related workforce-development strategies performed since the early 2000s, not including those being conducted at the national and local levels under the auspices of the National Fund for Workforce Solutions. (Those evaluations are discussed in Chapter 12 of this volume.) I review the multisite Public/Private Ventures–Aspen Institute and other sectoral evaluations and ongoing career-pathway and related studies. I then assess the current state of knowledge for sector partnerships and identify gaps in our knowledge about the effectiveness of these strategies and how to improve them. I end with several concluding observations and a cautionary note.

Findings from Sectoral, Career-Pathway, and Related Evaluations

Sectoral strategies have been operating in a growing number of regions, states, and cities in recent decades. Yet, despite investments in data collection and documentation, the evidence base to support them and their expansion remains thin. Appropriately, much of the early work focused mainly on their implementation and on measuring participation and labor-market outcomes, rather than their impacts. Rigorous impact evaluations are generally not warranted until the program intervention they seek to assess has reached a level of maturity and stability that lends itself to such estimation (Rossi et al., 2004). That said, real progress has been made on estimating the impacts of these strategies in recent years. To date, there have been a small handful of rigorous experimental and quasi-experimental evaluations of sectoral strategies.

This section focuses both on lessons from the implementation and effects of sectoral strategies and career-pathway programs in several broad categories aligned with the areas they seek to affect, including participation in education and training services; labor-market outcomes for job seekers and employers; and regional competitiveness. Unfortunately, there is little to offer in the last category, as important as it may be. Although a number of measures of regional competitiveness are widely used in the economic-development literature, such outcomes and impacts simply have not been evaluated with any rigor for sectoral strategies.

Lessons from Implementation Studies

Numerous studies of sectoral, career-pathway, and related strategies have been published since the early 2000s, many of them focused on a particular initiative or group of sites, including Shifting Gears and Breaking Through Initiatives. There have also been national implementation studies of large regional sectoral efforts, such as the *High-Growth Job Training Initiative and the Workforce Innovation in Regional Economic Development (WIRED) Initiative* (e.g., Eyster et al., 2010; Almandsmith et al., 2009; and Hewat and Hollenbeck, 2009). The following discussion summarizes key findings from these studies under four major headings: leadership and commitment; target populations; partners and resources; and services.

Leadership and Commitment

- As many program studies have concluded, strong, shared leadership and program "champions" (Almandsmith et al., 2009; Bragg et al., 2007; Glover et al., 2012), good-governance structures, and joint decision making (Hewat and Hollenbeck, 2009; Hollenbeck et al., 2009) all play roles in supporting the implementation of these strategies and programs.

- Colleges with a record of commitment to developing and implementing innovative practices appear most able to sustain them (Liebowitz and Taylor, 2004).

- Some of the more established sectoral and career-pathway networks—e.g., QUEST, ARRIBA, Capital IDEA—have benefited from strong, highly visible community support, via the Southwest Industrial Areas Foundation and its local affiliates, that translates into political and financial support for sustainability as well (Glover and King, 2010).

Target Populations

- Career-pathway and career-pathway bridge programs generally follow through on their commitment to serving a diverse, low-skilled adult population, including especially English-language learners, public-assistance recipients, the unemployed, recent immigrants, and youth (Bragg et al., 2007; Leibowitz and Taylor, 2004; Strawn, 2011).

Partners and Resources

- Career-pathway programs leverage and build on local strengths (including relationships with employers and community groups) and mobilize resources for adult learners. Partner relationships are seen as crucial to their sustainability over time (Bragg et al., 2007).

- Not surprisingly, community colleges are a key partner in career-pathway programs (Jenkins, 2006; Bragg et al., 2007). They also play a strong role in most sectoral strategies (Conway et al., 2010; Glover and King, 2010; Hewat and Hollenbeck, 2009).

- Sectoral strategies ascribe their success to their sharpened focus on growth sectors offering career-advancement opportunities, but career-pathway programs have also been found to be more effective when targeting regional labor markets and sectors that provide high-wage employment and career-advancement opportunities (Glover and King, 2010; Glover et al., 2012; Hewat and Hollenbeck, 2009; Hollenbeck et al., 2009; Maguire et al., 2010; Rab, 2003).

- For sectoral and related strategies, strongly engaging employers as partners early in the process was essential (Eyster et al., 2011; Glover and King, 2010; Hewat and Hollenbeck, 2009; Hollenbeck et al., 2009; Woolsey et al., 2012). Hiring and retaining instructors from the targeted industries were also important (Eyster et al., 2012).

- Strong advance planning and ongoing communication among partners is important to designing and supporting the necessary activities and services (Hewat and Hollenbeck, 2009; Hollenbeck et al., 2009).

- Access to adequate resources and the capacity to leverage nongovernmental support are important for program operations and sustainability (Hewat and Hollenbeck, 2009; Hollenbeck et al., 2009).[1] Social networking among extended partner groups is one form these resources may take (Hewat and Hollenbeck, 2009; Hollenbeck et al., 2009).

- Engaging key partners—not just employers but also unions, workforce-development boards, community-based organizations, and foundations—was also noted as important for career-pathway bridge programs (Strawn, 2011).

Services

- Comprehensive support services are essential to student success in career-pathway programs: Without access to a wide array of supports (e.g., financial aid, academic and career guidance or coaching, counseling, job placement, transportation and child care assistance, and mental health services), low-skilled students are unlikely to persist in or complete their studies (Bragg et al., 2007; Glover et al., 2012; Smith et al., 2012a; Liebowitz and Taylor, 2004; Strawn, 2010).

- Integrated institutional structures, in which adult education, workforce development, developmental education, and non-credit programs are more coordinated, are important to college and career program success (Liebowitz and Taylor, 2004). Alternatively, integrated service strategies contribute to the success of career-pathway programs (Glover et al., 2012; Smith et al., 2012a; Rab, 2003).

- The role of career coaches and explicit peer-support approaches has also been instrumental in helping low-skilled adults (Glover et al., 2012; Smith et al., 2012a; Strawn, 2010).

- Developmental or remedial education is considered to be a supplement to career-pathway programs by some (Bragg et al., 2007) and an integral part of their approach by others (Glover et al., 2012, Smith et al., 2012a; Strawn, 2010).

- Shorter, streamlined programs of study, including shortened learning modules and career-pathway "bridge" programs—programs that are contextualized, combine basic skills and career-technical skills, use new or modified curricula, and employ new delivery modes (for example, dual credit)—contribute to student success (Liebowitz and Taylor, 2004; Glover et al., 2012; Smith et al., 2012a; Strawn, 2010). Or, as one seasoned program director puts it, "Time is our enemy."

Finally, the following quote sums up an important point about career-pathway programs and applies to sectoral strategies as well (Jenkins, 2006, p. 6):

This model ... cannot be purchased off the shelf. The specific form and content of a career pathway will depend on the particular industries targeted, the requirements of employment and advancement in the target sectors, and the existing infrastructure for education and workforce development in those sectors. Building a career pathway is *a process of adapting existing programs and services, and adding new ones*, to enable students to advance to successively higher levels of education and employment in the target sectors. Where it is most effective, the career pathways process helps to transform institutions and organizations involved in education, workforce preparation and social services. The process strengthens cooperation among them in ways that improve their capacity individually and collectively to respond to the needs of local residents and employers. [Emphasis added]

Education and Training-Program Effects

Sectoral and related programs have increased participation in post-secondary education and occupational-skills training for participants, as compared with members of comparison and control groups in some instances. They have also led to higher rates of credential and degree attainment. Lessons from implementation studies of large national efforts, such as the High-Growth Job Training Initiative and the WIRED Initiative, are summarized above. But efforts to estimate the outcomes and especially their net impacts through the application of rigorous designs have not worked out all that well (Eyster et al., 2010). Program effects from selected experimental and quasi-experimental evaluations are summarized in *Table 1*.

Table 1: Program Effects from Selected Sectoral, Career-Pathway, and Bridge Evaluations

Study I Authors	Maguire et al. 2010	Smith et al. 2012	Smith & King 2011	Miller et al. 2005	Roder & Elliott 2011	Zeidenberg et al. 2010
Design	Experiment (Intent-to-Treat)	Quasi-experiment (Treat-on-Treated)	Quasi-experiment (Treat-on-Treated). ROI	Experiment (Intent-to-Treat)	Experiment (Intent-to-Treat)	Quasi-experiment & Diff-in-Diff (Intent-to-Treat & Treat-on-Treated)
Program	Sectoral; JVS-Boston, WRTP, Per Scholas	Sectoral; Capital IDEA	Sectoral; Capital IDEA	Sectoral/ Career Pathway; CET Replication	Career Pathway/Bridge/ Sectoral; Year Up	Bridge, I-BEST
No. of Sites	3	1	1	4 hi-fidel. of 12	3	1 state
Sample	2004-05 cohort, sample of 1,014	2003-2008 cohorts; 879 participants	2003-2004 cohorts; 332 participants	1995-1999 cohorts; 1,400 youth	2007 cohort of youth enrollees	2006-08 1st-time I-BEST Enrollees; 2005-07 DID

Participation	32-point increase (73% v. 41%)	n.a.	n.a.	145 more hrs of training; no impact on total program time	No difference in college-going or credits	17-point increase in service receipt
Completion/ Credential Attainment	75%	n.a.	n.a.	21-point increase in credentials	n.a.	10-point increase in likelihood of college credits; 7.5 point increase in OCC certification earned at 3 yrs; no AA effect

Most process studies report that sectoral and related programs exhibit high rates of participation in program services and yield similarly high completion and credential rates. However, few of the more rigorous evaluations of these programs actually track increased participation, completion, or credential rates or report them in any great detail. As shown in *Table 1*, the Public/Private Ventures–Aspen Institute experimental evaluation of three prominent sectoral programs estimated that they produced a statistically significant 32-point increase in education and training services participation relative to control group members accessing similar services in their communities (Maguire et al., 2010). The CET Replication evaluation conducted by Miller et al. (2005) found that participating youth received 145 more hours of training than youth in the control group, although overall time in the program was not significantly higher. Moreover, they also found that the program led to a statistically significant 21-point increase in the rate of credential receipt. The experimental Year Up evaluation conducted by Roder and Elliott (2011) found no effects on the rates of college attendance or credit receipt. Finally, the quasi-experimental evaluation of Washington State's I-BEST Program completed by Zeidenberg et al. (2010) estimated a 17-point increase in service receipt, a 10-point increase in the likelihood of earning college credits, and a 7.5-point increase in the rate of occupational certifications earned three years after students' initial enrollment. However, they found no statistically significant effects on the number of associate's degrees earned. Strawn (2011) summarizes the 2010 I-BEST results as follows: "I-BEST students are 56 percent more likely than regular adult basic education and ESL students to earn college credit, 26 percent more likely to earn a certificate or degree, and 19 percent more likely to achieve learning gains on basic skills tests—or more simply, as Washington puts it, I-BEST moves students 'farther and faster.'"

Labor-Market Outcomes and Impacts

It's important to examine the evidence on labor-market effects for job seekers (students) and employers, as well as for regional economies. *Table 2* summarizes these labor-market impacts. As above, the findings presented here are based only on more rigorous experimental and quasi-experimental evaluations. (Note that "n.a." signifies "not applicable" or "not available," while "n.s." indicates a statistically insignificant difference.)

Table 2: Labor-Market Impacts from Sectoral, Career-Pathway, and Bridge Evaluations

Study/Authors Period	Maguire et al. 2010 Yr 2 Post	Smith et al. 2012 4.5 Yrs Post	Smith & King 2011 7.5 Yrs Post	Miller et al. 2005 4.5 Yrs Post	Roder & Elliott 2011 2 Yrs Post	Zeidenberg et al. 2010 3 Yrs Post
JOB SEEKERS						
Any Employent	5-point increase (84% v. 79%)	12.3-point increase (74.3% v. 62.5%)	10.9-point increase	Positive impacts at 2.5 yrs; 0 impact at 4.5 yrs	n.s.	n.s.
Sector-related	n.a.	n.a.	n.a.	Men & women shift to target sectors	Most worked in targeted (e.g., IT) sectors v. controls	n.a.
Hours	250 hrs	n.a.	n.a.	fewer hrs for men	12 pt increase in FT v. PT	n.s.
Job Retention	1.3 mos.	n.a.	n.a.	n.a.	n.a.	n.a.
Career Advancement	n.a.	n.a.	n.a.	n.a.	n.a.	n.a.
Wages	Increased % in higher wage jobs	n.a.	n.a.		$2.26 more per hr (21.9%)	n.s.
Earnings	$4,011 more per yr (29%)	$3,036 more per yr 11.9%	$4,892 more per yr	0 by 4.5 yrs	$3,461 more per yr (30%)	n.a.
Fringe Benefits	-10-pt increase	n.a.	n.a.	n.a.	n.s.	n.a.
Monetary UI Eligibility	n.a.	12.3 pts.	10.8-point increase	n.a.	n.a.	n.a.
UI Claims	n.a.	n.s.	n.s.	n.a.	n.a.	n.a.
ROI	n.a.	n.a.	10 yr & 20 yr	n.a.	n.a.	n.a.
Taxpayer IRR	n.a.	n.a.	9% & 17%	n.a.	n.a.	n.a.
Society IRR	n.a.	n.a.	39% & 43%	n.a.	n.a.	n.a.
EMPLOYERS						
Productivity	n.a.	n.a.	n.a.	n.a.	n.a.	n.a.
Efficiency	n.a.	n.a.	n.a.	n.a.	n.a.	n.a.
Profits	n.a.	n.a.	n.a.	n.a.	n.a.	n.a.
REGIONS						
Competitiveness	n.a.	n.a.	n.a.	n.a.	n.a.	n.a.
Job Growth	n.a.	n.a.	n.a.	n.a.	n.a.	n.a.

Job seekers' employment. Most of the programs studied were estimated to yield statistically significant increases in employment from two to seven and a half years after the program. Neither Year Up nor I-BEST produced significant effects on rates of employment. WTRP trainees were more likely to obtain union jobs, a special focus of the program. Trainee outcomes were further enhanced by JVS-Boston's emphasis on paid internships. Both the CET Replication and Year Up resulted in significantly more individuals working in the sectors targeted by these programs, as noted in more detail below.

Job seekers' earnings. Sectoral and related strategies generally produced significant increases in earnings, ranging from 12 percent to 30 percent over control or comparison group members from two to seven and a half years after enrollment. WTRP participants earned 24 percent more than controls over the two-year study period and 27 percent more in the second year, largely from working more hours and drawing higher wages; WTRP participants were much more likely to work in jobs paying both $11 and $13 per hour than controls. JVS-Boston training generally produced earnings impacts for the two-year period overall, resulting mainly from gains in the second year. Participants were more likely to be working more months and hours and in higher-paying ($11 per hour or more) jobs than controls. Per Scholas trainees also earned more than controls in year two by working more months and hours and in higher-paying ($11 per hour) jobs; they were also more likely to work in jobs offering benefits.

In the Smith et al. (2012b) and Smith and King (2011) studies focused on Capital IDEA, earnings increases also led to significant increases in monetary eligibility for unemployment insurance of 11 to 12 points, an important outcome for low-income workers who became eligible for a key part of the "first tier" safety net.

Year Up participants earnings overtook those of the control group six quarters after program entry and exceeded them by 30 percent in the second year, largely as a result of trainees' working in jobs that were full- rather than part-time (12 points more) and paying higher wages ($2.26 per hour more). There were no significant differences in the rate of employee-benefit receipt between treatment and control group members.

Job quality. Very limited aspects of job quality—wage rate, fringe benefits, and full- versus part-time status—have been measured to date and only in a few studies. Maguire et al. (2010) report that, on average, participants worked more in jobs paying higher wages—14 points more in jobs paying at least $11 per hour and 8 points more in jobs paying at least $13 per hour—and experienced almost a 10-point increase in the share of jobs offering fringe benefits over the two-year study period.

Career advancement. The available studies provided few insights into career advancement based on the measures used, although movement into higher-wage jobs and earnings growth in later years of these studies (e.g., Maguire et al., 2010; Smith et al., 2011) are certainly suggestive.

Finally, Smith and King (2011) estimated return on investment from three major perspectives for the Capital IDEA program, producing internal rate of return (IRR) figures of 9 percent for taxpayers and 39 percent for society over ten years—nearly eight years of which were based on actual follow-up data—and 17 percent for taxpayers and 43 percent for society over twenty years. Returns for individual participants were even higher, at 73 percent and 74 percent for ten and twenty years, respectively.

Subgroup Impacts

While average impacts on major outcomes are of interest to policy makers and researchers, subgroup impacts are at least as important to consider. In workforce evaluations conducted over several decades, estimated program impacts on employment and earnings have often varied substantially by gender, age, race and ethnicity, and other dimensions. Findings from emerging studies of sectoral strategies, career-pathway and bridge programs, which present subgroup results, appear to fit this expected pattern of variation. One key finding is that, where estimated and reported, these programs produced substantial earnings impacts across most subgroups of interest.

Three Sector-Based Programs

Maguire et al. (2010) evaluated three sector-based programs that differed widely in terms of the type and duration of the treatment as well as the populations they served. WTRP in Milwaukee emphasized relatively short-term training for positions in the health care, construction, and manufacturing sectors and stressed access to better-paying union jobs. It served roughly equal shares of men and women, roughly 80 percent of whom were African American. Only 12 percent had less than a high school education, about half had been incarcerated, and 40 percent had been on welfare at some point. More than three-fifths were young adults ages eighteen to twenty-six, a less-educated group than WTRP participants as a whole. In contrast, JVS-Boston mainly provided longer-term (five and a half months) training for positions in medical office (mostly female) and computerized accounting (mostly male) jobs[2] and served a population that was primarily female (almost 90 percent) former welfare recipients (61 percent). Only 8 percent of JVS-Boston participants had not completed high school. Almost half were young adults ages eighteen to twenty-six, and some 41 percent were immigrants. The final program studied, Per Scholas in Brooklyn, New York, trained participants to be computer technicians with A+ certification in New York City's IT sector. Participants were mostly men (75 percent) and minorities (91 percent), 26 percent of whom were immigrants. About three-fifths of Per Scholas trainees were young adults, while only 17 percent were ex-offenders. As per the requirements of area IT employers, all participants had (or tested at) at least a high school education at entry.

Miller et al. (2005) evaluated the CET Program Replication demonstration based on the successful San Jose, California, program that provided training in a worklike setting with strong employer involvement. CET Replication sites served youth in varying labor-market settings. Per Miller et al., compared with the original program in San Jose, replication sites tended to serve a broader, more employable youth population and to operate in a stronger labor market and a more competitive environment where area youth were offered more training options. Impacts were presented for four of the twelve sites that replicated the CET model with the highest fidelity; all four were in California. Not surprisingly, these high-fidelity sites also produced the greatest increases in education and training services and in credentials received.

Roder and Elliott (2011) evaluated Year Up, a program operated by a non-profit organization headquartered in Boston. Year Up provides a year of training and work experience in the information technology and investment-opportunities sectors for young adults (eighteen to twenty-four years old) living in urban areas.[3] The program seeks to provide youth participants with access to jobs offering higher wages and career-advancement opportunities. Year Up has developed a network of sites across the country that relies on private rather than public sector support. A majority (57 percent) of Year Up participants were males, most were minorities (50 percent African American, 34 percent Latino), and all had at least a high school diploma or a GED. Nearly a quarter spoke a language other than English or were not U.S. citizens, while 18 percent lived in public housing. The overwhelming majority (88 percent) of Year Up youth had some work experience, mainly in low-wage food-service and retail jobs.

Impacts by Sector

- WTRP participants placed in health care and construction earned substantially more than those working in manufacturing, and earnings impacts followed different patterns in these sectors: In health care, earnings gains appeared in the second year and were associated with working more months in jobs paying more than $11 per hour and offering benefits, while construction trainees earned more over the entire two-year period, mainly from working in much higher-wage ($13 per hour and above) jobs than controls. Employment and earnings impacts were not reported by industry sector for either JVS-Boston or Per Scholas.

- Year Up participants made significant inroads in the targeted industry sectors: 22 percent were employed in the Information Technology (IT) sector, compared with 2 percent for controls, and 15 percent obtained positions in investment opportunities, compared with none for controls. In addition, fully 94 percent of Year Up trainees who were hired by participating employers obtained jobs in the two targeted sectors, compared with 2 percent of controls.

Impacts by Gender

- Female WTRP trainees earned more, mainly by working in higher-wage jobs. Male trainees in Per Scholas earned more in year two by working in higher-wage jobs paying at least $11 per hour in both years and jobs paying at least $13 per hour in the second year, suggesting some career advancement.

- While women CET participants tended to post significant employment and earnings gains at thirty months, possibly resulting from a shift out of retail trade jobs, these gains had completely faded by the fifty-four-month follow-up. Male CET participants actually suffered negative impacts on employment and earnings that may have resulted from their holding out for better jobs following training.

- Results were not reported separately by gender for Year Up, although nearly three-fifths of participants were males.

Impacts by Age Group

- Two groups of young adults trained by JVS-Boston outearned their control-group counterparts by working more months and more hours in jobs paying at least $11 per hour. Earnings gains for eighteen- to twenty-four-year-olds were significant only in the second year. Young adults ages eighteen to twenty-four in Per Scholas earned significantly more than controls in year two by working more months in jobs paying at least $11 per hour.

- Despite some suggestions that CET may have produced employment and earnings gains for younger youth (those eighteen or under), these results did not hold up to sensitivity testing.

Impacts by Race and Ethnicity

- African American WTRP participants earned more than controls by working in higher-paying jobs. African American JVS-Boston participants tended to outearn controls in the second year, primarily as a result of working more hours. African American Per Scholas trainees did not earn more than controls in the study but were tending to outearn them in the latter months of year two. In contrast, Latino trainees outearned controls by 36 percent in year two by working more and in jobs paying at least $11 per hour.

Other Subgroup Impacts

- Welfare recipients served by JVS-Boston enjoyed significant earnings gains in year two by working more months and hours than controls, not by working in higher-paying jobs.

- Immigrants who participated in JVS-Boston training did not experience significant earnings gains overall or in either year measured. Immigrants served by Per Scholas earned substantially more than controls over the two-year study period, for a number of reasons: working more, working more months, working more hours, and working in higher-paying ($11 and $13 per hour) jobs.

- Formerly incarcerated WTRP participants earned 44 percent more than controls over the study period, primarily by working more months and hours and working in higher-paying ($11-and $13-per-hour) jobs. Ex-offender Per Scholas trainees also earned more in year two by working more, working more months, and working in higher-paying ($13-per-hour) jobs than controls.

- Early negative impacts for high school graduates in CET tapered off by the fourth year; by the end of the fifty-four-month follow-up, there were no significant differences by education level.

Employers

Both the Aspen Institute's Workforce Strategies Initiative and the Commonwealth Corporation have invested considerable time and energy in developing practical resources for workforce-development practitioners—programs and employers—to use to measure the effects of workforce investments on employers. These materials are firmly grounded in years of program development and measurement experience across a wide range of sectors ranging from health care, hospitality, and manufacturing to early childhood education, human services, and financial services (e.g., Soricone and Singh, 2011). The Aspen Institute's *Business Value Assessment* handbook (2005) and the Commonwealth Corporation's *Measuring Business Impact* guide (Soricone et al., 2011) readily acknowledge that they are appropriately viewed as extensions of private sector–style evaluation (e.g., Jack Phillips, Don Kirkpatrick), rather than grounded in highly rigorous benefit-cost or return-on-investment analysis conducted of human-capital investment and other programs by economists (e.g., Boardman et al., 2010). While they offer excellent advice on devising measures and indicators of business/employer effects—e.g., reductions in vacancy and turnover rates, orientation time—and even suggest that practitioners consider applying more rigorous evaluation designs, including random assignment–based experimental and quasi-experimental methods, their applications to date are largely in the realm of gross outcomes and pre/post analysis.[4]

Productivity

None of the studies conducted to date has rigorously measured whether these strategies or programs have resulted in increased productivity for employers or had measurable impacts on worker productivity over time beyond pre/post measures.

Efficiency

Nor has any of the studies rigorously measured whether these strategies or programs have produced greater efficiency or lower costs for employers over time beyond relatively simple pre/post measures.

Profits

None of the studies has rigorously measured whether these strategies or programs have produced greater profits for businesses in the near or longer term.

Regional Impacts

Just as evaluations conducted to date have not tackled employer-related outcome or impact measurement with any real degree of success, they have left regional economic competitiveness unaddressed. As Hollenbeck and Hewat (2010) stated in relation to the WIRED evaluations: "In our opinion, some significant issues that have not been addressed ... include the costs in terms of resources and time that have gone into the partnerships. Without cost information, it is impossible to gauge benefits against costs or estimate roughly a return on the federal investment."

Systems

Finally, it is important to note that sectoral and related strategies, including career-pathway programs, have been implemented with an explicit overall aim of bringing lasting change to the way job seekers and employers are served by workforce systems. Such impacts are less amenable to measurement through the usual experimental or quasi-experimental evaluation designs. Far too many confounding factors affect policy and program implementation at all levels, even though for policy makers and program leaders spanning post-secondary education and training sectors, these may be some of the most important achievements they hope to attain. These critical effects are likely to be assessed through more qualitative implementation studies.

A Research Agenda for the Next Decade

While we are beginning to learn more about sectoral and related workforce strategies and their effects on workers and employers, there is much more we need to know about them if we are to make sound policy and resource decisions, especially in the face of ever-tighter public budgets and growing cost pressures on employers. In the following discussion, I lay out two sets of need-to-know topics. The first outlines a research agenda that basically argues for continuing work that is already under way, while the second lists topics that have yet to be addressed thoughtfully and/or deliberately.

Continuing Research

Studies of Newer and More Established Sectoral and Related Programs

The number of sectoral efforts has grown rapidly over the past decade, from around two hundred or so cited by the late Cindy Marano and colleague Kim Tarr (2004) to more than one thousand currently (Mangat, 2010), and they are now operating in at least half of the states across a wide array of industry sectors. Our knowledge of their outcomes and impacts for job seekers, employers, and regions simply has not kept pace. Many of these programs are too new and far too small to merit a robust experimental evaluation, although outcomes and quasi-experimental impact estimation would be appropriate if adequate funding were available (for example, see Smith et al., 2012b, and Smith and King, 2011).

Funding is definitely an issue that must be addressed. Resources available for evaluation in the budget for the U.S. Department of Labor's Employment and Training Administration have plummeted since the late 1990s. The department created a Chief Evaluation Officer position in 2011 and has been pressing for more rigorous evaluations of the initiatives it funds, including the $147 million Workforce Innovation Fund (WIF) grants made in June 2012.[5] But, absent a substantial (and very unexpected) increase in funding, it is unlikely that the Department of Labor will be able to do this on a sufficiently large scale in future years.

Importantly, a number of the twenty-six WIF grantees are new sectoral, career-pathway, and bridge programs, including, for example:

- Growing Regional Opportunity for the Workforce (GROW): Expanding the Border for Lower-Skilled Adults, which is seeking to transform the workforce system in the five-WIB region along the Texas–Mexico border with $6 million in WIF funds. GROW aims to improve education and employment outcomes by tailoring programs and services to specific subpopulations, improving coordination of case management and support services, implementing pathways aligned with identified employer needs in key sectors, and enhancing systems capacity. The Ray Marshall Center is conducting the implementation analysis and multi-year quasi-experimental evaluation of GROW with Jobs for the Future.

- The Los Angeles Reconnections Career Academy (LARCA) is aligning multiple youth programs, initiatives, services, and resources to address area-youth dropout and unemployment challenges with $12 million in WIF funds. A consortium of WIBs, the mayor's office, the Community Development Department (CDD), and other workforce, education, human services, and business partners, LARCA will address basic and work-readiness skills gaps; educational and career guidance and mentoring needs; occupational and career-pathway development needs; and a wide array of supportive service requirements. Social Policy Research Associates is conducting an experimental and implementation evaluation of LARCA.

- The Illinois Pathways Initiative: Moving Regional Sector Partnerships to Scale in Manufacturing is a $12 million collaboration of a number of workforce and education agencies.[6] It builds directly on an earlier Illinois pathways initiative as well as its work as part of both the Shifting Gears and Advancing Opportunities initiatives. The effort is attempting to scale up six to eight regional manufacturing-sector partnerships and also features structured career-pathway and bridge programs. The evaluation components include an implementation evaluation, an outcomes evaluation, and a quasi-experimental impact evaluation.

The Trade Adjustment Assistance Community College and Career Training (TAACCCT) initiative is a closely related effort funded by the Department of Labor in collaboration with the U.S. Department of Education.[7] As of mid-2013, the U.S. Department of Labor Employment and Training Administration (ETA) had awarded grants in two rounds to eighty-six individual community colleges or consortia of colleges spanning all states. A third round of grantees was selected in fall 2013. TAACCCT goals include meeting industry needs by pursuing sector strategies and fostering career pathways for workers who are or have been affected by trade, as well as certain low-skilled, low-income adults, goals that are clearly reflected in the project descriptions. A number of the grantees also are providing contextualized instruction in basic skills. Each of these grantees is required to have an external evaluator and, in the third round, to develop an employment results "scorecard." Projects are funded for up to thirty-six months, with an additional twelve months at the end for evaluators to track participant outcomes and complete their analysis. As with the WIF program, TAACCCT grantees are required to conduct a rigorous third-party outcome-and-impact evaluation employing either experimental or quasi-experimental methods;[8] the Department of Labor is also funding a national evaluation of the TAACCCT program.

In addition, the Innovative Strategies for Increasing Self-sufficiency (ISIS) project is a promising initiative along these lines. Funded by the U.S. Department of Health and Human Services, the Open Society Foundation, and others, ISIS identified a number of promising strategies—many of them sectoral and career-pathway programs around the country—that they will be evaluating over the next several years, employing leading-edge experimental designs (Fein, 2012). Projects being evaluated by the ISIS team, led by Abt Associates, include the following:

- Carreras En Salud, an established health care pathway program for limited-English adults in the Chicago area, also features a bridge program.

- I-BEST, Washington State's Integrated Basic Education and Skills Training program, provides customized training in selected occupations at the state's thirty-five community and technical colleges and employs English-language instruction contextualized in an occupational setting with paired instructors. ISIS is evaluating I-BEST implementation and impacts at Bellingham Technical College.

- Valley Initiative for Development and Advancement (VIDA), located in Texas's Lower Rio Grande Valley, trains students in high-growth fields, such as allied health, technology, business, education, social services, manufacturing, and specialized trades. VIDA also operates an intensive sixteen-week College Preparatory Academy for otherwise-eligible students who test below skill levels required for college admission.

- Year Up provides low-income youths aged eighteen to twenty-four, who have a high school diploma or GED, with training and job experience for entry-level jobs in information technology, financial services, and other high-growth sectors partnering with community colleges, employers, and specialized service providers. Year Up consists of a customized six-month training program at local program offices, followed by a six-month internship with a local employer, both requiring full-time participation. ISIS is evaluating all Year Up sites nationally.

ISIS should be able to provide rigorous evidence on near-, medium-, and longer-term impacts on participant employment, earnings, and other outcomes of interest, as well as program benefits and costs. ISIS is not addressing employer or regional effects.

Finally, the U.S. Department of Health and Human Services is supporting the 2011–2015 national impact evaluation[9] of the Health Professions Opportunity Grant (HPOG) programs, which are supported by $67 million in grants. HPOG grantees are implementing sectoral, career-pathway, and bridge programs in twenty-three states.[10] Abt Associates and Urban Institute are conducting the national HPOG implementation and impact evaluation.

In 2011 the Department of Health and Human Services also awarded five HPOG–University Partnership grants to university teams working closely with some of the HPOG program grantees to better understand and measure their results.[11] Lindsay Chase-Lansdale at Northwestern University's Institute for Policy Research and I are co-principal investigators of a four-year, quasi-experimental, mixed-methods evaluation of Career*Advance*®, a two-generation sectoral, career-pathway, and bridge program that is training low-income, low-skilled parents of Head Start and Early Head Start children served by the Community Action Project of Tulsa County.[12] We are examining (1) short- and longer-term family, parent, and child outcomes and impacts and (2) how variation in program participation is linked to differential patterns of educational attainment, employment, and family health and well-being.

Long-Term Impacts

Measuring and evaluating strategies and programs over sufficiently long periods of time to gauge their true impacts is absolutely critical. As King and Heinrich (2011) have pointed out, one of the major shortcomings of most workforce-program evaluations is that they tend to adopt post-intervention follow-up periods that are too short. Doing so biases impact findings in favor of less-costly, low-intensity interventions, as in the case of the 2001 report on the National Evaluation of Welfare-to-Work Strategies (NEWWS) that led policy makers to support "work first" as a strategy (Hamilton et al., 2001), when longer-term results actually favored skills investments (King, 2004). Of course, this is not always the case, as evidenced by the longer-term Job Corps findings that showed that impacts had in fact decayed over a longer time period. The existing evidence to date suggests that sectoral strategies potentially produce large, long-lasting impacts on employment, earnings, and other measures of interest. Maguire et al. (2010) found that employment and earnings of the treatment group exceeded those of controls substantially in year two, while Smith et al. (2012b) estimated large quasi-experimental impacts on these same outcomes that persisted more than seven years post-program and showed no signs of diminishing. Whether other strategies will prove as effective in other institutional or labor-market contexts over long time periods remains an open question that needs to be rigorously addressed.

Program Performance Metrics and Measures

Ten states, working with the Center for Law and Social Policy, recently launched the Alliance for Quality Career Pathways (AQCP) to (1) develop and field-test a set of voluntary quality benchmarks and metrics; (2) create a self-assessment tool based on the framework, and; (3) communicate about the value of high-quality career pathways and the resulting quality career-pathway framework. With funding from the Joyce and Irvine foundations, AQCP is creating a framework to complement "howto" career-pathway guides (Center for Postsecondary and Labor Market Success, 2013a and 2013b).[13] AQCP's comprehensive framework (2013b) explicitly builds on existing indicator/measurement systems and features four major components (2013b):

Continuous Improvement

- Criteria for high-quality systems and programs

- Quality indicators signaling how well core elements of both systems and programs support achievement of desired participant outcomes

Performance Measurement

- Shared Interim Outcome Metrics that mark progress toward achieving desired longer-term participant outcomes

- Shared Performance Metrics, common metrics across education, training, employment, and other public, private, and philanthropic systems in the career-pathway system

The AQCP effort is still in its beginning phases. Remaining issues and questions include the following (Center for Postsecondary and Labor Market Success, 2013b, p. 14):

- Gathering more information on data that state and local career-pathway systems are collecting and metrics they have developed, as well as how they are using these metrics.

- Understanding more about what states and local career-pathway systems feel are the most important missing elements of a comprehensive measurement system.

- Determining how close states and local systems are to implementing a measurement capability appropriate for career pathways, including multiple educational settings and funding sources. Gauging the progress they are making in developing the capacity to follow participants over time and across institutions.

New Research

Employer and Regional Outcomes, Impacts, and Mechanisms

There have been only minimal efforts to date to delineate and measure the outcomes and impacts of sectoral and related strategies on employers and the regions in which they operate, much less the actual mechanisms through which these outcomes and impacts occur. Aspen's work to assess the value of such strategies to businesses, funded by the Mott and Ford Foundations, has been pioneering (Aspen Institute, 2005). While the existing efforts have been helpful, much remains to be done, including refining and operationalizing outcome measures of interest for employers and regions affected by sectoral strategies and career-pathway programs. The measures may be clearer for employers than for the larger regions. For employers, increased productivity, efficiency, and profitability are the key measures. Devising a sufficiently rigorous design to estimate impacts on these indicators with confidence is quite difficult. As noted above, researchers at the Aspen Institute, Commonwealth Corporation, the Ray Marshall Center, and other organizations with considerable experience with both workforce development and performance measurement and evaluation have been struggling with these issues for decades. They have had much greater success in developing appropriate measures and indicators than in implementing rigorous evaluation designs using them. For regions, the measurement issues are even greater, given the many confounding factors at work in every region.

It would also be advisable to tailor measurement strategies and indicators to the particular needs and foci of the industry sectors targeted by these strategies. Sectors may prioritize human resource goals and outcomes quite differently. For example, health care employers in some areas of the country tend to be more concerned with filling hard-to-fill positions, often through a grow-your-own strategy, while manufacturing employers tend to focus more on increasing productivity, reducing costs, and positioning themselves for expansion into new markets. Measurement approaches should be tailored accordingly.[14]

In addition, more insight is needed into the nature of sector partnerships and the conditions that lead some employers and industry sectors to be more interested in pursuing them than others. Also, does employer engagement in such partnerships follow a "life cycle," which varies by sector and other traits?[15]

Based on an intensive review of Washington State's Skills Panels, Cheney et al. (2008) outlined a thoughtful framework for evaluating sectoral strategies for the National Governors Association as part of the Accelerating Adoption of State Sector Strategies Initiative with the Corporation for a Skilled Workforce (CSW) and the National Network of Sector Partners. This framework and the resulting "dashboard" recommend ways to measure effects for employers and their industry group; current or prospective employees; educators and the education and training system; and the Skill Panel partnership itself (pp. 11–12). Data to support measurement and evaluation at each "level" would encompass the following:

- Evidence of Progress: member, participant, and participant qualitative perspectives on the value of their particular skill panels.

- Products and Services: narrative delineations of products and services provided by skill panels.

- Impact and Outcomes: quantitative data collection on select metrics directly measuring the value to employers, employees, educators, and skill-panel partnerships.

Benefit-Cost Analyses of Mature Programs

As noted, rigorous impact estimates for sectoral strategies have only recently begun to emerge. Few benefit-cost or return-on-investment (ROI) analyses of these strategies have been conducted (Smith and King, 2011). Once impacts are found to be more commonplace among the mature programs operating around the country, more work should be done to measure, document, and communicate ROI results to policy makers, program administrators, and other funders.

In addition, it is clear that these programs and strategies require substantial investments of time, energy, and resources on the part of multiple partners to succeed. Researchers should gather detailed cost information on a number of sectoral and career-pathway projects and partnerships to assess their net returns to participants, taxpayers, and society more generally.

Another area that merits further research is the potential macroeconomic or general equilibrium impacts that result from implementing these strategies. That is, in addition to outcomes and impacts for those participating in and directly affected by the programs, are impacts resulting in the wider economy as well? In their evaluation of WIRED, Hollenbeck and Hewat (2010) noted: "If benefits are accruing within WIRED regions, does that mean that other regions of the country have less economic growth, or is there complementarity such that positive economic growth in WIRED regions stimulates non-WIRED regional growth?"

Scalability and Sustainability

While sectoral and related strategies are expanding to more regions, states, and local labor markets, we know little about the conditions that contribute to (or impede) this expansion. Are there necessary and sufficient conditions—e.g., minimum market size, institutional flexibility, leader/champions, flexible funding streams—that must be present in order for these strategies to expand successfully into new areas? In addition, once such strategies take hold in an area, what are the factors or conditions that are critical for their sustainability over time? As noted, an overwhelming majority (85 percent) of existing sectoral partnerships have been in operation for three or more years (Mangat, 2010). But does this necessarily imply that they have reached a point where they are likely to be maintained well into the future? What would it take for this to be the case? Are specific activities and services key to sustaining sector partnerships or, as some observers have suggested, is it, rather, the support for the partnership's convening function itself that makes the difference? CSW (2012) raises additional questions, including: To what extent are participating employers willing to fund sector strategies? And does employer funding alter the focus of sector partnerships? Scalability and sustainability issues also are articulated in Maguire et al. (2010).

Career-Advancement Effects

To date, researchers have documented the outcomes and estimated the labor-market impacts of sectoral and some related strategies over two to eight years with varying degrees of rigor (Maguire et al., 2010; Smith et al., 2012a). No one has yet directly measured the effects on career advancement. Do participants in such strategies and programs make greater career progress than their counterparts, moving into positions of increasing scope and responsibility, accessing enhanced training and development opportunities on the job and off, garnering better benefit packages, and other advantages? Part of the difficulty, of course, is that our systems for measuring occupations of employment are less robust than those for gauging earnings and industry of employment.

Effects of Credentials and Training Relatedness

There is debate about the value of placing individuals into positions closely related to the fields in which they have trained. In fact, employment and earnings success in the labor market vary widely by field of study. Dadgar and Weiss (2012) find that long-term certificates and associate's degrees yield substantial returns in health care and a number of other fields, but not in low-paying fields like childcare. Earlier work by Smith et al. (2010) found that program completers accounted for almost all of the earnings impact associated with Capital IDEA's success. More research is needed to analyze and understand the effects of placing individuals in growth fields from sectoral and career-pathway programs and ways in which different credentials affect their labor-market success (Maguire et al., 2010).

Eroding Employer Support for Training

While some evaluations have found that sectoral and career-pathways programs yield substantial labor-market returns for participants (and hopefully for employers and regions), they have done so largely in industry sectors and labor markets that were experiencing strong growth and expanding job opportunities. There is some evidence that employers may be responding to the new labor-market context since the Great Recession and sluggish recovery by hiring fewer workers and backing away from their commitment to training-from-within and pursuing more buy-from-without strategies (see Cappelli, 2012). (See Osterman, Chapter 2, for more on this subject.) What effect might this new labor-market dynamic have on employers' receptivity to workers newly trained in sectoral and career-pathway programs? Is this phenomenon present in the particular sectors in which these strategies and programs have been and are being implemented around the country?

Systemic Impacts[16]

After more than two decades of involvement in establishing and evaluating sector partnerships, it is clear to me that they are having effects that extend well beyond job seekers, employers, and the local and regional labor markets in which they operate. The process and results of these partnerships affect the behavior of those directly involved, as well as other actors. Some of the more systemically oriented questions that might be part of the research agenda include the following: How do industry sector strategies tend to affect both private and public sector investments in education and learning over the short and longer term? How do state, regional, and local leadership and related policies influence employer and employee investment in learning and skill development? What impact do industry sector–based approaches have on community agility, compared with communities or regions where industry sector-based approaches are not utilized? And, finally, are sector strategies more valuable for building skills or for improving labor exchange? This last question has particular saliency in light of Cappelli's (2012) observations about how employer hiring practices have been changing since the Great Recession.

Concluding Observations

Sectoral, career-pathway, and bridge programs all appear to have logic models that suggest positive effects on education and training service participation, as well as labor-market outcomes and impacts over time. The early results from a handful of rigorous experimental and quasi-experimental evaluations are very encouraging, but the body of evidence to date is relatively thin for such a broad and expanding array of program interventions, especially in terms of the effects on employers, systems, and regional competitiveness. There is still a great deal that needs to be learned about the mechanisms by which these programs work and their longer-term impacts.

That said, it is clear that current and planned research projects and highly rigorous longitudinal, mixed-methods evaluations—supported by both federal departments and major foundations—will yield a large body of evidence on many aspects of sectoral and related strategies over the next five to ten years. By the time we get there, new and unexpected questions will have emerged from this body of research that will need to be examined. Areas that will surely merit greater attention even in light of these research efforts are employer and regional competitiveness effects, as well as scalability and sustainability issues.

Finally, I think it's important to end on a cautionary note, one that echoes my concluding section in a chapter I wrote more than a decade ago, based on a study of successful training programs in Illinois and Texas conducted for the U.S. Department of Labor (King et al., 2000). We had found that local programs were far more successful in terms of their longer-term employment and earnings outcomes,[17] if they had certain features in common, including an intense focus on skills training in high-demand occupations in growth sectors, close relationships with training providers, especially community colleges, and concern with helping participants attain longer-term economic self-sufficiency through skills attainment and the supports necessary for them to do so—that is, key elements of today's sectoral and career-pathway programs. The caution offered then, which is appropriate now as well, is that if every program in the country were to adopt these approaches, there is no guarantee that all of them would be as successful. To some extent, the situation then and now is that these strategies, despite their expansion, are still "leading edge" rather than typical. Do the effects of these initiatives hold up in times of severe recession and anemic economic recovery? Will they be as effective if taken to scale? Are they effective in widely varying labor-market contexts? Will they be sustained in what some are calling the "new normal"? Only time (and, of course, more research) will tell.

Notes

1. It is important to note that the Washington State Board for Community and Technical Colleges has addressed the need for more resources to support the planning and coordination of its highly touted I-BEST bridge programs by funding them at 1.75 times the normal rate per full-time-equivalent student as long as he or she is part of a recognized career-pathway program (Zeidenberg et al., 2010, p. 4).
2. These were combined into a medical-office program halfway through the program.
3. Jobs trained for in the information technology industry included computer installation, repair, and networking, while investment-opportunities industry jobs mainly consisted of investing and managing portfolios.
4. The "to date" qualification is important. The Aspen Institute, Commonwealth Corporation, the Ray Marshall Center, and others have attempted to apply more rigorous

evaluation designs in recent years to estimating net impacts of sectoral strategies on job seekers and employers but without much success. It has proved difficult methodologically as well as practically.

5. For more on the Department of Labor's WIF procurement, its grantees, and their evaluation plans, see http://www.doleta.gov/workforce_innovation/grant_awards.cfm/. The Employment and Training Administration seems to have gone a bit too far in its first round of WIF projects, requiring that most projects—even relatively small, neophyte programs—employ random-assignment evaluation designs. Desires for rigor notwithstanding, this seems ill advised.

6. See http://www.doleta.gov/workforce_innovation/pdf/grantees/IllinoisDeptofCommerce_abstract.pdf.

7. The USDOL/ETA website has more information about the TAACCCT Initiative: http://www.doleta.gov/taaccct/.

8. The Ray Marshall Center is currently involved in evaluating three of the TAACCCT grants: the Training for Regional Energy in North Dakota Consortium of five state and tribal colleges centered in Bismarck (evaluation led by the Corporation for a Skilled Workforce, CSW); the Gulf Coast IT Consortium in Louisiana and Mississippi (evaluation led by the Aspen Institute); and a third grant led by Tulsa Community College (also with CSW).

9. For more on the HPOG evaluation, see http://www.acf.hhs.gov/programs/opre/research/project/health-profession-opportunity-grants-hpog-impact-studies.

10. Information on HPOG program grants can be accessed at http://www.acf.hhs.gov/programs/ofa/programs/hpog/about.

11. For more on the HPOG-UP grantees and their projects, see http://www.acf.hhs.gov/programs/opre/research/project/university-partnership-research-grants-for-the-health-profession.

12. Evaluation partners include Hiro Yoshikawa of New York University (until recently at Harvard's Center for the Developing Child) and Jeanne Brooks-Gunn of Columbia University.

13. The Council for the Advancement of Adult Literacy has also suggested some useful metrics for use with career-pathway programs (CAAL, 2010).

14. I'm grateful to Nancy Snyder of Commonwealth Corporation for this insight.

15. These comments are drawn in part from a 2012 Corporation for a Skilled Workforce working paper, which I contributed to as a CSW board member.

16. This discussion also draws upon Corporation for a Skilled Workforce (2012).

17. The study looked only at outcomes, not impacts.

Bibliography

Abe, Yasuo, and Fannie Tseng. 2005. *The Characteristics of Career Paths among Out-of-School Youth from the Center for Employment Training Replication Project Sites*. Oakland, CA: Berkeley Policy Associates, September.

Accelerating State Adoption of Sector Strategies: An Eleven-State Project to Promote Regional Solutions to Worker and Employer Needs, Phase I Project Report. 2008. Washington, DC:

NGA Center for Best Practices, National Network of Sector Partners, and Corporation for a Skilled Workforce, May 12.

Almandsmith, Sherry, Mary Walshok, Kay Magill, Linda Toms Barker, Pamela Surko, Mary Vencill, Tommy Smith, Hannah Betesh, David Drury, Tricia Cambron, and Kristina Lara Thomas Goldring. 2009. *The Power of Partnership: American Regions Collaborating for Economic Competitiveness, 2009 Generation I WIRED Interim Evaluation Report.* Oakland, CA: Berkeley Policy Associates, November 9.

Alssid, Julian L., Meliss Goldber and Sarah M. Klerk. 2010. *Building a Higher Skilled-Workforce: Results and Implications from the BridgeConnect National Survey.* Barrington, RI: Workforce Strategy Center, November.

———, David Gruber, Davis Jenkins, Christopher Mazzeo, Brandon Roberts, and Regina Stanback-Stroud. 2002. *Building a Career Pathways System: Promising Practices in Community College-Centered Workforce Development, Executive Summary.* Barrington, RI: Workforce Strategy Center, August.

Aspen Institute. 2005. *Business Value Assessment for Workforce Development Organizations: Handbook, Version 1.0.* Washington, DC: Aspen Institute, Workforce Strategies Institute, Documenting Demand-side Outcomes Project, October.

Baider, Allegra, Vickie Choitz, Amy Ellen Duke-Benfield, Marcie W. M. Foster, Linda Harris, Elizabeth Lower-Basch, Neil Ridley, and Julie Strawn. 2010. *Funding Career Pathways and Career Pathway Bridges: A Federal Policy Toolkit for States.* Washington, DC: Center for Law and Social Policy, October. Revised Edition.

Biswas, Radha Roy, Jack Mills, and Heath Prince. 2005. *Building Skills, Increasing Economic Vitality: A Handbook of Innovative State Policies.* Boston: Jobs for the Future, January.

Boardman, Anthony, David Greenberg, Aidan Vining, and David Weimer. 2010. *Cost-Benefit Analysis: Concepts and Practice.* New York: Pearson Series in Economics. 4th Edition.

Bragg, Debra D., Christine D. Bremer, Marisa Castellano, Catherine Kirby, Ann Mavis, Donna Schaad, and Judith Sunderman. 2007. *A Cross-Case Analysis of Career Pathway Programs That Link Low-Skilled Adults to Family-Sustaining Wage Careers.* St. Paul, MN: National Research Center for Career and Technical Education, University of Minnesota, October.

Bruno, Lee, Ying Jin, and Dwayne Norris. 2010. *Building Career Ladders for the Working Poor through Literacy Training.* Washington, DC: American Institutes for Research, July.

Campbell, Brett. 1994. *Investing in People: The Story of Project QUEST.* San Antonio: Communities Organized for Public Service (COPS) and Metro Alliance. Accessed February 12, 2013. http://www.cpn.org/topics/work/quest1-2.html#ch1.

Cappelli, Peter. 2012. *Why Good People Can't Get Jobs: The Skills Gap and What Companies Can Do About It.* Philadelphia: Wharton Digital Press.

Center for Postsecondary and Economic Success at CLASP. 2013a. *The Alliance for Quality Career Pathways Approach: Developing Criteria and Metrics for Quality Career Pathways: A Working Paper.* Washington, DC: Center for Law and Social Policy, February.

———. 2013b. *A Framework for Measuring Career Pathways Innovation: A Working Paper.* Washington, DC: Center for Law and Social Policy, February.

Cheney, Scott, Stacey Wagner, and Lindsey Woolsey. 2008. *Evaluating Industry Skills Panels: A Model Framework.* [Olympia, WA:] Washington State Training and Education Coordinating Board, June.

Chisman, Forrest, Garrett Murphy, James Parker, and Gail Spangenberg. 2010. *Longitudinal Data Collection in Career Pathways Programs: Core Indicators and Elements, Policy Brief.* New York: Council for the Advancement of Adult Literacy (CAAL), May 27.

Conway, Maureen, Amy Blair, Stephen L. Dawson, and Linda Dworak-Muñoz. 2007. *Sectoral Strategies for Low Income Workers: Lessons from the Field.* Washington, DC: Aspen Institute, Workforce Strategies Initiative.

———, Amy Blair, and Matt Helmer. 2012. *Courses to Employment: Partnering to Create Paths to Education and Careers.* Washington, DC: Aspen Institute, Workforce Strategies Initiative.

Corporation for a Skilled Workforce. 2012. "CSW's Next Generation Sector Strategy Focus." Ann Arbor, MI: Draft internal CSW working paper, June 20.

Dadgar, Mina, and Joy Weiss. 2012. *Labor Market Returns to Sub-Baccalaureate Credentials: How Much Does a Community College Degree or Credential Pay?* New York: Columbia University, Teachers College, Community College Research Center Working Paper No. 45, June.

Deaton, Brian, and Robert McPherson. 1991. *Design of Project QUEST.* Austin, TX: Center for the Study of Human Resources, University of Texas at Austin, September.

Eyster, Lauren, Demetra Smith Nightingale, Burt Barnow, Carolyn O'Brien, John Trutko, and Daniel Kuehn. 2010. *Implementation and Early Training Outcomes of the High Growth Job Training Initiative: Final Report.* Washington, DC: Urban Institute Center on Labor, Human Services, and Population.

Fein, David J. 2012. *Career Pathways as a Framework for Program Design and Evaluation: A Working Paper from the Innovative Strategies for Increasing Self-Sufficiency (ISIS) Project, OPRE Report #2012-30.* Washington, DC: Office of Planning, Research and Evaluation, Administration for Children and Families, U.S. Department of Health and Human Services, May.

Foster, Marcie, Julie Strawn, and Amy Ellen Duke-Benfield. 2011. *Beyond Basic Skills: State Strategies to Connect Low-Skilled Students to an Employer-Valued Postsecondary Education.* Washington, DC: Center for Postsecondary and Economic Success, Center for Law and Social Policy, March 4.

Ganzglass, Evelyn, Keith Bird, and Heath Prince. 2011. *Giving Credit Where Credit Is Due: Creating a Competency-Based Qualifications Framework for Postsecondary Education and Training.* Washington, DC: Center for Postsecondary and Economic Success, Center for Law and Social Policy, April 19.

Giloth, Robert P., ed. 2004. *Workforce Intermediaries for the Twenty-First Century.* Published in association with the American Assembly, Columbia University. Philadelphia: Temple University Press.

Glover, Robert W., and Christopher T. King. 2010. "The Promise of Sectoral Approaches to Workforce Development: Towards More Effective, Active Labor Market Policies in the United States." In Charles J. Whalen, ed., *Human Resource Economics: Essays in Honor of Vernon M. Briggs, Jr.* Kalamazoo, MI: W. E. Upjohn Institute for Employment Research, pp. 215–251.

————, Christopher T. King, and Tara C. Smith. 2012. *Expanding the CareerAdvance® Program in Tulsa, Oklahoma.* Austin, TX: Ray Marshall Center for the Study of Human Resources, Lyndon B. Johnson School of Public Affairs, University of Texas at Austin, January.

————, Tara Carter Smith, Christopher T. King, and Rheagan Coffey. 2010. *CareerAdvance®: A Dual-Generation Antipoverty Strategy, An Implementation Study of the Initial Pilot Cohort July 2009 through June 2010.* Austin, TX: Ray Marshall Center for the Study of Human Resources, Lyndon B. Johnson School of Public Affairs, University of Texas at Austin, August.

Hamilton, Gayle. 2002. *Moving People from Welfare to Work: Lessons from the National Evaluation of Welfare-to-Work Strategies.* New York: MDRC, July.

Harris, Linda, and Amy Ellen Duke-Benfield. 2010. "Building Pathways to Postsecondary Success for Low-Income Young Men of Color," In Christopher Edley, Jr., and Jorge Ruiz de Velasco, eds., *Changing Places: How Communities Will Improve the Health of Boys of Color.* Berkeley, CA: University of California Press.

————, and Evelyn Ganzglass. 2008. *Creating Postsecondary Pathways to Good Jobs for Young High School Dropouts: The Possibilities and the Challenges.* Washington, DC: Center for American Progress, October.

Henderson, Kathryn, Crystal MacAllum, and Mustafa Karakus. 2010. *Workforce Innovations: Outcome Analysis of Outreach, Career Advancement and Sector-Focused Programs.* New York: NYC Center for Economic Opportunity.

Hewat, Nancy, and Kevin Hollenbeck. 2009. *Nurturing America's Growth in the Global Marketplace through Talent Development: An Interim Report on the Evaluation of Generations II and III of WIRED.* Report submitted to U.S. Department of Labor, Employment and Training Administration. ETA Occasional Paper 2009-19. http://research.upjohn.org/reports/2.

Hollenbeck, Kevin, and Nancy Hewat. 2010. "Evaluation of Regional Collaborations for Economic Development: Lessons from the Employment and Training Administration's WIRED Initiative." *Employment Research* 17(3): 1–4. http://research.upjohn.org/empl_research/vol17/iss3/1.

Jenkins, Davis. 2006. *Career Pathways: Aligning Public Resources to Support Individual and Regional Economic Advancement in the Knowledge Economy.* Barrington, RI: Workforce Strategy Center, August.

————, Matthew Zeidenberg, and Gregory Kienzl. 2009. *Educational Outcomes of I-BEST: Washington State Community and Technical College System's Integrated Basic Education and Skills Training Program: Findings from a Multivariate Analysis, CCRC Working Paper No. 16.* New York: Community College Research Center, Teachers College, Columbia University, May.

Jobs for the Future. 2010. *The Breaking Through Practice Guide.* Boston: JFF, Spring.

King, Christopher T. 2004. "The Effectiveness of Publicly Financed Training in the United States: Implications for WIA and Related Programs." In Christopher J. O'Leary, Robert A. Straits, and Stephen A. Wandner, eds., *Job Training Policy in the United States.* Kalamazoo, MI: W. E. Upjohn Institute for Employment Research.

————, with Jerome Olson, Leslie Lawson, Charles Trott, and John Baj. 2000. "Training Success Stories for Adults and Out-of-School Youth: A Tale of Two States." In Burt S. Barnow and Christopher T. King, eds., *Improving the Odds: Increasing the Effectiveness of Publicly Funded Training.* Washington, DC: Urban Institute Press, February, pp. 129–184.

————, and Carolyn J. Heinrich. 2011. "How Effective Are Workforce Development Programs? Implications for U.S. Workforce Policies." Paper preented to the APPAM Fall Research Conference. November.

Lea, Cathryn. 2004. "BEST Benefits: Employer Perspectives." Boston: Commonwealth Corporation. Research and Evaluation Brief, Vol. 2, Issue 4, October.

Liebowitz, Marty, and Judith Combes Taylor. 2004. *Breaking Through: Helping Low-Skilled Adults Enter and Succeed in College and Careers.* Boston: Jobs for the Future and the National Council for Workforce Education.

Maguire, Sheila, Joshua Freely, Carol Clymer, Maureen Conway, and Deena Schwartz. 2010. *Tuning In to Local Labor Markets: Findings from the Sectoral Employment Impact Study.* Philadelphia: Public/Private Ventures. http://www.aspenwsi.org/wordpress/wp-content/uploads/TuningIntoLocalLaborMarkets.pdf.

Mangat, Ravinder. 2010. *Sector Snapshot: A Profile of Sector Initiatives, 2010.* Oakland, CA: National Network of Sector Partners, Insight Center for Community Economic Development. http://www.insightcced.org/uploads/publications/ wd/Sector-Snapshots.pdf.

Marano, Cindy, and Kim Tarr. 2004. "The Workforce Intermediary: Profiling the Field of Practice and Its Challenges." In *Workforce Intermediaries for the Twenty-First Century*, edited by Robert P. Giloth. Published in assocation with the American Assembly, Columbia University. Philadelphia: Temple University Press.

Miller, Cynthia, Johannes M. Bos, Kristin E. Porter, Fannie M. Tseng, and Yasuyo Abe. 2005. *The Challenge of Repeating Success in a Changing World: Final Report on the Center for Employment Training Replication Sites.* New York: MDRC, September.

————, Mark van Dok, Betsy L. Tessler, and Alexandra Pennington. 2012. *Strategies to Help Low-Wage Workers Advance: Implementation and Final Impacts of the Work Advancement and Support Center (WASC) Demonstration.* New York: MDRC, September.

National Governors Association Center for Best Practices. 2002. *A Governor's Guide to Cluster-Based Economic Development.* Report prepared by Stuart A. Rosenfeld. Washington, DC: NGA Center for Best Practices.

Prince, David, and Davis Jenkins. 2005. *Building Pathways to Success for Low-Skill Adult Students: Lessons for Community College Policy and Practice from a Statewide Longitudinal Tracking Study.* New York: Community College Research Center, Teachers College, Columbia University, April.

Rab, Sara. 2003. "Building a Career Pathways System: Promising Practices in Community College–Centered Workforce Development: Research in Brief." *Educause Quarterly*, No. 1.

Roberts, Brandon, and Derek Price. 2012. *Strengthening State Systems for Adult Learners: An Evaluation of the First Five Years of Shifting Gears.* Chicago: Joyce Foundation, December.

Roder, Anne, and Mark Elliott. 2011. *A Promising Start: Year Up's Initial Impacts on Low-Income Young Adults' Careers.* New York: Economic Mobility Corporation, April.

Rossi, Peter H., Mark W. Lipsey, and Howard E. Freeman. 2004. *Evaluation: A Systematic Approach, Seventh Edition.* Sage Publications.

Schultz, Caroline, and David Seith. 2011. *Career Advancement and Work Support Services on the Job: Implementing the Ft. Worth Work Advancement and Support Center Program.* New York: MDRC, April.

Sherrill, Andrew. 2012. "Workforce Investment Act: Innovative Collaborations between Workforce Boards and Employers Helped Meet Urgent Local Workforce Needs." Washington, DC: U.S Government Accountability Office, Testimony before the Subcommittee on Employment and Workplace Safety, Committee on Health, Education, Labor and Pensions, U.S. Senate, February 16.

Sherwood, Kay. 2009. *Helping Low-Wage Workers Access Work Supports: Lessons for Practitioners*. New York: MDRC Practitioner Brief, November.

Smith, Tara Carter, Rachel V. Douglas, and Robert W. Glover. 2012a. *The Evolution of the CareerAdvance® Program in Tulsa, Oklahoma*. Austin, TX: Ray Marshall Center for the Study of Human Resources, Lyndon B. Johnson School of Public Affairs, University of Texas at Austin, October.

————, and Christopher T. King. 2011. *Exploratory Return-on-Investment Analysis of Local Workforce Investments*. Austin: Ray Marshall Center for the Study of Human Resources, Lyndon B. Johnson School of Public Affairs, University of Texas at Austin, August.

————, Christopher T. King, and Daniel G. Schroeder. 2012b. *Local Investments in Workforce Development: 2012 Evaluation Update*. Austin: Ray Marshall Center for the Study of Human Resources, Lyndon B. Johnson School of Public Affairs, University of Texas at Austin, January.

Soricone, Lisa, and Navjeet Singh. 2011. *Measuring Business Impact: Lessons Learned from Workforce Development in Massachusetts*. Boston: Commonwealth Corporation, September. http://www.commcorp.org/resources/documents/Measuring%20Business%20Impact%20-%20Lessons%20Learned%2009.20111.pdf.

————, Navjeet Singh, and Rebekah Lashman. 2011. *Measuring Business Impact: A Workforce Development Practitioner's Guide*. Boston: Commonwealth Corporation, November. http://www.commcorp.org/resources/documents/MBI_Guidebook_1215.pdf.

Stephens, Rosanna Perry. 2009. *Charting a Path: An Exploration of the Statewide Career Pathway Efforts of Arkansas, Kentucky, Oregon, Washington, and Wisconsin*. Seattle: Seattle Jobs Initiative, May.

Strawn, Julie. 2011. *Farther, Faster: Six Promising Programs Show How Career Pathways Bridges Help Basic Skills Students Earn Credentials That Matter*. Washington, DC: Center for Law and Social Policy, Center for Postsecondary and Economic Success, August 23.

————. 2010. *Shifting Gears: State Innovation to Advance Workers and the Economy in the Midwest*. Chicago: Joyce Foundation, July.

U.S. Government Accountability Office. 2012. *Workforce Investment Act: Innovative Collaborations between Workforce Boards and Employers Helped Meet Local Needs*. Washington, DC: USGAO, Report GAO-12-97, January.

Woolsey, Lindsey. 2011. *Moving Beyond the Count: Maryland's Skills to Compete Initiative, A Case Study*. Ann Arbor, MI: Corporation for a Skilled Workforce, June.

————, Garrett Groves, Martin Simon, Larry Good, and Eric Seleznow. 2012. *State Sector Strategies Coming of Age: Implications for State Workforce Policymakers*. Washington, DC: National Governors Association Center for Best Practices, with the Corporation for a Skilled Workforce and the National Skills Coalition.

Zeidenberg, Matthew, Sung-Woo Cho, and Davis Jenkins. 2010. "Washington State's Integrated Basic Education and Skills Training Program (I-BEST): New Evidence of Effectiveness." CCRC Working Paper No. 20. New York: Community College Research Center, Teachers College, Columbia University, September.

12

Journeys and Destinations: The National Fund for Workforce Solutions Evaluation

Mark Popovich

From the earliest days of the "Race to Space" through today, ground control depended on telemetry systems to be their eyes and ears. Sensors, guidance systems, and communications equipment combined to instantaneously collect and report essential data. Those findings would inform decisions to "throttle up," to "abort," and even to terminate the vehicle if it strayed beyond safety parameters. Were engines delivering expected thrust? Were gyroscopes maintaining the correct direction and attitude? Would the package reach the intended orbit? Each launch was managed as an experiment—especially in the early days but even today. It required careful management and access to real-time information, along with the capacity to review all system components after the fact.

On an unseasonably warm day in September 2007, something quite different from a rocket ship began its maiden journey. In a conference room at the National Press Club, a core of national sponsors announced the formation of the National Fund for Workforce Solutions. This initial unveiling followed more than a year of preparation and discussion that included securing $15 million in commitments from three foundations, as well as the U.S. Department of Labor.[1]

Shortly thereafter, a telemetry system of sorts was designed and activated for the National Fund to monitor significant developments and performance parameters. The plan combined a national third-party evaluation with the efforts of local site evaluators. Essential components included core definitions, common data descriptors, and a data reporting and management system. All were marshaled to monitor the performance of this new approach, assess its components, and accurately chart its journey.

This new initiative, because it differs markedly from traditional national philanthropic programs, is a journey or experiment. Six years in, it has achieved significant accomplishments, faced considerable challenges, and provided lessons about the contours of effective practices and approaches. Much of this is captured in the National Fund evaluation reports.

This chapter reviews many specific elements of the National Fund evaluation. Preceding the current effort, there was already an extensive literature of varied evaluation evidence from workforce-development efforts (see King, Chapter 11). However, as the National Fund differs from its antecedents in design and implementation, the conclusions and ideas generated from the evaluation also differ in degree and kind. Perhaps the National Fund evaluation will offer insights others can use as guidance as workforce-development efforts and systems seek to reform and boost their effectiveness.

The remainder of this chapter is grouped into five sections:

- Review of the National Fund's principles, goals, and operating approaches.

- Discussion of the formation of the evaluation process and methods.

- Detailed review of selected evaluation findings;.

- An overview of evaluation experiences of an experienced urban site (Skill-Works) and a new initiative in a rural setting (Central Wisconsin).

- Key observations derived from the evaluation.

Principles, Goals, and Operating Approaches

Telemetry requires gyroscopes and fixed positioning to accurately determine position, velocity, and direction. In a similar fashion, an evaluation derives its bearings from firmly moored principles and priorities.

From the launch and continuing to the present, the sponsors worked together to clarify and communicate the National Fund's core principles, specific goals, and operating approaches. In practice, the strategy's originators drew on a sometimes hard-won experience in workforce development and related grantmaking.[2] And the pilot grants announced in fall 2007 expanded efforts in six communities. Each had been established with support from the Ford, Rockefeller, and Annie E. Casey foundations and had a track record of accomplishments.[3]

Key aspects of the National Fund can be broken down into three categories: principles, goals, and approaches.

Principles

A key principle of the National Fund was that reforms were needed in workforce-development policy, including changes on both the national and the local or regional level. The public workforce and related systems are bound by policies and regulations that often make it hard to have them work together constructively on the ground as part of a more seamless, coherent system.[4] The National Fund sites and regions are working to do so and thereby illustrate the gains reform can yield. This objective is referred to as a key part of the National Fund's systems-change agenda.

Another principle is that the National Fund is not a prescriptive model. Rather, it embraces a variety of approaches consistent with its principles and operating approaches. And finally the National Fund emphasizes assisting lower-wage workers and job seekers to find and keep jobs that improve earnings and benefits.[5] It is not, however, proscribed to only serve their needs.

Goals

The National Fund launched with a national goal of raising $50 million for five or more years.[6] With a four-to-one match requirement at each local site, that total increases to $250 million. That scale is certainly a milestone for philanthropic funding for workforce development and employment services.[7]

The National Fund made it a goal to help fifty thousand people either land jobs or advance in careers that offer family-supporting earnings[8] and to serve one thousand employers in finding, recruiting, and training the workers with the skills they need to succeed.[9] The investors hoped to do so by supporting thirty local or regional sites.[10]

Approaches

The National Fund was a platform for attracting and leveraging resources at the national and regional or local levels, including the requirement that local sites generate a fourfold match of the national funding. A high local co-investment helps ensure close management attention at that level and may help build resiliency in cases where National Fund support ends.

The National Fund offered sites funding that could be spent more flexibly than other workforce funding sources, which were often cramped by regulations.[11] More traditional public programs can make it difficult to accomplish key functions, including assessing local opportunities and challenges, convening disparate agencies and leaders, weaving together various programs into a more effective strategy, and filling gaps by offering some new forms of support or services.

The National Fund approach helps empower local decision makers to customize implementation based on their unique challenges, opportunities, and priorities. They are challenged to devise approaches tailored to their conditions that are consistent with the National Fund's core principles and operating approaches.

Finally, the National Fund works to meet the needs of both the demand (employers) and supply (workers) sides of the labor market. That was key, as it has long been established as a hallmark of more effective workforce-development and employment efforts.[12] This approach orients the National Fund to focus on specific job sectors that are growing, another proven approach in the workforce arena.

Forming the National Fund Evaluation

It is important to begin by sketching the National Fund's approach to evaluation. Richard McGahey represented the Ford Foundation from the earliest discussions through the launch of the National Fund and beyond; his experience in planning and conducting complex evaluation projects was crucial[13] as he led the effort to develop and implement the initial evaluation plans.[14]

Organizers of the initiative created an evaluation plan that provided overall direction and, in the early operating phase, partnered with Jobs for the Future to provide shared staff.[15] With limited staff, the National Fund needed consultants under contract for evaluation and issued a request for proposals that set evaluation goals, timelines, and priorities. After a review, the National Fund retained Workforce Learning Strategies in collaboration with Program and Policy Insight LLC under a five-year contract.[16]

The consultant team's primary tasks were to complete the details of the evaluation design, finalize metrics to be tracked, specify common definitions of key terms,[17] operate a data-management system to collect site-level data, and provide technical assistance. Once in operation, the consultants collaborated with the national investors and National Fund staff to refine the focus of the evaluation. And, of course, their main tasks included assessing the quantitative and qualitative data, analyzing results, and reporting annually on outcomes, progress against goals, and emerging issues.

Applications from local sites for National Fund support required a discussion of evaluation plans and capacities.[18] Following evaluation protocols and collaborating with the national evaluation effort—including data reporting—were also conditions of continued National Fund support.[19] Indeed, local evaluators were a key data source for the national evaluation.[20] Local evaluation partners also helped sites focus and learn on key issues while serving as a tool for reflective action, learning, and increasing local capacity.[21]

Questions that framed the evaluation efforts for the National Fund included the following:

- Core Principles: To what degree were the principles put into practice? Did fidelity to principles relate positively to capacity, performance, and other key metrics?

- Goals: The National Fund was launched with specified goals. What progress was made toward achieving those goals, both across the initiative and at individual sites?

- Lessons: Can quantitative and qualitative information be marshalled to derive, with some rigor, lessons about the overall approach, strategies, and tactics?

- Monitoring Performance and Allocating Resources: How were individual sites progressing toward their goals? Were there promising or lagging aspects to site or workforce-partnership performance? Did these results prove relevant to allocating limited resources—such as additional or renewed grant funding, technical assistance, or coaching help focused on specific issues?

- Policy Momentum: The primary federal workforce-development program was overdue for reauthorization and was (and is) suffering from stagnant or declining funding. Did the National Fund "prove" the efficacy of a different set of principles that could reanimate the policy debate? Could it provide policy approaches to reform the underperforming and underappreciated federal workforce-development program?

Practical considerations led to the decision that participant-level data would not be required by the national evaluation from the participating sites or funding collaboratives.[22] Rather, the national evaluation relied on summary data. In some ways, this limited the analytical capacity of the national evaluation. To some degree, this is changing for some local and regional sites under terms of the grant from the Social Innovation Fund, due to the requirement for impact assessments.[23]

Throughout the National Fund's pre–Social Innovation Fund years, the sites shared annual summary data with the national evaluation consultants. The independent national evaluation team compiled the data, developed qualitative insights from interviews and site visits, and discussed results and summary outcomes with the evaluation committee and national investors. The National Fund releases formal annual reports, often in the late summer or early fall.[24]

Evaluation Findings

The evaluation tracked progress of the National Fund along its implementation journey and served to continuously orient the effort along the pathway. It portrayed individual site progress and, when summarized together, the overarching performance of the National Fund.

This section reviews results from the National Fund with results available from *The National Fund for Workforce Solutions: Data Brief 2013*. Where added detail was necessary or useful but was not available from the brief, information was drawn from the fourth-year evaluation.[25]

Progress on Specific Goals

The National Fund grew from an initial national commitment of $15 million, which served to launch local or regional matches. As of the end of 2012, the National Fund could count almost $200 million in pooled and leveraged funds from local or regional sites. Between 2010 and 2011, the number of investors in local or regional sites grew to 431—more than doubling 2008 totals.[26] In 2012 the tally of local investors dipped to 383. At the same time, however, well over half of the local sites were then supported by ten or more funding organizations. And these local supporters demonstrated a diverse base. Through 2012 just over half of the funders for local sites were philanthropic organizations, but public agencies (20 percent) and employers and employer associations (15 percent) were also well represented.

People Served

By the end of 2012 the sites were progressing toward the goal of serving 50,000 people through job placement or career advancement in positions that offer family-supporting wages. From inception through 2012 the National Fund sites claimed 42,299 newly reported participants against the original goal of 50,000. The 2012 total of 12,645 individuals served was a 7 percent increase over 2011. However, the 2011 total of 11,880 was a jump of 64 percent above the 2010 figure. As *Figure 1* illustrates, the momentum in annual increases was dramatic and sustained. [27]

Figure 1: Number of Newly Reported Participants, 2008–2012

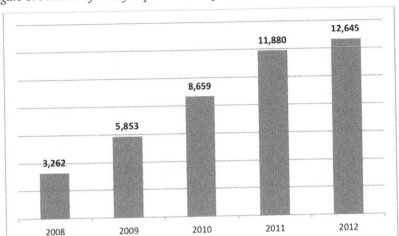

Wages earned at placement is one assessment of progress toward "family-supporting" wages.[28] The wage at placement for non-incumbent participants (job seekers) is displayed in *Table 1*. It indicates that 2,346, or just less than 30 percent, were placed in jobs paying at least $15 per hour. However, the relatively large percentage (10 percent) with missing data may tend to skew that figure lower. The 2011 data from the fourth-year evaluation revealed a more nuanced view. Uneven results across sites and regions and different workforce partnerships—also reflecting different industries or sectors—were evident. Just over one-fifth of the workforce partnership—twenty-two in number—reported that 50 percent or more of the placed participants were in jobs with wages greater than $15 per hour. Across three years of data, the share of job seekers placed in jobs with hourly wages over $10 but under $15 per hour and over $15 per hour was fairly stable. For comparison, the median hourly wage for all occupations in 2011 was $16.57 per hour.[29]

Table 1: Wage Level at Placement

	2010	2011	2012	2012 No. of Job Placements
< $10/hour	15%	27%	25%	2,099
$10.00–$14.99/hour	36%	37%	37%	3,118
$15–$19.99/hour	11%	13%	14%	1,209
>$20/hour	11%	17%	14%	1,137
Unknown/Missing Data	27%	7%	10%	842

Who Is Served

The national evaluation also compiled information on who is served. The data suggest that the strategies were indeed focused on the target audience. From 2008 to 2012 the share of male participants increased from 33 percent to 43 percent (along with 49 percent female and 8 percent whose gender was not reported). This gender balance reflected at least in part the shift away from a predominant focus on health care to include participation in such industries as construction and manufacturing as the economy recovered somewhat. African Americans remained the largest racial or ethnic group served—36 percent in 2012 (with racial data on 27 percent unknown or missing). Almost one-third of the workforce partnerships serviced more than 50 percent African Americans, according to the 2011 report. Most job seekers were poor or low-income; 42 percent had no wages at enrollment, and a further 18 percent had wages under $15 an hour.[30] Since 2008 the share of participants with a high school diploma or less steadily increased from 45 percent and now hovers at or just above 50 percent. More than half of all the partnerships served a participant population made up primarily of individuals with a high school diploma or less. See *Figure 2.*

Figure 2: Educational Attainment of Entering National Fund Participants by Year

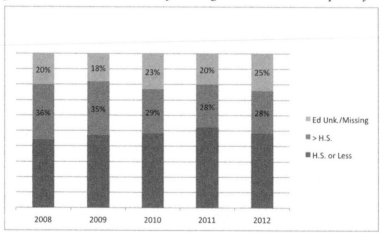

Degrees, Credentials, and Skills Training

Occupational or educational credentials are valuable to individuals and businesses and are often a prerequisite for jobs. And of course jobs that offer higher wages, better conditions, and career-advancement opportunities may be more accessible to job seekers or incumbent workers who present these qualifications.

Figure 3: Newly Reported Degrees and Credentials by Year

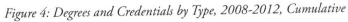

As *Figure 3* displays, a growing number of National Fund participants had completed these credentials as the initiative grew in scale and some sites matured and deepened their focus in these areas. From a low level in the National Fund's first year, with some growth in 2009 and 2010, the base was set for a large jump in 2011 and further growth in 2012. The 10,471 newly reported degrees and credentials attributed to 2012 would be a high fraction, compared with the 12,645 newly reported participants in the same year. However, the newly reported participants and newly reported credentials are not directly comparable. Participants may receive multiple credentials in a single year, and participants who entered the programs at the sites in one year may get their credential and be reported in a later year. The type of credential, degree, or certificate also varies across a wide array, as might be expected in the National Fund's diverse system. Over the full span of the initiative, occupations-skills certificates and credentials account for more than half of all degrees and credentials, as seen in *Figure 4*.

Figure 4: Degrees and Credentials by Type, 2008-2012, Cumulative

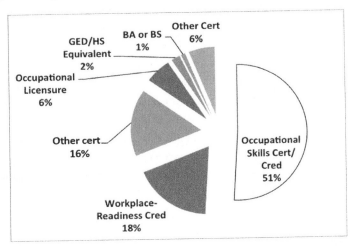

These skills are often in demand in the labor market. The high concentration in this area is encouraging and may be linked to higher wages at placement in jobs or advancement for incumbent workers. At the other end of the spectrum, workforce-readiness credentials (18 percent of all credentials and degrees) may be most relevant to individuals with poor job histories. Completing a course may help prepare them for some lower-paid entry-level jobs. In most cases, however, getting higher-level skills would be necessary to move forward toward careers in positions that offer family-supporting wages and benefits.

Job Placements

In 2012 the participating National Fund sites operated ninety-six sector-based partnerships, which reported that 11,694 job-seeker participants achieved job placements. That was a marked increase of 52 percent over the 2011 level of 7,671 (39 percent of the total) placed in employment.[31] Certainly, the slowly improving economy helped. But the investment by local sites and individual workers was also paying off.

Business Impact

The National Fund long ago exceeded its original goal of serving 1,000 employers; as of 2012, 4,064 were reported as having been served in some way. As *Figure 5* indicates, the momentum in engaging additional new employers accelerated from the initial years through 2011, with the numbers plateauing after that. The mix of services was evolving, however. In 2012, for the first time, assessment of employer needs was the most frequently provided service (57 percent in 2012 and 56 percent in 2011). Recruitment, screening, and referral of job applicants continued to be an important service to employers but declined from 60 percent in 2011 to 53 percent in 2012. Other services were provided to smaller segments of the employer group, including 29 percent for new-hiring training in basic skills, 26 percent for training of new hires in occupational skills, 15 percent for development of career-ladder programs, and 14 percent for training-plan development. The largest share of employers served was in construction (32 percent), followed by health care (26 percent). Manufacturing, however, grew quickly from a small base as the number of manufacturing firms served increased by 200 percent from 2010 to 2011. In the third-year evaluation, the national evaluators worked with local evaluation partners to gather additional data about employers engaged in National Fund activities and services. Surveys of 173 employer respondents indicated high satisfaction levels (*Figure 6*) as well as the top outcomes employers reported achieving through this assistance (*Table 2*).[32]

Figure 5: Number of Newly Reported Employers by Year

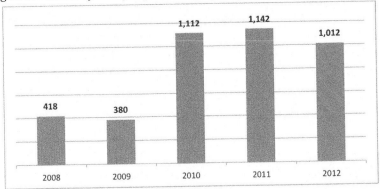

Figure 6: 75% of Employers Are Highly Satisfied or Satisfied with Services from Local/Regional National Fund Sites

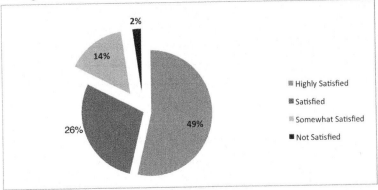

Based on 2010 survey of 177 employer respondents.

Table 2: Top Employer Outcomes from Assistance

Survey Data Collected in 2010[33]	N = 177 employer respondents
Employer Outcome	% of Employers Reporting
Reduce labor shortages	46
Support worker advancement	46
Reduce skill shortages	43
Improve quality or other standards	39
Improve productivity and competitiveness	34
Improve employee retention	34
Reduce turnover	30
Support for business expansion	26
Improve revenues	20

Targeting Industry Sectors

By 2011 the sectors most frequently targeted were health care, manufacturing, and construction. The variety and scale of the targeted industries evolved from the early years through 2011. *Table 3* displays that change.

Table 3: Workforce Partnerships by Industry or Sector

Sector	% 2008	% in 2011
Automobile Repair	0	10
Biotechnology	19	13
Construction	19	45
Energy	0	29
Financial Services	8	13
Health Care	51	97
Hospitality	3	19
Information Technology	3	22
Logistics/Transportation/Distribution	8	19
Manufacturing	14	52
Other	11	23

Fostering Collaboratives

The National Fund launched with initial grants to six sites. As of 2012 the focus spread beyond a distinct concentration in the Northeast and the West Coast to all regions as the number of local sites rose to thirty-two, with twenty-nine included as active and reporting annual progress.[34] The number of local investors funding these sites increased to 431 in 2011—a 136 percent rise since 2008—but dipped to 383 as of 2012. See *Table 4* to track the growth in the number of sites and the geographical spread of the National Fund.

Table 4: History of Sites Added to the National Fund

Cohort/Date	Northeast	South	Midwest	West
Carryover from prior pilot	Baltimore Boston New York Pennsylvania Rhode Island			SF Bay Area
October 2007	Washington, DC		Chicago	Los Angeles San Diego

October 2008	Hartford Philadelphia	Dan River	Central WI Cincinnati Denver Des Moines Milwaukee Omaha Wichita	Seattle
2009–2011	Newark	Manatee/Sarasota	Detroit	San Joaquin
2011 (SIF)		Atlanta Greenville Jackson/Delta Louisville Mobile New Orleans Shreveport		

Evaluation Experiences of Two National Fund Sites

During the formation and conduct of the evaluation, the evaluation committee members were drawn from among the initiative's national foundation investors. The sites and direct ground level, however, are where the work is done. Those at the local level have a different and valuable viewpoint of the national evaluation.

Table 5: Two Diverse National Fund Communities

	United States	*Boston Metro Region*	*South Wood County Area*
Population	314,000,000	4,600,000	45,741
Population Density	82 per sq. mile	942 per sq. mile	95 per sq. mile
Population Growth, Decade	+10%	+ 4%	–1%
Median Household Income	$51,413	$52,792	$38,367
Unemployment 2013	7.3%	6.8%	6.6%
Employment, Largest Sectors		Educationand Health Services Prof and Bus. Services	Sale and Office Production, Transport, and Material Handling
Employment Change, 2000 to Recent	+7.0%	+40%	–2% –32% Mfg Jobs
Poverty Rate	16%	10.7%	10%

This section offers perspectives from two very different local sites: Boston's SkillWorks and Central Wisconsin's Workforce Central, from the South Wood County area. The two sites were selected precisely because they had widely varying experiences as part of the National Fund.

The Boston SkillWorks Experience

Boston is an urban, relatively higher-income region with fast-paced job growth. The strong base of educational and health care institutions generates the biggest share of jobs. Many of these positions offer relatively good pay, attractive benefits, and stability. However, these jobs and those in many other growing sectors require higher educational attainment and/or occupational certifications and licensures. At the same time, there are significant numbers of individuals and families living at or well below poverty levels, and their circumstances and labor-market conditions make it difficult for them to prepare for, secure, and maintain attachment to family-sustaining jobs. Some employers also report facing ongoing challenges in finding and retaining workers with the skills they require. Boston's SkillWorks was formed to help address employment challenges in the region, a purpose to which it continues its strong commitment.[35] (See Leung, Chapter 7, for a thorough history of SkillWorks.)

SkillWorks was part of the initial launch of the National Fund, thanks to the Boston organization's long experience and strong track record. Planning for Skill-Works began in 2001, and it launched in 2003—well before the National Fund's launch in 2007. Those early efforts were led and supported by local philanthropy, with augmenting support from city and commonwealth public funds and grants from some national foundations. Local leaders created a strong collaborative of financial contributors, created a compelling action plan, and amassed accomplishments. The Boston results, combined with those of other early adapters, provided a strong rationale for the National Fund's goals to support similar approaches at more sites. In SkillWorks's first five years (2003 to 2008), the initiative helped 3,000 people start on career pathways that could lead to jobs offering family-supporting wages, more than 500 found new employment, 800 earned wage increases, and 250 were promoted. Along the way, forty-two employers engaged with Skill-Works, and some improved their practices or increased their workforce-training investments. SkillWorks also advocated for increased public-sector investment, and its efforts helped create the Workforce Competitiveness Trust Fund, which committed $18 million to sector-based programs in Massachusetts in the last five years and was recapitalized with $5 million more in state appropriations in 2012.[36]

Early on, SkillWorks established evaluation processes and procedures. The SkillWorks evaluation initially combined the strengths of Abt Associates and Mt.

Auburn Associates, an expert in economic-development analysis. (The Phase II evaluation contract was to Mt. Auburn Associates alone.)

The products from SkillWorks's evaluation began with a baseline report in 2004.[37] The evaluation noted even then that some of the goals of the initiative are shorter-term and more targeted to specific stakeholders (job seekers, low-income workers, and employers).[38] From the outset, the collaborating Boston funders recognized that there needed to be broader and sustainable changes in how the workforce system operated for the initiative's full impact to be realized.[39] This aspect of SkillWorks's goals was a focus for the evaluation from the first report. The evaluation team noted accomplishments and challenges in the initial year of efforts by the three implementation partners (workforce partnerships) and the public-policy advocacy work. They also began to identify limitations to the evaluation design and focus. The report, for example, identified particular challenges entailed in assessing the impacts of the partnerships and systems-change work. These included developing more standardized metrics, honing outcomes of interest to employer partners, and improving the capacity of the partnerships to track and report consistent and verifiable data relative to these measures on an ongoing basis.[40] Efforts by the evaluation team, combined with the SkillWorks staff and leadership, to improve metrics began with the report's release. The implementation partners' data development and reporting capabilities were further supported by SkillWorks's capacity-building activities.

SkillWorks joined the National Fund and received its first three-year grant award in 2007. In 2008 and 2009 SkillWorks leadership assessed the initiative's progress and lessons and committed to a second five-year, $10 million joint effort. However, while the overarching principles and key areas for investment were sustained, there was also a crucial adjustment in focus. SkillWorks's funders determined to increase the emphasis on post-secondary credential attainment and to better connect basic-skills training to credentialing and post-secondary pathways. This decision was influenced by Phase I experience as well as by research showing the importance of key credentials in the Boston region's high-education, high-skill labor market.

The deepened emphasis on credentialing also reflected the intention to aim toward improving rates of advancement for lower-wage incumbent workers and wages for individuals placed in jobs. Throughout Phase I, the evaluation reports strongly suggested that meeting goals for educational certification and achieving family-supporting earnings levels was likely to take longer than the three-year timeframe for initial investment commitments under SkillWorks.[41]

The shift in emphasis of objectives in Phase II also prompted significant changes to the evaluation. The transition to Phase II was viewed as an opportunity to explore questions that interested SkillWorks's leaders beyond tracking and reporting the initiative's progress in overall terms. Doing so required assessment through tracking individual-participant progress over spans longer than a single program year.[42] As a result, more detailed participant-level data was required across all SkillWorks implementation partnerships and throughout Phase II. To track participants, a database was created that used social security numbers as the universal identifier. The data system was adapted from one originally created by the Commonwealth Corporation. It extends across all programs and uniquely identifies each participant. It allows tracking more information on outcomes over a longer time span.

Participant-level tracking was a major step beyond requiring summary data by program year. The system provided the capacity SkillWorks sought to bring data analysis to bear on key program and policy questions and to monitor participant progress and outcomes in more powerful ways. It also enabled SkillWorks's program team to run reports, monitor progress, and do some analyses directly, without requiring time from the external evaluation partner. This later change could, to some degree, free up the evaluation partner from more routine matters to support and analyze higher-order challenges and questions. This unique ability, however, entailed costs in complexity and time. Collecting, inputting, and updating participant-level data was certainly more complex and burdensome for the implementation partners running programs, and required more of the core SkillWorks staff's time. Partly reflecting this, the budget for evaluation and data increased somewhat in absolute terms between the two phases. The percentage of overall funding to this function evidenced a sharp jump from 4.6 percent in Phase I to 7.9 percent in Phase II.

Table 6: SkillWorks's Budget

	Phase I	Phase II
Full Initiative Budget	$14,100,000	$9,800,000
Evaluation and Data Budget	$650,000	$770,000
Evaluation and Data Percentage	4.6%	7.9%

SkillWorks's local evaluation was designed to learn about, document, and share results. The SkillWorks evaluators were viewed as adept at contributing to these goals by providing a third viewpoint on issues. With a vantage point beyond either investor or service provider, they often helped cut through the clutter of issues and information. The evaluators pointed out specific areas of weakness and challenge, as well as areas to celebrate. They also helped SkillWorks's collaborators focus decisions and identify questions about the work to be conducted in the next contract or grant cycle. A second tier of evaluation priorities included supporting management functions, such as monitoring grantee performance and progress.

The national evaluation requirements were established well after SkillWorks set its Phase I evaluation plans. Due to timing and some differences in data definitions and requirements, there was some misalignment at this point between the local and national processes. As SkillWorks moved into Phase II, the national evaluation process had already unfolded, requirements were defined, and alignment improved. Still, SkillWorks continued to rely primarily on the local evaluation to provide information and feedback about the effectiveness of their grantees and activities.

The national evaluation data summarize the results from Boston and all other sites, but the information is less detailed then Boston's participant-level database can generate. The national evaluation reports and products offer them an interesting field perspective, but their impact on SkillWorks appears to be limited. The Boston local evaluation has focused on a few key themes for analysis and reporting. It also may make reports and analyses more approachable and digestible.

The Central Wisconsin Workforce Central Experience

The South Wood County area of Central Wisconsin is rural,[43] with 1 percent of the population of Boston's metropolitan area. Median income is much lower, but so too are living costs. The economic base traditionally centered on natural resource–based industries. Agricultural production—such as cranberries and dairy products—supports a large and growing food-processing industry. Many of the firms in this sector are highly advanced manufacturers. Paper production in the region dates back to the late nineteenth century. For recent generations, large unionized plants offered high wages and good benefits. Papermaking was the community's economic cornerstone, but changes in ownership from a local family to an international corporation, combined with challenging market conditions, prompted deep downsizing between 2000 and 2010. As nearly 40 percent of total employment evaporated from the base by 2005, residents struggled to find new jobs. Many of the openings required different educational backgrounds and skills than the ones they had. As a result, many younger employees and residents left the area, leaving behind an aging workforce with specialized skills, looking for job that no longer existed.

The Incourage Community Foundation[44] and the local Chamber of Commerce combined efforts, beginning shortly after 2000, to help the community cope with and respond to this deep economic crisis, launching the Community Progress Initiative.[45] They worked on information sharing and creating a shared vision for the future, promoting culture change toward collective action, fostering new relationships, and leadership development. They also engaged in adaptive-skills training to promote citizen engagement in community problem solving.[46] This experience allowed the region to develop a proposal to join the National Fund. They strive to foster an innovative multi-sector workforce system that serves business and workers as part of an overall community and economic development effort. They seek to expand opportunities for people to prepare for and secure family-sustaining jobs and advance in a career. And they continue to develop a partnership of employers, educators, and service providers to meet the needs of the workforce, economy, and job market.[47]

The Central Wisconsin site joined the National Fund in its third round, in October 2008, as it expanded from ten to twenty-one sites. It was among the first two rural areas to enlist in the effort and remains one of only three in the initiative.

Between 2000 and 2008 the area lost about 39 percent of existing jobs. Employment fell, while underemployment and public-assistance claims rose. In 2008 a group of core partners came together, all of whom had received adaptive-skills training.[48] The group included the Incourage Community Foundation, Mid-State Technical College, the Heart of Wisconsin Business and Economic Alliance, and the North Central Wisconsin Workforce Development Board.

With a three-year grant award from the National Fund in October 2008, Central Wisconsin hired a project director and brought on Yellow Wood Associates as the local evaluation partner. Yellow Wood Associates is a Vermont-based expert in rural economic and community development. The first phase of Workforce Central's local evaluation entailed baseline assessments of conditions, systems, and service providers; convening and engaging key stakeholders; and researching best practices. The Central Wisconsin site also joined with the Milwaukee Area Funders Alliance to undertake joint efforts to create online tools that better connect people with public benefits available through federal and state assistance programs.[49] Also in this initial year, the site leadership refined goals, indicators, and measures. And the initiative decided to focus initially on the advanced manufacturing sector. The plan included specific training opportunities that were aligned with business strategies with the target sector. More broadly, the initiative focused on strengthening the network of social-service, education, and training providers to help residents improve their employability.

Fall 2009 seemed to mark a new phase for Workforce Central's efforts with the launch of its first sector-based approach to workforce development, the Manufacturing Partnership, which was guided by a network of eleven manufacturing chief executives. Services available included organizational training assessments, a good-practices guide, and collaborative training from Mid-State Technical College and the workforce-development system. Trainings included a food-manufacturing

science program, manufacturing-skills standard certification, and leadership training. Basic manufacturing fundamentals in safety, quality, production, and maintenance were also offered through Food Stamp Employment and Training Industrial
Manufacturing Certification. Basic skills in manufacturing safety, quality, production, and maintenance were also offered through Food Stamp Employment and
Training Industrial Manufacturing Certification.

Table 7: Workforce Central Budget[50]

	Inception through 2012
Full Initiative Budget	$2,300,000
Evaluation and Data Budget	$324,000
Evaluation and Data Percent	14%

In 2010, Workforce Central hired the Center on Wisconsin Strategy
(COWS) to be its local evaluator. This nonprofit think-and-do tank is based at
the University of Wisconsin–Madison. It was a promising partner mostly due to
COWS's twenty years of experience with industry-partnership models, as well as
their expertise in workforce policy and practice evaluation. Under the agreement,
COWS would assess Workforce Central's strategies and programs and work with
the National Fund evaluation effort.

From the start, the leaders of Workforce Central have emphasized an evalua-
tion-as-learning process.[51] The theory of change was clarified with assistance from
the Aspen Institute's Community Strategies Group. The process of evaluation and
development of its specific theory of change became an important and unifying
force. That helped, for example, the social-service, education, and training providers see themselves as part of the workforce system. It aided in delineating their part
in a larger overarching system.

With the launch of a rural workforce-funders collaborative, the National
Fund emphasis on collecting and reporting detailed outcome measures was not a
strong fit. In the initial years of development and refinement, Workforce Central's
goals were defined at a high level. As COWS joined the effort, it focused on honing measurements to track progress on those goals, which reflected the interests
of different stakeholders. Those efforts culminated in a January 2012 report that
included such metrics as the number of people employed and trained but also
incorporated qualitative measures drawn from the viewpoints of workers, trainers,
and employers. The local evaluation report included many specific lessons, findings, discussions of implications, and details of best practices.

From Workforce Central's perspective, the local and national evaluations
were not strongly connected, initially. As one of the local leaders observed, "The

national evaluators were looking for outcomes for the hardest to serve. Employers were telling us to focus on incumbent workers, particularly in light of the 2008 recession." There was also an adjustment period in the early days after the initial National Fund award to Workforce Central, as some local investors had little experience with supporting evaluation. Over time, experience helped to ease concerns in both areas.

This site credits the national evaluation with keeping it connected to other sites as part of a network engaged in common work and challenges. The national reports, with summaries from across the sites, raise the visibility of Workforce Central's impact nationally.

In late 2010 Workforce Central was among ten existing National Fund sites to receive a multiyear funding commitment with resources from the Social Innovation Fund (SIF). The SIF funding includes a requirement for a quasi-experimental design impact evaluation process. That approach and design goes well beyond the national evaluation's methods and available data. Workforce Central was selected as one of a handful of sites for this expanded evaluation work. COWS saw the potential for the SIF impact evaluation to persuasively demonstrate the value of the National Fund model. With that evidence in hand, the information could be more readily disseminated nationally and give credence and legitimacy to this approach to workforce development. The data requirements for the site are consistent with past national evaluations. However, the SIF grant did prompt the site to implement its own data-collection system so that participant-level data could be collected and reported while maintaining confidentiality.

Lessons and Issues from the National Evaluation

At this stage of the National Fund, it's time to consider whether the work and evaluation are worth the effort. Were the experiment's accomplishments worth the commitment of funding, effort, and the challenges confronted? A debt is owed to the evaluators—at the national and site levels—as the information to answer that question developed from their dedication.

This final section highlights six observations derived from the author's association with the national evaluation effort from the beginning.

The National Evaluation Links Effectiveness to Fidelity with the Initiative's Core Principles

For the fourth-year evaluation, the national investors worked with the evaluation team to refocus the analyses. The aim was to examine the National Fund's major hypothesis that implementation of key principles leads to positive outcomes for job seekers, incumbent workers, and employers. The first step was to develop criteria to assess how the principles were being implemented. These criteria allowed evaluators to classify or rate each collaborative and workforce partnership connected to the National Fund. For outcomes for individuals, quantitative data through December 2011 is the source. All other ratings rely on qualitative information from interviews, site visits, written reports, and other documents.

The analysis determined that three quarters of collaboratives garnered ratings of high to moderate overall conformity with National Fund principles. Interestingly, the fidelity ratings did not vary systematically by the date the site joined the National Fund cohort. There was, according to the evaluators, a positive relationship between collaborative and partnership fidelity. But due to data dispersion, the relationship should not be considered a strong linear association.

Sufficient data were also available to rate 80 of the 125 workforce partnerships operating within the National Fund. The great majority (66 percent) target low-income, low-skilled individual and receive the highest fidelity rating. A further 26 percent get a moderate rating. Three-quarters received high to moderate ratings on both employer engagement and career advancement. And 67 percent achieve moderate or better ratings on sustainability. Only 15 percent of the partnerships received the highest overall fidelity rating, as partnerships needed perfect scores on all criteria to reach that plateau.

The National Fund's theory of change predicts a positive relationship between fidelity to the principles by partnerships with overall outcomes. The analysis provides strong evidence that this is true and holds for programs for both job seekers and incumbent workers. The national evaluators conclude that "the broad findings … suggest that high fidelity partnerships are more likely to yield higher overall outcomes that include participant, employer, and system change."[52] There was also a positive relationship between workforce partnership and collaborative fidelity. Two thirds of partnerships achieving high fidelity scores are working with collaboratives ranking in the top third in their conformance to the National Fund's vision and principles. The interplay of collaboratives and partnerships is key. At the same time, the relative roles and responsibilities of collaboratives and partnerships are quite varied across the thirty-two sites.

Finally, the evaluation showed that systems-change efforts are strengthened by the National Fund principles, with evidence showing a fairly strong relationship between conformance to National Fund principles and success in effecting system change in public policy, programs, and institutions and among employers.

Evaluation of the National Fund Is a Valuable but Complex Challenge

The tools of evaluation may be better attuned to assessing a model program or design. To varying degrees, the National Fund's assessment encompasses elements of program evaluation, goals-based evaluation, process evaluation, and impact evaluation—albeit to a lesser extent. That is a wide range of assignments. And it is implemented through an evaluation across a large scale that also embraces decentralization and a diversity of approaches.

Despite that complexity, the National Fund evaluation is a key tool for learning and managing the effort at the national and local or regional levels. It is a navigational guide for addressing a host of issues, including gauging progress toward achieving goals, assessing contributions of sites and workforce partnerships, facilitating adjustment of goals, and verifying and helping to increase impacts at all levels. The evaluation has helped to clarify the efforts' focus and strategies, facilitated comparisons over time, and produced output and outcomes data useful for dissemination and promotion. Finally, the evaluation helped heighten awareness of the value of workforce-development and employment investments, particularly with economically disadvantaged incumbent workers and job seekers; highlighted the need for an expanded role for employers as investors and decision makers in these efforts; and illuminated lessons to guide further adoption and replication.

Most important, the national evaluation generates the evidence essential to promoting an agenda for reforming and refocusing the workforce-development, training, education, and employment-services systems. It demonstrates what can be accomplished within the "silos" and restrictions of existing policies and programs. And it defines bright spots and innovative practices and directions that deserve additional investments.

The relative value of the national evaluation is straightforward to describe but more complicated to assess. The annual contract costs for national evaluation partners varied from a low of $350,000 in the first year of 2007–2008 to a high of $500,000 in 2008–2009, and has settled in the $400,000 to $443,000 range in subsequent years. This compares companies with an annual overall budget of $7.7 million.[53] The concurrent spending for local-evaluation capacity is not readily available. However, based on a review of budget plans across a variety of sites and regions, these are modest, with a few exceptions. For example, SkillWorks invested more and required more intensive reporting.

The National Fund Demonstrates the Level of Demand for Reform

The growth of the National Fund to thirty-two diverse sites or regions is like an iceberg. It illustrates the tip of a larger, unseen mass below. National philanthropic initiatives are sometimes a draw because of the funding resources they offer. With the National Fund, grant sizes are quite modest ($150,000 or less annually). And even those modest, albeit flexible, resources are entwined with significant requirements. More recently, however, a handful of communities approached the National Fund to join in the learning and adopt the model. They are doing so either without the need for grant support or with the knowledge that grant support is not assured. The model is proving effective, and the ideas behind it are compelling. Reform through systems change is happening across almost all sites, even within the many constraints of existing policies and programs.

More Rigorous Impact Assessment and Comparative Cost Effectiveness Are Missing Pieces

As discussed earlier in this chapter, decisions shaping the national evaluation in the earliest stages reflect the priorities and needs forecast at that time. An impact assessment was considered too complex and costly. It was also a lower priority, given prior evaluations of sector-based workforce-development programs. As such, the design did not include collection of participant-level data. However, the award from the Social Innovation Fund entails a requirement for a quasi-experimental design impact assessment for select National Fund sites. The contract is awarded and work is under way to conduct that assessment at sites in Wisconsin, Ohio, and Pennsylvania. Data from the sites will be combined with information from state employment data sets. Together they will yield a representative control group and allow evaluators to compare outcomes for individuals participating or not participating in the National Fund sites' services. The prospects for analyzing the cost-effectiveness of the approach are dimmer, however, due to the complexity of how the sites are financed. Those sites receive national funding, as well as cash and in-kind matches from local sources. Evaluators may be able to use grants-management budget reports to track the former. But the cash or in-kind local match funding, which often comes from a variety of sources, is difficult or impossible to measure. Spending of National Fund grants is usually reported within broad categories. There are few if any cases with reports of sufficient detail to allow allocation of spending between types of services or between services and systems-change efforts.

The National Fund Should Meet the Challenge of Speeding the Ramp-Up of New Sites

A grant from the National Fund provides initial flexible resources to help organize and recruit a funders' collaborative, assess local challenges and opportunities, and choose first priorities for funding through workforce partnerships. The model is appealing and is proving effective. It is, however, also complex and time-consuming to implement. According to the national evaluation data, the vast majority of new sites or regions take at least twelve to eighteen months to begin offering services at significant scale. Because it is such a decentralized approach that requires customization, there are likely limits to how much quicker the set-up phase can be completed. Some combination of technical assistance or capacity building, tools and publications capturing lessons learned, and other interventions should be considered to quicken the pace at the initial site-development stage.

2013 Marks a New Phase for the National Fund That May Also Shift Evaluation Priorities

The national evaluation was always viewed as a tool useful at both the national and the local level, with philanthropic organizations serving as major partners at both levels. Within the foundation landscape, accountability internally and to the public is an important requirement. It is also a key management tool for operating a complex strategy at the national or local level. However, the national investors were the direct client for the evaluation. The core group engaged in shaping annual plans was limited to national investors and National Fund staff. The national evaluation team and National Fund staff consistently shared evaluation results with the sites and fielded suggestions, concerns, and recommendations from local partners. But general input is a poor substitute for direct engagement. In 2013 the National Fund governance structure will change. National investors will be a minority of the committee, and the voices of sites and others will be louder and directly involved. The new committee will have authority for guiding the national evaluation. One direction of change might be to recraft the evaluation to be a more useful and used tool of management for the local and regional sites.

Conclusion

The National Fund and its evaluation were charting a way forward that presents real promise. It was a guide that was applicable to designing and implementing more comprehensive strategies to meet the needs of both lower-wage workers and employers. With this initiative, local and national philanthropy combined resources in an award-winning effort that demonstrated the value of this new combination of institutional arrangements, strategies, and functions. Over five years, the evolution and scaling of the effort was impressive. There is significant evidence to support the theory of change. And as the initiative passes into the next phase, prospects are indeed quite exciting.

The need for change is certainly great as well. As America struggles with an anemic recovery from the Great Recession, economic and job growth is far too weak. At the same time, the public sector is locked into budget cutting rather than investing in the stagnant economy. From Washington to most statehouses and in many city council chambers, poor revenue projections and high demand for services combine to create enormous budget pressures.

This is a public-policy climate that demands innovation. Policies must deliver results that matter and can be felt. Investing in human capital through workforce development and employment services must be part of the key to unlocking growth. The National Fund's approaches and lessons provide a way forward for many more places.

Appendix: Local Evaluation Contacts (as of June 2012)

Site	Site Contact and Organization	Local Evaluation Partner
Atlanta	Cinda Herdon-King United Way Atlanta	Kelly Hill Nexus Research Group
Baltimore	Martha Holleman Association of Baltimore Area Grantmakers	Ann St. George Abt Associates
Boston	Loh-Sze Leung Boston Foundation	Devon Winey Mt. Auburn Associates
Central Wisconsin	Rick Merdan Incourage Community Foundation	Michele Mackey Center on Wisconsin Strategies
Chicago	n/a	Rhae Parkes RJFP Consulting
Cincinnati	Ross Meyer United Way of Greater Cincinnati	Chris Spence New Growth Group
Dan River	Julie Brown Dan River Region Collaborative	Brandi Tweedy
Denver	n/a	Beth Mulligan Corona Insights
Des Moines	Helen Grossman United Way of Des Moines	Chris Spence
Detroit	Jennifer Irish Live United of Southeastern Michigan	Jane F. Morgan JFM Consulting
Greenville	John Baker Greenville Works	Leise Rosman Corp. for a Skilled Workforce

Site	Site Contact and Organization	Local Evaluation Partner
Hartford	Kim Oliver Capital Workforce Partners	Devon Winey Mt. Auburn Associates
Jackson (Delta)	Aisha Nyandoro Foundation for the Mid South	Cassandra Drennan
Los Angeles	n/a	Pat Lee Vital Research
Louisville	Cindy Read KentuckianaWorks	In Transition
Manatee-Sarasota (FL)	Mireya Eavey Career Edge Funders	Bonnie Beresford Capital Analytics
Milwaukee	Karen Gotzler Urban Strategies	Terry Batson U.W.–Milwaukee
Mobile	Laura Chandler Southwest Alabama Work- force Development Council	Not specified
New Orleans	Ellen Lee Greater New Orleans Foundation	Not specified
New York	Stacy Woodruff-Bolte Public/Private Ventures	Stacy Woodruff-Bolte Public/Private Ventures
Newark	Regina Bardoza, Greater Newark Workforce Funders Collaborative	Charyl Yarbrough Heldrich Center
Omaha	Jami Anders-Kemp	Not specified
Pennsylvania	Steve Herzenberg Keystone Center	Not specified
Philadelphia	Seth Green, United Way of Southeastern Pennsylvania	Barbara Fink Branch Associates
Rhode Island	n/a	Catherine Dun Rappaport Abt Associates
San Diego	Jessica Mosier San Diego Workforce Partnership	Sonia Taddy Harder & Company
San Francisco	Jessica Pitt San Francisco Foundation	Kathy Booth The RP Group
San Joaquin	Dennis Prieto, San Joaquin Valley Workforce Funders Collaborative	Stergios Roussos, Alliance for Com- munity Research and Development
Seattle	Chris Pierson SkillUp Washington	Annie Laurie Armstrong, Business Government Community Connections
Shreveport	Paula Hickman Community Foundation of North Louisiana	Helen K. Wise Institute for Human Services and Public Policy, LSU
Washington, DC	Sarah Oldmixon Community Foundation of the National Capital Region	Carrie Markovitz Abt Associates
Wichita	Keith Lawing Workforce Alliance of South Central Kansas	Beth Tatarka Austin Peters Group

Notes

1. The Hatcher Group (2007). The initial fiscal commitments came from the Annie E. Casey, Ford, and Hitachi foundations, with supplemental support for evaluation from the U.S. Department of Labor.
2. Waldron (2008), pp. 2–6.
3. Ibid., p.6.
4. U.S. Government Accountability Office (2011), pp. 4–6. By one count of federally funded employment and training programs, there are forty-seven different efforts across nine agencies with combined budgets exceeding $18 billion as of FY2009.
5. The Hatcher Group (2007); Baran et al. (2009)
6. The Hatcher Group (2007).
7. The commitment from the national foundations is sufficiently large that it engendered anxiety about secondary impacts. Many of the philanthropies committed to the National Fund provide base support to the workforce-development field. Such a large allocation to implementing the National Fund might affect resources available to research, advocacy, evaluation, and other programs. While funding availability may have been limited in some cases, the National Fund clearly expanded the attention to and the scale of funding to this purpose, as well as enlarging the pool by engaging new funders. This is true at the national level but also particularly the case among community foundations, United Way agencies, and others at the local or regional levels.
8. The Hatcher Group (2007); Baran et al. (2009).
9. Both the press release by the Hatcher Group on behalf of the National Fund and the first annual evaluation report confirm the goal of one thousand businesses. This was later amended to double that to two thousand based on operating experience.
10. Baran et al. (2009). A competitive grant awarded to the National Fund from the Corporation for National Community Service and the new Social Innovation Fund in late 2010 also provided resources—as well as requiring additional matching funds—for ongoing support to some existing sites and also to expand to six to eight new communities in the South or Southwest regions. Additional funding from the same source was awarded in August 2012. With funding from the national investors, local matching resources, and the two Social Innovation Fund grants, the National Fund is engaging thirty-two sites or regions as of early 2013.
11. Site directors and local philanthropic leaders also report that recognition as part of a national initiative is important and valued. They suggest that participation in the National Fund, as well as the implicit endorsement from recognized and respected national foundations, facilitated recruitment of leaders and fundraising.
12. The Annie E. Casey Foundation (2004), pp. 6–9; Combes-Taylor and Rubin (2005), pp. 6–15.
13. In addition to political and policy experience in the U.S. Senate and House, McGahey was engaged in evaluation efforts for two years at the U.S. Department of Labor, five years at Abt Associates, and six years first as a program officer and then as director of impact assessment at the Ford Foundation.
14. Until spring 2013, the national investors operated with an overall Investors Committee shouldering broad oversight and grant decision-making authority. Subcommittees took lead responsibility in specific areas. For the first evaluation committee, Richard McGahey was chair, and Robert P. Giloth (The Annie E. Casey Foundation) and I

were members. After McGahey's departure, the evaluation committee continued with a membership of this author, Robert P. Giloth (The Annie E. Casey Foundation), Chauncy Lennon (Ford Foundation), Kim Ostrowski (Prudential), and Whitney Smith (Joyce Foundation). Both National Fund Deputy Directors, first Steve Adams and then Navjeet Singh, brought added experience in evaluation and provided staff support. National Fund 2.0 was launched in spring 2013, accompanied by a new advisory body and subcommittee structure. The initiative is guided by a new Partners Council. The new group is diverse, including direct involvement by five site representatives, four national foundations, an employer from a local site, and the Jobs for the Future president/CEO. The representatives are: Michael Gritton, KentuckianaWorks, Louisville, KY; Marci Hunn, Harry and Jeanette Weinberg Foundation; Loh-Sze Leung, SkillWorks, Boston; Ross Meyer, Partnership for a Competitive Workforce, Cincinnati; John Padilla, Annie E. Casey Foundation; Mark Rigdon, JPMorgan Chase; Kelly Ryan, Incourage Community Foundation, South Wood County, WI; Marlene Seltzer, Jobs for the Future; Whitney Smith, Joyce Foundation; Jennie Sparandara, Job Opportunity Investment Network, Philadelphia; and Peter Strange, Messer Construction Company, OH. "Partners Council Holds First Meeting," *National Fund Monthly*, May 2013. The Partners Council is also supported by five committees: Executive, Budget/Development, Investor, Policy, and Evaluation. Memo from Fred Dedrick, February 13, 2013. As of mid-2013, Kelly Ryan, president of the Incourage Community Foundation, is chairing the new Evaluation Committee.

15. Through the initial planning and operating years, the National Fund budget allocation for staff, as well as spending for activities beyond grants to sites, was limited by consensus of the national investors. This reflected the intersection of practical concerns and priorities. A core staff complement dedicated solely to the National Fund evolved later. The National Fund staff operates as a program within Jobs for the Future.

16. The original team included seven individuals from three collaborating but distinct organizations: from Workforce Learning Strategies, Barbara Baran, Stephen Michon, and Suzanne Teegarden; from Program and Policy Insight LLC, Leanne Giordono and Kendra Lodewick; and from University of California at Davis, Chris Benner and Manuel Pastor. By the second evaluation report, released in June 2010, the first two organizations and five individuals continued as the project team. The five-year agreement with Workforce Learning Strategies (WLS) and Program and Policy Insight LLC (PPI) came to a conclusion with the release of the fourth-year evaluation report. WLS declined to extend its direct involvement in the ongoing evaluation to cover at a minimum the fifth year of National Fund operation. The National Fund continued a contract with PPI (Giordono and Lodewick), with FutureWorks East (Stephen Michon) as a coauthor. They completed *The National Fund for Workforce Solutions: Data Brief 2013* in April 2013. The report covers the National Fund from inception and first-year reporting through the full fifth year of operations.

17. The national evaluation consultants prepared common definitions and reporting forms for sites or regions and to support local evaluators. *The National Fund for Workforce Solutions Data Dictionary* was updated most recently in November 2010. Both are valued technical assistance, particularly for local evaluators at new sites. This was somewhat less true and a source of some friction in the early stages of work with the six communities that had operated before the National Fund. Differences between these communities and the new regime necessary for the National Fund evaluation were worked through under the leadership of the national evaluation consultant team.

18. Submissions from sites seeking funding required this information and more. Site visits, including an assessment of evaluation capacity, were completed prior to funding approval from the National Fund.

19. A memorandum of understanding (MOU) was required prior to funding for any site joining the National Fund. From the initial grantmaking to current practice, the MOUs explicitly required the site to align regional measures with national measures; contract with a local third-party evaluation partner; analyze each element of the site's approach; work with national evaluators to design local criteria that would adopt the National Fund's common performance metrics; provide data on individual outcomes using the common database; verify data reliability; and provide technical assistance to workforce partnerships locally on data collection and reporting. For an example, see "Memorandum of Understanding with Los Angeles Workforce Funder Collaborative, October 1, 2007–September 30, 2010."

20. Site contacts (grantee organizations) and their local evaluation partners are identified in Appendix I. The national evaluation effort was made possible in considerable part by their ongoing data collection, reporting, and liaison with the evaluation team. This approach started and was strengthened during the evolution of the National Fund. For example, in 2011, in supplementing the usual reporting materials, the national evaluators designed protocols for interviewing and data collection from employers. In most cases, the local or regional sites choose to conduct those employer contacts directly through their local evaluators rather than via contact with those employers by the national evaluation team. However, most local evaluations did not assess funding collaborative and systems change. Some did limited work focused on employers. The common questions reports from local evaluators were valuable, and the national evaluation team also conducted interviews, site visits, and document reviews, as well as analyses of information and data provided by the local evaluators.

21. This lesson was identified by Jennifer Riggenbach of the Incourage Community Foundation.

22. Chief among these considerations is the modest size of grants to the sites from the National Fund—not exceeding $150,000 annually. The complexity of the strategies is a second factor. These strategies usually encompass more than one provider of services. Coordinating reporting and unifying key definitions in these cases is complicated and often costly in time and funding. Third, the data handling and capacity to analyze participant-level data for an initiative of this scale and scope exceeded the budget for evaluation. And fourth, participant-level reporting was not necessary for the evaluation's primary purposes: guiding implementation at the national and local level, apportioning technical assistance and other support, and tracking achievement against the overarching numerical goals.

23. The Social Innovation Fund requires a quasi-experimental design evaluation by a third-party consultant of the fund's grant recipients' projects. In 2011, following a request for proposals and interviews with the top-rated applicants, the National Fund selected IMPAQ International to conduct this evaluation at selected sites in Wisconsin, Pennsylvania, and Ohio.

24. The schedule for the first annual report was somewhat different. The data covered from the date of the grant agreement with the site through December 31, 2008. Data were shared with the national evaluators in January/February 2009. While the consultant team shared preliminary results with the national investors, the final formal report was issued in December 2009.

25. Baran et al. (2012a, 2012b, 2012c) and Giordano, et al. (2013). Most of the quantitate results—particularly those about outcomes for individuals served—are drawn from the beginning date of each site and extending through December 2012. Quantitative data come from the National Fund's Web-based reporting system. Qualitative data is derived from a set of common questions for response from local evaluators, as well as interviews, site visits, written reports, and other documents from the local or regional collaboratives and partnerships.

26. Baran et al. (2012a), p. 1. The one-year growth in the number of funding organizations to the sites between 2010 and 2011 was 36 percent, the largest number of new investors since the start of the initiative. Also see Giordono et al. (2013), p. 4.

27. Giordono et al. (2013), p. 14. The totals for years prior to 2011 differ from earlier evaluation reports. The changes reflect refinements in definitions. For example, a significant number of individuals reported as served in the New York City Workforce1 Transportation Sector for airport-related jobs were included in the early year total. Later reports were revised and exclude them.

28. The Evaluation Reports in 2011, 2012, and 2013 show unknown or missing data on placement rates, wages, hours, and benefits at placement from a small number of workforce partnerships. Due to missing data, the results for selected indicators are presented excluding two partnerships with the largest amounts of missing data.

29. U.S. Department of Labor (2011).

30. Baran et al. (2012a), p. 33. This section uses data from 2011, as comparable breakouts are unavailable from report covering 2012.

31. There are different definitions of job placement between the National Fund and some other programs, such as the Workforce Investment Act. Those variations hinder direct comparison of placement rates across these programs.

32. Baran et al. (2011), p. 59.

33. Ibid., p. 58.

34. By 2012 Opportunity Chicago, Los Angeles Workforce Funders Collaborative, and Skill Build Colorado had reached the end of their funding period and did not report data. Skill Up Rhode Island and Greater Washington Workforce Development Collaborative (District of Columbia) no longer received National Fund support but continued as active and reporting.

35. These two primary goals are highlighted on SkillWorks's Web site, www.skill-works.org.

36. The accomplishments cited here are derived from http://www.skill-works.org/about-history.php.

37. Abt Associates and Mt. Auburn Associates (2005).

38. Ibid., p. 7.

39. Ibid., p.14.

40. Ibid., p. 118.

41. Author's interview with Loh-Sze Leung, April 12, 2013.

42. Ibid.

43. Central Wisconsin was the first rural site added to the National Fund. That site category came from a decision by the National Fund's Investors Committee to encourage diversity among sites and to include specific provisions more tailored to fit the different challenges and opportunities in rural regions. Later a second rural site, San Joaquin Valley (CA), also garnered National Fund support.

44. At the time, it was the Community Foundation of Greater South Wood County. The name was changed to the Incourage Community Foundation in early 2012. Use of the current name throughout this chapter is an effort to clarify their identity and roles.

45. This chronology draws on the summary in Yellow Wood Associates (2009), pp. 1–3.

46. FSG and Network Impact (2013), pp. 23–26.

47. Mackey et al. (2012), pp. 13–19.

48. Information provided by Jennifer Riggenbach, Incourage Community Foundation.

49. Information from Jennifer Riggenbach, Incourage Community Foundation.

50. Information provided by Kim Shields, Incourage Community Foundation, e-mail, September 30, 2013.

51. Author's interview with: Kelly Ryan, CEO, and Jennifer Riggenbach, chief collaboration officer, Incourage Community Foundation; and Michele MacKey, senior associate, Center on Wisconsin Strategy, April 22, 2013.

52. Baran et al. (2012b), p. 23.

53. Financial data provided by National Fund staff.

Bibliography

Abt Associates and Mt. Auburn Associates. 2005. *Baseline Report of the SkillWorks Initiative*. Boston: SkillWorks Funders Group.

The Annie E. Casey Foundation. 2004. *Good Jobs and Careers: What Communities Need to Do to Train and Move Low-Income, Low-Skilled People into Good Jobs and Careers*. Baltimore: The Annie E. Casey Foundation.

Baran B., S. Teegarden, S. Michon, L. Giordono, and K. Lodewick. 2010 (the most recent update). *National Fund for Workforce Solutions Data Dictionary*. Boston: National Fund for Workforce Solutions.

Baran, B., S. Michon, S. Teegarden, L. Giordono, and K. Lodewick, C. Benner, and M. Pastor. 2009. *Implementing the National Fund for Workforce Solutions: The Baseline Evaluation Report*. Boston: National Fund for Workforce Solutions, December.

———. 2011. *Implementing the National Fund for Workforce Solutions: Third Annual National Evaluation Report*. Boston: National Fund for Workforce Solutions, August.

———. 2012a. *Implementing the National Fund for Workforce Solutions: Data Brief for the Fourth National Evaluation Report*. Boston: National Fund for Workforce Solutions, April.

———. 2012b. *National Fund Principles: Collaborative and Partnership Achievements, Fourth Annual National Evaluation Report*. Boston: National Fund for Workforce Solutions, August.

———. 2012c. *Systems Change Activities and Achievements: Fourth Annual National Evaluation Report*. Boston: National Fund for Workforce Solutions.

Combes-Taylor, J., and J. Rubin. June 2005. *Engaging Employers to Benefit Low-Income Job Seekers: Lessons Learned from the Jobs Initiative*. Boston: Jobs for the Future.

FSG and Network Impact. 2013. *Case Studies: How Four Community Information Projects Went from Idea to Impact, Revitalization in Central Wisconsin*. Miami: John S. and James L. Knight Foundation.

Giloth, Robert P., ed. 2004. *Workforce Intermediaries for the Twenty-first Century.* Published in association with the American Assembly, Columbia University. Philadelphia: Temple University Press.

Giordono, L., K. Lodewick, and S. Michon. 2013. *The National Fund for Workforce Solutions: Data Brief 2013.* Boston: National Fund for Workforce Solutions, June.

Hatcher Group. 2007. "$50 Million Workforce Initiative Launched by Foundations, Business and U.S. Department of Labor." Press Release, September 4.

Hebert, S., and T. Waldron. 2007. *Strengthening Workforce Policy: Applying the Lessons of the Jobs Initiative to Five Key Challenges.* Baltimore: The Annie E. Casey Foundation.

Mackey, M., S. Peterson, and L. Dresser. 2012. *Workforce Central: Evaluation.* Center on Wisconsin Strategies and Incourage Community Foundation.

U.S. Department of Labor, Bureau of Labor Statistics. 2011. *National Occupational Employment and Wage Estimates: United States.* May, http://www.bls.gov/oes/2011/may/oes_nat.htm.

U.S. Government Accountability Office. 2011. *Multiple Employment and Training Programs: Providing Information on Colocating Services and Consolidating Administrative Structures Could Promote Efficiencies.* Washington, DC: GAO-11-92, January.

Waldron, Tom. 2008. *The National Fund for Workforce Solutions: A History of Collaboration.* Baltimore: The Annie E. Casey Foundation.

Yellow Wood Associates. 2009. "Workforce Central Phase One Evaluation." Wisconsin Rapids: Workforce Central.

13

Building Capacity to Prepare America's Workers for Twenty-first Century Jobs

Sheila Maguire and Patricia Jenny

Organizations seeking to create economic opportunities for low-income workers and job seekers need to incorporate a range of capacities. They must be able to understand the dynamics of the labor market and develop working relationships with local businesses; they must infuse that understanding of business throughout their own organization; and they need to develop a variety of strategies to help connect low-income workers and job seekers with real local business needs.

This work is not easy. Organizations involved in workforce development need staff that is well-prepared to handle the interests of both businesses and workers. They must provide job seekers and workers with support and advice while helping businesses assess their needs. They should be aware of larger industry trends and, in many cases, work collectively, often by sector or subsector, to develop joint employer initiatives. Organizations also must target their talent search to low-wage workers and unemployed people from low-income communities. In some cases workforce organizations broker and/or provide jointly funded employer training programs, and connect businesses to relevant government support. In addition, workforce organizations design and operate training curricula; utilize adult learning and training techniques; conduct effective outreach to low-income communities; and provide or refer to reliable support services, including child care, transportation, housing, and legal assistance, depending on the needs of the workers or job seekers.

Finding the funding to underwrite the costs of their services is another important role for workforce-development organizations. This funding is often from third-party public and private funders, who determine which outcomes must be measured. In fact, workforce organizations must be able to understand two data sets: performance outcomes and labor-market information. As one of the first fields to be funded by federal and state governments on the basis of outcomes (such as placement, retention, and wage advancement), a critical organizational capacity is to understand and use this data for program improvements, as well as to get paid. Workforce organizations also must be able to manage multiple funding contracts and outcome databases, deal with slow and unreliable payments for services, and work with many different city, state, and federal agencies to advance organizational and client paperwork. In addition, workforce organizations must understand their local labor market in terms of both longer-term trends and employment patterns, and short-term shifts that will affect their programs.

A range of workforce intermediaries or sector partnerships, as they are typically known, have emerged to help frontline workforce organizations coordinate these diverse skills and actors. This intermediary function can be played by community-based organizations, chambers of commerce, employer associations, labor-market partnerships, community colleges, and government agencies, including some Workforce Investment Boards (WIB). They offer services directly or broker partnerships.

Given the complexity of these tasks, it is no surprise that evaluations of workforce-development programs frequently attribute successes and failures to the capacity of the organizations offering services. Yet discussions about the effectiveness of workforce development often remain fixed on the type of services that result in success as measured by job placement and retention for job seekers or workers, with far less focus on improved business outcomes. While it is important to understand what kinds of services, and in what doses, are most effective for disadvantaged job seekers and low-wage workers, as well as to understand the real benefits to businesses of services, it also is important to advance our understanding of how to build the capacity of groups to deliver these services.

We, the authors of this chapter, have spent more than ten years on such capacity-building efforts. Pat Jenny, as the chairperson of the New York City Workforce Funders, coordinated grants of nearly $3 million for capacity-building projects from the group's collaborative fund. Sheila Maguire, along with a team of colleagues, designed and led capacity-building efforts as a senior staff person at Public/Private Ventures and is currently engaged in learning groups in New York, Seattle, and Washington, D.C.

In this chapter, we suggest that one of the key challenges in building capacity is developing the ability within organizations to bridge the divide among business, government, and social services. We argue that investing in the workforce-development field's ability to provide this critical function for both business and workers—particularly in times of austerity—is also prudent. Creative, flexible organizations and/or partnerships will need to find new ways to develop, broker, and pay for services. Organizations skilled in meeting employers' hiring needs must move beyond the initial hire to helping businesses more effectively train, manage, and support their workforce. Economic-development and business-led organizations must develop the capacity to partner and/or develop workforce services.

New efforts in sectors typically characterized by low wages and high turnover also will require new skills and strategies. These types of jobs are being created in larger numbers after the Great Recession and are projected to grow as a proportion of the overall labor market. Capacity-building efforts can help organizations spread newly acquired knowledge, techniques, and tools; provide insider intelligence about industry trends; offer methods for working with small and medium-sized local businesses; exchange curricula; provide training for frontline, supervisory, and management staff; and invest in emerging leadership.

But on the ground, workforce organizations face a range of barriers to implementing effective programs. They all face difficult business operations, given the complexity of administering multiple performance-based contracts. Because so many factors affect an organization's performance, it is difficult to determine what difference specific capacity-building initiatives are making.

In this chapter, we first introduce a framework for thinking about capacity building in the workforce-development field that we hope will provide practitioners, funders, and policy makers a useful tool for furthering their own efforts. Using this framework, we will describe the NYC Workforce Funders' initiatives to improve the capacity of workforce-development organizations. We will share the basic approaches used and our reflections on their effectiveness and the challenges these efforts faced. We also will draw from two formal evaluations and from participant feedback provided through surveys and focus groups, as well as a study of New York City's frontline workforce-development staff conducted by the Fiscal Policy Institute and the Workforce Professionals Training Institute. Finally, we will make practical recommendations calling for the immediate development of a common framework to evaluate workforce capacity-building efforts; a complementary strategy of developing a network among the many professionals already engaged in this work; and a sharp focus on developing the skills of frontline staff. Finally, we will suggest developing a policy-advocacy approach, as many have before us, to leverage funding that can help provide the resources that support such work.

A Framework for Workforce Development and Capacity Building

Many supporters of sector partnerships and workforce intermediaries have made companion investments in capacity building in a variety of ways. Foundation and government-sector strategy initiatives have included technical assistance. Publicly and privately sponsored evaluations, for example, often offer trainings, conferences, or on-site technical assistance. Training academies have been offered on the local, state, and national level by the Aspen Institute, the Corporation for a Skilled Workforce, the National Governors Association, and the National Network of Sector Partners, which also offered a biannual conference for practitioners. Foundation grants have allowed the National Skills Coalition to advance a policy agenda that supports sector practice. The National Fund for Workforce Solutions has provided funding to kick-start local funders' collaboratives that in turn spur the development of local sector-focused strategies, including local capacity building. Provider coalitions at the state and local levels also offer training workshops and conferences.

In the workforce field, the term "capacity building" covers a multitude of different interventions targeted at various levels. In fact, "capacity building" is a commonly used phrase that means different things to different people. Public or private funders design and deliver capacity building to accomplish different goals (e.g., increase numbers of people served, improve quality of services, and develop management functions). Capacity-building programs are delivered in different formats, from group sessions to one-on-one technical assistance. The National Council of Nonprofits defines "capacity building" as: "activities that improve and enhance a nonprofit's ability to achieve its mission and sustain itself over time."

In discussing capacity-building efforts in this chapter, we will examine five levels, derived in part from previous frameworks for thinking about the concept:[1]

- The *individual* level, referring to the structure of the jobs, as well as the skills, knowledge, and abilities of individual professionals.

- The *organizational* level, including functions, systems, and procedures of agencies providing employment services.

- The *program* level, referring to specific service-delivery mechanisms and program design.

- The *field* level, meaning the capacity of a group of organizations to act together on common issues.

- The *systems* level, referring to the major actors that together create and fund the group of services available in a community for job seekers, including government and philanthropy.

Figure 1: Five Levels of Capacity-Building Efforts

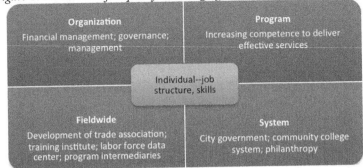

Table 1: An Initial List of Capacities Required for Effective Workforce Intervention

Individual	<ul><li>Manage computerized performance-management data</li><li>Understand career paths in industries in which they work</li><li>Work effectively with local businesses, providing them with useful human-resource services</li><li>Maintain appropriate distance, and engage with clients who have many barriers to employment</li><li>Teaching and group-facilitation skills</li><li>Organizing skills for working with the community and employers</li><li>Basic skills, particularly writing skills that enable staff to effectively complete documentation</li></ul>
Adaptive Organization	<ul><li>Create a data-driven decision-making approach, including fostering a culture of continuous-improvement procedures</li><li>Manage multiple funding contracts and outcomes databases</li><li>Deal with slow and unreliable payments for services</li><li>Work with many different city agencies to expedite billing and client data entry</li><li>Install continuous-improvement procedures</li><li>Anticipate and respond to changes in public policy and labor-market trends</li></ul>

Strategic Program	• Understand and respond to the dynamics of the labor market
	• Develop working relationships with local employers
	• Infuse employer intelligence throughout organization, including frontline workers
	• Design and operate relevant technical, vocational, and work based training curriculum
	• Understand and practice education and training techniques
	• Provide effective career counseling
	• Ensure effective job-brokering services
	• Conduct effective outreach to low-income communities
	• Provide access to support services, including child care, transportation, housing, and legal assistance
	• Collaborate effectively with a range of partners
Field Building	• Share information on best practices
	• Advocate at city, state, and federal level, for more resources as well as resources that support effective programs
	• Provide labor-market information
	• Address important and systemic problems
	• Train frontline workers
	• Provide forums for leadership to work collaboratively
System	• Create partnerships between the public sector and philanthropy
	• Establish formal relationships between a set of employers in a community or industry and training providers
	• Rationalize a confusing array of programs, and coordinate funding sources at the local level

Table 1 identifies the capacities needed at each of the five levels. Of course, capacity-building activities do not always fall neatly into one category or another. In fact, many efforts may have built capacity in more than one category. We offer this framework simply as a way of thinking about the many dimensions of capacity building necessary to move the workforce-development field forward. In each of these categories, while the target of some capacity building is the individual professional, other training efforts are focused on organizational teams and systems. Successful workforce development, like other human services, depends on competent individual professionals working in an integrated system that utilizes effective communications. Throughout the chapter, we will identify the distinctions between training programs focused on individual professionals and those that are designed to create better systems.

New York City Funders and Workforce Development

Before describing capacity-building efforts in New York City using this framework, we will provide a brief background and history of the New York City Workforce Funders' individual and joint efforts to effect change.

Workforce-development services are provided to New York City job seekers by a mix of organizations and institutions, with funding from the federal government and New York City and State governments as well as from private philanthropy. Because of New York City's size and its history of contracting out social services, hundreds of large and small nonprofits operate employment programs, including job readiness, job development, and skills training, in addition to the training programs taught at community colleges. These nonprofits use government contracts as well as private foundation grants to support their programs.

All types and sizes of organizations provide employment services in New York City. They range from community groups that hang a shingle from a storefront and run job-placement services to large human-service organizations that operate on a citywide basis. In addition, several organizations have become intermediaries, serving as connectors between city government and community groups that can provide case-management services, and between community groups and employers. Employment providers in New York include nonprofit organizations, proprietary firms, community colleges, and union-affiliated training programs.

In 2001 a group of foundations and corporate charities with interest in employment issues formed a funders' network and a collaborative fund for grant making in order to improve the effectiveness of workforce-development services and create a more functional and accessible citywide system. The group is now known as the NYC Workforce Funders and includes, among others, the following: the Altman, Clark, Bernard F. and Alva B. Gimbel, JPMorgan Chase, Tiger, Rockefeller, and Mizuho USA foundations, and the New York Community Trust. Its quarterly meetings include state and city officials, foundation staff interested in employment issues, workforce providers, and leaders of local and national initiatives. Meeting agendas focus on timely issues in the field, such as the future of the GED in New York state or the city's response to Hurricane Sandy, or feature results from new initiatives. A subgroup of funders also contributes to a collaborative fund at the New York Community Trust that makes grants to initiatives and capacity-building programs developed by the NYC Workforce Funders.

Over time, the level of private resources in the local workforce-development field has grown significantly, due in part to the presence of the funders' network and its partnership with the city of New York. The increase in private support, especially for direct skills training, has offset, in part, the steady decline in federal money through the Workforce Investment Act (WIA). Surveys of private funders have documented an increase in private grants for workforce-development projects from $18.5 million in 2004 to $58.3 million in 2012. During the same time period, federal allocations for adult, youth, and dislocated-worker employment programs through WIA dropped from $96 million in 2004 to $60 million in 2012. According to a report published by the mayor's office, ten city agencies administer workforce services, with a total investment of $336 million in 2010.[2]

Under Mayor Michael Bloomberg's leadership, New York City has moved from a laggard to a leader in the workforce-development arena. In particular, the transfer in 2004 of the adult employment programs to the New York City Department of Small Business Services (SBS), one of the city's economic-development agencies, rejuvenated the city's management of the federally funded adult WIA programs. The move infused a once-moribund program with an entrepreneurial culture. (The youth employment programs were transferred to another city agency, the Department of Youth and Community Development.) Albeit[3] a number of years after other cities, New York created an ambitious one-stop network of Workforce1 Career Centers throughout the five boroughs that placed fourteen thousand New Yorkers in jobs in 2012. It also reached out to the philanthropic sector to create program innovations.

In late 2004 the NYC Workforce Funders began meeting with Commissioner Robert Walsh of SBS to discuss how they could work together. The result of these conversations was the creation of the Workforce Innovation Fund, the virtual home of the public-private partnership. While the private funders had long been interested in testing sector employment strategies, discussions with city officials convinced them that the concept was worth an investment. The first project was the New York City Sectors Initiative, a $3.2 million, multiyear demonstration of a sector employment strategy. Foundations contributed $1.4 million and city government $1.8 million to the project. SBS and eleven private foundations acting as the Workforce Innovation Fund selected the Metropolitan Council on Jewish Poverty to operate health care training programs and the State University of New York Downstate to develop biotechnology sector-training programs. Public/Private Ventures (P/PV) both managed and prepared a formal evaluation of the New York City Sectors Initiative.[4] While the total number of individuals trained (363) and placed in jobs (167) was modest, the initiative contributed to widespread acceptance of the sector employment approach in New York City among public officials, private funders, and workforce-development providers and cemented a sturdy partnership between private philanthropy and SBS. The city decided to try sector-focused one-stop centers, and private funders and workforce providers began to support and design more sectorlike projects.

In 2006, when the city's budget was flush, the mayor created the Center for Economic Opportunity (CEO), following a report from a commission that identified workforce development as an effective route out of poverty. Partnerships with private philanthropy have been a key part of these programs. CEO has supported a range of programs, including a suite of ambitious efforts for young adults as well as sector employment strategies, expanding the traditional focus of the federal workforce system on quick job placement. Using CEO resources, the city established Workforce1 Career Centers, focused on three sectors: transportation and distribution, health care, and manufacturing. The transportation Workforce1 Career Center in Queens went quickly to scale, serving thousands of job seekers, and eventually merged with the manufacturing center.

In 2009 CEO became a grantee of the federal Corporation for National and Community Service and the Social Innovation Fund. This brought millions of additional federal dollars for workforce development to New York City and allowed CEO to replicate a number of adult and youth employment programs in other cities.

During this same period, as the city government was expanding its role in workforce development, private philanthropy in New York City began connecting to employment funders in other cities. In 2007 the NYC Workforce Funders became a part of the new National Fund for Workforce Solutions, created by a group of national foundations to strengthen workforce partnerships through direct support of local collaboratives, technical assistance, research, and advocacy. The New York City Workforce Innovation Fund continues to be a grantee and local collaborative of the National Fund, which supports the New York health care intermediary described later in this chapter.

At various points since the 1990s, philanthropy has convened groups in retreat settings to review the state of affairs in workforce development and determine next steps. In 2011 the NYC Workforce Funders began an assessment of its successes and remaining challenges in improving workforce-development services in the city. To that end, funders gathered a group of workforce leaders to plan a retreat, and together they developed a set of principles to guide the design of new initiatives. Eighty-nine public officials, funders, and workforce providers met in October 2011 in Cooperstown, New York, to identify new initiatives that embody a set of principles:

- Place employers' labor force needs front and center.

- Create a more streamlined system of organizations providing job services by:
  - cultivating more effective partnerships among groups with particular expertise,
  - bringing individuals' projects to scale, and
  - establishing service networks with multiple entry points for customers.

- Develop additional intermediaries with providers and employers.

- Use data for greater accountability.

- Develop better communications.

The NYC Workforce Funders met on several occasions after Cooperstown to analyze the findings from the meeting, and made three planning grants for the design
of new initiatives that embody the principles. In addition, it supported the New
York Association of Training and Employment Professionals to conduct training
on advocacy and lobbying for a group of forty organizations. The goal was to
improve workforce professionals' understanding of the legislative process, appropriations, elements of an effective education-and-advocacy strategy, and sophisticated understanding of the legislative environment in Albany and Washington,
D.C. Most attendees found the sessions quite valuable. A second round of training started in late 2012 and continued through June 2013 for a smaller group of
twenty-five individuals from ten workforce-development organizations.

Finally, the NYC Workforce Funders supported a group of nine workforce
professionals to create a new vision for workforce development in New York City.
The draft report has been reviewed by funders, public officials, and nonprofits and
was to be the subject of a yearlong communications campaign to inform the 2013
mayoral election. Its goal is to improve the capacity of the workforce-development
system to prepare disadvantaged New Yorkers for a twenty-first-century economy.

Capacity Building and the New York City Workforce System

Since 2001 the NYC Workforce Funders have developed capacity-building
initiatives for workforce-development practitioners at the five levels identified
above: organizational, program, field, individual, and system. The NYC Workforce Funders was formed to build a more effective system of workforce services
in New York City and did not set out with a road map for its capacity-building
investments. The group built on successes, learned from mistakes, and took advantage of opportunities that presented themselves along the way. The quarterly
meetings of the NYC Workforce Funders also created a common understanding
of current policy and practice among foundation officers and guided the group's
collaborative grant making. In this section, we describe these initiatives.

It is important to note that the impetus for these efforts came from different
players in the field. We do not intend to imply that we are including all of the
many capacity-building initiatives that are under way in New York City, either in
the nonprofit world generally or in the workforce field. The efforts we include in
this chapter are those that have involved, to a greater or lesser degree, the NYC
Workforce Funders.

As the city changed its workforce-development programs and reflected the job-placement focus of the Workforce Investment Act, its vendors became larger organizations that could handle higher volumes. But private philanthropy retained its support of skills training in independent nonprofits throughout the city. Private support for capacity building, accordingly, focused increasingly on a set of twenty to twenty-five organizations that had become more sophisticated in weaving public and private sources of support together.

The NYC Workforce Funders and member foundations have funded capacity-building efforts at all five levels in order to achieve a synergistic effect on a large and complex system. The following sections describe the specific efforts in more detail. Two of the initiatives, focused on financial-management skills and board development, aimed to improve the management capacities of nonprofits offering workforce services (organization category). Three efforts focused on helping organizations and, in some cases, public agencies develop outcomes measures to improve performance and involve employers more effectively (program category). Private foundations in New York City (both collaboratively and independently) also funded the development of several fieldwide institutions: a trade association and an institute that provides training to frontline workers. In addition, the New York City Workforce Investment Board (the mayor-appointed group of business and nonprofit leaders who advise the city's workforce system) worked with the Center for Urban Research at the City University of New York to establish the Labor Market Information Service (field-building category). We include two efforts, the New York City Sectors Initiative and the New York Alliance for Careers in Healthcare, in the systems category. *Table 2* provides an overview of the capacity-building efforts we will discuss.

Capacity-building efforts across all these categories concentrate on training more competent individual professionals as well as developing more effective programmatic approaches, communication, financial, and networking systems. Individuals were trained to run competent organizations; to understand labor-market dynamics and how to help low-skilled job seekers navigate through more effective programs; understand how to use available resources and practice continuous improvement; and work for accessible and helpful systems in government and private businesses. Systems were the focus of intervention at all four levels as well: business operations at the organization level; program design, feedback loops, and so on at the program level; communications, networking, and training systems at the field level; and finally partnerships among employers, government, and the nonprofit sector at the system level.

The figure below illustrates each level of capacity building undertaken by the New York City Workforce Funders, followed by sections describing each one, including key early lessons learned, as well as remaining challenges.

Table 2: Overview of New York City Capacity-Building Programs

Category	Initiative	Project Description
Individual	Workforce Professionals Training Institute	The institute provides professional development opportunities for workforce-development staff and technical assistance to workforce-development organizations/local workforce systems in order to improve capacity and strengthen performance.
	Workforce Leaders Academy	Funded by The Clark Foundation, WLA sought to strengthen the New York City workforce-development system by cultivating a community of leaders from the nonprofit, public, and education sectors skilled and equipped to deliver more effective services to New York City's job seekers, low-wage workers, and employers. Five cohorts of 25 practitioners.
Program	New York City Workforce Innovation Fund—Sector Strategies Practicum	Nineteen organizations participated in two cohorts of a yearlong institute designed to enable staff teams to develop, refine, and operate effective sector programs.
	Benchmarking Project	Forty-two organizations participate in a project to identify meaningful benchmarks in workforce development so that practitioners, funders, and policy makers can be better informed about what constitutes "good" performance.
	WIA Youth Technical Assistance Initiative	From 2001 to 2005 the NYC Workforce Funders supported Seedco and the Youth Development Institute to work with WIA youth contractors to build their capacity to provide stronger workforce services to young people.

Category	Initiative	Project Description
Fieldwide	New York City Employment and Training Coalition	This trade association promotes effective employment and training practices and shares best practices with state and local workforce-development policy makers.
	Workforce Professionals Training Institute	*See* Building the Workforce-Development Profession at the Individual Level *below*
	JobsFirstNYC	This intermediary uses available community, corporate, private, and public resources to bring out-of-school and out-of-work young adults into the economic life of New York City.
	New York City Labor Market Information Service	The service develops research and tools that help policy makers and practitioners engaged in workforce development, education, and economic development make sense of the labor market and make informed decisions that benefit their constituents and the city's economy.
System	New York City Work-force Innovation Fund—New York City Sectors Initiative	Established by the SBS and the NYC Work-force Funders to create an innovative sector strategy for the New York City workforce-development system, the Innovation Fund supported two three-year initiatives managed by the Metropolitan Council on Jewish Poverty and SUNY Downstate.
	New York City Work-force Innovation Fund— New York Alliance for Careers in Healthcare	The New York Community Trust and the Innovation Fund created a workforce "meta-partnership" of the key trade associations representing three major health care subsec-tors—acute care, primary care, and long-term care—and a major union. The alliance works with employers to design training programs for low-income job seekers and incumbent workers.

Building the Workforce-Development Profession at the Individual Level

Frontline workers (case managers, career advisors, job developers, account managers) serve people who face substantial barriers in such areas as education and skills, housing, mental health, child care, transportation, and legal challenges. Despite this, there are few fieldwide standards and practices in terms of job re-sponsibilities, professional development, and management approach, or educa-tional requirements. While capacity-building efforts can enhance program designs or strengthen organizational systems, the skills and capacities of individual front-line workers are also key elements of success.

As we have described above, many social programs need workforce staff who are skilled at helping disadvantaged job seekers and low-wage workers achieve success in the labor market. Increasingly these workers also need to work as human-resource consultants to local businesses. The creation of the Workforce Professional Training Institute (WPTI) was driven by concern about frontline workers' skills. Board members of the New York City Employment and Training Coalition, described later in this chapter, as well as staff from P/PV and the New York State Association of Employment, saw the need to develop services focused on the skills of frontline workers, particularly job developers. Since that time WPTI has trained more than five thousand individuals from 375 organizations, with three in four organizations sending staff to multiple training sessions. Organizations that were trained at WPTI include the largest and smallest groups providing employment services in New York City. Among WPTI's most popular classes have been "Beyond Paystubs and Metro Cards," "Working with Employers," "Becoming Outcomes Driven," and "Assessment and Goal Setting." WPTI also provides consulting services on building teams, curriculum development, job development, recruitment and retention, and marketing to organizations, and offers customized training for providers through contracts with several city agencies.

For five years beginning in 2005, The Clark Foundation funded the Workforce Leaders Academy in order to strengthen the New York City workforce-development system by cultivating a community of leaders from the nonprofit, public, and education sectors skilled and equipped to deliver more effective services to New York City's job seekers, low-wage workers, and employers. Nationally recognized program, research, and policy leaders from around the country came to New York and worked with the Academy cohort to examine practical and strategic issues in labor markets and the economy, workforce research and policy, employment-program strategies, outcomes management, and other topics in workforce development. Participants engaged in joint and individual action learning projects.

Early Lessons

Although there has been no systematic evaluation, investments in training frontline staff have at a minimum put the field on notice that a more informed and better-trained workforce can help raise the quality of services provided to job seekers and workers. Alumni of the Leaders Academy recognize the importance of their network and acknowledge the greater confidence they have in their own performance. WPTI's program evaluations consistently show that participants learn new and useful information and raise their skill levels as human-service professionals. Finally, there is greater affiliation to a field of practice among workforce professionals due to the development of these training courses.

Remaining Challenges

Despite this progress, frontline workforce professionals experience high turn-over and even dissatisfaction with their jobs. In November 2012 WPTI and the Fiscal Policy Institute (FPI) released the findings of a survey of frontline workers ("Deep in the Trenches") that aimed to better understand the workforce profession, including its demographics and the employment practices of organizations in the field.[5] A multichoice, open-ended survey of 182 frontline workers in New York City was conducted, as well as interviews with workforce-development managers and small group discussions with frontline workers.

Nearly half of the respondents indicated they were somewhat or very likely to look for a job at another organization within the next year, 61 percent when the time horizon was extended to three years. Sixty-four percent of respondents wanted to advance within their current organization, but only half had a clear idea of what was required. Some might suggest that workforce development is badly in need of a sector intervention itself as workforce personnel face some of the same challenges that many other employers typically involved in sector initiatives face: few pipelines delivering workers with the specific skills needed to perform critical functions; no clear career pathways for workers to advance; limited opportunities for skills training and leadership development; and staff turnover, particularly difficult given the importance of relationship building in working with workers and businesses.

Developing More Competent Organizations

In 2003, based on initial work by the Tiger Foundation, the NYC Workforce Funders created a Financial Management Training Program designed and managed by the Nonprofit Finance Fund and Fiscal Management Associates. It ran until 2008. The two organizations provided nonprofit business analyses and reviews of fiscal infrastructures for twenty-two workforce-development organizations in three cohorts. The groups were selected based on demonstrated need and level of commitment to the project. Over the course of the consultancies, Fiscal Management Associates observed and made recommendations on each agency's fiscal staffing and systems and procedures, and worked with the agencies to implement changes. The Nonprofit Finance Fund analyzed financial conditions from five years of audits and helped organizations understand their balance sheets in order to make informed business and program choices. Because there was no formal evaluation done, it is not possible to quantify the long-term effect of this effort. However, private and public funders recognized that the twenty-two participating organizations were better able to articulate their financial positions, focus on key financial challenges and priorities, attract additional resources, and manage organizational change.

In 2011 the NYC Workforce Funders selected VCG Governance Matters to operate the Board Governance Initiative to strengthen the boards of directors of workforce-development agencies by adding corporate executives who could diversify funding and bring the employer's perspective to all programming. VCG selected eight organizations out of fourteen that applied to participate in consultation with the funders. Staff from the eight organizations attended an orientation meeting, at which they provided baseline information. After a group meeting of the whole cohort, VCG worked individually with each board chair and executive director to assess the strengths and weaknesses of the boards of directors and identify strategies for making them more effective. The work plan included new board member recruitment goals, plans for creating committees or advisory groups, and training and fundraising goals. At the time of writing this chapter, results were mixed on adding new board members, expanding fundraising by the board, and training new board members. An evaluation survey was planned for the next cohort of board members in 2014.

Early Lessons

For technical assistance directed to individual organizations, it is important to embed as much as possible of the training and new expertise into an organization's systems. Otherwise, the newfound abilities or improvements can be lost as staff members depart. In the case of financial management, wholesale reviews of accounting systems, billing, and so on can lead to suggested system changes that survive any personnel changes. Or, in some cases, they will lead to the creation of new staff positions. Such changes would bring longer-lasting benefits than result from simply training existing staff. Similarly for board governance, establishing policies or committees or new standards for board members is as important as identifying new members for a board. This type of technical assistance requires a trainer who can get to know an organization's systems, assess their effectiveness, and make specific recommendations for augmenting or changing them. This is a more expensive and time-consuming approach to capacity building than training a group of staff from multiple organizations.

Technical assistance to improve financial systems or board governance will not necessarily lead to more program clients in jobs. This is why improving the operations of organizations is not enough to build the capacity of a fully functioning workforce-development system. The NYC Workforce Funders therefore have provided other levels of capacity building as explained in the sections below, focusing on techniques for improving programs in individual organizations, as well as efforts to lift the standards or raise the bar for the whole field.

Remaining Challenges

Technical assistance delivered to single organizations is perhaps the most common sort of help provided, at least in New York City, and nonprofits can access it from citywide management-assistance providers. The NYC Workforce Funders has experimented with cohort approaches to delivering this assistance in order to allow peer professionals to get to know and help one another. One question to be answered is about the relative merits of the individual versus the group approach for building capacity: When is one better than another?

In a time of declining public resources, New York City nonprofits and foundations face quandaries about the need to support such a large number of organizations. While management-assistance providers continue to help groups raise more support and become better organizations, the larger issue of considering alliances, partnerships, and even mergers supersedes the intrinsic value of technical assistance. For New York City, with its long history of tens of thousands of nonprofits operating throughout the five boroughs, it does illustrate the need to consider how individual technical assistance contributes to the effectiveness of a broader system before making that investment.

The NYC Workforce Funders has determined that we need to assess whether these capacity-building programs actually do create more effective organizations. We will design and install a cost-effective mechanism of tracking outcomes for the current board-governance clients. For any future investments in capacity building we will commit to supporting an assessment of its effects.

Building Strategic Program Capacity

The NYC Workforce Funders made a number of investments to develop or strengthen workforce programs. These capacity-building efforts have been offered in a group setting (cohort-based), as noted above, with the idea that this might not only be cost effective but also provide the opportunity to create networks and partnerships across and among organizations in the field.

The first grants made from the collaborative fund, in 2001, were aimed at helping youth employment organizations provide better programs for their clients. At that time, many organizations stood to gain significant new funding from WIA, and many private funders were concerned that the organizations had no systems or the proper staff in place to spend it well. Along with the regional office of the U.S. Department of Labor and two city agencies, the funders selected Seedco and the Youth Development Institute to manage a series of workshops for the fifty-three youth-serving organizations that the city contracted with to provide comprehensive workforce-preparation programs. While Seedco focused on how to implement the city's new performance-based contracts (as distinct from fee-for-service contracts, through which a contractor is paid to deliver services regardless of the outcomes), Youth Development Institute taught the contractors best approaches for engaging youth and helping them develop job skills. The program continued into 2006.

A formal assessment[6] of the WIA Seedco and Youth Development Institute program was carried out by the Heller School for Social Policy and Management at Brandeis University. As noted in this evaluation, there were no statistically significant relationships between the New York City Department of Employment's judgments about performance levels of its youth employment providers and the number of training sessions attended by agency staff. But surveys of participants showed that over the years the technical approach became more intensive and targeted to senior-level staff. Seedco and Youth Development Institute combined workshops with intensive one-on-one technical assistance. Group workshops focused on job development and action planning. Agencies also formed support networks among themselves. According to surveys that Seedco administered, 60 percent of respondents agreed that Seedco and Youth Development Institute's assistance helped them improve contract performance.

In 2008 the NYC Workforce Funders also worked with P/PV and the Aspen Institute to create the Sector Strategies Practicum (SSP), a yearlong training program for organizations interested in developing sector employment strategies. The New York City Sector Initiative and other prior efforts to introduce New York City workforce-development agencies to the concepts embedded in sector strategies, such as understanding and meeting the labor force demands of employers, improving job quality, and providing intensive skills training, revealed a gap in experience and interest in trying more sophisticated approaches to helping lower-skilled job seekers get jobs. The funders were interested in designing a longer-term training program that would capture the imagination of New York City workforce professionals.

The design of the practicum was based on the national Sector Skills Academy, which brings individual leaders together from across the country, and was adapted to assist teams from organizations across the city develop or refine their sectoral approach. Two cohorts (the 2008–2009 cohort had nine organizations, and 2009–2010 had ten) were selected through a competitive process. Each practicum started with a three-day retreat, followed by a series of workshops for staff and partners. Participating organizations were introduced to a set of planning tools (developed for the national academy) and created new or improved existing sectoral approaches. At the end of the practicum each organization presented its strategies to a panel of national experts and local funders in a daylong event. While the first cohort was focused on a range of sectors, the second concentrated on health care in the hope that providing targeted information about one sector might prove more beneficial to organizations. Each year's activities were kicked off with a public workshop aimed at increasing awareness of the role of sector strategies and at recruiting a cohort of interested organizations.

In order to understand better the role of SSP in helping organizations develop their capacity to develop and implement programs, focus groups were held with staff who participated. Feedback indicated that participants had gained a better understanding of the important players in the workforce-development system, especially employers and educational institutions, and the importance of getting buy-in to the sector approach from all levels of an organization. Practicum members said they had learned how to collaborate with other organizations and were interested in continuing. They also identified specific areas of staff training that would be helpful, which Workforce Professionals Training Institute (see below) incorporated into its curriculum development.

Building from another national initiative, the NYC Workforce Funders also invested in a citywide effort to increase the capacity of workforce organizations to use data to improve performance. The Benchmarking Project, funded by the Annie E. Casey Foundation, is designed to shed light on the performance of workforce organizations by pooling and analyzing data from programs across the country. As of 2011, two hundred organizations had voluntarily completed a survey of aggregate data for 330 programs, including information about participant demographics, services, and job placement and retention results. In return for submitting data, organizations receive reports with anonymous outcomes comparisons to those of similar programs across the country. Through a grant from the NYC Workforce Funders, recruitment was targeted to New York City providers, resulting in forty-three organizations contributing data. Participants representing twenty of these organizations took part in bimonthly forums focused on how to develop a more outcomes-focused, data-driven culture. Five organizations received one-on-one technical assistance, which involved staff at multiple levels in identifying short- and long-term success outcomes and indicators.

The Benchmarking Project also worked with eight NYC youth-serving organizations to identify progress milestones that correlate with participants' achievement of a GED or employment. It published a report on the findings in 2010.[7] Based on data-driven improvement processes developed by the Institute for Healthcare Improvement (IHI) and working with the Workforce Professionals Training Institute, practice-improvement teams were launched in eight NYC organizations, including several groups that serve young adults. In 2011–2012, with input from a significant number of providers and funders, a shared-outcome tool was designed to standardize information reported to NYC private funders, and an initial pilot was undertaken.

Early Lessons

The NYC Workforce Funders' first capacity-building program for youth employment organizations showed that a large-scale program that delivers a little assistance to many organizations is not very beneficial. Its later efforts were more structured and worked with fewer groups. Both the Sector Strategy Practicum and the Benchmarking projects were different from the come-one, come-all approach of the WIA Youth Employment effort, in which not every group participating in capacity-building activities had expressed a clear need and desire to work with technical-assistance providers.

For group technical assistance aimed at developing new strategies and/or programs, it is important to target organizations ready for change, as well as the specific staff people who have the authority and support to make change happen. Getting the right organizations and people involved maximizes the chances of implementing new approaches based on the informational and group-learning sessions offered. For example, organizations were required to apply to participate in the Sector Strategies Practicum and were assessed for readiness. Also, organizations selected for participation in the Benchmarking Project were required to submit performance data, assess their current capacity, and identify clear goals for participation.

Finally, involving organizational teams that include a mix of staff (frontline, mid-level, executive), as happened in the Sector Strategies Practicum, provides an opportunity for team reflection and planning away from the day-to-day pressures of organizational life.

Creating a dynamic peer-learning environment using appropriate adult learning technologies is at the heart of effective cohort technical assistance. Enabling practitioners to share candidly starts with visiting presenters sharing the "unplugged" version of their programs' successes and failures. Engaging participants in joint problem-solving using case studies, confidential peer groups, site visits, and "capstone" projects (student-led projects for a client) can help transform ideas into action. Cohort capacity-building also provides opportunities for networking and new-partnership development and helps create a field identity among participating staff, although turning increased awareness into sustained action outside the formal sessions requires ongoing support—a lesson that reflects the rich experience of the IHI approach.

Remaining Challenges

Organizations attempting to develop new approaches may find they are swimming upstream against policies that were enacted during a time of economic growth, such as WIA and welfare reform. Efforts to develop new strategic and program interventions are often undermined by the relentless pressure for immediate job outcomes. Participants in SSP focus groups noted the ongoing tensions between pressures to place job seekers into immediate employment versus doing the long-term work required to understand the needs of employers. Burdensome reporting demands, like collecting pay stubs from participants, tie up already-pressed workers from assisting job seekers and local businesses.

Establishing Fieldwide Organizations

Workforce development is often criticized as a highly fragmented field in which programs are funded by an array of federal government departments and agencies. It is hardly surprising that so many government programs include workforce services, given strong evidence that connecting people to employment can ease some of society's most pervasive problems. For example, welfare benefits are now tied to participation in work activity; the Second Chance Act funds employment assistance, among other services, to help reduce recidivism; and jobs are viewed as a strategy for improving life in public housing projects and reducing homelessness. Workforce services are needed by a wide range of people who come under the jurisdiction of different government agencies, which in turn contract with a large number of organizations to provide those services. At the same time, the programs, services, and measures of success used by government agencies have made it difficult for workforce-development employees and leaders to develop codified practices and a common professional identity.

Since 1999 four citywide entities have been established to serve the needs of the many organizations and city agencies that provide workforce-development services to New Yorkers. The first, the New York City Employment and Training Coalition (NYCETC), began as a volunteer-led staff group from agencies that contracted with the city. In 1999, with a grant from the New York Community Trust, staff was hired with the idea that one of the prerequisites of developing a field was a full-fledged trade association that could bring its diverse organizations and professionals together to advocate for policy change and keep members up to date on developments at the federal, state, and local levels. By 2013, led by a board made up of executive directors and leaders of nonprofits, community colleges, and union-affiliated training programs, the coalition had increased membership to two hundred organizations, hosted an annual workforce conference, created a policy agenda, and held discussions with mayoral candidates.

A second citywide organization, WPTI, was launched in 2005 and focused on developing frontline workers' skills. WPTI's work was described above.

Fueled by concern about the growing number of young people in New York City who are neither in school nor working, the Tiger Foundation and the

NYC Workforce Funders supported the preparation of a business plan that led to the creation in 2006 of JobsFirstNYC. The initial funding for this intermediary was provided by the Clark and Tiger foundations. Its overall goal is to serve as a "market maker" to rationalize what was viewed as a disjointed set of services for young adults, with a particular emphasis on making business a key partner, raising consciousness about the out-of-work and out-of-school young adult crisis, and improving the work of organizations and individuals focused on the needs of young adults. For example, in 2010 the Bronx Opportunity Network, a collaborative of eight community organizations serving young adults in the South Bronx, worked with Bronx and Hostos community colleges to improve passing rates of young people on the CUNY COMPASS placement exams. JobsFirstNYC has also commissioned several reports, including an analysis of high-demand occupations that might be relevant for young adults[8] and a study of the views of employers of young people and the workforce system.[9] In 2013 JobsFirstNYC launched an effort to adapt sector strategies to more effectively serve young people.

Although it is not supported financially by the NYC Workforce Funders, another critical entity that serves the workforce-development community is the New York City Labor Market Information Service (NYCLMIS). Formed in spring 2008 as a joint endeavor of the New York City Workforce Investment Board and the Center for Urban Research at the City University of New York, NYCLMIS provides labor-market intelligence for a range of public and private clients as well as the field at large. Its goal is to help workforce and education policy makers and providers use labor-market intelligence to align their efforts with employer demand. To that end, NYCLMIS develops research and information tools and provides technical assistance and strategic consultation. Its report on employment in the transportation sector[10] helped guide the work of the city's transportation one-stop center, and in 2009 NYCLMIS published practitioner-friendly briefs on the job prospects in nine industry sectors in the city. NYCLMIS synthesizes volumes of available labor-market and economic information through monthly reports on various aspects of the New York City labor market and has helped raise the field's understanding of how economic data can drive good program planning.

Early Lessons

These citywide entities have served as critical building blocks for improving the effectiveness and professionalism of what many have acknowledged is a fragmented and disjointed workforce system in New York City. Collectively, these four entities help meet the needs of direct service organizations by advocating for supportive public policies, providing timely and relevant labor-market information, training staff, and bringing together key stakeholders on the issue of young-adult unemployment. For example, WPTI has implemented capacity-building efforts for SBS and the Department of Youth and Community Development, as well as for a wide range of initiatives, including the Benchmarking Project, CEO's WorkAdvance, and a City Council-created program called New York City Works, serving as a local nexus of knowledge about frontline-worker practice. Likewise, NYCLMIS has guided several local organizations and CUNY campuses involved in the career-pathway program funded by the U.S. Department of Labor in their use of labor-market data and provided joint training with WPTI. It works strategically with CUNY to improve the alignment of degree and non-degree programs with opportunities in New York City's labor market. Finally, JobsFirst NYC aims to improve outcomes for young adults by bringing together the many players that provide services to design a more effective system and to rationalize a diverse set of funding sources.

However, to ensure the success of these organizations, leaders from across the field, many of whom run direct service organizations, also have invested significant time in serving on boards (in the case of WPTI and NYCETC), as well as envisioning and implementing joint action. These practitioner-leaders, who understand that their organizations' futures are also tied to the future of the workforce field as a whole, are critical to success.

Remaining Challenges

WPTI, NYCETC, and JobsFirstNYC are small organizations with big tasks. Due in part to their size, they are highly dependent on strong leadership that can work collaboratively across a historically competitive field. It has been difficult to find talented leadership to take on these roles, which require a combination of knowledge of the field, collaborative skills, and willingness to take fiscal risks. Dealing with the inevitable turnover in leadership can be disruptive.

Funding also presents significant challenges. In an outcomes-driven environment, it is important, and difficult, to quantify the effects of such entities, and in each case this creates different challenges. Prioritizing investments in sustaining fieldwide entities regularly competes with the demand to fund direct services. In some cases, generating fee-for-service incomes has been a critical aspect of an organization's stability. Measuring the impact of its work is an important strategic goal for each organization. As described above, the impetus for creating each of these entities has come from practitioners, private funders, and the public system itself. While each has a role in helping to advance the field, it is important that their services are well coordinated to ensure that there is not unnecessary duplication or competition.

Toward Building a Better System

The mission of the NYC Workforce Funders since its inception has been to create a more effective system of workforce-development services for job seekers, including publicly and privately funded programs. While the group has made progress on increasing the capacity of the adult-employment system in New York City, changing the relationship between training providers and employers has been more difficult.

Since 2004 the NYC Workforce Funders has been engaged in several joint initiatives with local and state government. As noted, the first joint effort between philanthropy and the city was the New York City Sectors Initiative, which introduced sector employment strategies to local government as well as to nonprofit providers. The experience of managing the demonstration taught players in the public, philanthropic, and nonprofit sectors how this approach can achieve better outcomes.

Since 2011 the creation of the New York Alliance for Careers in Healthcare, known as NYACH, has performed the same function for government, philanthropy, nonprofits, and others by advancing the notion of workforce partnerships. NYACH was designed during 2010 by the New York Community Trust (the Trust) to exploit the large number of jobs in the New York City health care industry at multiple levels (acute care, primary care, long-term care, and direct care). The theory behind NYACH is to work through the trade associations serving these discrete areas of health care to identify employers who need help in redefining labor-force needs, especially in the wake of health care reform. Once these employers are identified, NYACH links them to the services and organizations involved in the workforce-development field. In 2010 the Trust made a series of grants to three trade associations and the Workforce Development Corporation, a nonprofit established by the city to launch the initiative. The NYC Workforce Funders and SBS joined the Trust late in 2010 to support the initiative through the Workforce Innovation Fund and to prepare a proposal to the National Fund for Workforce Solutions for NYACH.

NYACH has a small staff that is located in city government. Since 2011 it has succeeded in bringing together employers through their trade associations, the labor unions, community colleges, and city government to redesign curricula and launch seven new training programs that will help New Yorkers secure health care jobs while addressing the needs of the health care providers who employ them. By increasing their understanding of the needs of the health care workforce, this new initiative has built the capacity of almost every agency or institution that has been involved in the project, placing it in the category of system-level capacity building.

Its presence in the city's SBS has provided new opportunities for spending customized training funds. SBS has committed these funds to the training programs developed by NYACH because SBS officials have been involved with the rigorous process of designing the programs to meet the specific needs of healthcare employers.

Additionally, NYACH has brought health care employers to the City University of New York to help rewrite curricula to meet employers' changing labor-force needs in light of state and federal health care reform. The health care trade associations NYACH worked with have an enhanced understanding of the importance of workforce development, accelerated by the demands of health care reform.

Creating a financing system that is accessible, includes sensible reporting requirements, and inspires innovation is an important goal for the public system. The complex, overlapping, and fragmented workforce-development funding system impedes effective program design. Demonstrating the value of more cohesive approaches through pilot projects is an excellent and time-tested role for private philanthropy.

Early Lessons

Establishing a good partnership between private philanthropy and the public sector allows the transfer of knowledge, increased flexibility, and expanded ability for both sides to create innovation in the field. Working on projects together allows lessons learned to be absorbed immediately into large public funding systems. Examples include changing how individual training allowances are provided or spent and leveraging more public funding for sector strategies.

It is also important to involve employers as partners in ventures that add value to their business operations. While they may not be able to attend meetings to plan a program, if they can improve their operations or save money they will be open to other approaches for finding workers. Trade associations can be a good entry point for employers. But the associations must have the resources to invest time in identifying hiring issues and designing better training programs. Grants to associations to bring on staff who worked with employers in the health care arena have been an effective investment. Prior to those investments, workforce development was not on employers' radar screen.

Introducing private employers to the world of workforce development and/or community colleges can lead to more effective training programs and consequently more job placements. Structuring an interaction around a specific hiring problem is a good start.

An intermediary is necessary for demanding the quid pro quos from employers; if training is designed to meet their needs, they must guarantee jobs, provide release time, or make some other investment in the project. Traditional workforce providers find it difficult to get out of the "charity" approach when approaching employers. Developing the capacity to work with employers remains challenging, although significant progress has been made. Finally, meeting the labor-force demands of employers can lead to training of higher-skilled incumbent workers or job seekers. For example, in the New York Sector Initiative, one of the two grantees focused on the biotechnology industry, which requires college degrees for entry level positions in labs. In the case of NYACH, one of the training programs will provide an internship for graduate bachelors in nursing. But meeting employers' demands in a business negotiation is necessary to create true partnerships.

Remaining Challenges

Changing the practices of government or foundations is a long-term goal. While the New York City Workforce Funders has managed to establish good relationships with the city's adult-employment agency and among the foundations that support workforce, the task of including employers in conversations, meetings, and initiatives is far from complete. As a combined system of public and private funders and contracted providers, workforce-development services in New York City still require more robust capacity to interact with private employers. NYACH is perhaps the most promising effort to date. But the challenge of establishing additional workforce partnerships in other sectors remains.

Recommendations

Workforce development has roots in many different policies and professional practices and involves organizations and individuals who come from a diverse set of professional experiences and academic backgrounds. Building the capacity of the field is a long-term endeavor that involves weaving together funding sources as well as organizational, programmatic, fieldwide, and system practices. In order to advance this process, we recommend that workforce-development practitioners, funders, and policy makers consider four actions:

Develop a capacity-building network.

Investments in building the capacity of workforce organizations have been made in a variety of ways. Foundation and government initiatives frequently include technical assistance and capacity-building activities. Efforts such as those described in this chapter are taking place in many locales across the country. There are, however, few opportunities for those engaged in these efforts to pool experiences, share tools, and advance practice. By developing such a network, those few resources that are available for capacity building could be maximized. Creating a platform for collaboration could bring about significant efficiencies. This network should consist of people engaged in ongoing capacity-building efforts, and while online collaboration would be an important aspect, in-person meetings might foster relationships that could result in meaningful partnerships and sharing. Affiliating such a network with existing efforts to connect professionals engaged in capacity building, such as the Alliance for Nonprofit Management, would also ensure that those working on capacity building in the workforce field are linked to and can learn from efforts in other fields.

Develop a framework for evaluating the effectiveness of capacity building.

On the ground, workforce organizations face a range of barriers to implementing effective programs. These organizations all contend with challenging business operations, given the complexity of administering multiple performance-based contracts. Because so many factors affect an organization's performance, it is difficult to determine which specific capacity-building initiatives are making a difference, especially since so many variables can influence an organization's performance. As noted in this chapter, finding the resources to invest in capacity building is a challenge. And resources to evaluate the effectiveness of these programs are even scarcer. There is an urgent need, however, to develop meaningful approaches to assessing effectiveness so that appropriate investments can be made and measured. A key task for members of the capacity-building network recommended above would be to develop a framework for evaluating their own efforts. Building on the work already undertaken among capacity-building professionals[11] can inform and shape evaluative approaches in the workforce field. Developing common frameworks for defining success and encouraging those involved in capacity-building efforts to use such frameworks could catalyze the critical first step along the road to evaluation: using outcomes to improve performance. Participants in capacity-building efforts should also be engaged in developing this framework. External evaluations of mature capacity-building efforts initiatives could also be undertaken.

The Benchmarking Project is an example of a capacity-building initiative that has the potential to serve as an ongoing assessment tool. A recent report of the Benchmarking initiative, published in May 2013, noted key patterns associated with "success" in job placement or retention. For example, the data collected from two hundred workforce organizations across the country showed that occupational skills training leading to industry-recognized certifications tended to have

higher performance, that work-experience opportunities resulted in better job retention, and that programs with post-employment services had better placement
and retention results.[12]

As noted above, we will start formal assessment of capacity-building investments with the board-governance clients in the summer of 2013. The NYC Workforce Funders is committed to investing in assessment of all its capacity-building
grants going forward.

*Focus investments on developing skills of frontline staff, including
higher-education curricula and training workforce-development
professionals.*

The quality of workforce-development services for the business customer and
job seeker is largely dependent on the skills of frontline workers. This sparked the
creation of the WPTI, described in this chapter. But typically, individuals take
jobs in workforce-development programs with little or no formal training to prepare them for their roles (for example, adult learning, human resources, career
counseling, sales). WPTI/FPI's survey found a strong desire for training among
frontline workers in New York City and a strong interest in a certification that
would be recognized by government agencies and other stakeholders shaping local
workforce policy. It is worth noting that while 63 percent of respondents indicated it would be difficult to find time for the demands of a certification while on the
job, 66 percent noted a willingness to use their time outside of work to complete
certification. There are, in fact, a number of certifications offered in the workforce
field (although none has gained widespread recognition) that could help guide
further work in this area.

The capacity of the field could also be elevated if relevant skills and knowledge were integrated into associate's, bachelor's, or master's degree programs and if
formal links to workforce-development organizations were established. Certificate
programs at community colleges or four-year institutions could also play a role
in preparing workers for jobs in the field. Establishing certifications and professional qualifications can help ensure that everyone serving in a frontline position
has requisite knowledge. In addition, a set of standards creates a ladder that allows
professionals to improve their skills and move up.

*Advocate for the inclusion of public resources for technical assistance
as part of any publicly supported workforce-development program.*

Public agencies that manage other program areas, such as community development, the arts, or education, often include resources to support capacity build-

ing for those organizations that work in the field. This chapter has illustrated how capacity building has been part and parcel of the overall expansion of workforce-development services in New York City. While a large philanthropic community exists in New York to support capacity building, that is not the case in most cities. Establishing some organizational or programmatic technical assistance for publicly funded programs can accelerate the achievement of outcomes for workforce-development contractors and grantees.

Conclusion

While this chapter focuses on the capacity-building work done in New York City, many similar efforts are under way across the United States. City and state-wide organizations similar to WPTI, NYCETC, and NYCLMIS are working to serve other communities of workforce practitioners. Efforts to provide organizations, government systems, employers, field leaders, and frontline workers with the knowledge, skills, and connections to produce better outcomes for low-income job seekers and workers have been initiated by private philanthropy and organized by local practitioners or advocates. And new partnerships have been launched in specific industries designed to serve a range of workforce entities. But these efforts, like the systems they serve, are often fragmented and offered in legislative, industry, geographic, or organizational silos. Workforce-development organizations, leaders, and frontline workers operate across these silos. A long-term and sustained effort at building the capacities of these individuals and organizations is critical to advancing the effectiveness of workforce strategies and could hold the key to the integrated workforce system that many experts and policy makers have so long sought.

Notes

1. Letts, Ryan, and Grossman (1999).
2. City of New York (2011), p. 29.
3. Report from SBS to the NYC Workforce Investment Board (December 2012).
4. Woodruff-Bolte and Farley (2012).
5. Parrott and Mattingly (2012).
6. Smith, Kingsley, and Bailis (2003).
7. Miles and Woodruff-Bolte (2012).
8. Stix and Von Nostitz (2012).
9. Frye et al. (2012).
10. Hirsch (2008).
11. Connolly and York (2002).
12. Miles and Woodruff-Bolte (2013).

Bibliography

City of New York. May 2011. "One System for One City: The State of the New York City Workforce System Fiscal Year 2010." http://www.nyc.gov.

"City of New York Workforce Development Quarterly Report." December 2012. Report from SBS to the NYC Workforce Investment Board.

Connolly, P., and P. York. 2002. "Evaluating Capacity-Building Efforts for Nonprofit Organizations." *OD Practitioner* 34, no. 4.

Frye, C., M. Foggin, S. Zucker, and M. Lee. 2012. "Going Beyond the Bottom Line: Employer Perspectives on the Young Adult Workforce Development System in New York City." New York: JobsFirstNYC.

Hirsch, L. 2008. "Employment in New York City's Transportation Sector." New York: Center for Urban Research, City University of New York.

Letts, C., W. Ryan, and A. Grossman. 1999. *High Performance Nonprofit Organizations: Managing Upstream for Greater Impact.* New York: John Wiley & Sons.

Miles, M., and S. Woodruff-Bolte. 2012. "Understanding Interim Progress Milestones in Young Adult–Serving Workforce Development Programs." Philadelphia: Public/Private Ventures.

———. 2013. "Apples to Apples: Making Data Work for Community-Based Workforce Development Programs." Ann Arbor: Corporation for a Skilled Workforce.

Parrott, J., and M. Mattingly. 2012. "Deep in the Trenches: Understanding the Dynamics of New York City's Front Line Workforce Development Staff." New York: Fiscal Policy Institute and Workforce Professionals Training Institute.

Smith, Pam, Chris Kingsley, and Lawrence Neil Bailis, Ph.D. September 2003. "Assessment of NYCT/WDF Training and Technical Assistance for Youth Employment Programs in the City of New York." Boston: Heller School for Social Policy and Management, Brandeis University.

Stix, M., and G. Von Nostitz. 2012. "Now Hiring." New York: Center for an Urban Future.

United States Department of Labor. 2010. "Catalogue of Available Certifications: Employment and Training Administration."

Woodruff-Bolte, S., and C. Farley. 2012. "Building Effective Workforce Collaborations: Findings and Lessons from the New York City Sectors Initiative." Philadelphia: Public/Private Ventures.

14

Reforming the Supply Side of Sector Strategies: Innovations in Community Colleges

Evelyn Ganzglass, Marcie Foster, and Abigail Newcomer

Ten years ago the editor of *Workforce Intermediaries for the Twenty-first Century*[1] posed three scenarios for expanding the reach of reforms that advance the career prospects of low-skill workers and promote business prosperity:

- Expanding the capacity of sector partnerships to advocate for changes to public education and training services to make them more responsive to workforce needs.

- Mobilizing the significant and underutilized resources of community colleges to spread adoption of best practices across the colleges' adult education, college-level workforce education, and business-responsive customized training programs.

- Pursuing a venture capital approach through local funding collaboratives and other approaches for increasing the number, diversity, and capacity of workforce intermediaries to promote needed changes.

This chapter focuses on systemic reforms that community colleges have undertaken to improve the relevance of their education and training offerings to priorities in their regional economies and to more effectively bridge "silos" in education, training, and human-services delivery systems as a means of better serving a diverse student body. The examples highlighted provide evidence that, at least in leading-edge states and communities, a combination of "inside," "outside," "top-down," and "bottom-up" reform strategies have been working to set in motion reforms that provide employers with a pipeline of skilled workers and individuals with flexible pathways to career advancement.

Before discussing these reforms, we provide an overview of the scope and scale of community college workforce education and training activities, describe a number of national community college reform initiatives, and review the types of barriers faced by community college students as they struggle to attain the skills and credentials needed for economic success. We end the chapter with forward-looking observations about issues that the nation must address to enhance the skills of a rapidly evolving U.S. workforce.

Scope and Scale of Community College Workforce Education and Training Activities

Economists estimate that 65 percent of jobs will require some level of post-secondary education by 2020, with 30 percent of those jobs requiring only some college or an associate's degree.[2] This growing demand for more educated workers, coupled with the comparatively low cost of community colleges, has made these schools an essential asset in workforce-development efforts. In 2012–2013 average tuition and fees at community colleges were less than one-third of the average cost of tuition and fees at a four-year public institution and one-tenth of the average cost of a year at a four-year private nonprofit institution.

Students and businesses across the United States are taking note of these trends. In 2012 more than eight million students—four out of every ten under-graduates—attended one of the 1,132 public, independent, and tribal community colleges in the United States[3] to get the skills and credentials they needed to obtain a better job or advance in their careers. Millions more were enrolled in non-credit education and training within a community college.

The mission of community colleges has changed over time—and still varies significantly by state and region—though it is common for them to serve as a vehicle for workforce and economic development for a local region and its residents.[4] As such, most of these colleges operate under a policy of open admission that allows all students to attend, though the vast majority of enrolled students (99 percent of associate degree seekers and 94 percent of certificate seekers) have a high school diploma or its equivalency.[5]

Community colleges traditionally have provided credit-bearing instruction leading to certificates, two-year associate's degrees, and, more recently, bachelor degrees in a wide range of academic and occupational fields. Colleges also offer a large number of non-credit, occupation-specific courses. According to estimates by the American Association Community Colleges, in the 2011–2012 academic year nearly 40 percent of community college students were enrolled in non-credit courses. These non-credit offerings include short-term certificate programs and training leading to industry certification and state licensure requirements in a wide range of occupational fields and industries.

Community colleges play other functional roles. Local businesses often turn to community colleges for their workforce-development needs: Many community colleges provide training on a fee basis to industry on health, safety, and a wide variety of other topics for employees, as well as the classroom-training components of some apprenticeships. In a number of states, community colleges operate the states' economic development–focused customized training programs.

Community colleges also have a tradition of providing training efforts targeted to the needs of special populations. Some community colleges are Eligible Training Providers under the Workforce Investment Act (WIA) and thus are eligible to receive Individual Training Account vouchers in payment for training provided to low-income adults, dislocated workers, and other WIA participants. While the number of colleges that have programs on the Eligible Training Provider List (ETPL) varies significantly by state, it is estimated that 85 percent of community colleges operate programs on the ETPL. Colleges also report participating directly in WIA programs: 27 percent participate in youth programs under WIA, 62 percent provide adult-education programs, and 63 percent participate in Dislocated Worker programs.[6] Additionally, some colleges have been partners in welfare-to-work programs and programs targeted to returning veterans and other special populations. Moreover, in recognition of the growing importance of postsecondary education to achieving economic success, twelve states now administer their adult-education programs and their community and technical colleges through the same agency in the hopes that more low-skilled adults in adult-education courses will ultimately transition to credit-bearing postsecondary education.

National Efforts to Strengthen Community Colleges

The philanthropic community and the federal government have undertaken numerous initiatives to promote reforms in community colleges.

Recognizing the importance of increasing the educational attainment of U.S. workers, President Obama early in his administration challenged all Americans to commit to at least one year of education beyond high school. He also set a goal for the United States to have "the highest proportion of college graduates in the world by 2020."

President Obama has supported legislation to allocate significant funding for competitive grant programs that support strategies to improve college completion

and degree attainment among America's workers. In the federal economic stimulus package, the American Recovery and Reinvestment Act of 2009 (ARRA, or the
Recovery Act), substantial new resources focused on creating education and training pathways to for-credit and non-credit postsecondary credentials.

The Health Career and Education Reconciliation Act of 2010 allocated nearly
$2 billlion in competitive Trade Adjustment Assistance Community College and
Career Training (TAACCCT) grants to help trade-impacted and other workers acquire the skills and credentials necessary to prepare them for high-wage, high-skill
employment. Three rounds of TAACCCT competitive grants have been made to
support increased access to postsecondary credentials and training in community
colleges, including promoting the use of career pathways,[7] stacked and latticed credentials and other reforms. Additionally, nearly $100 million was made available
through the Workforce Innovation Fund, which sought to improve the alignment
and design of education and training systems, including a focus on improving linkages between education and training services through a career-pathways approach.
Last, Health Profession Opportunity Grants (HPOGs) were made available
through the passage of the Patient Protection and Affordable Care Act of 2010.
HPOGs are designed to support the development of career pathways to health
professions for Temporary Assistance for Needy Families recipients and other low-
income individuals.

Also in 2010 the White House, together with the U.S. Department of Education, convened a national Community College Summit led by Dr. Jill Biden, wife
of Vice President Joe Biden. This national summit served as a broad call for innovation among policy makers and practitioners and marked the launch of three
new community college initiatives:

- Skills for America's Future, which is creating a national network of partnerships among employers, community colleges, industry associations,
  and other stakeholders to ensure that Americans receive the training necessary to meet the needs of employers and have the opportunity to get and
  keep good jobs.

- Aspen Prize for Community College Excellence, whose goal is to honor
  institutional excellence, stimulate innovation, create benchmarks for measuring progress, and incent scaling of effective strategies for improved program completion, transition to four-year institutions, and employment
  outcomes.

- Completion by Design, which works with competitively selected community colleges in Florida, Ohio, and North Carolina to transform their
  students' experience and significantly increase completion and graduation
  rates for low-income students under twenty-six while holding down costs
  and maintaining access and quality.

The departments of Labor, Education, and Health and Human Services also pursued non-legislatively mandated activities to support the president's national degree-attainment goals. Much of this work has been around the pursuit of career pathways, a model growing in popularity among states and regions that offers a more aligned and integrated way of delivering education, training, and supportive services that help low-skilled adults and youth earn marketable credentials and access good-paying jobs. The administration has supported this model by helping states embed career pathways into their existing formula-funded systems through several projects and initiatives. Together these agencies hosted a series of Career Pathways Institutes that provided eleven states with a forum for interagency collaboration and access to technical assistance and national experts in career pathways. The departments also released a joint public letter to encourage states to align state resources and federal funding streams and build partnerships in the support of career pathways. Individually, each department has pursued major technical-assistance initiatives to further this work.[8]

Private investment by national foundations has had a considerable influence on the design of community college reforms and the capacity of states and colleges to change policy and practice. Major national and regional education foundations, such as the Bill & Melinda Gates Foundation, the Lumina Foundation, and the Joyce Foundation, have placed a strategic focus on improving postsecondary attainment and invest strategically in a host of nonprofit organizations, colleges, and state governments to work together and advance their goals.

Barriers Facing Community College Students

Many community college students struggle to access and persist in school because of poor preparation, the struggle to balance the multiple demands of school, work, and family responsibilities, and inadequate financial, social, and academic supports.

Demographics of Community College Students

Forty percent of community college students are low-income, and more than four in ten are the first in their families to go to college.[9] These students often lack the information, confidence, and family support to help them navigate the college environment. Research on community college students finds that many are bewildered by the complexity of choices they face in postsecondary education.[10]

These students have not been well served by the education system before they arrive on campus. About two-thirds or more of community college students enter lacking the basic skills and/or English-language skills needed to succeed in college.

Nearly 60 percent of students take at least one developmental-education (remedial) course while in college. For most students, these developmental-education
courses are a dead end. Less than 25 percent of students who enroll in remediation complete a degree or certificate within eight years.[11]

Once on campus, many students are juggling multiple responsibilities. More
and more community college students are older and have work and family responsibilities, one reason 59 percent now attend only part-time.[12] While there is a great
deal of variation across colleges, in 2008 (the last year for which data are available)
47 percent of students were "independent,"[13] 42 percent of students were over age
twenty-four,[14] and 23 percent were parents.[15] Almost one-third (29 percent) of
full-time and 37 percent of part-time students are caring for dependents for eleven
or more hours per week.[16] These students bring life experience, which enhances
their educational experience but also require more flexible schedules and service-
delivery modes to accommodate their other responsibilities.

Community college students are also likely to work while attending school.
More than 80 percent of community college students work while in school to cover college and family costs; about one-third work full-time.[17] According to 2010
data from the Center for Community College Student Engagement, 42 percent of
part-time community college students worked more than thirty hours per week.[18]
While part-time jobs can help students build work habits and make connections
that will lead to future employment, excessive work can interfere with college attendance and success, leading to prolonged time to completion and even drop-
ping out. Students who miss class to go to work are likely to fall behind in their
schoolwork and get grades that reflect their poor attendance. But students who
refuse work shifts that conflict with their classes may be fired or may simply find
themselves scheduled for so few hours that they cannot pay their bills.

Financial Barriers Facing Community College Students, and Their Impact

Unmet financial need among community college students is a barrier to
student access and success. While these tuition and fees are significantly lower
than those at four-year public institutions, other costs of attending community college—including basic living expenses, transportation, and textbooks—are
still substantial. In 2010–11 a year at a community college was estimated to cost
$14,637, compared with $20,339 for the average undergraduate at a public, four-
year university.[19] For students who are supporting families, the cost is even higher,
as housing, food, and child care costs add to the total.

Financial aid can help to cover these costs, but community college students receive relatively little. As a result, the financial burden on students at community colleges is very high, despite assumptions of affordability and lower tuition costs. After accounting for available financial aid, 80 percent of community college students still have unmet need, compared with 54 percent of students in public four-year college students.[20] The average full-time community college student was projected to have had more than $6,000 in unmet need in 2010–2011.[21]

Non-credit Courses and Credit-Accumulation Barriers

Close to 40 percent of all community college enrollments are in non-credit courses. Non-credit offerings include occupational programs, pre-college-level developmental, and adult-education and English as a second language (ESL) courses, as well as vocational courses.[22] About half of non-credit courses are in occupational, vocational, or technical fields.[23] While non-credit courses serve industry needs and help students gain the knowledge and skills they need to get or keep a job, or even lead to valuable industry certifications, non-credit courses often are dead ends for students in terms of their transferability. Students may never be able to receive credit for these courses in programs of study leading to educational credentials, such as associate's degrees, that are stepping-stones to further postsecondary education and often required for better-paying jobs with advancement potential.

Taken together, these factors impede students' ability to persist and succeed in gaining valuable postsecondary credentials. Federal higher-education statistics indicate that fewer than three in ten students who start at community colleges full-time graduate with an associate's degree in three years.[24] There are no federal data on completion rates for the more than half of community college students who attend part-time. However, an analysis of data from thirty-three states found that the four-year completion rate for part-time community college students was 8 percent, compared with 19 percent for full-time students.[25] These data may be overstating the problem, because they do not take into account that many students leave for employment once they get the skills or industry credential they need and others transfer to other institutions before they get their associate's degree.

Emerging Supply-Side Innovations in Community Colleges

California's Edge Campaign defines a sector strategy as an organizing principle that provides incentives and support for the alignment of workforce, education, and economic-development policies around major regional industry sectors to address the needs of both businesses and individuals. The goal is to weave together a patchwork of workforce-development programs around sector-focused career pathways for workers. Doing so makes more efficient use of limited public resources; provides access to a full range of skill-attainment coursework for students, jobs seekers, and incumbent workers; improves labor-market outcomes; and meets the needs of regional industries and economies.[26]

The community college reform efforts discussed in this chapter all aim to achieve sectoral alignment. Just as sector strategies are diverse in their focus, these community college reforms differ in their scope and the target employers and populations they aim to serve. However, they all aim to improve the responsiveness of community college offerings to diverse economic and student needs. Many are designed to address different aspects of the student experience, from preparation and initial assessment to degree or certificate completion. Although these reforms are related and may be taking place in the same state or community college simultaneously, each is defined by one of four primary goals:

- Improving the relevance of community college offerings.

- Creating sector-based pathways to marketable credentials and good jobs.

- Connecting industry and educational credentials and non-credit learning to credit-bearing education.

- Strengthening student supports to promote persistence and completion.

Improving the Relevance of Community College Offerings

States and individual colleges have taken a number of steps to improve the responsiveness of their educational offerings to changing local economic needs. For example, California and Washington State have created Centers of Excellence in community and technical colleges, which create new and relevant programs and curricula, understand skills gaps, and connect with business and industry partners. In California these centers also conduct environmental scans and customized reports for community colleges. Washington's ten Centers of Excellence focus on targeted industries that drive the state's economy and, guided by industry representatives, act as brokers of information and resources related to their targeted industry for employers, community-based organizations, economic-development organizations, community and technical colleges, secondary-education institutions, and four-year colleges and universities.

The Washington Centers of Excellence are closely linked with Industry Skill Panels, regional business, labor, and education partnerships that examine workforce needs in their industries and foster solutions to meet those needs. Centers of Excellence host four of the skill panels: those for the marine, construction, energy, and enology/viticulture industries. Since their introduction in 2000, skill panels, which receive their funding through the Workforce Training and Education Coordinating Board, have been able to catalyze considerable investments and expand collaborations to improve workforce skills and talent pipelines for key Washington industries. For example, Centralia College's training programs used the industry skill standards for plant operators and plant mechanics developed by the skill panel to cut in half the number of hours required for becoming a certified journeyman through a union-management agreement. As of 2013, there were thirty-five skill panels in sixteen industries.

State efforts such as those in California and Washington complement sectorfocused initiatives undertaken by community colleges themselves to improve curriculum and instruction. Such efforts range from the Automotive Manufacturing Technical Education Collaborative—which includes an international group of auto manufacturers, their supply chains, and thirty-two community colleges and labor organizations across thirteen states—to much smaller regional partnerships in health care, energy, and other industries.

Creating Sector-Based Pathways to Marketable Credentials and Good Jobs

Sector-based career pathways are one of the fastest-growing education and training reforms to better meet employers' need for skilled workers and transform and align disconnected components of education and training systems to optimize students' progress.

It's important to differentiate career pathways from sector strategies. They share a dual-customer focus on employers and job seekers. They both focus on a specific industry or cross-sector occupation based on needs in regional labor markets. They are both guided and implemented by a partnership of key public- and private-sector players, including multiple employers, labor representatives, and public-sector agencies related to education and human services. They also both often involve intermediaries to make connections and facilitate the systemic change needed to address changing economic needs. However, despite these similar features, there are differences. Sector strategies may deal with a wider set of issues of concern to local partners than education- and training-focused career-pathways initiatives. And career pathways have a clear focus on longer-term education that can be "chunked" into smaller segments for workers and job seekers who are balancing work, family, and education.

Just as sector strategies differ in the scope and population targeted, the scope of career-pathway reforms and target populations served ranges from a focus on improving the transition from high school to college, to facilitating the reemployment of veterans and dislocated workers. For students with multiple challenges, the career-pathways approach focuses on better integrating the services of adult-education, youth-employment, workforce-development, and community college systems that serve these populations. In many states and communities, community colleges have played an important role in the development and implementation of career pathways, often serving as the providers of extensive non-credit and for-credit coursework and supportive services, such as advising and financial-aid assistance. In a growing number of states, they are also the primary providers of basic-skills instruction for adults and youth with limited skills or limited English proficiency.

Creating a career-pathway system requires redesigning most of the way that education, training, and employment services are delivered to be more demand-driven, integrated, aligned, and participant-centered. Many pathways employ evidence-based and promising student-centered approaches to instruction and occupational training, including competency-based instruction; accelerated programs; flexible service-delivery options, such as a choice of course scheduling and delivery modes and modularized courses; and appropriate and meaningful assessment of participant skills and needs. Many career pathways emphasize the use of supportive services, such as child-care assistance, transportation, and academic advising and navigation, to help students continue along the pathway while juggling work and family obligations.

Adopting a career-pathways approach requires education and training partners to transform the way they interact with one another and with the business community. Creating a career-pathway system entails radically deepening collaboration with employers and coordination among agencies, institutions, and organizations. Thus, an essential tenet of all career-pathways initiatives is the significant and ongoing engagement of employers in career-pathway development and implementation.

Successful career-pathway systems are built and maintained by a partnership among local or regional employers or industry partnerships, agencies, organizations, and institutions that are committed to building, scaling up, and sustaining demand-driven career pathways. One of the specific indicators that career pathways are attuned to industry demand is that they are linked to sector partnerships, where they exist. Another indicator is that the local or regional partners use labor-market intelligence on current and future demand to inform the development and ongoing relevance of career pathways.

While many career-pathways initiatives are an integral part of state or regional sector strategies, committed and sustained employer involvement varies and is an ongoing struggle, especially during periods of slack labor-market demand. The following examples illustrate variations in how the career-pathways approach is being implemented as an integral aspect of a sectoral approach to economic and workforce development:

Career Pathways in Virginia

Virginia approaches career pathways through an economic-development lens, with the explicit goal of creating a workforce that is customized to the needs of industry and responsive to regional labor-market demand. This interagency effort was developed out of a Governor's Task Force in 2008 that brought together leaders from the Office of the Governor, the Virginia Department of Labor and Industry, the State Council of Higher Education, the Virginia Community College System, the Virginia Department of Education, the Virginia Economic Development Partnership, and other state agencies to create a set of coordinated strategies to build a statewide workforce development and education pathway.

The principal purpose of these efforts was to create a workforce that is customized to the needs of industry and responsive to regional labor-market demand. Through a combination of state, federal, and private investments, Virginia is expanding on this work to create industry-specific career pathways in each region of the state. These activities include scaling up the promising PluggedInVA model, which combines basic-skills instruction and GED preparation with industry certifications and for-credit coursework. Participants in this program graduate with a GED, an industry certification, a Career Readiness Certificate, a digital-literacy certificate, at least twelve community college credits, and experiences with local employers.

The Virginia Peninsula Strategic Plan for Career Pathways in Advanced and Precision Manufacturing Technologies is an example of a regional partnership organized around the goal of the task force, bringing together the Peninsula Council for Workforce Development, Thomas Nelson Community College, and the Virginia Community College System to create a world-class technical workforce by providing integrated career pathways for youth and adults.[27]

Career-Pathway Bridge Programs

Career-pathway bridge programs are an extension of the career-pathways approach, designed specifically as a first step into a longer-term career pathway for adults and youth with low basic skills or poor English-language proficiency. Career-pathway bridges use new curricula, innovative delivery modes, and joint planning and instruction to bridge the skills gap that can prevent individuals with limited basic skills from entering and succeeding in postsecondary education. Well-designed bridges incorporate most of the elements of career pathways, such as support services and a strong role for employers. In addition, because they are intended to provide a seamless on-ramp for lower-skilled individuals, bridges use evidence-based strategies for accelerating student success, such as integrated education, dual enrollment, and contextualized learning.

At the lower levels of adult basic education and English-language instruction, career-pathway bridges (sometimes called pre-bridges in this context) tend to focus initially on career exploration and planning, or on introducing students to broad concepts, vocabulary, and career opportunities in a specific sector. For example, a health care pre-bridge might include medical terminology and visits to healthcare workplaces so that participants learn about the range of job opportunities in that sector. These types of pre-bridges tend to be delivered solely by basic-skills instructors, either within adult basic education or developmental education. Higher levels of career-pathway bridges are typically more narrowly focused, because their goal is to help students prepare for and succeed in specific occupational certificate programs within a career pathway. These bridges are typically jointly planned and delivered by basic-skills and career-technical-education instructors.

Shifting Gears in Illinois

As part of the multistate Shifting Gears Initiative supported by the Joyce Foundation, the Illinois Community College Board (ICCB) and other workforce-development partners launched a statewide effort to support the development of career-pathway bridge programs for low-skilled adults in adult education and developmental education. These bridge programs integrate basic-skills instruction with occupational instruction in one of the sixteen career clusters identified by the state. To ensure consistency and quality of bridge programming throughout the state, the ICCB and the Illinois Department of Commerce and Economic Opportunity adopted a common definition of bridge-program core elements for use in adult, career, and technical education, and WIA program funding and reimbursement structures.

Building on these and other education and workforce reforms, the state and the Illinois Business Roundtable launched the Illinois Pathways initiative in 2012 to create regional career pathways that allow workers to progress from entry-level to more advanced jobs through the use of stackable industry-recognized credentials. Statewide public-private partnerships, known as Learning Exchanges, in targeted STEM sectors aligned to the state's economic and workforce-development objectives will coordinate investments, resources, and programs.

FastTRAC in Minnesota

Minnesota FastTRAC is an example of statewide adult career pathways designed to help workers with very low skills increase their foundational skills and eventually acquire industry-recognized credentials and employment. Initiated in 2007 through the Shifting Gears initiative, the FastTRAC model is supported by a public-private and cross-system collaboration to focus on the needs of low-skill adult learners and make FastTRAC bridge programming available at every two-year state college in Minnesota. The model includes a series of credit-based courses and supportive services that help participants at all skill levels get on a pathway to earning marketable skills and preparing for high-wage employment. Programming is delivered through a network of organizations and institutions that work together to provide education and training services, including the Minnesota State Colleges and Universities system, Adult Basic Education, the Department of Employment and Economic Development, and local workforce-development partners, human services, and community-based organizations. FastTRAC also connects to local employers and sector partnerships through local workforce investment boards. Minnesota FastTRAC Adult Career Pathway has gained significant traction among high-level state leadership; its statewide expansion was supported by the Governor's Workforce Development Council, and new, dedicated funding for the initiative was proposed by the governor to the state legislature in 2012.

Research and Evaluation of Career Pathways and Career-Pathway Bridges

There has been a significant amount of experimentation with career-pathway approaches at the state and local levels, and there is early and promising evidence of student success, credential attainment, and positive labor-market outcomes. However, the confusing array of definitions and system-building and programmatic strategies pursued under the career-pathway banner is a barrier to identifying and then scaling effective policies and practices.

A descriptive study[28] of Oregon's career-pathway program found that despite unusually high levels of unemployment in the state from 2008 to 2010, when the first career-pathway cohorts completed certificates, 44.5 percent of certificate completers entered employment at $12 per hour or more within four quarters of completing their certificate, with many completers earning more than $15 per hour. Of those that entered employment, 48.1 percent were continuously employed for four quarters at $12 per hour or more. Their average wage was $17.68 per hour. In some regions of the state, the average wage of career-pathway completers was higher than both the regional average entry-level wage and the median wage for the region.

The most rigorous research to date is on the effectiveness of career-pathway bridge programs. A 2010 study by the Community College Research Center at

Columbia University[29] evaluated the effectiveness of Washington State's I-BEST (Integrated Basic Education and Skills Training) program, which pairs basic-skills and career-technical instructors in the same classroom to teach integrated occupational-certificate and basic-skills content. I-BEST is commonly cited as the first basic-skills program to take a systemic and integrated approach to contextualized basic-skills instruction, seeking to improve the rate at which students who have initially low basic skills improve their occupational skills and earn college credentials. The study, which used statistical controls to compare the outcomes of I-BEST students to those of their peers in regular basic-skills courses, found that I-BEST students are 56 percent more likely than regular adult basic education and ESL students to earn college credit, 26 percent more likely to earn a certificate or degree, and 19 percent more likely to achieve learning gains on basic-skills tests. More simply, as Washington puts it, I-BEST moves students "farther and faster."

In addition to the I-BEST study, considerable research exists on individual elements of bridge programs, such as dual enrollment, enhanced student services, and learning communities. This research suggests that these can be effective strategies for improving student completion of basic-skills coursework and for increasing enrollment in and completion of college-level courses. While the impact of any one of these strategies alone is often modest, the I-BEST experience lends weight to the idea that such strategies may have more impact when combined, as they are in career-pathway bridges.

An evaluation of the Illinois Shifting Gears bridge programs by the Office of Community College Research and Leadership at the University of Illinois found that programs that provided career orientation, admissions assistance, transportation assistance, and advising were more likely to have higher student completion rates than those that did not. The evaluation also identified three major barriers to improved student completion: individual student-level factors, such as preparation and multiple personal and work responsibilities; institutional barriers, such as poor use of assessments; and poor alignment of federal education and training funding streams.

While experimentation continues, the U.S. Department of Health and Human Services is pursuing a random-assignment evaluation of career pathways under the Improving Strategies for Self-Sufficiency (ISIS) project. Findings from the ISIS evaluation are expected to be released in 2016.

Connecting Industry and Educational Credentials and Non-credit Learning to Credit-Bearing Education

Employer demand for better alignment of educational curricula and credentials with industry requirements, coupled with efforts to create stackable career-

pathway credentials that have value in both industry and education, is contributing to increased use of competency or mastery of knowledge and skills, rather
than the credit hour, as the standard by which to measure instruction and award
credentials. Other factors leading in this direction are career-pathway and career
pathway-bridge innovations that bring together in new ways academic and occupational content that previously has been divided into credit-bearing and non-
credit offerings, increased use of online instruction, and recognition that older
students bring with them relevant knowledge and skills learned through life and
work experiences. These non-education-based experiences may include on-the-job
learning, or training provided by professional associations and societies, employers, unions, the military, or community-based organizations.

States and institutions are using a number of approaches for bridging the
divide between non-credit learning and credit-bearing courses, which we break
down into two overarching strategies: integrating work-based learning into courses of study and dual enrollment.

Integrating Work-Based Learning and Credentials into Courses of Study

State and institutional efforts to create "stackable" credentials and embed
industry-recognized credentials in credit-bearing courses of study rely on mapping the appropriate curriculum pathways, building on any demonstrated skills,
licensure, and certificates and certifications, then validating those certifications.
When combined with an academic credential, this approach is proving effective in
advancing workers along career pathways.

Credit for prior learning (CPL) is the oldest, though still underutilized, approach for awarding credit retroactively. CPL includes a variety of methodologies,
such as portfolio assessments, standardized exams, and use of credit recommendations made by institutional or third-party evaluators using nationally recognized
criteria to recommend credit equivalencies for non-credit learning. A 2010 Council on Adult and Experiential Learning study of more than sixty-two thousand
adult students at forty-eight institutions nationwide reported that students with
CPL had higher graduation rates, better persistence, and shorter time to degree,
compared with students without CPL credits. According to the study, student advisors believe that earning CPL can motivate students to persist in their studies
and complete their degrees. It also serves as a motivating factor for students to
know that they have already learned at the college level.[30]

Forsyth Technical Community College (FTCC) in North Carolina uses
a newer model for awarding credit to experienced workers, the National Association of Manufacturers-endorsed Skills Certification System. FTCC has aligned

the curriculum in four of its manufacturing-related programs of study with these industry-based certifications. The advanced manufacturing pathways developed through this alignment process enable students to earn numerous industry certifications while simultaneously earning college credit for many of the courses they take. The college is exploring several feeder options for the manufacturing-related programs in the certification system. First, high school students can earn college credit free of tuition through a dual-enrollment program. College leadership is also exploring the possibility of translating students' experiences in non-credit customized training for incumbent workers to college credit, so that individuals can get a jump-start on a certificate or degree program.

Kentucky Community & Technical College System (KCTCS) has created multiple entry and exit points for students by building associate's-degree programs on multiple credentials, certificates, and diplomas. KCTCS also implemented fractional credit of as little as 0.2 credit hours and modularization for both classroom and online education. As a result, 60 percent of participants in state-run customized training with industry now earn some form of academic credit. KCTCS has expanded its efforts to corporate and apprenticeship training programs, incorporating them as "embedded credentials" leading to higher levels along a career pathway within a particular field of study. For example, the KCTCS Information Technology Program enables students who complete and pass an industry's standard certification examination (e.g., CISCO Certified Network Administrator), administered by an industry-authorized certification testing center, to earn up to twenty-four credit hours toward an associate's degree.

Indiana's twenty-three-campus Ivy Tech Community College system uses a certification crosswalk to award a consistent amount of educational credit for a wide range of industry certifications, including apprenticeships, provided through third-party certification organizations. The crosswalk helps students with proper documentation avoid the lengthy review process and the fee associated with portfolio assessment of prior learning. The crosswalk also saves campuses time and money, because they do not have to review each student's prior learning. The crosswalk is being used to award educational credit for students in WorkINdiana, Indiana's career-pathway program targeted to pre-postsecondary occupational training in high-demand fields, which is administered through regional consortia of adult education, community colleges, and workforce development and community nonprofits and provides basic-skills students can access. In Wisconsin, Regional Industry Skills Education (RISE) centers on creating career pathways that offer new technical certificates and diplomas embedded within existing one- and two-year diploma and degree programs. RISE provides an avenue for local technical colleges to break longer programs into shorter modules and certificates that are easier for adults to complete quickly by creating a new, streamlined process for approving technical diplomas and recognizing occupational certificates that are embedded within existing Wisconsin Technical College System State Board–approved programs. Wisconsin also awards educational credit for apprenticeship-related instruction. Apprentices can earn thirty-nine credits through an apprenticeship program, which can be applied toward the sixty-credit Journeyworker Applied Associate in Science degree.

Dual-Enrollment Programs

Dual-enrollment career-pathway bridges enable basic-skills students to begin earning a postsecondary occupational credential right away, without having to first complete a sequence of adult-basic-education, English-language, or developmental-education services. Like dual-enrollment options for high school students, students enrolled in these bridge programs work to master pre-college reading, writing, math, or English-language skills while also beginning their postsecondary program coursework. In this way, students can enter a program of study from the very beginning of their postsecondary experience while at the same time receiving support to improve their basic skills.

This approach is showing results. New research finds that the sooner students enter a program of study, the more likely it is that they complete a certificate or degree or transfer to a four-year institution. Specifically, research finds that students who entered a program of study in their first or second term were twice as successful as students who did not enter a program of study until their second year at completing a certificate or an associate's degree or transferring.[31] South Texas College in McAllen, for example, offers basic-skills students the opportunity to earn college credits and occupational certificates through dual enrollment in contextualized English-language and math classes, technical Spanish classes (which cover occupational knowledge and vocabulary in the students' native language), and college-level occupational courses. Through this dual-language bridge model, basic-skills students without a high school diploma or GED can complete three occupational courses in green-construction career pathways, which include HVAC/refrigeration, plumbing, and electrical. While the initial classes in the "on-ramp" portion of these pathways are non-credit, students automatically receive college credit for them on enrolling in the next level in the pathway.

Strengthening Student Financial Supports to Promote Persistence and Completion

While community colleges are experimenting with new ways of providing students the education and training they need, they are also innovating in meeting students' non-academic challenges, which can be personal or financial in nature and can impede their persistence and completion. Personal supports address child care, transportation, and other challenges that arise as students balance the demands of participation in training with work and family. Career-preparation supports help identify students' interests and assist them in exploring careers and developing education and training plans to meet their career goals. Financial supports, apart from financial aid, help students make ends meet while attending school. This latter type of support is gaining attention as the cost of postsecondary degrees increases and lower-income students are less able to afford college. As discussed earlier, low-income students who receive financial aid have a gap between their aid and the amount they need to support themselves and their families.

Some of these efforts are tied in to career-pathways and other programs designed to provide supports for at-risk students. For example, Gateway Community and Technical College in Kentucky, one of the colleges participating in the multi-site Benefits Access for College Completion (BACC) initiative, connects low-income students in their health-career pathway and bridge programs on campus to an array of public benefits.[32] BACC is designed to test whether the combination of financial aid and enrollment in public support—such as options under the Affordable Care Act, Medicaid, the Children's Health Insurance Program, the Supplemental Nutrition Assistance Program, the Special Supplemental Nutrition Program for Women, Infants and Children, and the free and reduced-price school-lunch program for children—can increase graduation rates among low-income community college students juggling work, studies, and family responsibilities. The participating colleges are integrating screening and application assistance for these programs with the services and supports they already provide, so that the strategies they develop are sustainable and scalable. They also are partnering with local and state human-services agencies to streamline the process of applying for support.

A number of community colleges are combining academic and career supports with personal and financial ones. Some are doing the majority of this work on campus, while others are building strong partnerships with community-based organizations, such as nonprofit social-service organizations, workforce nonprofit organizations, private foundations, and businesses.

One such partnership, being implemented as part of the Courses to Employment (C2E) demonstration,[33] is the Automobile Career Pathways Project. This project, operated by the Workforce Development Council of Seattle–King County and Shoreline Community College, offered a General Service Technician certificate program. Participants had access to a career navigator, who helped them obtain resources to cover tuition, other academic expenses, rent, child care, and transportation. The career navigator also assisted students with career planning and worked with faculty to arrange internships for students during the program and employment opportunities after program completion. Results of C2E show that the additional assistance these partnerships can provide to adult and other nontraditional, frequently low-income learners can make it possible for them to complete job training and secure employment with higher wages.[34]

Supply-Side Innovations Moving Forward

Educating low-income workers and job seekers at community colleges continues to be vital to meeting the growing demand for more educated workers. The changes that have been seeded over the last ten years within community colleges and in collaboration with partners show promise in addressing key barriers to skill and credential attainment and improving access to family-sustaining employment for low-income workers and job seekers. Unlike previous siloed approaches to connecting people to employment, the current reforms bridge the divide between workforce development and postsecondary education. They are guided by a shared goal among partners of participant progress and success in both education and employment. These reforms aim to provide more holistic and student-centered services that tackle the complicated challenges faced by many low-income people as they seek to advance economically. Remaining true to the dual-customer focus that traditionally guides U.S. workforce-development programs, they also aim to serve employers and remain responsive to specific and dynamic labor-market contexts.

The challenge moving forward is to scale and sustain proven strategies and practices. Eventually, these reforms should become the new way of doing business in community colleges, in the broader workforce-development community, and in the employer community. To achieve this goal requires several steps—private-sector leadership, adequate and aligned funding, addressing trade-offs, continuous improvement and shared accountability, and continued focus on access and completion for disadvantaged students—described in more detail below.

Committed and Sustained Private-Sector Leadership at Multiple Levels

Collaborative leadership by the public and private sectors in leading states can make a difference in creating more targeted and comprehensive service delivery for low-income workers and job seekers. It is unclear whether sector partnerships, career-pathway initiatives, or other intermediaries will be able to sustain, much less scale, employer involvement in the low-skilled-worker agenda. In any case, these efforts should be more closely joined so as not to compete with one another for

employer involvement and commitment. The challenge of sustaining employer involvement is exacerbated by current trends related to the globalization of the labor
market, changing human-resources practices, fewer internal career ladders within
companies, and the continuing weak job market in communities throughout the
country. We must create policies that make it attractive for employers to participate but avoid creating windfalls for employers or losing the focus on improving
the economic prospects or low-income workers.

Adequate and Aligned Funding

Despite tight budget environments for the foreseeable future, we need to increase the capacity of chronically underfunded workforce education and training
and human-services delivery systems to provide the necessary supports and other
services needed to more effectively meet the challenges of low-income workers and
job seekers. A combination of stagnant federal and state funding for some workforce education and training systems and deep cuts for others has left adult workers and students with few alternatives for gaining needed skills and credentials.
Policy changes in student financial aid have cut this option off for some students,
and community colleges have not been able to keep up with increased demand for
services due to budget pressures.

We also must focus on aligning existing funds in smart ways. Work should
continue toward removing federal and state policy and practice barriers to braiding
funding streams, but we must steer away from simplistic program consolidation
solutions. Consolidation proposals would likely lead to a reduction of available
resources and therefore diminish communities' capacity to provide multifaceted
interventions, such as those described in this chapter.

Addressing Trade-offs Inherent in Achieving Scale

Without an infusion of considerably more money, we must consider trade-offs between scaling more holistic interventions that help targeted groups of low-skill workers
and job seekers and providing narrower and presumably less expensive interventions to
a greater number of people. We also should consider what is meant by scale, given the
growing demand for skills and credentials among workers and job seekers; it's important that the supply of these workers not outstrip labor-market demand.

Commitment to Continuous Improvement and Shared Accountability

Despite constrained resources, we need to build a stronger base of evidence
about what works and foster a culture of evidence-based continuous improvement at the program, local system, and state levels. For example, the Achieving the

Dream National Reform Network of two hundred community colleges in thirty-two states and the District of Columbia—which promotes a data-driven culture of continuous improvement and institutional change, with the goal of improving outcomes, especially for students of color and low-income students[35]—is a start, but more needs to be done.

Shared accountability goes hand-in-hand with implementing evidence-based practices. Instead of siloed accountability systems tied to individual funding streams, we need a set of shared performance metrics to provide a cross system focus on how well these systems are working together to help people progress along education and career pathways. However, we still need to experiment with realistic ways to encourage collaboration among multiple providers and hold them jointly accountable for achieving participant progress and success.

Continued Focus on College Access for Low-Income, First-Generation, and Disadvantaged Students—Not Just Completion

While supporting student success is vital to ensuring that more low-income and disadvantaged students obtain credentials and degrees, a narrow focus on achieving high college-completion rates may lead states and institutions to focus on serving students most likely to graduate quickly with inexpensive, light-touch interventions. Improving access to community colleges for low-skilled, low-income, and other disadvantaged students should continue to be a priority for state and federal policy makers and local institutions.

Conclusion

Achieving these changes will not be easy, but as discussed in this chapter, community colleges and the broader workforce education and training community have come a long way in the last ten years. We have demonstrated that, with leadership from the public, private, and nonprofit sectors, it is possible to change the way systems and institutions function. We must continue on this course.

Notes

1. Giloth (2004).
2. Carnevale (2013).
3. American Association of Community Colleges (2012).
4. Dougherty and Townsend (2006).
5. Community College Research Center FAQs (2013).
6. Visher and Fowler (2006).

7. The ten-state Alliance for Quality Career Pathways, an initiative led by the Center for Law and Social Policy, supported by the Joyce and James Irvine foundations, defines career pathways as an approach for "connect[ing] progressive levels of basic skills and postsecondary education, training, and supportive services in specific sectors or cross-sector occupations in a way that optimizes the progress and success of individuals—including those with limited education, English, skills, and/or work experience—in securing marketable credentials, family-supporting employment, and further education and employment opportunities; ... help[ing] employers meet their workforce needs and help[ing] states and communities strengthen their workforces and economies" (CLASP 2013, p. 2).

8. These include Career Connections, Career Pathways Institutes, and Policy to Performance, which helped states align education and training systems for specific populations of students and workers, such as adult-education students.

9. American Association of Community Colleges (2012).

10. Scott-Clayton (2011), pp. 10–11.

11. Bailey and Cho (2010), p. 47.

12. U.S. Department of Education (2010b).

13. For purposes of federal financial aid, students are considered "independent" if they meet at least one of the following seven criteria:

- Be twenty-four or older by December 31 of the award year.

- Be an orphan (both parents deceased) or a ward of the court, or was a ward of the court until the age of eighteen.

- Be a veteran of the Armed Forces of the United States.

- Be a graduate or professional student.

- Be a married individual.

- Have legal dependents other than a spouse.

- Be a student for whom a financial aid administrator makes a documented determination of independence by reason of other unusual circumstances.

14. U.S. Department of Education (2010a).

15. Miller, Gault, and Thorman (2011), p. 10.

16. Center for Community College Student Engagement (2012), p. 6.

17. Staklis and Chen (2010), p. 36.

18. Center for Community College Student Engagement (2012), p. 6.

19. Baum and Ma (2010), p. 6.

20. Institute for College Access & Success (2009), p. 2.

21. Baum and Ma (2010), p. 15.

22. American Association of Community Colleges (2012) p. 1.

23. Vorhees and Milam (2005), p. 14.

24. U.S. Department of Education (2010c).

25. Complete College America (2011), p. 8.

26. California EDGE Campaign Legislative Workforce Policy Group.

27. Memorandum of Understanding, Virginia Peninsula Strategic Plan for Career Pathways in Advanced and Precision Manufacturing Technologies, revised February 2, 2012.

28. "Pathways in Oregon: A Descriptive Study of the Statewide Initiative & Initial Cohort of Completers," Worksource Oregon, March 2013.

29. Accelerating Opportunity is supported by the Bill & Melinda Gates Foundation, the Joyce Foundation, the W.K. Kellogg Foundation, the Kresge Foundation, and the Open Society Foundations.

30. Klein-Collins (2010), pp. 7–8.

31. Jenkins and Cho (2012). These findings are based on an analysis of transcript records, student level characteristics, test scores, and institutional-transfer information for a sample of first-time college students in an anonymous group of community colleges in the same state in 2005–2006.

32. Benefits Access for College Completion is funded by a consortium of funders that includes Open Society Foundations, the Ford Foundation, the Lumina Foundation, the Kresge Foundation, and the Annie E. Casey Foundation. It is managed by CLASP and the American Association of Community Colleges.

33. C2E was implemented by the Aspen Institute's Workforce Strategies Initiative, with support by the Charles Stewart Mott Foundation.

34. Conway, Blair, and Hemler (2012), p. 5.

35. See http://www.achievingthedream.org/network.

Bibliography

American Association of Community Colleges. 2012. "Community College Fact Sheet."

Bailey, T., and S.W. Cho. 2010. *Developmental Education in Community Colleges.* Community College Research Center, Columbia University.

Baum, S., and J. Ma. 2010. *Trends in College Pricing.* College Board.

California EDGE Campaign Legislative Workforce Policy Group. *Sector Focused Career Pathways.* http://californiaedgecampaign.org/wp-content/uploads/2012/03/SECTOR-handout-3-1FINAL.pdf.

Carmichael, M. 2012. "Food Banks Confront Hunger at Community Colleges." *Boston Globe.* May 12.

Carnevale, Anthoy P., Nicole Smith and Jeff Strohl. June 2013. Recovery: Job Growth And Education Requirements Through 2020, Georgetown Public Policy Institute, Center on Education and the Workforce.

Center for Community College Student Engagement. 2012. *A Matter of Degrees: Promising Practices for Community College Student Success (A First Look).* Austin: University of Texas at Austin, Community College Leadership Program.

Cheney, S., S. Wagner, and L. Woolsey. 2008. *Evaluating Industry Skill Panels: A Model Framework.* Corporation for a Skilled Workforce and PAROS Group.

CLASP. 2013. *Alliance for Quality Career Pathways "Beta" Framework: Public Version.* July 15.

Complete College America. 2011. *Time Is the Enemy: The Surprising Truth about Why Today's College Students Aren't Graduating … and What Needs to Change.*

Community College FAQs 2013. Community College Research Center, Teachers College, Columbia University.

Conway, M., A. Blair, and M. Helmer. 2012. *Courses to Employment: Partnering to Create Paths to Education and Careers.* Aspen Institute, Workforce Strategies Initiative.

Dougherty, Kevin J. and Barbara K. Townsend. "Community College Missions: A Theoretical and Historical Perspective" in New Directions for Community Colleges, Special Issue: Community College Missions in the 21st Century, Volume 2006, Issue 136, Wiley Periodicals, Inc., pages 5-13, Winter 2006.

Giloth, Robert P., ed. *Workforce Intermediaries for the Twenty-First Century.* 2004. Published in association with the American Assembly, Columbia University. Philadelphia: Temple University Press.

Institute for College Access & Success. 2010. *Quick Facts about Financial Aid and Community Colleges, 2007–08.*

Jenkins, D., and S. Cho. 2012. *Get with the Program: Accelerating Community College Students' Entry into and Completion of Programs of Study.* CCRC Working Paper No. 32. Community College Research Center.

Klein-Collins, R. 2010. *Fueling the Race to Postsecondary Success: A 48-Institution Study of Prior Learning Assessment and Adult Student Outcomes.* Council on Adult and Experiential Learning.

Lee, David. Feeding America, October 1, 2012.

Liston, C., and R. Donnan. *Center for Working Families at Community Colleges: Clearing the Financial Barriers to Success.* MDC.

Miller, K., B. Gault, and A. Thorman. 2011. *Improving Child Care Access to Promote Postsecondary SuccessAmong Low-Income Parents.* Institute for Women's Policy Research.

Scott-Clayton, J. 2011. *The Shapeless River: Does a Lack of Structure Inhibit Students' Progress at Community Colleges?* Community College Research Center, Columbia University.

Staklis, S., and X. Chen. 2010. *Profiles of Undergraduate Students: Trends from Selected Years, 1995–96 to 2007–08.* Report prepared for the U.S. Department of Education, National Center for Education Statistics, under contract (No. ED-CO-0033) with MPR Associates, Inc.

U.S. Department of Education, National Center for Education Statistics, 2009 Integrated Postsecondary Education Data System (IPEDS). 2010a. Table 201: "Total fall enrollment in degree-granting institutions, by control and type of institution, age, and attendance status of student: 2009." Digest of Education Statistics.

———. 2010b. Table 202: "Total fall enrollment in degree-granting institutions, by level of enrollment, sex, attendance status, and type and control of institution: 2009." Digest of Education Statistics.

———. 2010c. Table 39: "Graduation rates at Title IV institutions, by race/ethnicity, level and control of institution, gender, degree sought, and degree completed at the institution where the students started as full-time, first-time students: United States, cohort years 2003 and 2006."

Visher, Mary G. and Donna Fowler. December 2006. *Working It Out, Community Colleges and the Workforce Investment Act.* Institute for the Study of Family, Work and Community, MPR Associates.

Vorhees, R.A., and J.H. Milam. 2005. *The Hidden College: Noncredit Education in the United States.* Vorhees Group.

Waters Boots, S. 2010. *Improving Access to Public Benefits: Helping Eligible Individuals Get the Income Supports They Need.* The Annie E Casey Foundation.

Woolsey, L., and G. Groves. 2013. *State Sector Strategies Coming of Age: Implications for State Workforce Policymakers.* National Governors Association Center for Best Practices, Corporation for a Skilled Workforce, and National Skills Coalition.

15

Workforce Intermediaries and the Apprenticeship System: Lessons and Implications from the Construction Industry

Matt Helmer and Maureen Conway

Registered Apprenticeship has been a valuable approach to employment training for more than seventy-five years in the United States. Enacted in 1937, the National Apprenticeship Act (Fitzgerald Act) has led to the creation of more than 25,000 Registered Apprenticeship programs across the United States. In 2011 approximately 130,000 individuals entered one of these programs, and nearly 400,000 overall were active in one.[1] Registered Apprenticeship programs provide employers with pipelines of skilled workers and individuals with an opportunity to "earn and learn" through a training model that combines related technical or classroom instruction (RTI) with structured, paid on-the-job training (OJT) experiences. By design, apprenticeship training responds to employer demand, both in training content and in the number of workers who are equipped with needed skills.

Apprenticeship positions can be found in a range of industries, but the building trades continue to be the sector that uses the apprenticeship system most. Many associate building trades apprenticeship programs with unions—and indeed unions do sponsor a disproportionate number of apprentices, given their market share—but non-union employers also use the apprenticeship system. Each year apprenticeship programs in this sector enroll thousands of apprentices who will become carpenters, electricians, laborers, plumbers, and more. After completing between three and five years of OJT and RTI, many of these apprentices earn a nationally recognized credential and become a highly skilled, and often highly paid, craftsman or journey worker.

Building on the success of apprenticeship in the building trades, industries such as manufacturing, culinary trades, information technology, and health care have built apprenticeship programs. For example, MultiCare, a nonprofit health care organization based in Pierce County, Washington, that includes four hospitals and more than ninety outpatient clinics and service centers, has created its own apprenticeship programs to help train health-unit coordinators, computed-tomography technicians, and engineering-maintenance mechanics.[2]

Many state government agencies are also increasingly viewing apprenticeship as an important component of their workforce- and economic-development strategies. In South Carolina, the Apprenticeship Carolina initiative, part of the South Carolina Technical College System, provides employers in the state with free access to expert consultants and technical assistance to create customized Registered Apprenticeship programs in a variety of industries. Employers may also receive a tax credit of up to $1,000 per apprentice per year for each apprentice they hire, for up to four years of training per apprentice. According to Apprenticeship Carolina, the initiative has spurred a 528 percent increase in the number of apprenticeship programs in the state and a more than 450 percent increase in the number of apprentices.

Still, the dominant industry offering apprenticeships, and among workforce intermediaries and sector initiatives working with the apprenticeship system, remains the building trades. Therefore, this chapter will focus primarily on the experience and lessons learned from work in that industry sector.

Workforce intermediaries seeking to connect workers to Registered Apprenticeship opportunities often operate a pre-apprenticeship program, which the U.S. Department of Labor defines as follows: "a program or set of strategies designed to prepare individuals to enter and succeed in a Registered Apprenticeship program and has a documented partnership with at least one, if not more, Registered Apprenticeship program(s)."[3] Our interest in this chapter centers on how pre-apprenticeship programs support access to and success within apprenticeship programs for low-income workers. Pre-apprenticeship programs are an important part of efforts to help low-income individuals and historically excluded populations gain access to apprenticeship opportunities.

While the appeal of earning money while learning a trade is certainly great, the rigors of combining work and learning in most apprenticeship programs are substantial, and workers need to be prepared to meet these demands. Further, there is often a limited number of apprenticeship openings in the various building trades each year, and given the quality of opportunity offered, these openings are highly competitive. Pre-apprenticeship programs screen, assess, train, and prepare workers to compete for apprenticeship slots, as well as other construction-related jobs. A key function of pre-apprenticeship programs is to ensure that workers are well-informed about the realities, challenges, and opportunities of work in the construction industry so individuals can make an informed choice about whether apprenticeship is a good fit for their life circumstances and career goals.

In this chapter, we discuss the benefits of the apprenticeship model as typically operated in the building-trades sector, with a particular focus on the construction industry. We examine the challenges low-income workers face in completing an apprenticeship program and in building a career in building-trades industries, as well as the ways that pre-apprenticeship programs may mitigate these challenges. We conclude with some thoughts on how apprenticeship and pre-apprenticeship programs could be better utilized to open opportunity to low-income workers in the building trades, but also more broadly in other sectors. We believe there is opportunity to expand and adapt apprenticeship models to meet the needs of today's economy and to efficiently prepare the workforce to meet the rigors of tomorrow's jobs.

Overview of Registered Apprenticeship

The Registered Apprenticeship is an employer-driven training system that combines job-related technical instruction (RTI) with structured on-the-job training (OJT). Individual businesses or employer associations, some of which partner with labor organizations through collective bargaining, sponsor apprenticeship programs. If a union is involved, a joint apprenticeship and training committee (JATC) including representatives of labor and management designs and administers the apprenticeship program. The committee sets standards for training, including the occupations, length of training, selection procedures, affirmative-action plan, wages, and number of apprentices to be trained.

Registered Apprenticeship is often referred to as an "earn and learn" training model. Apprentices have the opportunity to learn on the job in a structured learning environment with an assigned mentor while earning a wage and receiving classroom instruction. RTI is provided by such institutions as apprenticeship training centers, vocational technical schools, and community colleges. Apprenticeship programs vary in length from one to six years, but most last around four years, or eight thousand hours of combined OJT and RTI. Apprentices receive an industry-issued, portable, and nationally recognized credential upon completing a Registered Apprenticeship program. This credential certifies occupational proficiency. In the construction industry, apprentices become known as journey workers on completion.

The U.S. Department of Labor's Office of Apprenticeship (OA) and independent State Apprenticeship Agencies (SAAs) administer Registered Apprenticeship programs. OA and SAAs register apprenticeship programs that meet federal and state standards, issue Certificates of Completion to apprentices, assist in the development of new apprenticeship programs through technical assistance and marketing, and monitor programs to ensure that safety and training standards are met. These regulations and program parameters are established under the National Apprenticeship Act and are designed to protect the welfare of the apprentice.

Program sponsors identify and define the qualifications needed to enter their apprenticeship program and develop an entry process. Minimum qualifications in construction often require the applicant to possess a high school diploma or GED, be at least a minimum age (usually eighteen but in some instances as young as sixteen), pass a drug screen, be physically able to perform the job duties, and pass an aptitude test demonstrating a certain level of math and reading skills. Previous work experience may also be a consideration, and a successful interview may be needed to enter some apprenticeship programs.[4]

Registered Apprenticeships in Construction and Disadvantaged Workers

Benefits of Apprenticeships

Registered Apprenticeship programs in the construction industry hold several distinct benefits for disadvantaged workers looking to upgrade their skills and pursue a career in the industry. First, many workers cannot afford to stop working to pursue additional training and skills-development opportunities. As an apprentice, workers are not only trainees but also paid employees who receive incremental wage increases throughout the course of their apprenticeship. As paid employees, most apprentices also receive benefits, such as health insurance and paid leave. In addition, given the tight integration of learning and employment, apprenticeship programs reduce the risk that a worker is training for an occupation for which there is insufficient demand, or that a worker is learning outdated skills.

Second, apprenticeship accommodates different learning styles through its combination of classroom and applied learning opportunities. In the classroom, apprentices receive instruction from skilled journey workers. In some cases, traditional instructors may also be employed to help apprentices develop math skills or work on other academic skills. On the job site, apprentices work under the tutelage of a skilled craftsman, who may serve as an informal mentor. In many building-trades apprenticeship programs, apprentices are rotated among different employers. This affords apprentices an opportunity to be exposed to different types of construction work, learn from different journey workers, and ultimately gain a broader skill set in their trade.

Third, apprenticeship programs increasingly partner with community colleges. One study found that nearly one-quarter of construction apprentices now receive their classroom or related technical instruction from a community or technical college.[5] Apprenticeship programs partnering with community colleges sometimes offer apprentices college credit for their apprenticeship training.[6] In some instances, completing the coursework required by an apprenticeship program allows an apprentice to be eligible to receive an associate's degree from the partnering community college or to need only one or two more courses to complete the degree. By offering credits and degrees in addition to their certificate for completing an apprenticeship, colleges offer apprentices a broader range of options to pursue postsecondary education and career opportunities outside the construction industry.

Apprenticeships in construction offer a path not just to good-paying jobs but to careers in the construction industry. As apprentices, workers are on a clear career pathway leading to the completion of their apprenticeships and to the opportunities available to them with their apprenticeship credentials. Journey workers may pursue varied opportunities in the construction sector to apply their skills as a carpenter, an electrician, a plumber, or whatever trade they learned. In addition, many experienced journey workers develop careers operating their own businesses, supervising construction projects, organizing and representing workers for unions, developing and managing construction contracts, providing building-maintenance services, or designing and/or managing apprenticeship programs.

Diversity in Construction Occupations and Apprenticeship

Firms in the construction industry have traditionally relied on social networks for hiring. Family members and friends, as a result, have often been given preference over job and apprenticeship candidates who do not have these connections. This persistent dynamic in the industry has resulted in relatively slow progress in bringing diversity to the building trades.

The construction industry has attempted to correct these practices, but women and minority groups, such as African Americans, have long been excluded from jobs in the industry and remain underrepresented in the sector today. According to the Bureau of Labor and Statistics, only 9 percent of construction workers in 2012 were women, 5.6 percent were African American, and less than 2 percent were Asian.[7] Hispanics, on the other hand, were overrepresented in the building trades. More than 24 percent of construction workers were Hispanics, though this group makes up only 15 percent of the overall workforce.

African Americans and women also are underrepresented in construction apprenticeships. An analysis by the Aspen Institute of more than 120,000 apprenticeship agreements initiated between 2006 and 2007 found that only 2.5 percent were initiated by females and 8 percent by African Americans.[8] As discussed later, pre-apprenticeship programs that build and leverage their own networks within the construction industry offer women and minorities potential pathways into apprenticeships and jobs in the building trades.

Challenges of Construction Apprenticeships

A construction apprenticeship is an intensive educational and employment experience that spans between three and five years. The challenges apprentices experience on the road to completing and becoming journey workers are numerous. For many workers seeking an apprenticeship in the construction industry, however, the challenges begin before they apply.

Apprenticeship accounts for a very small percentage of jobs in the construction industry. In 2011 the federal Office of Apprenticeship registered 130,000 new apprentices in all industries.[9] While most of these apprentices were in the construction industry, they nonetheless constituted a very small percentage of the nearly 5.5 million workers in the industry in 2011.[10] Given this relative scarcity, apprenticeship slots are highly sought after, and entry is very competitive, particularly when the construction industry is slow and many programs have reduced the number of apprentices being accepted.

An applicant must meet a number of requirements in order to qualify for entry into an apprenticeship program. In addition to the minimum skills qualifications, employers sponsoring or working with apprenticeship programs may require that apprentices have a driver's license and access to their own vehicle so that they can travel to changing job sites. For many workers aspiring to careers in construction, these transportation challenges can quickly end their goal of entering an apprenticeship.

The apprenticeship application process may also be unclear to those coming from outside the industry. Apprenticeship programs often have set times each year when they invite potential apprentices to apply, or they may have specific locations that interested individuals need to visit to apply. For those who have friends and family in the trades, the knowledge of where, when, and how to apply is available to them through their personal networks. For those without networks in the industry and particularly for populations (such as women and African Americans) who have been excluded from the industry, however, the process of how to apply for entry into an apprenticeship program can be opaque, making entry into a construction apprenticeship more difficult.

Apprenticeship itself is a demanding employment and education opportunity, and the challenges of apprenticeship continue once training and employment begins. Significant rates of non-completion or cancellation among apprentices attest to the challenges of this pathway. An analysis of more than 120,000 apprenticeship agreements initiated between 2006 and 2007 finds that 46 percent of the agreements had been cancelled by May 2012 and 18 percent were still active. Only 36 percent had been completed.[11] The recession undoubtedly played a big role in high numbers of apprentices being cancelled in this study. Apprentices depend on employment for the OJT portion of their training and, of course, for a paycheck. The recession hit the construction industry particularly hard, leading to a steep drop in construction employment. The recession aside, these cancellation rates may not be unusual: State-level data and previous research show that the industry has always battled issues with cancellation and that rates of 40 or 50 percent are not uncommon.[12]

A variety of challenges contribute to the high dropout rate among apprentices. In the building trades, the cyclical nature of the industry poses particular challenges. Regular periods of unemployment and layoffs are the norm in construction, as the work can be seasonal and work stoppages can happen for weather-related reasons. Thus, an apprentice may start in a time of strong demand, but as the economic cycle turns, it may become very challenging to complete the range of work experience needed to fulfill apprenticeship requirements, and discouraging to spend time unemployed. All workers in the industry struggle to plan for gaps in income, but this is particularly difficulty for low-paid apprentices, and even more so for those with poor financial literacy.

Apprentices also struggle with the scheduling demands of an apprenticeship, which can involve working during the day, going to school in the evenings, and doing homework on the weekends. Particularly for apprentices with families, juggling the responsibilities of family, work, and school can pose challenges. Apprentices often cite arranging and paying for child care as a particularly difficult barrier.

Strong basic academic skills may also play a role in keeping up with an apprenticeship. Recent research found that individuals who entered an apprenticeship agreement with less than a high school diploma tended to cancel at higher rates than those with a higher level of education.[13] And finally, adjusting to a particular workplace culture and environment can also pose challenges. Hazing of new apprentices is widely practiced. While much hazing is good-natured, it sometimes crosses the line into harassment, racism, and sexism.

In short, persistence and completion in apprenticeship programs combine the challenges low-income individuals face in persisting and completing post-secondary credentials with the challenges faced by individuals adjusting to the culture and pressures of a career in a new industry, often while still struggling with the limited financial resources characteristic of entry-level job holders.

Workforce intermediaries, discussed in the next section, have the competencies to help individuals address these challenges. Many operate or are affiliated with pre-apprenticeship programs, and these efforts can play an important role in creating pathways to apprenticeship and may help support retention and completion in apprenticeship programs.

Workforce Intermediaries and Pre-Apprenticeship Programs: Creating Pathways to and through Apprenticeship

Given the strong appeal of apprenticeship for low-income and disadvantaged workers as well as the many challenges these workers face in gaining entry into and succeeding in an apprenticeship program, it is not surprising that an array of initiatives has developed to help low-income workers in this arena. We refer to these programs as pre-apprenticeship programs, and in many ways these initiatives are a specific type of workforce intermediary. In this section we describe pre-apprenticeship programs and how they support the success of workers and industry in their labor markets.

Overview of Construction Pre-Apprenticeship Programs

Pre-apprenticeship programs in the construction industry are designed to recruit, screen, train, and place low-income, minority, or female candidates for careers in the construction industry. Graduates of pre-apprenticeship programs may enter an apprenticeship program, enroll in additional training or post-secondary education, or be placed in another construction or non-construction-related job.

These outcomes are dependent on labor-market conditions and opportunities. For example, labor markets with high union density tend to have relatively more apprenticeship opportunities. Similarly, areas experiencing strong economic growth or substantial investment in new buildings and infrastructure are likely to have a larger number of apprenticeship slots in response to strong demand for workers.

In addition to these market factors, potential apprentices' skills, interests, and goals and their personal situation and ability to manage the rigors of apprenticeship must also be considered. Pre-apprenticeship programs develop unique blends of support services and skill-building activities into a successful program depending on the worker populations they serve, the industry stakeholders they partner with, and the structure of their local construction labor market.

Pre-apprenticeship programs are quite common across the United States. In 2008 the Aspen Institute's Workforce Strategies Initiative (AspenWSI) fielded a survey to learn about pre-apprenticeship efforts and received responses from 260 operators of pre-apprenticeship initiatives from around the country. These efforts were located in community-based nonprofits, community colleges, public agencies, labor unions, and other types of organizations. Programs in the survey reported leveraging a wide array of funding streams to support their work.

Populations Served by Pre-Apprenticeship Programs

As noted earlier, the construction industry, with a workforce that is predominantly white men, has long been viewed as homogeneous. Construction unions and employers, which have often relied heavily on networks of friends and family to recruit new workers and apprentices, have also faced challenges with diversity. Through concerted efforts at both the local and the national level, the construction industry is beginning to increase the diversity of its workforce. There is much work left to do, and many pre-apprenticeship programs began and persist today with the goal of helping diversify the construction workforce and provide career opportunities in the industry to women and minorities. According to the AspenWSI pre-apprenticeship survey, nearly 33 percent of programs reported specifically designing their program for women. Almost 40 percent of respondents said their programs are designed specifically to serve ethnic minorities. For women and minority workers who are "nontraditional" in the construction industry, pre-apprenticeship programs serve as an important on-ramp into a sector where they have long been underrepresented.

Services Provided by Pre-apprenticeship Programs

Respondents to the AspenWSI pre-apprenticeship program survey had a common focus on providing a variety of services to workers and job seekers to prepare them for work in the building-trades sector. Respondents typically reported a number of common training elements, including, among others, an overview of work in the industry; an introduction to one or more of the various trades, including the tools and materials used; information on the apprenticeship system and apprenticeship-test preparation; math and basic-skills remediation; and safety training. Many initiatives also reported offering a number of support services, including case management and assistance with transportation costs. As described below in the example of Oregon Tradeswomen, Inc., pre-apprenticeship programs often customize these services, training elements, and activities to meet the needs of the workers they support and to align their efforts with employers' needs in their labor market.

Oregon Tradeswomen, Inc.

Located in Portland, Oregon Tradeswomen promotes the success of women in the trades through education, leadership, and mentorship. Long segregated from the construction workforce, many women may not know much about or consider job opportunities in the construction industry. In response, Oregon Tradeswomen, which was founded by women who had successful careers in the trades, conducts targeted outreach and recruitment to promote knowledge of opportunities for women in the trades. With sponsorship provided by the local construction industry, Oregon Tradeswomen has organized the annual Women in Trades Career Fair for more than twenty years. The fair provides nearly two thousand adult, middle school, and high school women and girls the opportunity to learn about careers in the construction trades, meet employers, and participate in hands-on activities and workshops taught by women industry professionals.

The fair is a primary means by which Oregon Tradeswomen recruits women for Pathways to Success, its seven-week pre-apprenticeship program. Students in the program participate in training for six-and-a-half hours per day, three days weekly. The length and timing of training are intentionally designed to help women with children, an existing job, or an immediate need to go to work. As with most other pre-apprenticeship programs, the Pathways curriculum includes a mix of classroom and hands-on training. Through thirty-five hours of hands-on training, students practice working with a variety of tools under the guidance of a skilled instructor, who also educates the students on the job-site expectations they will encounter in the industry. Training content is designed to build strong math and measuring skills, key to succeeding in any construction job. And participants build strength and physical endurance through twenty-five hours of physical education and training.

Importantly, a significant amount of time is devoted to helping students learn about the construction culture, what it is like to work as women in the trades, and some of the unique barriers and situations women must overcome to be successful in their careers. Instructors are all experienced female professionals, and participants are prepared to encounter and navigate instances of sexism on the job site. The program also includes five field trips to visit apprenticeship training facilities and job sites and numerous presentations by other industry stakeholders. Through these site visits and presentations, participants learn about the work and culture of the different construction trades, as well as how to apply and interview for apprenticeships and other job opportunities in the industry.

The vast majority of pre-apprenticeship initiatives have connections to Registered Apprenticeship programs in their area. Placement into an apprenticeship, however, is not necessarily the next step for many pre-apprenticeship participants.

According to the Aspen Institute's survey of pre-apprenticeship programs, just 26 percent of programs reported that more than 50 percent of their participants are placed into apprenticeship programs, while 36 percent of programs reported that less than 25 percent of their participants are placed in apprenticeship slots. While the survey was conducted during the recession, when apprenticeship slots were scarce, the reality is that pre-apprenticeship programs help their participants achieve a variety of outcomes outside of apprenticeship. Many programs focus on helping constituents achieve such outcomes as educational goals and direct employment in construction or other industries. Importantly, pre-apprenticeship programs recognize the rigors and challenges of apprenticeship, and many see their role as helping trainees make an informed choice as to whether they are truly ready and motivated to take on that challenge.

Phone interviews and site visits with Oregon Tradeswomen and other programs revealed that an important goal for programs is to provide high-quality information to potential apprenticeship applicants so that they make an informed decision as to whether a career in construction is right for them, and whether they are ready to take on the demands of an apprenticeship. Program leaders described their work as a service, both to industry and to workers, to try to facilitate a good fit between a worker and a potential apprenticeship opportunity. For workers who might not be ready to take on the rigors of apprenticeship, or who simply decide that the building trades are not for them, programs might help connect them with other employment opportunities or with opportunities to pursue post-secondary education. Oregon Tradeswomen partners with a variety of employers and associations, including both union and non-union segments of the market, in order to provide workers with as many high-quality job and apprenticeship opportunities as possible.

Supporting Apprentices after Placement

Recently, the challenge of apprenticeship retention, mentioned earlier, has gotten the attention of pre-apprenticeship programs, employers, and some state government agencies around the country. Since women and minorities, groups often served by pre-apprenticeship programs, have noticeably lower apprenticeship retention and completion rates, new efforts to support these workers are being piloted and assessed. These efforts to support apprentices include mentoring programs, continued case management and referrals to social-service agencies, additional math tutoring and other academic supports, financial counseling, and assistance with work supports (including helping apprentices address the costs of child care and transportation).

Oregon Tradeswomen, for example, links newly placed apprentices to women in the trades who serve as mentors. They also provide regular meet-ups or networking opportunities where women in the trades can come together to discuss their experiences and share resources. These kinds of services are often viewed as "post-placement" and can be challenging to fund, but program leaders are hopeful that some early indications of success will shore up support for these efforts.

In Cincinnati, Partners for a Competitive Workforce (PCW)—a partnership of businesses, workforce investment boards, chambers of commerce, secondary and post-secondary educational institutions, service providers, and philanthropic funders—supports multiple pre-apprenticeship initiatives in the area. In particular, PCW has partnered with union and non-union apprenticeship providers to launch an innovative pilot to support new apprentices and reduce cancellation rates among first- and second-year apprentices. As an initial effort, PCW provided seed money to Easter Seals, which operates a pre-apprenticeship initiative, to hire a retention counselor. The model is designed to replicate the success of a job-coaching program PCW established with local health care providers that contributed to halving turnover among frontline health care workers.

During the two-year pilot project, the counselor has provided a cohort of fifty-seven construction apprentices in union electrician-apprenticeship programs and non-union electrician-apprenticeship programs, with supplemental counseling, tutoring, and other forms of assistance.[14] Apprentices participate in group and one-on-one sessions and stay in contact through telephone and e-mails with the retention counselor. The counselor organizes and conducts math-tutoring sessions to help academically unprepared apprentices and convenes peer-group meetings to cover such topics as scheduling, employer expectations, joking on the job site, suggestions for employers, the most common firing offenses, bridging the generation gap, and the construction career ladder. The counselor, in part, acts as a sounding board for issues that apprentices would rather not discuss directly with program staff or their employer. The counselor also tries to motivate and boost the confidence of apprentices who doubt their ability to complete their programs. Gas cards are provided at the group meetings to help offset the costs of transportation. As of June 2013, over 80 percent of the fifty-seven apprentices had remained in their apprenticeship programs twenty months after they began their training. Project leaders are optimistic about these numbers; previous research found that 55 percent of men and 74 percent of women in construction apprenticeship programs in the region cancel.[15] Efforts such as these hold potential to benefit not only the workers but also employers and industry partners who invest time and resources in apprentices' training.

Work with Industry Partners

Pre-apprenticeship initiatives are also tailored to the conditions in their regional labor market and to meet the needs of specific sets of employers. In a set of site visits, AspenWSI observed that successful building-trades pre-apprenticeship programs build and maintain industry networks across their labor-market region that include individual businesses or contractors, joint apprenticeship training committee representatives, trade association leaders, local building-trades union leaders, project owners, and public officials involved in managing public infrastructure or construction projects. Pre-apprenticeship programs take varied approaches to building these networks and relationships, depending on the characteristics of their labor market and the assets of their organization. Many organizations have staff members that have experience in the building trades, and their relationships may form the starting point for building a larger network over time. Other organizations may have, for one reason or another, gotten involved in a large project that had high visibility in a region, and from there continued developing relationships and working with the industry.

The strength of building-trades unions in an area often affects how organizations build their industry network. In areas with high union density, programs may build and leverage union relationships as a foundation to develop relationships with apprenticeship programs, industry associations, and contractors. In areas with low union density, a pre-apprenticeship program may build its industry network through a non-union trade association, such as the Associated Builders and Contractors (ABC), in order to reach contractors who are association members. Due to long-standing tensions between the union and non-union segments of the labor market, balancing and managing these relationships can be difficult for pre-apprenticeship programs. Thus, programs build relationships carefully and clearly communicate their goals and approach, in order to maintain the trust in their industry relationships that is essential to their ability to help their constituents find employment.

Regardless of the approach to building an industry network, these types of relationships are critical to a pre-apprenticeship program's success. Strong industry relationships help programs forecast industry demand, stay attuned to changes in the skills workers need, develop curricula and training that respond to changing needs, and locate job opportunities for their participants. Pre-apprenticeship programs often engage individuals with industry experience as staff members, consultants, or volunteers, to help ensure that the screening, assessment, training, and supports provided to participants align with industry needs. Below, we describe how one program, JumpStart, works within its local construction industry and discuss how industry benefits from pre-apprenticeship initiatives.

JumpStart in Baltimore, Maryland, is a thirteen-week pre-apprenticeship initiative managed by the Job Opportunities Task Force (JOTF). JumpStart's unique relationship with the Baltimore Metro Chapter of the ABC, the industry trade group for non-union employers, gives the initiative a strong position inside the local industry. The relationship between JumpStart and ABC began after research into the construction industry in Baltimore showed low-income residents faced significant barriers to obtaining employment in construction but that there were family-sustaining jobs available if these barriers could be overcome.

Baltimore residents typically needed improved math skills but also had a very low awareness of the kinds of jobs available in the industry and what is required to access those jobs and succeed in them. A local committee, led by JOTF, convened to address the issue and consider strategies for connecting residents to these opportunities. Ultimately, the committee distributed a Request for Quotation to launch a pre-apprenticeship program targeting low-income adults in Baltimore and selected ABC to operate the program. As part of the initiative, ABC is contracted by JOTF not only to provide the training in the pre-apprenticeship classroom but also to provide job placement and retention services. Recruitment for participants into JumpStart's pre-apprenticeship training is managed and coordinated by Catholic Charities of Baltimore, which has strong connections to low-income neighborhoods in the region. JOTF manages and monitors the overall operations of the initiative and advocates for policy changes that would facilitate greater success when needed.

Graduates of JumpStart are placed in ABC's pool of potential employees and linked to ABC's network of hundreds of construction contractors. A performance-based contract with ABC also provides financial incentives to ABC for placing graduates into employer-sponsored apprenticeships. ABC actively provides follow-up retention services and works with JumpStart graduates who do not enter an apprenticeship immediately to ensure that the job experience, skills, and networks they are building will lead to an apprenticeship placement and an opportunity to become a licensed professional in the future.

For local construction contractors, JumpStart offers a pool of workers who have been pre-screened, assessed, and trained with industry input. Graduates have also already completed their OSHA 10 and have been certified in first aid/CPR, reducing expenses for potential employers. In addition, the initiative offers links to minority workers, allowing contractors to diversify their workforces. For contractors working on projects with local-hiring goals or subject to public scrutiny, this ability to have a qualified and diverse workforce can be very important to meeting project requirements and to successfully competing for work.

Finally, JumpStart helps ensure that the initial investments and time spent by employers in hiring someone are met with resources and work supports to help the new employee stay on the job. JumpStart offers graduates assistance with purchasing tools and clothing and any additional work-related fees or expenses they may encounter early in their career. Since reliable transportation is critical to a construction worker's ability to be on time for work and to travel to multiple job sites, JumpStart also provides workers with resources to obtain their driver's license and partners with Vehicles for Change to provide graduates the opportunity to purchase a car at a low cost and interest rate.

Engagement of Pre-Apprenticeship Programs in the Regulatory and Policy Arena

Construction work is often heavily regulated through zoning, building codes, and other policies and by infrastructure or economic-development projects that are publicly financed. As pre-apprenticeship initiatives develop their services for their industry and worker constituencies, they often become involved in efforts to change regulatory frameworks and government and industry policies as they see ways in which these policies could work better for employers and workers.

A variety of public policies influence construction projects and associated employment practices. For pre-apprenticeship programs, policies of particular interest include those that connect training opportunities to projects, encourage local hiring, and increase demand for apprentices and the use of the Registered Apprenticeship system. Some pre-apprenticeship programs seek opportunities to weigh in when the terms of a major construction project are being debated and agreed on by various stakeholders, such as the project owner, the community, contractors, and labor unions. The results of these deliberations can have important implications for the demand for apprentices.

In the construction industry, there are several policy or contract vehicles that can be negotiated to shape how a project manages its workers and benefits the local community. One such vehicle, a Project Labor Agreement (PLA), is often used to set the key terms, hiring practices, pay, and working conditions for a construction project. Community Workforce Agreements (CWAs) are PLAs that include targeted hiring components, which may mandate that a certain percentage of the hours on a project be worked by local residents, minorities, or women. These agreements are legally binding collective-bargaining agreements between one or more labor organizations (such as a local Building Trades Council) and the owner of a construction project, which is sometimes a government entity. Contractors and subcontractors working on the project must abide by the terms set forth in the CWA. According to PolicyLink, more than one hundred PLAs have been negotiated in public and private projects over the last eight decades.[16]

Community benefits agreements (CBAs) are agreements between a construction project developer and community-based organizations representing the interests of the local residents. CBAs are also legally binding but, in addition to local or diversity hiring goals, may address a variety of community concerns, such as mitigation of traffic or pollution issues or setting aside space for low-income housing, local small businesses, child-care centers, or other community facilities in a development. The Partnership for Working Families provides useful definitions and helpful clarifying discussion of the distinctions among these types of agreements.[17]

A final type of policy mechanism is the Apprenticeship Utilization Requirement (AUR), which guarantees that apprentices work a certain percentage of the total construction labor hours on a construction project. AURs can be constructed and implemented through bidding specifications, project labor agreements, or memoranda of understanding. Below we offer examples to illustrate how these policy vehicles have helped pre-apprenticeship programs broaden the pool of high-quality employment opportunities available to low-income and underrepresented workers.

A number of pre-apprenticeship programs help with both the design and the implementation of CWAs. Some pre-apprenticeship programs work as part of large coalitions to help develop and implement CBAs that support the training placement of low-income, minority, and female job seekers into jobs and apprenticeship opportunities, while in other areas a program may work on an issue on its own. Oregon Tradeswomen, described above, played an important role in creating and implementing a CWA to ensure that local residents, including women and minorities, were placed in jobs for Portland's Clean Energy Works project, which weatherized homes throughout the metro area. In Milwaukee, WRTP/BIG STEP, an intermediary and provider of pre-apprenticeship training described in Chapter 6, helps contractors identify and hire the workers they need to meet the requirements set forth in the CWA, by ensuring that local and minority residents have access to high-quality training that is aligned with the needs for a particular construction project. Their deep understanding of the industry and their close relationships with a number of training providers, industry leaders, and community organizations positions them well to tailor programs to respond to projects and to ensure that local residents are prepared to succeed on the job site and employers have access to the workers they need to fulfill their obligations under the policy agreement.

Building Futures, an initiative in Rhode Island that operates a pre-apprenticeship initiative, works to ensure that construction jobs created by public investments benefit local residents. Building Futures is engaged in activities to support the city of Providence's First Source Hiring ordinance, which was passed to ensure that employment opportunities for local residents are created when public funding of a construction project occurs. To increase the number of available apprenticeships and the use of apprenticeship training in the community, Building Futures works with construction-project owners and repeat users of construction services, such as hospitals, government, private developers, and schools, to implement AURs. Building Futures also works with project owners to help them identify, evaluate, and hire construction companies that are known to offer quality apprenticeship programs to their workers. In this way Building Futures works to ensure that there is continued demand for the individuals they prepare in their pre-apprenticeship programs, and that public construction expenditures are leveraged to provide opportunities needed by local residents.

Regulation of Pre-Apprenticeship Programs by Government and Industry

While apprenticeship programs are regulated and meet requirements to be registered, little attention had been given until recently to the role that pre-apprenticeship programs play. Lately, however, both government entities and industry stakeholders have expressed concern about programs that fail to connect to apprenticeship programs in their area or that simply provide ineffective screening and training and do not align with industry needs. In 2012 the Employment and Training Administration in the U.S. Department of Labor provided guidance on quality standards for pre-apprenticeship, including training and curriculum aligned with industry, the incorporation of hands-on training in the program design, access to support services for pre-apprentices, strategies to support the long-term success of underrepresented populations, and facilitated entry or articulation from the pre-apprenticeship program into an apprenticeship.

Some construction-industry stakeholders have also started to set standards among pre-apprenticeship programs. The AFL-CIO Building and Construction Trades Department's Standing Committee on Apprenticeships, which includes participants from all the building trades represented in that labor federation, developed the Multi-Craft Core Curriculum (MC3) for pre-apprenticeship programs. The standardized curriculum covers the common skills and capacities needed to enter a building-trades apprenticeship through 120 hours or eight modules of training. Topics covered include an orientation to apprenticeship, an overview of the construction industry, introduction to construction tools and materials, CPR and first-aid training, OSHA safety certification, blueprint reading, math skills, and a history of organized labor in the industry. Pre-apprenticeship programs using the curriculum must obtain approval from the local or state Building Trades Council.[18] (Fairchild, Chapter 9, which describes the Emerald Cities Collaborative, offers more detail on the MC3 curriculum.)

Final Thoughts on Construction Pre-Apprenticeship Programs

Pre-apprenticeship programs have played a critical role in opening up apprenticeship and career opportunities in the construction industry to low-income individuals, minorities, and women. By building strong industry relationships and networks, programs have created industry-specific assessment, career counseling, and training services that prepare a diverse population to enter and succeed in an industry whose workforce for decades has traditionally been white men. To complement these practices, many programs have engaged in the public-policy arena to create demand for apprentices and ensure that jobs created by public investments provide opportunities to local residents, women, and people of color. Industry partners have, in turn, benefited from access to a pre-screened, trained, and diverse pool of workers.

In workforce-development circles today, the conversation is often steered toward developing career pathways and stackable credentials. While these efforts are undoubtedly valuable, developing these pathways with sufficient employer input and buy-in is often difficult. And sometimes a lack of employer engagement in this sphere has led to pathways and credentials being developed that fail to match the realities of how people advance and what credentials are valued in the labor market.

In contrast, apprenticeship training is linked to employer demand, so apprentices are mostly assured that the skills they are developing are valued and needed in the labor market. The structure of apprenticeship offers a reliable and transparent career ladder for apprentices to climb. For low-income workers in training, financial stability is a big concern. Most community college students who drop out of school do so because the responsibilities and stress of work and school are too difficult.[19] The financial benefits of being able to earn a living while in training as an apprentice cannot be underemphasized.

Nonetheless, apprenticeship opportunities remain relatively scarce. In construction, apprentices constitute a small percentage of the workforce; in other industries, apprentices are even less common. For individuals who do become apprentices, the road to completing a long, intensive, and demanding training and employment experience often means several years of juggling work, school, personal, and family commitments. In the building trades, apprentices also must learn to plan for and navigate periods of unemployment as they move from job to job. As policy makers, investors, and practitioners look to expand apprenticeship opportunities to more low-income workers, a close examination of what is working and what can be improved is worthwhile. Below we offer some initial ideas for making apprenticeship work better for today's workers, particularly for low-income and historically underrepresented workers who enter apprenticeship through pre-apprenticeship programs.

Policy Recommendations

The "earn and learn" model of apprenticeship offers enormous potential to workers wishing to improve their career prospects. For employers, it offers a reliable pipeline of skilled workers for their businesses. As the original earn-and-learn, demand-driven approach to workforce development, apprenticeship holds much more potential than is currently being realized. Based on the experience of workforce intermediaries in the construction industry and that of the construction industry in apprenticeship, we offer the following recommendations:

Expand the Apprenticeship Model into Other Industries

For decades the building trades have operated an apprenticeship model that has provided workers with training and career opportunities while offering industry a reliable source of skilled labor. All of this has largely been done in the absence of public investment. Today the apprenticeship model is used in other industries, such as manufacturing, health care, automotive repair, and culinary occupations. But growth of apprenticeship into these industries has been slow and small in scale relative to the size of the workforce in these industries.

Sectors such as health care seem to be a good fit for expanding apprenticeship. Many nursing and other health care occupations, in addition to requiring classroom training, often in a community college setting, require on-the-job learning through clinical programs. Due to the scheduling demands of school and clinical programs and the heavy academic workload, it's hard to succeed in these programs while working. Many health care workers also often remain stuck in lower-paying occupations, such as home health aides and nursing assistants, because of the challenges of working and advancing their training at the same time. Health care providers also face challenges. Many hospitals and skilled nursing facilities have trouble finding the workers they need and may experience high turnover. In areas where multiple languages are spoken or people have different cultural backgrounds, health care providers often struggle to find practitioners who can provide culturally competent care to the community or can communicate with patients and family members effectively. Creating more nursing apprenticeships could address all of these concerns to some extent by providing a paid training experience leading to a good-paying career in the sector for low-income workers, while also helping hospitals and others address high recruitment costs, skill shortages, challenges related to cultural competence, and retention issues.

Expanding apprenticeship into health care would require some changes. For example, existing licensing systems for certain health care occupations may need to be redesigned or rethought in some communities, and employers may be unwilling to take on apprentices. Reimbursement rates are another challenge:

Companies that provide healthcare services are generally paid for the service provided by insurance companies or government programs like Medicare and Medicaid. Rates are negotiated by the insurers and are regulated by state and federal bodies. Rates are based on the specific service, not on the hours of labor. In many cases, implementing employee pay structures where healthcare apprentices earn incremental wage increases as their skills increase would require renegotiation of reimbursement rates, a process that is already highly politicized.[20]

Despite these challenges, the use of apprenticeship in health care is expanding, and more of these barriers could be removed for further expansion with concerted effort by policy makers, workforce-development leaders, and employers.

Other fast-growing industries that are expected to add jobs in the coming decade also seem to be good candidates for the apprenticeship model. For example, many businesses face challenges recruiting and retaining skilled information technology workers, such as computer programmers, software developers, and database administrators. Women, African Americans, and Hispanics are also often underrepresented in some of these jobs.

Two other fast-growing sectors, retail and restaurant work, require a great deal of on-the-job learning already. But many low-wage, entry-level jobs in these sectors lack pathways to higher-paid positions in operations and management. Most workers in these industries, particularly women and minorities, are left behind in dead-end jobs without hope for skills development or career advancement. Meanwhile, both industries have extremely high turnover rates. Exploring apprenticeship in some of these sectors to create more structured pathways to better-paying positions and careers while helping address employers' turnover and recruitment issues seems worthy of investment.

Public matching funds might help incentivize uptake of the approach among employers. Much as the public invests in technical and occupational training in secondary and post-secondary institutions, public funds could also be used to support registered apprenticeships that work to build similar skills in the workforce. South Carolina offers an example of this policy approach, putting resources toward expanding the model into such sectors as manufacturing. Public investments could provide tax incentives or public workforce-training dollars to employers who invest in and train their workers through apprenticeship. Government resources could also be used to conduct studies on the feasibility of apprenticeship models' growing and going to scale in other industries, and to market apprenticeship to employers.

Develop Pre-Apprenticeship for Other Industries While Encouraging Expanded Apprenticeship

Pre-apprenticeship programs in construction have helped many disadvantaged and historically excluded populations enter construction apprenticeships. As apprenticeship expands into other industries, many potential apprentices may face similar barriers. A large proportion of today's workers need assistance to brush up on basic skills, develop professional networks, and find resources to manage child care, transportation, and other work-related expenses in order to be successful. Pre-apprenticeship programs have demonstrated potential in helping workers to address these barriers. As we look to grow the apprenticeship model in construction and expand it to other industries, investors and policy makers need to ensure that the pathways into apprenticeship, regardless of the industry, are open and accessible. Providing investments to support and build on the success of pre-apprenticeship initiatives by expanding the model into other industries would be a good place to start.

Provide More Support Services and Retention Supports to Apprentices

Cancellation rates of apprentices in the construction industry are a problem that needs to be addressed. As the apprenticeship model grows, more attention needs to be paid to supporting apprentices through the completion of their training. This includes more investment in mentors and retention counselors that help apprentices understand and navigate this unique work and school experience. Support services that help apprentices shore up their academic skills or manage family demands and responsibilities while earning entry-level wages could also be critical to apprenticeship retention and success. More resources for this work are clearly needed, preferably coupled with research on which services are most in demand and most effective. Better supports would ensure smoother transitions from pre-employment to employment and success, maximizing the benefits of investing in pre-employment training.

Conclusion

Workforce intermediaries and sector initiatives often struggle to identify and remain current regarding industry demand and the implications for pre-employment training programs. As a demand-driven model, apprenticeship overcomes this challenge. The opportunities provided by apprenticeship, however, have sometimes bypassed low-income workers, people of color, and women. Pre-apprenticeship programs are an important means by which low-income and histori-cally excluded groups can find a pathway to the valuable career opportunities ap-prenticeship offers. In addition, many older workers with family responsibilities need opportunities to develop new skills while maintaining a regular paycheck and benefits. Pre-apprenticeship programs can help these workers enter a new line of work and provide the supports they need to successfully enter and complete an apprenticeship. Meanwhile, employers today seek both skills and experience in new hires; apprenticeship systems can provide new workers who bring both to the table. Policy makers, workforce-development professionals, philanthropy, employ-ers, and others should creatively explore, experiment, and invest in opportunities to expand apprenticeship and pre-apprenticeship programs in order to meet the demands of today's labor market.

Notes

1. Office of Apprenticeship, Employment and Training Administration, U.S. Department of Labor, "Registered Apprenticeship National Results: Fiscal Year 2011," accessed December 20, 2012, http://www.doleta.gov/OA/data_statistics.cfm.

2. For more information on MultiCare's apprenticeship programs, see Bronwyn Mauldin, "Apprenticeship in the Healthcare Industry," October 31, 2011, accessed January 2, 2013, http://www.lni.wa.gov/TradesLicensing/Apprenticeship/files/pubs/Apprentice-shipsHealthcareIndustryMauldin.pdf.

3. Training and Employment Notice No. 13-12, "Defining a Quality Pre-Apprenticeship Program and Related Tools and Resources," Employment and Training Administration, U.S. Department of Labor, November 30, 2012. http://wdr.doleta.gov/directives/at-tach/TEN/TEN_13-12_Acc.pdf.

4. For more information on Registered Apprenticeship, see Office of Apprenticeship, Employment and Training Administration, U.S. Department of Labor, "What iIs Reg-istered Apprenticeship?" accessed December 20, 2012, http://www.doleta.gov/OA/ap-prenticeship.cfm.

5. Robert I. Lerman, "Training Tomorrow's Workforce: Community College and Appren-ticeship as Collaborative Routes to Rewarding Careers," Center for American Progress, December 2009, accessed May 10, 2013, http://www.americanprogress.org/wp-con-tent/uploads/issues/2009/12/pdf/comm_colleges_apprenticeships.pdf.

6. The National Labor College accepts up to eighty-four credits toward a bachelor's degree from coursework completed as an apprentice. The college also offers up to thirty credits through its prior-learning assessment program for training done outside the classroom, such as that done on the job site in an apprenticeship. For more information, please visit http://nlccommunity.wordpress.com/2012/10/01/helmetstohardhats/.

7. U.S. Department of Labor, Bureau of Labor and Statistics, *Current Population Survey*, accessed September 6, 2013, http://www.bls.gov/cps/cpsaat18.htm.

8. Matt Helmer and David Altstadt, "Apprenticeship Completion and Cancellation in the Building Trades," Aspen Institute, 2013, accessed September 30, 2013, http://www.aspenwsi.org/wordpress/wp-content/uploads/aspen_apprenticeship.pdf.

9. Office of Apprenticeship, Employment and Training Administration, U.S. Department of Labor, "Data and Statistics," accessed January 7, 2013, http://www.doleta.gov/OA/data_statistics2011.cfm.

10. U.S. Department of Labor, Bureau of Labor and Statistics, *Current Employment Statistics*, accessed January 8, 2013, http://data.bls.gov/timeseries/CES2000000001?data_tool=XGtable.

11. Helmer and Altstadt, "Apprenticeship Completion."

12. See Cihan Bilginsoy, "The Hazards of Training: Attrition and Retention in Construction Industry Apprenticeship Programs," ILRReview 57, no. 1, Article 3 (2003), accessed December 10, 2011, http://digitalcommons.ilr.cornell.edu/ilrreview/vol57/iss1/3, Cihan Bilginsoy, "Registered Apprentices and Apprenticeship Programs in the U.S. Construction Industry between 1989 and 2003: An Examination of the AIMS, RAIS, and California Apprenticeship Agency Databases," University of Utah, Department of Economics Working Paper Series, Working Paper No. 2005-09, May 2005, accessed January 3, 2012, http://economics.utah.edu/publications/2005_09.pdf; and U.S. Government Accountability Office, "Registered Apprenticeship Programs: Labor Can Better Use Data to Target Oversight," Report to Congressional Requesters, GAO-05-886, August 2005, accessed January 12, 2012, http://www.gao.gov/products/GAO-05-886.

13. Helmer and Alstadt, "Apprenticeship Completion."

14. PCW partners with the Ohio Valley Associated Builders and Contractors to support non-union apprentices in various trades and with the International Brotherhood of Electrical Workers–National Electrical Contractors Association in Cincinnati to support union apprentices.

15. Keisha Steward and Theresa O'Brien-Turco, "Changing the Outcome: Closing the Gap to Completion in Greater Cincinnati's Apprenticeship Programs," PAD 793, Capstone Project, December 6, 2010, accessed December 10, 2011, http://www.competitiveworkforce.com/files/Teri_O_Brien_RAP_Retention_Report_-_Changing_the_Outcome.pdf.

16. Sarah Treuhaft and Victor Rubin, "Economic Inclusions: Advancing an Equity-Driven Growth Model," Big Ideas for Job Creation Project, accessed September 6, 2013, http://www.bigideasforjobs.org/wp-content/uploads/2013/06/4a_Treuhaft-Rubin_Policylink-Report_Sectoral-Industry.pdf.

17. Partnership for Working Families, Community Benefits Law Center, "Community Benefits Legal Dictionary," accessed July 12, 2013, http://www.forworkingfamilies.org/cblc/dictionary.

18. T. Burress, T. Gannon, and R. Kapadia, "Community-Based Organizations and Union Apprenticeship Programs: Creating Pathways to Careers in the Unionized Construction Trades for Minorities and Lower-Skilled Workers," Greenways Initiative Technical Assistance Webinar, Jobs for the Future, April 2011, accessed May 16, 2013, http://www.jff.org/sites/default/files/CommBasedOrg-UnionApprentProg_040212.pdf.

19. J. Johnson, J. Rochkind, A. Ott, and S. Dupont, "With Their Whole Lives Ahead of Them," New York: Public Agenda, prepared with support from the Bill & Melinda Gates Foundation, accessed October 31, 2013, http://www.publicagenda.org/pages/with-their-whole-lives-ahead-of-them-methodology.

20. Mauldin, "Apprenticeship in the Healthcare Industry."

16

Will Workforce Policy Finally Catch Up to Sector Practice?

Andy Van Kleunen

*Today, President Obama announced the Community College to Career Fund, an $8 billion investment ... that would train two million workers with skills that lead directly to good jobs.... The program would also help high-growth industries address the issues they face in hiring skilled workers by funding **regional or national industry groups tasked with identifying workforce needs in their respective fields**, and developing solutions like standardized worker certification, new training technologies, or collaborations with industry employers to better define careers pathways for workers. [February 13, 2012; emphasis added.]*[1]

This volume has documented the impact that sector strategies have had on the workforce-development field over the past decade. What has not been clear until recently, however, was whether the policy makers in charge of our nation's workforce policies had even noticed.

Dismissed for years by reformers in Washington as a "boutique" strategy that could not go to scale, sector-based intermediaries now are a regular reference point for federal officials talking about a retooled national skills strategy. But while D.C. policy makers have embraced the concept of sector partnerships, they have been reluctant to adopt the practice in law as a fundamental pillar of the federal workforce-development system. Competitor nations like Canada and the United Kingdom have long used sector councils as the mandated means to certify industry-recognized credentials, chart advancement pathways across firms, and target public training investments toward their greatest impact.[2] Yet here in the United States, sector partnerships are considered an optional add-on, receiving occasional monetary support for limited periods of time, subject to the vagaries of changing administrations and recurrent fiscal crises.

If they are so well regarded, why have sector partnerships not been adopted as a central organizing feature in the deployment of our workforce-development, career and technical education, and higher-education policies? The usual response— "the United States is not Europe"—no longer seems relevant, given the successful investment of hundreds of millions of dollars (public, private, and philanthropic) in such initiatives throughout the country. So what is the real reason for the disconnect between sector policy and practice? The following offers some possible explanations: differing perspectives dating back fifteen years between workforce reformers and sector innovators over the structure of a new federal workforce system; the lead role played by states to advance sector initiatives within a workforce system that was nevertheless largely defined by federal funding and regulation; and the contradictory role that federal-agency grants played in seeding the sector field, raising congressional suspicion about the operation of such initiatives outside their legislative authority.

Policy Debates during the Birth of Sector Strategies

During the 1990s, the first sector intermediaries were being developed in the field while a political debate was raging in Washington. After the 1994 midterm elections, a newly elected, conservative-led Republican majority in Congress embarked on an aggressive effort to trim what it saw as a bloated welfare state. Federal job-training programs offered an easy target in that campaign: They were focused on workers and the poor, and conservatives felt they illustrated government's unwarranted intrusion in the private-sector marketplace of labor supply and demand.

Liberals certainly did not agree with ending the federal role in workforce development, but their political support was tepid at best, tempered by questions raised by critics and proponents alike about the structure and efficacy of some of these programs:

- Conflicting Silos: Critics from the right railed against the number of federal training programs, but even proponents were concerned about the confusing array of federal programs faced by individuals in need of employment assistance.

- Business Engagement: Critics cited recurrent employer complaints about the lack of consultation by colleges and training programs in the development of curricula, but even proponents were concerned that the business community was not willing to speak up for federal policies presumably intended to meet their hiring needs.

- Training versus Employment: Critics invoked their "work first" mantra in their portrayal of the chronically unemployed using serial enrollment in training programs as a way to postpone getting a job, but even proponents were concerned about the number of poor and laid-off individuals who had graduated from multiple training programs without gaining a foothold within a local industry.

Without a mobilized caucus of supporters, federal skills programs were highly vulnerable. A small cadre of workforce reformers in Washington—members of Congress and the Clinton administration who had supported or administered these programs—tried in vain to stem the assault. Congress moved ahead with dramatic funding cuts and new statutory restrictions that rolled back federal support for workforce training in a number of areas: prohibitions on training for the poor under the new Temporary Assistance for Needy Families (TANF) welfare law; severe cuts to services for unemployed workers under the Wagner-Peyser Act and to training and school-to-work programs for young people; and the move by the House to consolidate 150 Labor and Education programs, including the Job Training Partnership Act (JTPA), the primary federal workforce-development program, into a few reduced block grants to the states.[3]

It was within this contentious environment that workforce reformers in the Senate negotiated the far less sweeping incorporation of JTPA and several other federal workforce programs into the Workforce Investment Act (WIA) of 1998.[4] Reformers presented WIA's passage as a victory, in that it addressed some of the above-noted concerns of critics while preventing the wholesale dismantling of existing workforce programs. For example, rather than conceding on program elimination and consolidation, WIA addressed the "conflicting silos" issue by creating One-Stop Career Centers, which would allow a range of job seekers to access a variety of separate federal programs in one physical location with the help of an on-site counselor. WIA achieved new "business engagement" by mandating that private-sector employers hold the majority of seats on new Workforce Investment Boards (WIBs) that would oversee the administration of programs accessed under the WIA banner. To counter "training versus employment" critiques, WIA adopted a "sequence of services," in which counseling and job-search assistance were prioritized over training as the first step to help job seekers find employment.

These were astute legislative responses that enacted system reforms while preventing workforce development's harshest critics from eliminating the programs entirely. For sector innovators who saw some of the same gaps in existing work-force programs, these were not the solutions they were testing in the field. Innovators had dealt with "conflicting silos" by developing private-sector or nonprofit intermediaries that brought together different funding streams—including those beyond WIA's statutory reach—to create a basket of services that met the particular needs of workers and employers in a targeted industry. Their "business engagement" did not take place in the administrative oversight of public programs but in intensive collaborations across a range of competing employers from the same industry in order to rationalize their conflicting skill, credential, and advancement standards. At the same time, sector innovators resisted the new limits on training—not just those under WIA, but under TANF as well—asserting that better employment outcomes would come not from rejecting training but from developing shared training and retention strategies across an industry's employers.

Under normal circumstances, the successes of these innovations in the field would have been celebrated by workforce reformers in Washington. But the politically tenuous standing of the new WIA system instead prompted nervousness among reformers concerned that the sector field's approach did not mimic WIA's structure. Some reformers feared that the new sector intermediaries would be perceived as a *replacement* for, rather than a complement to, the WIA system. One "New Democrat" think tank already had proposed as much, to the consternation of reformers in their party.[5] And once some successful sector programs were passed over for funding by local WIBs, some intermediary proponents embraced the label of being more effective alternatives to WIA.[6] For those fighting to protect workforce programs in Washington, this seemed politically naïve and potentially destructive.

Workforce Intermediaries and WIA Reauthorization

Some of these tensions between reformers and innovators emerged at the 2003 American Assembly on Workforce Intermediaries, particularly in deliberations about whether the intermediary functions performed by sector partnerships were different from or redundant to those provided by WIBs and One-Stops. To bridge this disconnect, a number of American Assembly participants returned to Washington and began working on a legislative proposal intended to clarify the *distinct but complementary* roles these sector-based intermediaries could play within an evolving WIA infrastructure.[7] It started from the premise that any effective local workforce-development system needed three specialized capacities:

- For Worker Services: A workforce system, first and foremost, must deliver the full range of services—including industry-approved training—that different individuals will need in order to qualify for and succeed at skilled employment. To fulfill that function, WIA used contracts and Individual Training Accounts (ITAs) to fund a range of education and support service providers (community-based organizations, community colleges, labor unions, etc.).

- For Public Access and Oversight: A workforce system must provide public access points whereby job seekers can be assessed and referred to the appropriate services. It also must ensure that these services are delivered efficiently and equitably. Under WIA, local One-Stop Centers and state-run Employment Service offices were to provide these access points, while state and local Workforce Investment Boards fulfilled the administrative, oversight, contractor evaluation, and reporting functions.

- For Industry Engagement: Finally, a workforce system must have the capacity to keep pace with a changing labor market and the needs of various employers, large and small, across various industries. *This is the capacity that was missing from the baseline WIA infrastructure* but which could be incorporated into a reauthorized WIA with some dedicated capacity for sector-based intermediaries that could better connect firms, WIBs, and training providers for each of several different local industries.

The proposal presented these as complementary functions, each requiring different capacities and expertise. It also called for distinct performance measures for each function: *individual outcome* measures (e.g., employment, earnings, credential attainment) to assess the impact of worker services, *system performance* measures to assess whether a range of workers was enjoying equitable access to WIA services, and *industry engagement* measures to assess the extent to which a diversity of firms within a key industry worked with the local workforce system.

The authors hoped the framework could provide some common ground upon which both reformers and innovators could advocate for WIA reforms as the law approached its five-year reauthorization. Unfortunately, there were much larger political dynamics at play in 2003 that would prevent WIA's renewal. In what was to become the first act in a decade-long drama, WIA's initial reauthorization was derailed not by substantive differences between Democrats and Republicans on how best to meet workers' or businesses' skill needs but by larger political fights for which WIA merely provided one expendable arena for battle: the push to downsize the federal government by consolidating social-service programs into state block grants, "charitable choice" and claimed infringements on the religious liberties of federally funded service providers, and ending the unionized merit staffing of state employment services.

Even amid the partisan din there were some isolated moments of bipartisan agreement in the WIA debate. For example, during the House Education and Workforce Committee's mark-up of the Republican majority's WIA bill, only two amendments won bipartisan support, one of them being Rep. Rob Andrews's (D-NJ) "Business Partnerships" amendment, which was loosely modeled on the sector-based workforce intermediary proposal.[8] Sector partnerships' bipartisan appeal was confirmed, even if the WIA bill to which it was attached was not.

Over in the Senate, where there was more room for bipartisan dialogue, sector proposals faced different obstacles. Reformers on the Senate Health Education Labor and Pensions (HELP) Committee who had negotiated the original WIA bill in 1998 were hesitant to embrace sector intermediaries as a change to the baseline WIA infrastructure they had created. Senators outside the HELP Committee introduced a number of sector proposals, including two by Sen. Maria Cantwell (D-WA), whose state had become an early sector innovator (see below).[9] Yet reformers on the committee resisted the bills' incorporation into their WIA reauthorization frameworks. Reformers did ultimately write sector partnerships into their bills as "allowable activities"—that is, optional efforts that states and locals could pursue, albeit without any additional funding or distinct performance measures. But the partnerships were never given their own capacity or complementary standing to WIBs, One-Stops, and service providers.

States Move Past Congressional Reforms

Not willing to wait for Washington or WIA's reauthorization, a number of state governments, under both Republican and Democratic governors, already had begun looking to sector-based intermediaries to enhance the new workforce system's industry responsiveness:

- Washington: In 2000, under Governor Locke (Democrat), Washington established a statewide infrastructure of Industry Skill Panels (ISPs). These panels brought together multiple firms in the same sector to advise local WIBs on how to designate WIA funds for their industry, and then worked with the WIB, community colleges, and other service providers to put their training plans into action.[10]

- Pennsylvania: In the 1990s the Commonwealth had supported union-sponsored efforts to re-employ workers displaced by the contraction of the state's industrial base, including its steel sector. Governor Schweiker's administration (Republican) subsequently experimented with sector-targeted strategies in its initial implementation of WIA, which Governor Rendell (Democrat) later took to scale with an annual $20 million state investment, supplemented by federal WIA and private-sector dollars, in a statewide "Industry Partnership" initiative.[11]

- Massachusetts: In 2000, with a push from sector advocates and the long-term care industry, Governor Swift (Republican) oversaw enactment of the Extended Care Career Ladder Initiative, a statewide effort in which industry, unions, and community-based organizations (CBOs) collaborated to address both skilled workforce shortages and job quality in that sector.[12]

- Illinois: Inspired by community-based sector leaders in and around Chicago, the state legislature and Governor Blagojevich's administration (Democrat) adopted in 2003 a statewide Critical Skills Shortage Initiative, using WIA discretionary dollars for grants to local workforce investment areas to support sector partnerships in targeted industries.[13]

- Michigan: Informed by foundation-sponsored sector-based programs in the state, Governor Granholm (Democrat) established in 2004 a statewide Regional Skills Alliance strategy, utilizing both public and philanthropic dollars to make grants to consortia of WIBs, employers, and service providers to develop regional industry strategies.[14]

Sensing a tipping point in the states, the Charles Stewart Mott Foundation partnered in 2006 with the National Governors Association (NGA) and national technical-assistance providers in the creation of a State Sector Skills Academy to capture and promulgate these efforts. The NGA enlisted the above states in the academy's first class to assess what generalized lessons could be learned from their various efforts, then shared these lessons with other states expressing an interest in developing their own statewide sectoral strategies. By 2008 eleven states had participated in the NGA academy, and by 2010 an additional fourteen states were either designing or implementing sector strategies.[15]

Importance of WIA Discretionary Dollars

But perhaps the single most important factor in the spread of these state-based initiatives was, ironically, federal funding: specifically, the 15 percent of a state's WIA adult and dislocated worker dollars that governors could use at their discretion after covering allowable state administrative costs. Most of the states pursuing a statewide sectoral initiative were funding them with 15 percent from WIA. Only a few—like Pennsylvania, Washington, and Massachusetts—were supplementing with substantial state funding. States found that adding their own resources not only extended the capacity of their sector efforts; it also increased industry, stakeholder, and, ultimately, state legislators' interest in those workforce efforts. Witness what happened when a newly elected Republican majority in

Pennsylvania's state legislature attempted to zero out Governor Rendell's budget request for Industry Partnerships (IPs). Employers participating in IPs from all over the Commonwealth came to Harrisburg to vouch for the program and to advocate for its continued funding. Thereafter, the effort had supporters in both parties in the legislature.[16]

Yet most states were pursuing sectoral strategies with resources made available by a federal policy that did not explicitly support the creation of partnerships, nor did it set performance and reporting standards to measure those partnerships' impact. The result was significant variation in the quality of sector-based efforts from state to state. Technical-assistance interventions like the NGA academy tried to establish some sense of recognized effective practice across states, but the adoption of such lessons—without mandated outcome indicators articulated in the law funding much of this activity—still led to great unevenness. So, too, did the inevitable shifts in gubernatorial administrations, which often led to the abandonment of discretionary programs established under a former administration, particularly when there was not a state legislature interested in sustaining the policy.[17]

Federal Grants in Lieu of Reauthorization

The WIA 15 percent money may have been the most common federal funding for sector intermediaries, but it was not the highest-profile source. That distinction belonged to a number of U.S. Department of Labor (DOL) grant programs established across three presidential administrations. While most of these grant programs did not explicitly intend to create sector partnerships, they nevertheless helped to fuel the sector field's expansion. Yet the episodic nature of grant programs that were born and then died with each successive administration prevented the compilation of a consistent base of practice that could be evaluated over time.

Clinton Sector Demonstration Grants

After WIA's passage in 1998, sector practitioners asked President Clinton's DOL to use its guidance and rule-making authority to include sectoral strategies in the set-up of new state and local WIA systems. While the federal Employment and Training Administration was hesitant to promote the strategy explicitly, it did agree to create a small, $50 million Sectoral Demonstration Grant program to test the model for future replication. Designed during the last year of the Clinton administration, the program was launched in 2001 shortly after the Bush administration took office. Thirty-eight projects were funded, most of them exploratory "formation" grants under which recipients were initiating a new sector effort. An evaluation of the program by the Aspen Institute and the Urban Institute showed some encouraging initial gains, but the grant program was discontinued by the Bush administration before most of the demonstrations could mature.[18]

Bush Demand-Driven Grants

The Bush administration was instead interested in pursuing its own industry-targeted workforce efforts. What's more, due to a recent change in federal visa policy, DOL had access to a growing pot of discretionary resources made available by the American Competitiveness and Workforce Improvement Act.[19] In 1998 the act authorized DOL to receive a portion of the H-1B visa fees paid by employers to import high-skilled immigrant workers to fund the training of U.S. workers for similar skilled positions. By 2002 the fees available to DOL had grown to more than $200 million annually after Congress, at the urging of the business community, raised the annual cap on H-1B visas from 65,000 to 195,000.[20] These added funds allowed DOL to develop a series of "demand-driven" grant programs that became signature workforce initiatives, including the following:

High Growth Job Training Initiative (HGJTI)

To make WIA more industry-responsive through engagements outside the standing WIA system, the Bush administration DOL in 2001 started to convene field meetings with groups of industry executives throughout the country. WIBs, notably, were not invited to these field discussions. From these discussions, DOL eventually identified fourteen "high growth" sectors for industry-targeted training grants totaling more than $295 million over a four-year period.[21] Grantees included businesses and trade associations as well as more traditional training providers and some sector-based intermediaries. DOL generally did not set standards for potential grantees—almost 90 percent of the funds were let on a non-competitive basis—in some circumstances choosing recipients that had clear industry expertise but little background in actual workforce training. As a Government Accountability Office (GAO) review noted, this led to significant unevenness across the grants, as did the general absence of explicit performance measures or outcome documentation requirements.[22] As a result, while HGJTI may have funded a number of good sector-based training efforts, it did not do much to raise the credibility of industry-targeted workforce efforts in the eyes of workforce reformers on Capitol Hill. It further re-enforced in the minds of some reformers that industry-targeted efforts came at the expense or exclusion of the WIA system.

Workforce Innovation in Regional Economic Development (WIRED)

WIRED grants were initiated during the second term of the Bush administration in an effort to push local WIBs to more effectively work with one another on a regional basis, as well as to better align with the needs of regional industries. In contrast to the awarding of HGJTI funds primarily to private-sector and nonprofit grantees, WIRED grants were made primarily to states (governors, state WIBs, state labor agencies), which in turn used the leverage to bring groups of local WIBs together with other industry and economic-development entities for regional planning purposes. Some thirty-nine regions received grants totaling almost $324 million between 2006 and 2008.[23] While these grants were often not sector-specific, several of them were used to assist industry-specific strategies already being developed by some states. For example, several of Michigan's Regional Skills Alliances were recipients of WIRED grants.

While these grants did not explicitly support sector-based intermediaries, they had elements similar to aspects of the sectoral approach and did in fact fund a number of sectoral efforts. But these were not sector partnership grants. While both the HGJTI and WIRED grants were explicitly industry targeted, consistent with the approach of sector-based intermediaries, they were not exacting about the types of workers to be served or the advancement impacts expected. WIRED grants likewise focused on regions, as opposed to local workforce areas, as the unit of workforce planning and deployment—again, consistent with the approach of sector-based intermediaries. But some felt that WIRED grants were more focused on organizing geography (i.e., redrawing local workforce investment areas) than on individual industries, which some saw as consistent with the Bush administration's controversial efforts to empower governors to eliminate local workforce investment areas. Hence, some of the good things that came out of these grants were overshadowed by how the grants were perceived by some WIA proponents.

Such controversy was heightened by the fact that DOL was plowing increasing amounts of resources (some $900 million total) into these competitive grant programs while calling for reduced funding for the baseline WIA system in its annual budget requests to Congress. Between 2002 and 2007 DOL sought cumulative cuts in WIA and related workforce training programs of almost $2.2 billion, or nearly 28 percent over the five-year period.[24] This confirmed to some that such grants were intended to undermine the legitimacy of the WIA system and thereby tarred industry-targeted funding (including for sectoral efforts) in the eyes of some reformers as bad for the baseline workforce system.

Obama Recovery Act and Regional Grants

By the time President Obama entered office in 2009, the sector intermediary field was in a much different place from the outset of the Bush administration. As the incoming administration and congressional Democrats assessed their prospects for re-employment strategies to counter the Great Recession of 2008, sector partnerships were included in the American Recovery and Reinvestment Act (ARRA). While workforce-development funding constituted a modest portion of ARRA ($4 billion out of a $787 billion package of spending and tax cuts), sector partnerships were a highly featured part of the Department of Labor's segment.

This was most evident in the $750 million issued by the department across a number of competitive grant programs, several of which explicitly encouraged the development of multi-stakeholder partnerships to develop and deploy training and employment strategies within a regional industry.[25] The Obama administration even went so far as to prioritize the industries for these partnership investments, focusing on the "green jobs" and health care sectors aligned with the clean energy and health care reform planks of the president's campaign. But this created challenges for grantees. This was particularly true for the green grants when the hoped-for "green jobs" never materialized, due both to the slow economic recovery and to Congress's rejection of the clean-energy demand policies (e.g., cap and trade) that would have spurred growth in those sectors.[26] Subsequent criticisms were lodged at the administration for attempting to "pick winners" among industries—not just by critics who dismissed federal training programs in general, but also by some workforce advocates who thought Washington should support industry-based training but leave it to local leaders to choose the targeted sectors.

Of less profile but potentially greater impact was DOL's further guidance that the larger portion of the $4 billion given out by formula to states and localities be prioritized for training, and that WIA systems consider structuring such training utilizing sector partnership and career-pathway strategies.[27] Unfortunately, the pressure for states to spend ARRA resources as quickly as possible allowed little time for changes on the ground. Those states that were using sector intermediaries generally continued to do so, and those that were not generally did not.

After ARRA, the Obama administration continued to experiment, albeit at much smaller scale, with grant programs geared toward industry-targeted regional partnerships. In 2010 the Department of Commerce led a joint agency grant initiative with DOL and the Small Business Administration that bore a striking resemblance to the regional alliances some sector partnerships had developed.

The Jobs and Innovation Accelerator Challenge (or Jobs Accelerator) made initial grants totaling $37 million to consortia consisting of community colleges or universities, WIBs, and economic-development agencies. Grants were given to twenty high-growth, regional industry clusters in such sectors as advanced manufacturing, information technology, aerospace, and clean technology. In addition, at the start of his second term, as the president looked to expand investments in community colleges to help re-employ two million out-of-work Americans, the administration proposed making more explicit that colleges receive such grants only if they were working with "industry or regional partnerships" of employers and other relevant stakeholders.[28] While this proposal did not address how such regional industry intermediaries would be developed, at least there was recognition from the White House that such intermediaries would better target these new training investments.

Sector Field Comes Back to Congress

Eight years of federal grants added up to a significant investment in sector intermediaries, broadly defined. But because there were no consistent standards across these various grant programs, they did not yield a recurrently tested model that might have proved to the skeptics in Washington the worth of the sectoral approach. To go to scale nationally, sector intermediaries needed a predictable source of support and evaluation that extended beyond the next presidential election cycle. Practitioners and advocates thus decided to take another run at developing a legislative proposal that would standardize federal investments in sector partnerships and make them a more regular part not just of the WIA system but of federal skills investments writ large.

Drawing on the principles of earlier proposals, the National Skills Coalition worked with a range of sector-based intermediaries and national organizations to develop a legislative framework modeled after existing state policies, like Pennsylvania's Industry Partnership initiative. Practitioners in Ohio and Maine were ultimately successful in getting Sen. Sherrod Brown (D-OH) and Sen. Olympia Snowe (R-ME) to introduce the Strengthening Employment Clusters to Organize Regional Success (SECTORS) Act of 2008.[29]

The bill, written as an amendment to WIA, incorporated certain aspects of prior state and federal grant programs while rejecting others. It allowed both states and local industry consortia to apply, with the expectation that initial investments of public resources would have to be balanced over time by private-sector investments as the partnership matured and demonstrated value to a local industry. The partnerships also would be encouraged to leverage public education and training resources from programs outside of WIA's current jurisdiction.

The proposal intentionally avoided mandating a specific organization type (e.g., WIB, trade association, community college) to serve as the convener or applicant, recognizing that the diversity of industries and actors on the ground required flexibility that allowed industry stakeholders themselves to decide who was best suited to lead the intermediary effort. SECTORS did, however, set specific standards for identifying the stakeholders that ultimately had to participate in the partnership for it to qualify for support: multiple firms within the industry (including small and medium-sized employers), along with a number of mandatory (e.g., WIBs, state workforce agencies, training providers, unions where appropriate) and optional partners.

The proposed local partnerships would engage in a number of activities, including ongoing analysis of the industry's current and future skill needs, identifying particular skilled occupations that employers throughout the sector were struggling to fill, and getting firms to reach common skill and credential standards that they would use to hire workers to fill those positions. The partnership would develop or advise shared capacity at local education and training institutions both to prepare new workers for hire and to help existing workers up-skill in order to advance along newly defined pathways across the industry. There would be required documentation of both worker placement and worker advancement as facilitated by the partnership's efforts. In addition, the bill identified a range of performance measures that would assess engagement with the local industry and its diversity of firms, as well as benefits to the surrounding community.[30]

Companion legislation was introduced in the House by Rep. Dave Loebsack (D-IA) and Rep. Todd Platts (R-PA), along with nineteen Democratic and Republican co-sponsors.[31] And once again, sector partnerships demonstrated their bipartisan appeal. Despite the highly contentious nature of the House in the 111th Congress, SECTORS was passed unanimously by the full body in July 2010 as part of a package of bills focused on reviving American manufacturing.[32] Key to the bill's passage had been the demonstration of support by both small and large manufacturers and several manufacturing trade associations. Subsequently, a group of local employers involved with local sector partnerships flew to Washington in collaboration with the National Skills Coalition and the National Fund for Workforce Solutions to see if they could persuade the Senate HELP Committee to take up the Brown-Snowe version of SECTORS and conference it with the House bill. Unfortunately, the Senate did not act on the bill before the expiration of the 111th Congress at the end of 2010.

Despite this setback, several of these local employers agreed to help create a new employer-led organization, Business Leaders United for Workforce Partnerships (BLU), to strengthen the voice of local business leaders in Washington workforce-policy discussions. BLU leaders—whose companies ranged from Fortune 500 corporations to fifty-employee metal-stamping shops—have since continued to meet with Congress, the White House, and federal agencies to share their experiences in the development of these industry partnerships and to advocate for their adoption as a tool in the regional targeting of federal workforce, career, and technical education and some higher-education investments.

As for the SECTORS Act, the legislation has subsequently been reintroduced with bipartisan co-sponsors in the 112th and 113th Congresses, but it has yet to be passed by either the House Education and Workforce Committee or the Senate HELP Committee as part of its baseline WIA reauthorization proposals.

A Return to 1990s Debates

While some continued to debate the finer points of WIA reauthorization, there emerged after the 2010 midterm elections a new threat to the very existence of federal workforce-development programs. In what seemed like a replay of the 1990s, a conservative resurgence asserted that President Obama's failure to reduce unemployment after the Great Recession, despite the investments made by ARRA, proved that an ineffectual and bloated federal government should get out of the business of workforce training and re-employment altogether.

Leading this charge was new House Budget Committee chairman and eventual vice presidential nominee Paul Ryan (R-WI), who proposed a far-reaching agenda to reduce the size and scope of the federal government with some particular attention to workforce-development programs. Ryan's budget blueprint echoed a chorus of critics who had begun citing a new GAO report cataloguing some forty-seven workforce-development programs across nine different federal agencies.[33] Ryan claimed the report proved the need to eliminate most of these programs, describing them as redundant, ineffective, and failing to meet employers' needs for skilled workers.[34] The full House subsequently passed legislation calling for the cessation of almost all WIA funding for a period of eighteen months and for the permanent consolidation of WIA and more than thirty other Labor Department workforce programs into an undifferentiated block grant to states with few federal prescriptions.[35]

Implications for State Sector Efforts

These were more devastating cuts than those proposed prior to the negotiated passage of WIA in 1998. While these cuts ultimately were not adopted by the Senate, workforce programs were clearly vulnerable. This was borne out by the collateral damage suffered by workforce programs after the high-stakes negotiations in 2011 between President Obama and congressional Republicans first to prevent a federal government shutdown and then to raise the federal debt ceiling. Labor programs suffered more than $1 billion in cuts in that process, including the elimination of the $300 million in discretionary WIA funding that many states had been using for their statewide sector strategies.[36] These reductions were followed two years later by "sequestration" cuts—the other half of the deficit-reduction measures negotiated in 2011—that further compelled states to roll back workforce-development efforts to only those activities that were mandated and/or lowered cost. The accumulation of these cuts over time while states were facing their own fiscal crises brought several of the country's signature state sectoral efforts to a halt.[37]

However, some states that were fully committed to the approach began to assess if there were other ways to maintain some type of statewide sector strategy even without additional federal resources. This second generation of state sector strategies began to look beyond WIA, to see if sector-based intermediaries might leverage public resources from other human-capital programs in exchange for better alignment not only with job-training programs but also with adult education, career and technical education, and higher-education programs. States experimented with establishing statewide sector committees to perform some of the functions of multiple regional intermediaries; raising new awareness of sector intermediaries among state legislators to potentially secure new state funding to replace depleted federal resources; providing regional industry data and programmatic technical assistance to local areas that wanted to develop or refine sector intermediaries; and leveraging additional private-sector and philanthropic resources to build new intermediary capacity.[38]

For some states, this marked a potential transition from viewing sector partnerships as an optional *grant-making strategy* to one of more fundamental *systemic reform*—a way to use industry partnerships to better target a range of publicly funded education and training programs. Compared with the late 1990s, these latest state responses have the potential for broader-based impact than some of the early state sector innovations. They also benefit from a decade of experience, in both the public and the private sector, in developing and applying such intermediaries.

However, it still seems unlikely that such efforts will achieve national scale or consistency of quality without some renewed and predictable federal investment. The past decade has shown that effective partnerships require standing capacity and continually renewed industry expertise that cannot be maintained without designated resources. Said resources are not as great as those required to actually train workers to the specifications developed by these partnerships, but their necessary predictability seems to require some type of federal funding to ensure quality intermediaries in every regional labor market. So, too, has the decade shown the potential value of a consistent, congressionally authorized set of national investments in industry-led intermediaries, with predictable and measurable performance standards that will live beyond the expiration of the next signature DOL discretionary grant program.

Potential New Allies in Congressional Debates

What are the prospects for winning new support for sector intermediaries in Congress, given the backlash currently faced by workforce-development programs on Capitol Hill? Certainly, the workforce-development field in general is in a much different place than in the 1990s. While it is not perfect, the WIA system is much more industry responsive than its predecessor JTPA, and until the Great Recession its worker-training and advancement outcomes had been moving in the right direction relative to WIA's early days. What's more, some of the WIA system's greatest success stories have been found in those places that have used available state, federal, and philanthropic resources to establish sector-based intermediaries. Not only have these partnerships shown encouraging results; they also have won over a new group of allies who were not there to defend federal workforce investments in the 1990s, including members of the business community who have become champions of the sector approach. The sector-partnership field itself has grown and matured over the past decade, due in part to the support of Democratic and Republican governors and state legislators who have become champions of sector intermediaries in their states. Unfortunately, these state policy makers have yet to leverage some of that political capital to advocate for federal support for sector intermediaries in Washington as well. If the partnerships developed on the ground over the past decade between industry, state policy makers, WIA administrators, and education and training providers could be replicated in Washington as part of a concerted advocacy effort to solidify federal investments in sector intermediaries, there seems to be a decent chance that workforce development's harshest critics could be rebuffed and a new vision for federal workforce-development policy could be advanced.

Conclusion

The reason the United States has not adopted industry-led, sector-based intermediaries as a fundamental element of its human-capital policies is not "American exceptionalism." As the past decade has shown, U.S. employers—just like their competitors overseas—are comfortable working with one another as well as with education and training providers and workforce investment boards to establish shared, industrywide workforce partnerships. The barrier in taking these partnerships to scale has not been a clash of economic cultures. Rather, much of it has been rooted in the political dynamics between various actors in Washington; between critics and proponents of federal workforce programs, between congressional authorizers and federal agencies jockeying for authority, and even between proponents of federal workforce programs who have had different tactical perspectives on the best ways to simultaneously protect and reform our federal workforce-development system. While states have shown their willingness to fill this federal void for a time by investing in or recognizing the value of sector partnerships, the past decade has shown that without a willing and consistent federal partner in those investments, the United States will never be able to bring the use of such intermediaries to scale or to ensure their effective and consistent deployment in a manner that would ensure the greatest leverage of our various federally funded human-capital programs.

Thankfully, there is a new set of allies who are ready to work with federal workforce-development champions to move the Congressional debate from one of program elimination to one of program improvement and alignment. If reformers and innovators can get on the same page about how to leverage these new partnerships, the next ten years could eclipse the past decade in terms of the growth and development of the sector-intermediaries field.

Notes

1. Slack (2012).
2. Watt and Gagnon (2005); UK Commission for Employment and Skills (2012).
3. *CAREERS Act* (1995).
4. Gragg and Kaleba (2011).
5. Atkinson (2003).
6. Giloth (2004).
7. Workforce Alliance and National Network of Sector Partners (2003).
8. Amendment to the Amendment in the Nature of a Substitute to H.R. 27, Offered by Mr. Andrews [Business partnership grant demonstration program], February 2005.
9. *ISEED* (2003), introduced by Sen. Cantwell (D-WA); SMARTER Act (2003), introduced as an amendment to WIA by Sen. Cantwell (D-WA) and Sen. Collins (R-ME).
10. Washington State Workforce Training and Education Coordinating Board (2005).
11. *Labor Relations Committee* (2010); Vito and Cleveland (2005).
12. Eaton et al. (2001).
13. Sheets (2005).
14. Michigan Department of Labor and Economic Growth (2004).

15. NGA Center for Best Practices et.al. (2008); Corporation for a Skilled Workforce (2010).

16. Supporters for the Industry Partnership (IP) program were not as successful in subsequent years after Governor Rendell was succeeded by Governor Corbett, who called for the elimination of the IP program. With vocal support from IP participants and bipartisan support in the legislature, Gov. Corbett eventually agreed to fund the program at $1.6 million annually, compared with the $20 million that it had originally received in the state budget.

17. Edelman et al. (2011).

18. Pindus et al. (2004).

19. The American Competitiveness and Workforce Improvement Act (ACWIA) was an amendment to the Immigration and Nationality Act that regulated the issuance of visas to various classes of foreign workers brought into the country by U.S. employers to fill workforce gaps. These included the 65,000 skilled immigrants who were allowed to be hired annually under the H-1B visa program. ACWIA authorized that 56 percent of the fees collected from employers for the issuance of these visas be set aside in a special Department of Labor account to train more U.S. workers for positions in these industries that were looking overseas for skilled workers.

20. The American Competitiveness in the Twenty-First Century Act of 2000 raised the annual cap on H-1B visas to 195,000 for three years (fiscal years 2001–2003) before reestablishing the 65,000 cap in fiscal year 2004.

21. The sectors were Advanced Manufacturing, Aerospace, Automotive, Biotechnology, Construction, Energy, Financial Services, Geospatial Technology, Health Care, Hospitality, Information Technology, Retail, and Transportation.

22. Government Accountability Office (2008).

23. Ibid.

24. Workforce Alliance (2007).

25. Ibid. (2009).

26. White, Dresser, and Rogers (2011).

27. USDOL Employment and Training Administration (2009).

28. In 2010 the Obama administration initiated its four-year, $2 billion Trade Adjustment Assistance Community College and Career Training (TAACCCT) grant program. In year three of the grants (2013), the administration wrote into the grant solicitation greater expectations for colleges' engagement of industry, including through sector strategies. In anticipation that the grant program might expire with the end of the Trade Adjustment Assistance program in December 2013, the White House proposed in its fiscal year 2014 budget a new $8 billion Community College to Career grant program, which would replace the TAACCT grant program and even more explicitly require regional or industry partnerships. See note 1, above.

29. SECTORS was originally introduced in the Senate as S.777. It has been subsequently reintroduced, with Democratic and Republican co-sponsors, in the 111th, 112th, and 113th Congresses.

30. National Skills Coalition (2013).

31. SECTORS was originally introduced in the House in 2009 as H.R.1855. It too has been subsequently reintroduced, with Democratic and Republican co-sponsors, in the 111th, 112th, and 113th Congresses.

32. National Skills Coalition (2011a).

33. Government Accountability Office (2011).

34. House Committee on the Budget (2012).
35. House Appropriations (2012); SKILLS Act (2013).
36. National Skills Coalition (2011b).
37. Edelman, et al. (2011).
38. Woolsey, et al. (2013).

Bibliography

Amendment to the Amendment in the Nature of a Substitute to H.R. 27 [Business partnership grant demonstration program]. 2005. Offered by Mr. Andrews.

Atkinson, R. 2003. "The Innovation Economy: A New Vision for Economic Growth in the 21st Century." Progressive Policy Institute.

Consolidated and Reformed Education, Employment and Rehabilitation Services (CAREERS) Act of 1995, H.R. 2332, 104th Congress. 1995.

Corporation for a Skilled Workforce. 2010. "Sector Strategies at a Tipping Point—A Fact Sheet." Ann Arbor, MI: Corporation for a Skilled Workforce.

Eaton, S., C. Green, R. Wilson, and T. Osypuk. 2001. "Extended Care Career Ladder Initiative (ECCLI): Baseline Evaluation Report of a Massachusetts Nursing Home Initiative." Cambridge, MA: JFK School of Government.

Edelman, P., H. Holzer, E. Seleznow, A. Van Kleunen, and E. Watson. 2011. "State Workforce Policy: Recent Innovations and an Uncertain Future." Washington, DC: Georgetown Center on Poverty, Inequality and Public Policy and National Skills Coalition.

Giloth, Robert P., ed. 2004. Workforce Intermediaries for the Twenty-First Century. Published in association with the American Assembly, Columbia University. Philadelphia: Temple University Press.

Government Accountability Office. 2008. "Employment and Training Program Grants: Evaluating Impact and Enhancing Monitoring Would Improve Accountability." Report GAO-08-486. May.

———. 2011. "Multiple Employment and Training Programs: Providing Information on Colocating Services and Consolidating Administrative Structures Could Promote Efficiencies. Report GAO-11-92. January.

Gragg, R., and K. Kaleba. 2011. "Training Policy in Brief: An Overview of Federal Workforce Development Policies." Washington, DC: National Skills Coalition.

House Appropriations for the Departments of Labor, Health and Human Services, and Education (Labor-H), 112th Cong. 2012.

House Committee on the Budget. 2012. "The Path to Prosperity: Restoring America's Promise."

Industrial Sector Employment and Economic Development Act (ISEED), 108th Cong. 2003. Introduced by Sen. Cantwell (D-WA).

Labor Relations Committee, Pennsylvania House of Representatives. 2010. On House Bill 2230, establishing the Industry Partnership program. Statement by Stephen Herzenberg, executive director of Keystone Research Center. February 24.

Michigan Department of Labor and Economic Growth. 2004. "Reshaping Michigan's Workforce: An Action Plan of the Michigan Department of Labor and Economic Growth." Lansing: Michigan Department of Labor and Economic Growth.

National Skills Coalition. 2011a. "SECTORS Act." Washington, DC: National Skills Coalition.

———. 2011b. "Washington Update: December 2011." Washington, DC: National Skills Coalition.

———. 2013. "The Strengthening Employment Clusters to Organize Regional Success Act of 2013, Section-by-Section Analysis." Washington, DC: National Skills Coalition.

NGA Center for Best Practices, National Network of Sector Partners, and Corporation for a Skilled Workforce. 2008. "Accelerating State Adoption of Sector Strategies: An Eleven-State Project to Promote Regional Solutions to Worker and Employer Needs." Washington, DC: NGA Center for Best Practices.

Pindus, N., M. Conway, C. Haskins, C. O'Brien, and I. Rademacher. 2004. "Evaluation of the Sectoral Employment Demonstration Program: Final Report." Washington, DC: Urban Institute and Aspen Institute for the U.S. Department of Labor.

Sectoral Market Assessment for Regional Training Enhancement and Revitalization (SMART-ER) Act, 108th Cong. 2003.

Sheets, B. 2005. "Linking Economic and Workforce Development: A Regional Sector Approach."

Slack, M. 2012. "President Obama's Plan to Train 2 Million Workers for Jobs in High-Demand Industries." White House Blog, February 13.

Supporting Knowledge and Investing in Lifelong Skills (SKILLS) Act, 113th Cong. 2013.

UK Commission for Employment and Skills. 2012. "UK Sector Skills Councils Annual Report, April 2011–March 2012." London: UK Commission for Employment and Skills.

USDOL Employment and Training Administration. 2009. "Guidance for Implementation of Workforce Investment Act and Wagner Peyser Act Funding in the American Recovery and Reinvestment Act of 2009 and State Planning Requirements for Program Year 2009." Training and Employment Guidance Letter (TEGL) 14-08. March 18.

Vito, S., and A. Cleveland. 2005. "Pennsylvania's New Performance Management Plan and Benchmark Report on Current Workforce Programs." Harrisburg, PA: Office of the Governor.

Washington State Workforce Training and Education Coordinating Board. 2005. "Industry Skill Panels 2005."

Watt, D., and N. Gagnon. 2005. "The Skills Factor in Productivity: How Canada's Sector Councils Are Helping Address the Skills and Labour Needs of Employers." Ottawa, Canada: Conference Board of Canada.

White, S., L. Dresser, and J. Rogers. 2011. "Greener Reality: Jobs, Skills and Equity in a Cleaner U.S. Economy." Madison: Center on Wisconsin Strategy.

Woolsey, et al. 2013. "State Sector Strategies Coming of Age: Implications for State Workforce Policymakers." Washington, DC: National Governors Association.

Workforce Alliance and National Network of Sector Partners. 2003. "Multi-Stakeholder Workforce Intermediary Grant Program: A Proposed WIA Amendment to Create a National Demonstration Program to Help Local Industy Partnerships Develop Targeted Workforce Strategies."

———. 2007. "Not Ready to Compete: Declining Federal Investments in a Skilled, Competitive Workforce, 2002–2007." Washington, DC: Workforce Alliance.

———. 2009. "ARRA Competitive Grants for Green Jobs Training: Training and Employment Notice Summary." Washington, DC: Workforce Alliance.

17

Workforce Intermediaries in a Slack Labor Market: Who Pays and for What?

Orson Watson

The concept of workforce intermediaries emerged during the 1990s boom in the U.S. economy, when employers experienced skilled-labor shortages and lower-skilled individuals dominated the available labor supply. At the time, the existing workforce-development system seemed structurally incapable of addressing this problem. Federal funding through the Workforce Investment Act (WIA) had redirected its focus from low-skilled populations to universal services emphasizing job matching and rapid employment. The multiplicity of sometimes conflicting public funding sources for workforce preparation created a fragmented, misaligned pastiche of services, including literacy, occupational training, and job matching. The main delivery systems for the existing training services—One-Stop Centers, community colleges, and community-based organizations—lacked strong relationships with employers and a general understanding of demand-side needs. In short, neither job seekers nor employers were having their needs adequately met by the system.

In an era of 5 percent unemployment, labor-market economists predicted an ominous impending shortage of skilled American labor capable of keeping pace with the current and projected demand created by industrial restructuring, robust annual economic growth rates, and the impending retirement of baby boom workers. Simultaneously, structural industrial fragmentation and human-resource disinvestment practices within the private sector—reportedly driven by global competition for lower human-resource costs—and the rapid integration of revolutionary computer-based technologies heightened firms' demand for workers who were pre-trained (externally and at someone else's expense) and ready to work. Employers' increased demand for skilled labor, coupled with a large supply of low-wage, low-skilled workers, illuminated a need for mechanisms that would both create a supply of work-ready workers and provide an external resource that would create a path to further skill, career, and, most important, wage advancement within firms or expanding industry sectors.

Armed with innovative philanthropic investments, pilot programs like San Francisco Works, the Wisconsin Regional Training Partnership, Focus: HOPE, and the Jane Addams Resource Center developed models that were deemed replicable and capable of increasing the future efficiency of the ailing U.S. workforce delivery system. These model programs worked closely with employers to analyze their specific skilled-labor needs and put together an integrated set of training and job-readiness services that prepared lower-skilled, high-barrier target populations for those jobs. The dual-customer strategy of these pilot programs seemed so logical that the required financing mechanisms for their long-term sustainability seemed self-evident. Workforce intermediary strategies would add so much labor-market value that the beneficiaries (government and philanthropy, employers—individually or through aggregated employer associations—and workers or job seekers) would willingly pay for their services.[1]

However, shifting economic, labor-market, and stakeholder priorities arising out of the Great Recession have raised questions about the continued validity of the original workforce-intermediary value proposition, raising questions about how to pay for the long-term sustainability of specialized, even boutique, workforce intermediary services. With the exception of the Aspen Institute's 2011 study on the financing of community college partnerships, sustainable financing for workforce-intermediary strategies has been a strikingly underresearched subject.

Based on interviews with representatives of philanthropy, funder collaboratives, the public sector, and training providers,[2] this chapter will revisit the original definition and value proposition for financing workforce intermediaries outlined in the "Financing Workforce Intermediaries" chapter of *Workforce Intermediaries for the Twenty-first Century*.[3] This chapter will test the original theory against the financing and recessionary realities of the last five years in an effort to address new critical questions about the realities faced by low-wage, low-skilled workers in the current labor market and the future financial sustainability of this important labor-market function.

What Is a Workforce Intermediary?

Despite extensive research, convenings, and reports on the subject, the term "workforce intermediary" remains controversial in the field of workforce development. In many respects, the term has morphed, and currently a wide range of organizations, programs, and initiatives self-identify as workforce intermediaries. Because the term "workforce intermediary" means different things to different audiences, it is necessary to revisit the original concept to clarify "what" needs to be financed.

In his paper "What Do Workforce Intermediaries Do?" Richard Kazis uses San Francisco Works as an example of a successful workforce intermediary based on its ability to:

- pursue a "dual-customer" approach: a commitment to promoting advancement by serving the needs of employers in need of qualified workers and lower-skilled workers or job seekers;

- organize multiple partners and funding streams toward common goals: the ability to bring together employers, educational institutions, social-service agencies, and other stakeholders to implement programs and policies to improve labor-market outcomes;

- provide and/or broker labor-market services to individuals and employers that include, but go beyond, job matching: the capacity to address identifiable labor-market problems by either providing necessary services directly or arranging for their provision by others; and

- project a vision that motivates and guides its partnerships and activities: mission-driven organizations guided by strongly held views on what both firms and their workers need to prosper in today's economic and policy environment.

Kazis subsequently identifies "a broad range of organizations" that function as workforce intermediaries, such as community-based organizations, chambers of commerce, employer associations, labor-market partnerships, community colleges, and government agencies, including some workforce investment boards.[4] While Kazis and others deliberately define workforce intermediaries by "what they do," there is built-in confusion about whether the term "workforce intermediary" refers to a specific type of organization (a noun) or a series of functions that a number of different types of organizations perform (an adjective). Throughout *Workforce Intermediaries in the Twenty-first Century*, the organization and the function are used interchangeably. However, the report generated by the subsequent 102nd American Assembly, entitled "Achieving Worker Success and

Business Prosperity: The New Role of Workforce Intermediaries," specifically defined "workforce intermediaries" as a strategic "approach":

> *[The Workforce Intermediary] approach does not require creating a new set of organizations or overhauling public systems but it does require the transformation of existing policies and programs so that they are more adaptable to local labor markets.*[5]

The function versus the organization is a critical distinction that seems to have gotten lost during the last ten years. A variety of organizations perform workforce intermediary functions. As a result, questions regarding the financing of workforce intermediary strategies need to be disentangled from issues related to the sustainable financing of the organizations that perform the function, because stand-alone workforce intermediaries remain rare (some would say nonexistent).

Their scarcity is largely due to the fact that core non-programmatic[6] workforce intermediary functions have become difficult to adequately finance. Thus workforce intermediary financing questions are about providing sustainable support for functions that are often buried within a variety of types of organizations. Despite the best intention and long-term vision of the American Assembly, ten years later there is still no financing mechanism or clear stakeholder incentive to provide all of the support needed to sustain workforce intermediary functions wherever they may reside.

Who Should Have Paid

From the beginning, workforce intermediary approaches have been supported by a diverse set of resources encompassing a set of distinct financing priorities and funding mechanisms. In workforce intermediary literature, this strategy is often referred to as "aligning funding resources." The original model anticipated that the short- and long-term sustainability of workforce intermediary strategies ultimately was to be financed collaboratively by the beneficiaries of the strategy: philanthropy, the public sector, employers, and workers.

- Philanthropy: Foundations have always played an important role in promoting workforce intermediary functions by providing programmatic start-up capital and financing not readily available through other sources.

- Public Funds: Public funds, such as WIA, Dislocated Worker funds, WIA Individual Training Accounts (or vouchers), Temporary Assistance for Needy Families, and state Department of Labor Education funds, have primarily been used to pay for direct services. In some cases, flexible secondary sources of public financing, such as WIA Governor's Discretionary 15 percent funds, have been applied to cover some of the costs of intermediary functions.

- Employer Contributions: Employers spend significant amounts on workforce training and development, but their investments are disproportionately focused on professional and executive-level workers at the expense of entry-level workers. Understanding the training needs of lower-skilled workers, workforce intermediaries attempted to become (eventually paid) advisors to employers needing to address the perilous mid-skilled labor gap. While several workforce intermediary initiatives have managed to raise some funds from employers through fee-for-service, corporate contributions, and tuition reimbursements, this funding source generally falls far short of anticipated revenue projections derived from the original model's employer value proposition.[7]

- Worker Contributions: Worker contributions in the form of direct training payments, such as tuition payments, Pell grants, and labor union training funds, also were projected to help fund worker training costs.

The ability to blend diverse funding streams into a unified portfolio has always been critical to the survival of workforce intermediary strategies. The diversity of the funding mix differed widely depending on regional priorities and shifting funding environments. (*Figure 1* highlights the multiple funding streams used by sites in the Courses to Employment initiative.) The flows of public, philanthropic, and private funding available through any one source is unpredictable and can shift dramatically on an annual basis. Developing and coordinating multiple funding streams, however, takes considerable amounts of time and staff expertise, representing an essential ongoing cost for workforce intermediary programs. These "overhead" or "indirect" cost activities, as well as the capacity to develop, monitor, and report on a range of funds, represent one of the more difficult areas to finance.[8]

Adding to the complexity is the fact that both public and philanthropic financing usually comes with multiple, not always overlapping restrictions on how funds may be used. For example, a workforce intermediary program may have one public funding source that supports only training for youth and another that supports only employment services to public-housing residents in a specific geographic area. Similarly, a philanthropic funder may have interest only in supporting training in a specific industry sector for targeted underserved populations. Restricting the percentage of a grant that can be applied to indirect or overhead expenses is also common practice among both public and philanthropic funders. Given the funding complexity, it is understandable why even during the boom years of the U.S. economy, the originally conceived workforce intermediary financing scenario never fully materialized.

Figure 1: Number of Courses to Employment Programs Using Funding Sources (FY 2008)

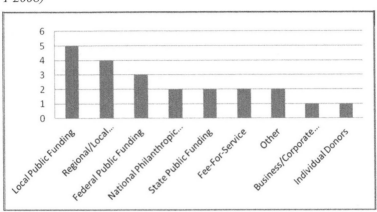

Source: Update: Courses to Employment, Number 2, The Aspen Institute, Workforce Strategy Institute, February, 2011.

In the interest of growing and accelerating investments in workforce intermediary strategies, the National Fund for Workforce Solutions (NFWS) was created in 2007. The NFWS (discussed at length in Dyer et al., Chapter 5, and Popovich, Chapter 12) provided seed funding for regional efforts to build a network of funder collaboratives capable of supporting the implementation and replication of workforce intermediary strategies at the local level.[9] The NFWS network of funder collaboratives pooled philanthropic and public-sector funds to support the expansion of workforce intermediary approaches and to advocate for policies that could help to sustain them. Most important, funder collaboratives played a key role in funding the most difficult-to-finance workforce intermediary functions, including:

- funding for general operating costs;

- funding for core intermediary functions;

- funding that provided sustainability, autonomy, and consistency;

- flexible funding that could service multiple populations; and

- a reliable source of long-term funding.[10]

In reality, however, over the last ten years, many workforce intermediary strategies have managed to exist (and in many cases prosper) by adhering to "robbing Peter to pay Paul" financing strategies. Difficult-to-fund costs are embedded within other, more fundable workforce-development functions and services. Many organizations have become adept at taking advantage of the "gray areas" of federal funding equations to cover critical overhead costs.

The Great Recession

The economic boom, historically low unemployment rates, and structural industry shifts of the 1990s produced a dual dilemma: Large numbers of workers needed skills training to access quality jobs while employers demanded more skilled and productive workers to remain globally competitive. Notions of the short-term nature of this phenomenon were countered by labor-market economists' projections of increased future demand for skilled workers as baby boomers retired. Experts estimated that the United States would face a shortage of roughly 15 million qualified workers by 2020.[11] Policy makers, academics, practitioners, and even employers posited that the inevitable skill and labor shortage would be so persistent that employers would be forced to invest in up-skilling the nation's low-wage, low-skilled labor to fill the gap. In response, the late 1990s witnessed what some called an "organic" explosion of innovative dual-customer workforce intermediary strategies designed to advance low-wage, low-skilled workers.

Had the growth trajectory of the U.S. economy and declining unemployment rates continued, the value proposition-derived assumptions about the financial sustainability of workforce intermediary approaches might have been realized. Unfortunately, the entire workforce intermediary approach suffered the bad timing of the Great Recession. Between the fourth quarter of 2007 and the second quarter of 2009, real GDP fell by more than 5 percent. The unemployment rate rose from a low of 4.4 percent in May 2007 to a high of 10 percent in October 2009, for a twenty-nine-month increase of 5.6 percentage points. From July 2007 to July 2009, unemployment doubled in twenty-four states and nearly doubled in eleven others.[12] (*Figure 2* shows the unemployment rate in the United States between 1990 and 2012.)

Figure 2: Unemployment Rate in the United States, 1990–2012

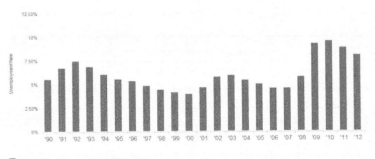

1 United States; 16 years and older; 1990 to 2012

Faced with unemployment increases far exceeding the 1973 postwar record, the federal government paid attention and responded. Although federal inflation-adjusted investments in worker training decreased by 30 percent between 1985 and 2005 (with increasing funding responsibility devolving to the state level), both the number of and funding for federal employment and training programs increased between 2003 and 2009, due largely to the American Recovery and Reinvestment Act (ARRA) of 2009. In fiscal year 2009, nine federal agencies spent approximately $18 billion to administer forty-seven programs, representing an increase of $5 billion from 2003.[13]

Although the federal government had become adept at dual-customer language and rebranded often ineffective workforce investment systems as the embodiment of responsive workforce intermediary principles, the top priority of ARRA and workforce spending was to keep people working and place dislocated workers in jobs that would open up as a result of stimulus spending. The goal of ARRA spending was less about long-term careers, skill development, and wage advancement and more about short-term rapid placement outcomes. In short, at the height of the recession all jobs (with or without advancement potential) counted.

After years of advocating (often unsuccessfully) for increased public workforce funding, many workforce intermediary program operators seized the financing opportunity by positioning themselves on the receiving end of the wave of ARRA dollars. Although (with the exception of a few pilot demonstration projects) ARRA workforce funding criteria was not designed with classic advancement functions in mind, many organizations used their underfunded workforce intermediary frameworks to provide the short-term job matching and retention services that the crisis funding sought. Although the immediate necessity of funding these critical interventions was unquestionable, many program operators inadvertently violated basic principles of the workforce intermediary approach and, in so doing, reverted to "training for training's sake" paradigms of the 1970s. While this approach provided a lifeline for underfunded programs and the appearance of "doing something" in the face of skyrocketing unemployment, this short-term shift from a demand-driven to a supply-driven focus ultimately failed to serve the supposed long-term skills advancement needs of both customers—employers and job seekers.

Funder Priorities and the Shifting Value Proposition

In retrospect, the rationale behind the expansion of workforce funding during the peak years of the recession was antithetical to many core principles of the workforce intermediary approach. According to the original model, funding for workforce intermediary functions should increase during a tight labor market when the demand for skilled workers is high, and it should shrink in a slack labor market when the demand for skilled labor is low. While cash-starved workforce intermediary programs were understandably grateful for the recessionary funding windfall, their attempts to use workforce intermediary functions for purposes for which they were not designed were doomed to generate poor outcomes. Workforce intermediaries could train to employer specifications, but the number of training slots available during the recession far exceeded employer demand for skilled labor. Unfortunately, the lackluster job-matching outcomes of many workforce intermediary programs during the recession generated (potentially unwarranted) questions about the overall effectiveness of strategies that could negatively impact long-term financing prospects: How do you prove that the model works when the economy does not?

As the ARRA funding subsided and emergency initiatives ended, the challenge of identifying and/or creating sustainable long-term financing mechanisms for workforce intermediary functions remained and in some areas became even more complex. There are two main reasons for this: The priorities and financing strategies of core funders have changed, and the dual-customer value proposition of workforce intermediary approaches was misaligned with funders' recession-fighting priorities.

The collapse of the stock market wiped out 20 percent to 40 percent of foundations' assets. After peak levels in 2008, overall giving by foundations dipped as they began multiyear efforts to rebuild their endowments. Simultaneously, the recession also generated increased demand for philanthropic funding to support immediate basic needs of low-income people. This dilemma sent many foundations into a flurry of strategic reevaluation and planning.[14] The result of this attempt to increase the impact of shrinking endowments has been a greater focus on outcomes-based grant making. Outcomes-based grant making has become the norm of national foundations over the last twenty years. Even the NFWS, which was conceptualized to provide Local Initiatives Support Coalition-type venture capital to launch local workforce intermediary initiatives, began with only a five-year commitment from national funder partners. Increasingly, however, place-based and community foundations (the core members of local funder collaboratives) have begun to follow the same trajectory. As a result, the long-term general operating support and flexible funding required to build the capacity of start-up workforce intermediary programs has been shrinking at both the national and the local level.

Public funders also have modified their strategies in response to state and local government budget shortfalls. A subtle but important paradigm shift has taken hold in which public funders offered through new programs like the Social Innovation Fund[15] also have become oriented toward time-limited innovation. In addition, both the philanthropic and public funding strategies specifically seek out "leveraged funding" opportunities that blend together public private and philanthropic dollars. The language of leveraged funding masks an underlying caveat that if one of the innovation-oriented investing partners quietly withdraws, the other funding partners could be left to bear the long-term cost. In short, everyone wants to fund innovation, and no one wants to provide long-term funding to sustain programs.

Employers who in theory could share the cost of valuable workforce intermediary service in a tight labor market either have no immediate direct interest in financially sustaining the programs or are "free rider" beneficiaries of a workforce intermediary system. This is particularly true with regard to the needs of non-traditional, high-barrier, low-wage, low-skilled workers. In the tight-labor-market years of the late 1990s and early 2000s, when intermediaries were scaling up, few managed to convince employers to pay for their value-added labor-market services. Furthermore, the slack labor market significantly reduced employers' interest in increasing the skills of their entry-level workforce.

The Post-Recession Skills Shift

After the recession, a new trend emerged that further clouds the picture about where shrinking workforce funds should be invested to benefit low-wage, low-skilled workers. The recent recovery has witnessed a trend in which the gap in employment rates between America's highest- and lowest-income families has stretched to its widest levels since the governments began tracking the data a decade ago.

Rates of unemployment for the lowest-income families (those earning less than $20,000) have reached 21 percent, nearly matching the rate for all workers during the Great Depression of the 1930s. Correspondingly, U.S. households with income of more than $150,000 a year have an unemployment rate of 3.2 percent, a level traditionally defined as full employment. At the same time, middle-income workers are increasingly pushed into lower-wage jobs. Many of them in turn are displacing lower-skilled, low-income workers who become unemployed or are forced to work fewer hours. In short, one part of America remains in depression, while another part is in full employment.

This labor market "bumping down" or "crowding out" is a domino effect that pushes out lower-income workers, pushes median income downward, and exacerbates income inequality. Because many mid-skill jobs are being lost to globalization and automation, recent U.S. growth in low-wage jobs has not come fast enough to absorb displaced workers at the bottom. Low-wage workers are older, higher skilled, and better educated than ever, with especially large jumps in those with at least some college-level training. Data on current and projected job growth in the economy indicate that this trend will continue. According to the Bureau of Labor Statistics, six of the seven fastest-growing jobs projected between 2010 and 2020 are in low-wage employment sectors (see *Table 1*). According to the McKinsey Global Institute, the U.S. economy will experience growth in jobs that require complex, personalized interactions, such as home health care aids, coupled with declines in routine transaction and production jobs that can be scripted and automated. Although the U.S. economy may still very well face an impending skills gap, post-recession labor-market conditions have made investments in skills advancement even less of a priority for employers.[16]

Table 1: Occupations with the Most Job Growth, 2010 and Projected 2020

2010 National Employment Matrix title	Employment		Change, 2010-20		Median annual wage, 2010
	2010	2020	Number	%	
Total, All Occupations	**143,068.2**	**163,537.1**	**20,468.9**	**14.3**	**$33,640**
Registered Nurses	2,737.4	3,449.3	711.9	26.0	64,690
Retail Salespersons	4,261.6	4,968.4	706.8	16.6	20.670
Home Health Aides	1,017.7	1,723.9	706.3	69.4	20,560
Personal-Care Aides	861.0	1,468.0	607.0	70.5	19,640
Office Clerks, General	2,950.7	3,440.2	489.5	16.6	26,610
Combined Food Preparation and Serving Workers, Including Fast Food	2,682.1	3,080.1	398.0	14.8	17,950

SOURCE: Employment Projections program, U.S. Department of Labor, U.S. Bureau of Labor Statistics, Occupational Employment Projections to 2020, *Monthly Labor Review*, January 2012.

According to Peter Cappelli, although employers still claim they can not find skilled workers, the definition of skill has shifted from basic competencies to duplicate job experience. In the current labor market, employers can afford to wait for the perfect candidate for reasons including the following:

- Productivity is rising with fewer workers, because firms have downsized and expect the remaining "grateful to be employed" workers to work harder.

- Employers are paying lower wages by shopping for ideal experienced workers hungry enough to accept lesser wages.

- Employers are defining job requirements so narrowly that applicants have to have direct experience in a similar job in order to get hired.

- By demanding experienced candidates who can contribute immediately with no training or start-up time, employers have shifted the burden of responsibility and the cost of training to external sources—the federal government, states, and the prospective employee.

In the current environment, employers can afford to be picky, applicants need to be overqualified, and skills are measured in terms of experience rather than education and training (Cappelli).[17]

Utilizing a more basic framework, some economists question whether the much-touted skills gap exists at all. According to basic supply-and-demand economics, real skills shortages trigger rising wages. Yet according to the Bureau of Labor Statistics, the number of skilled jobs in the United States has fallen, and so have the wages paid for them. Employers' difficulty recruiting highly skilled workers at rock-bottom rates constitutes a wage rather than a skills gap (Davidson). The more relevant question is: Why do American businesses feel compelled to not pay high enough wages to attract the workers they say they need?[18]

The post-recessionary labor-market trend is far more disturbing than a mere hollowing-out of the middle-skilled jobs that were the focus of workforce intermediary strategies. With the growth of jobs at the bottom of the labor market not matching the growth at the top, the low-wage people at the bottom who were the original target of workforce intermediaries are going to be continually squeezed. In the face of increased competition from higher-skilled workers moving down and a lack of wage growth at the bottom tier of the labor market, the rationale behind the 1990s skills-based career-advancement strategies needs to be revisited.

Workforce Intermediaries 2.0?

Unquestionably, the dynamics and impact of the slack labor market have caused a critical shift in the original value proposition of workforce intermediary strategies. A significant part of the problem is derived from the fact that despite their demand-led orientation, workforce intermediary strategies in reality largely consist of supply-side interventions—focused on "fixing" low-skilled workers rather than the business practices that create them. Beginning with the assumption that quality jobs exist but low-skilled workers lack the skills that match available jobs, the responsibility for acquiring the marketable skills is placed on the shoulders of the low-wage, low-skilled worker (with the support of programs financed by philanthropy and government). This has become problematic in the current environment of shrinking demand for labor at the middle of the labor market (the very jobs that are the advancement targets of workforce intermediaries) and increased competition at the bottom of the labor market.

Given the potentially long-term tight-to-slack labor-market trends, the original intent of workforce intermediaries—outlined the proceedings of the 102nd American Assembly and *Workforce Intermediaries for the Twenty-first Century*—need to be revisited. Both began with an urgent call to arms in the interest of long-term U.S. industrial competitiveness to avert an impending skilled-worker shortage. The entrepreneurial, outcomes-driven workforce intermediary strategies that they espoused stood in stark contrast to a traditional workforce system that was incapable of helping low-wage target populations achieve long-term skills, career, and income advancement.

While these approaches may have seemed like a silver-bullet solution during the 1990s tight labor market, post-recession there is a need to creatively rethink when, where, and how to invest increasingly scarce public and philanthropic workforce funds to achieve meaningful results. This is particularly so for the original intended beneficiaries of workforce intermediary strategies: high-barrier target populations of workers. The answers to these questions require workforce investors to face some cold realities and a possible return to the drawing board.

Skills acquisition has become even more critical post-recession, not only to high-barrier workers but to the broader socioeconomic cross-section of American workers. In the current labor market, "low-wage" and "low-skilled" are no longer synonymous. Over the last decade, while there has been increased pressure on individual workers to improve their skills, there has been decreased pressure on employers to create jobs that reward those skills. America still needs a better-skilled workforce, but it also needs an economy that is creating better jobs and is treating low-skill, low-wage workers more fairly.

With its intentional dual-customer language, its focus on industrial competitiveness, and a desire to make the case for businesses to voluntarily improve human-resource practices that advance low-wage, low-skilled workers, workforce intermediary strategies by definition have always been business friendly. In this attempt at cooperation and shared employer interest, old-fashioned employer regulation became a third-rail issue for the movement. With the lion's share of new-job creation at the increasingly competitive bottom of the labor market and unrewarded skills acquisition becoming increasingly beyond reach for many target populations, philanthropy and government have a critical role to play. In addition to making investments that enable the entry-level labor market to function more efficiently, philanthropy may need to make investments to reconstruct a regulatory framework that can protect the interests of all workers who are struggling to survive at the lower end of the labor market.

Current labor-market conditions require workforce stakeholders to systematically revisit the state of the low-wage American workforce with the same urgency and vigor that was mustered a decade ago at the 102nd American Assembly. At the very least, there is a definite need to revisit the perceived skills shortage and its implications for high-barrier, low-wage, low-skilled workers. Through this process, the effectiveness and impact of existing workforce intermediary strategies need to be re-evaluated to redefine needs, illuminate best practices, and strategize support for the creation and start-up of alternative, yet-to-be-identified strategies fitted to the new labor-market reality.

Notes

1. Colborn (2007).
2. The argument and conclusions contained in this paper were based on interviews with Geri Scott, program director of Building Economic Opportunities, Jobs for the Future; Jerry Rubin, CEO of Jewish Vocational Services Boston; Loh-Sze Leung, director of SkillWorks Boston; and Angel Bermudez, AHB & Associates.
3. Rubin, Seltzer, and Mills (2004).
4. Kazis (2004).
5. American Assembly (2003).
6. While traditional workforce funders provide support for program elements, funding for the research and relationship-building activities needed to align the workforce system with employer needs, and to bridge gaps in delivery systems, constitute the difficult-to-fund core workforce intermediary functions.
7. Jobs for the Future (2004).
8. Aspen Institute (2011).
9. The National Fund for Workforce Solutions created a pooled fund with investments from national investors to provide seed money and support to local workforce intermediary initiatives by providing financial support, technical assistance, evaluation, research, and other capacity-building services. The National Fund's initial investors were the Annie E. Casey Foundation, Ford Foundation, the Harry and Jeanette Weinberg Foundation, the Hitachi Foundation, JPMorgan Chase, the U.S. Department of Labor, John S. and James L. Knight Foundation, Microsoft Corporation, the Prudential Foundation, and the Walmart Foundation. www.nfwsolutions.org.
10. Prince (2007).
11. Manufacturing Institute (2005).
12. Rothstein (2012).
13. Government Accountability Office (2011).
14. Lawrence (2010).
15. The Social Innovation Fund, a program of the Corporation for National and Community Service, combines public and private resources to grow promising community-based solutions that have evidence of results in any of three priority areas: economic opportunity, healthy futures, and youth development. The fund makes grants to experienced grant-making intermediaries that are well positioned within communities to identify the most promising programs and guide them toward greater impact and stronger evidence of success. These grants typically range from $1 million to $5 million annually for up to five years. The intermediaries then match the federal funds dollar for dollar and hold open competitions to identify the most promising nonprofit organizations working in low-income communities that have evidence of compelling results.
16. Manyika et al. (2012).
17. Cappelli (2012).

18. In 2013, the Senate passed S.744-the Border Security, Economic Opportunity, and Immigration Modernization Act-with bipartisan support. Unfortunately, despite the House leadership's assertion that they are committed to passing an immigration reform bill in 2014, they still had not brought immigration legislation to the floor. In contrast to the Senate bill, House Republicans are taking a "piecemeal" approach to reforming the immigration system by moving discrete bills through the committee process. At the time of publication of this paper, five have passed out of committee, each aimed at reforming different parts of the broken U.S. immigration system.

Bibliography

American Assembly. 2003. *Keeping America in Business: Advancing Workers, Businesses, and Economic Growth.* Summary of the 102nd American Assembly. New York: American Assembly, Columbia University.

Aspen Institute. 2011. "The Price of Persistence: How Nonprofit–Community College Partnerships Manage and Blend Diverse Funding Streams." *Update: Courses to Employment* 2. February.

Bureau of Labor Statistics. 2012. Occupational Employment Projections to 2020. *Monthly Labor Review.* January.

Cappelli, Peter. 2012. *Why Good People Can't Get Jobs: The Skills Gap and What Companies Can Do About It.* Philadelphia: Wharton Digital Press.

Colborn, John. 2007. "Workforce Development and the Workforce Intermediary Function: A Discussion Primer." In *Financing Workforce Intermediaries: Working Papers,* edited by Heath Prince. Boston: National Fund for Workforce Solutions.

Government Accountability Office. 2011. *Providing Information on Colocating Services and Consolidating Administrative Structures Could Promote Efficiencies.* Washington, DC: GAO, January.

Jobs for the Future. 2004. *Workforce Intermediaries and Their Role in Promoting Advancement—Report on Advancement for Low-Wage Workers.* Boston: Jobs for the Future, January.

Manyika, James, Susan Lund, Byron Auguste, and Sreenivas Ramaswamy. 2012. *Help Wanted: The Future of Work in Advanced Economies.* McKinsey Global Institute, March.

Rubin, Jerry, Marlene Seltzer, and Jack Mills. "Financing Workforce Intermediaries." In *Workforce Intermediaries for the Twenty-First Century,* edited by Robert P. Giloth. Published in association with the American Assembly, Columbia University. Philadelphia: Temple University Press.

18

Knowing Together, Growing Together: Epistemic Communities and Equitable Growth

Chris Benner and Manuel Pastor

The great recession of 2007–2008 officially was declared over by June of 2009.[1] But economists measure recessions by changes in gross domestic product growth, while people judge the economy by job creation, and by that standard the turnaround did not come till the first quarter of 2010. Worse yet, the persistent impact of the recession on the labor market still was clearly evident in 2013, with continued high unemployment, tepid job creation, and evidence that the jobs created post-recession were disproportionately low-wage positions.[2]

While the employment data illustrate the difficulties facing the country, the economic crisis confronting us is rooted in a longer-term stagnation in economic growth as well as a sharp rise in inequality (Stiglitz 2012). Alongside this has come a broader crisis in political leadership that is linked not just to heightened partisanship but to a fragmentation in the very knowledge base that underpins public life. The result is a vicious cycle. As Harvard economist Benjamin Friedman put it, "We could be stuck in a perverse equilibrium in which our absence of growth is delivering political paralysis, and the political paralysis preserves the absence of growth."[3]

Yet there may be lessons for the nation—and the activities of workforce intermediaries—from the way in which this three-pronged crisis of low growth, high inequality, and political fragmentation varies across the country. Certain regions—what we term *just growth regions*—have shown particular resilience in the face of this economic restructuring. The reasons for their resilience are complex and often rooted in a number of structural factors, such as the nature of the sectoral mix of the regional economy, the educational level of the workforce, and the scale and role of public employment, all of which impact economic growth and the distribution of income. None of these is easy to simply will into existence. Sectoral diversity is hard to secure, educational capabilities change slowly, and local public sectors—long-suffering as the nation has moved toward more market-oriented strategies—are reeling from the impacts of the recession.

But another element may be more susceptible to action and directly relates to the activities of workforce intermediaries: the development of diverse epistemic communities. A clunky term, "epistemic community" refers to what you know and with whom you know it. In our recent research, we have found that diverse epistemic communities—diverse in both their membership and their sources of knowledge—can actually play an important role in enabling regions to sustain some degree of growth and improve social equity at a time when most regions in the country have experienced relative stagnation and/or growing inequality (Benner and Pastor 2012). This has an important implication for the role of workforce intermediaries: While certainly one of the key metrics for success involves actual placements of low-income workers, another is whether or not they create a conversation that builds a common understanding of regional economic challenges and opportunities among critical actors. In doing so, workforce intermediaries may provide critical solutions to our deeper national economic and political problems.

This chapter argues that this conversational and consensus-building role is especially critical in light of emerging shifts in the nation's economy that require regions to be resilient, flexible, and inclusive. We begin by elaborating on what we see as the three-pronged nature of our current economic crisis, highlighting the interlinked nature of the economy, inequality, and political fragmentation. We then review the experience of just growth regions, highlighting what we see as the contributions of diverse epistemic communities not just to achieving prosperity and inclusion but also to broadening civic consensus. We then offer suggestions about how workforce intermediaries can expand that civic role more effectively even while they stay focused on the initial critical issue of job opportunities, especially job opportunities for low-income workers. We conclude with some reflections on what all this might mean for a national economy and policy makers in desperate need of a new and more cohesive and coherent approach to the difficult economic, fiscal, and social challenges ahead.

Crisis and Challenge: A National Perspective

As national unemployment rates drop below 8 percent, it is more than tempting to focus on short-term fixes. But no sustainable solution will be found simply by tinkering with tax rates, spending patterns, or even job-training funds and strategies. The reason is that the downturn that manifested itself in 2008 was actually rooted in several very long-term and interrelated challenges: the economic crisis, the inequality crisis, and the political crisis.

The Economic Crisis

Figure 1: Index of U.S. Employment Change in 36 Months Following Recession Trough

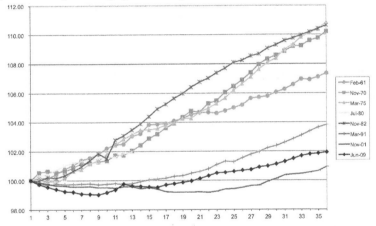

Source: U.S. Bureau of Labor Statistics, Payroll survey employment, Series CES0000000001.

The recovery following the Great Recession has been characterized as a "jobless recovery," a term that certainly resonates with both the lived experience of ordinary workers and the data trends of the last several years. However, this phenomenon of slow job growth following the end of a recession has been true for the last three economic recoveries, dating back to the early 1990s. *Figure 1* shows job growth in the United States from the end of the recession for all recoveries going back to 1961. During the recovery for the five business cycles from 1961 through the 1980s, job growth began with the end of the recession, and by three years after the beginning of the recovery, total jobs had increased by more than 7 percent in all the recoveries that lasted that long and by 10 percent in three cases. In contrast, in the three most recent business cycles starting in 1991, it took in all cases more than a year into an economic recovery for job growth to begin. By three years into economic recovery, in no case was total job growth greater than 4 percent, and in the recoveries starting in 2001 and 2009, the net jobs growth three years into the recovery was still less than 2 percent—still below peak employment prior to the beginning of the recession. Indeed, following the recession that began in March 2001, it took nearly four years for employment to recover to pre-recession levels, and current estimates are that it could take eight years to recover to pre-recession employment levels from the 2007 recession, much less match growth in the labor force.[4]

Some analysts suggest that this experience of a jobless recovery since the 1990s is the result of the increased diffusion of information technology throughout the economy. Companies are able to improve productivity and produce more with fewer people by using more machinery and computers, in the process impacting the quantity of jobs created as well as relative wages (Autor, Katz, and Kearney 2006; Brynjolfsson and McAfee 2011). This argument, however, ignores two other important bodies of evidence. The first is the widespread evidence, both in the United States and abroad, that the overall impact of technology on job levels is indeterminate—that it depends greatly on the context and on the unit of analysis. At a firm level, sophisticated use of information technology can lead to increased competitiveness and expanded job creation—as the case of Walmart clearly demonstrates—as much as it might lead to automation and job loss. At a national scale, countries with higher levels of productivity and technology sophistication demonstrably have higher growth rates, though again there are a variety of other factors, including trade patterns, exchange rates, and education policies that shape the overall relationship between technology diffusion and job creation (Bogliacino and Vivarelli 2010; C. L. Mann 2012; Mortensen and Pissarides 1998). Thus even if there is a relationship between technology diffusion and slow job growth in the United States in the decades of the 1990s and 2000s, it begs the question of why the increased productivity has not translated into greater economic competitiveness, as would be generally expected.

What is clear is that our economy is experiencing not simply a jobs shortfall but, rather, a more deeply rooted economic crisis. Overall economic growth rates in the country have declined substantially since 1970. In the decades of the 1950s and 1960s, the U.S. economy experienced average annual growth rates of more than 4 percent. This dropped to an average of 3 percent in the 1970s, '80s, and '90s. In the 2000s overall economic growth averaged only 1.57 percent a year, while in the first three years of the 2010s it averaged 2 percent annually.[5] Since the dramatic economic restructuring that began in the 1970s, it is clear that the overall U.S. economy, not just the labor market, has been underperforming.

The Inequality Crisis

Connected with the economic and jobs crisis, we also have experienced a dramatic growth in inequality. The evidence of this inequality is widespread. One of the most important indicators is evidence gathered by Emmanuel Saez and Thomas Piketty, based on data from the Internal Revenue Service, which is more accurate than U.S. Census surveys in measuring incomes at upper tiers of U.S. society. From the 1940s until the late 1970s the proportion of total income in the United States captured by the top 10 percent of income earners consistently remained in the 33 percent to 35 percent range. Starting in 1979, however, upper-income earners started gaining consistently higher proportions of total income, rising to a peak of 50 percent of total income going to the top 10 percent of income earners in 2007. Much of this was concentrated in the top 1 percent, which saw its proportion of total U.S. income rise from roughly 10 percent from the 1940s through 1981 to a high of nearly 24 percent in 2007 (Atkinson, Piketty, and Saez 2011).[6] Overall, the Gini coefficient, a measure of income inequality for wages, grew from .317 in 1987 to .340 in 2007.[7]

This inequality has many roots, including excess CEO and executive compensation at the top of the income ladder, and excess financialization, leading to outsized returns in the financial sector (Stiglitz 2012). But it also is due to stagnant and declining wages for large sectors of the workforce, with large shifts in returns to education. While real hourly wages grew an average of 2.6 percent per year between 1948 and 1973, they grew only 0.2 percent a year in the 1970s, 0.8 percent a year in the 1980s, 0.3 percent a year in the 1990s, and 0.9 percent in the 2000s.[8] For workers with less than a high school degree, wages declined more than 20 percent from 1973 to 2011, more than 7 percent for workers with only a high school degree, and nearly 5 percent for those with some college education. In 1973 these categories accounted for a full 95 percent of the labor force, and even by 2011, 66 percent of the labor force still had less than a college degree and earned wages that were lower in real terms than nearly forty years previous.[9]

The Political Crisis

One would hope that these deep crises of job creation and inequality might give rise to visionary and effective political leadership. Unfortunately, we seem to face a crisis in our political institutions that is nearly unparalleled in contemporary American politics (T. E. Mann and Ornstein 2012). While approval ratings of the president remain reasonable, the percentage of the American electorate that approve of the way Congress is handling its job has fallen dramatically in recent years.[10] One poll conducted in early 2013, following the gridlock over the so-called fiscal cliff and a particularly unproductive 112th congressional session, found that only 9 percent of respondents had a favorable opinion of Congress.[11]

Like the economic situation, this is not a recent phenomenon. Overall confidence in political institutions has declined from highs in the 1960s (with a short-lived surge following the 9/11 attacks), while voter-participation rates fell steadily over the two decades since the mid-1960s, with a brief resurgence in 1992, an uptick in 2004, and a surge in the election of President Obama in 2008. The current experience of either incremental change or political gridlock in which the nation staggers from crisis to crisis falls far short of the comprehensive and substantial steps that need to be taken to address our economic and social crisis on a scale that is really required.

Most frequently, the lack of progress is attributed to a high level of political partisanship (McCarty, Poole, and Rosenthal 2006). While the current relative unpopularity of one side of that equation could signal an opening for the agenda of the executive, taking advantage of party polarization runs the risk of feeding into and exacerbating what may be the most important underlying factor: a substantial growth in fragmentation of knowledge such that there has been a dramatic decline in agreement on basic facts needed for policy making, such as the role of taxation in economic growth, the impact of immigrants on society, and even the nature of global warming.

Part of the reason is an increase in "narrow casting" in the media: Since the 1970s, we have experienced a growing customization of media channels and fragmentation of news sources, starting first with the growth in cable television and accelerating dramatically with the growth of the Internet (Owen 2012). Readership of daily newspapers has declined across all age groups; of adults eighteen to thirty-four, fewer than 30 percent now read a daily newspaper, whether in print or on the Web.[12] Meanwhile, with the acceleration and increasing sophistication of algorithm-based customization of Internet-based information—on sites as varied as Google, Facebook, Amazon, and *The New York Times*—information that is "unwanted" is increasingly filtered out without the consumer even knowing (Pariser 2011).

We also have seen an increase in partisan and social sorting as more people seem to be moving to areas with more homogeneous political and social circumstances and thus are exposed to less diversity of opinions in their residential life as well (Chinni and Gimpel 2011). In 1976, for example, only about a quarter of America's voters lived in a county that a presidential candidate won by a landslide (20 percent of more), while in 2004 it was nearly half (Bishop and Cushing 2008). In 1970 only 15 percent of families lived in neighborhoods that were classified as either affluent or poor; by 2007 this had more than doubled, to 31 percent of families (Reardon and Bischoff 2011).

This fragmentation of information, we believe, has eroded a common base of knowledge about the very nature of the problems we face—both in the political leadership and in the broader public that elects them. Extreme examples of this fragmentation of knowledge have received substantial publicity. For example, 30 percent of Republicans said in a July 2012 poll by the Pew Forum on Religion and Public Life that they thought President Obama was Muslim—nearly double the percentage who thought so four years previous.[13] Similarly, more than a third of respondents in a 2006 survey by Ohio University believed that federal officials either assisted in the 9/11 terrorist attacks or took no action to stop them in order for the United States to go to war in the Middle East.[14] While these examples may be extremes at opposite ends of the political spectrum, we believe that the problem has a more subtle face throughout public discourse. When we can not agree on what the basic facts about the challenges are, disagreement about appropriate solutions naturally follows.

Connecting the Crises

Many observers seem to see the economic, inequality, and political crises as relatively disconnected. This implies that they could be dealt with either separately or, to the extent that they are connected, sequentially. We, in fact, think the challenge for policy makers and leaders is that these three crises are deeply interconnected.

There is emerging agreement, for example, that inequality and economic stagnation are linked. The connection between growth and inequality is familiar: Less employment means less bargaining power and thus lower wages. The relative prosperity in the latter part of the Clinton administration, for example, brought a narrowing of racial wage differentials that had not been seen since the early days of the civil rights breakthroughs. In recent years it has become more difficult to ignore the idea that inequality might itself damage economic prosperity.

The mechanisms are complex but not inaccessible. For one thing, inequality may be associated with lower demand—an aggregate gap that might be filled by a government willing to spend, although this has been problematic, given persistent deficits since the early years of President George W. Bush. Inequality also is associated with excessive financialization of the economy, particularly as the wealthy look for more creative (and more risky) ways to hold their assets. Finally, inequality is corrosive to social solidarity, creating political problems when it comes time to share either burdens or benefits (Frank 2012; Stiglitz 2012).

It stands to reason that growing inequality would be closely linked with our political crisis—and this insight seems to stand up to statistical analysis as well. In an intriguing paper, political scientist Eric Uslaner ran a series of multivariate regressions in which measures like trust and social cohesion were considered dependent variables while various measures of inequality and other control measures were entered as the independent variables (Uslaner 2012). Not only was rising inequality a significant predictor, but it explained a large share of the shifts (for example, up to a third of the decline in a generalized measure of trust between the late 1960s and the current era).

A rise in one measure of income inequality, the Gini coefficient, also was associated with a decline of faith in government institutions, as well as a fall in the sense that different racial groups share common interests. Of course, these various trends may be moving in the same direction because of an entirely different third factor common to them all, but the relationship between growing inequality and growing social distance makes intuitive sense to those who have seen the growth of gated communities, the growth of exurbia, and the continued geographic concentration of racial minorities and the re-emergence of the relative concentration of the poor (Kneebone, Nadeau, and Berube 2011).

On the other hand, the impacts of fragmentation on economic decision making are becoming increasingly clear: When everyone is so far apart in terms of both income and perspective, sensible agreements on tax policy, education investments, and industrial promotion are difficult to achieve. We need, in short, to address all three of these interlinked problems in order to make progress. And while it seems like this might be a tall order, we do not need to start from scratch: There are lessons evident in a handful of regions across the country that, over a sustained long-term period, have been able to create not only *growth* but *just growth*, which we define as expanded social inclusion as well as faster economic growth. Significantly, these regions have been overcoming the knowledge and civic fragmentation with implications that may be important for workforce intermediaries.

Crisis and Challenge: Regional Solutions

Long before the national meltdown helped to solidify the point, the notion that inequality might actually damage economic growth was gaining ground at a metropolitan scale in a growing number of regions across the country. In certain places, key metropolitan actors—including collaboratives of business, labor, civic, and community leaders—have advanced the idea that a more inclusive economic approach could actually strengthen the social consensus and human capital needed to compete in a global economy. Backing up that perspective has been a range of empirical studies, including one from the Federal Reserve that show that strategies that reduce social, geographic, and other disparities actually are correlated with broad economic success (Eberts, Erickcek, and Kleinhenz 2006; Voith 1998).

We ourselves have contributed to this literature with a series of studies on the relationship between growth and various measures of economic inequality and geographic disparity. In general, we have found that inequality dampens metropolitan growth, including in "weak market" regions, where many observers suggest that addressing issues of inclusion should take a backseat to first resuscitating a weak economy (Pastor and Benner 2008; Pastor 2006). Our argument instead is that equity concerns need to be at the front end of regional deliberations, an argument echoed recently in PolicyLink's work on the future of the American economy and demographics (Treuhaft, Blackwell, and Pastor 2011).

But if the inequality and growth dimensions are linked at the regional level, what is their relationship to the third element of political disconnection, discussed above? Under what conditions do the imperatives of fairness and the need to support economic drivers come together at the metropolitan level? What are the social and political arrangements, particularly given the lack of specifically regional government institutions, that allow this to happen in some regions and impede it in others? And what are the potential lessons for a U.S. economy seeking to stop the economic bleeding and the distributional divisions?

What Makes for "Just Growth"?

We set out to answer these formative questions in a recently completed study of *just growth* regions across the country. Utilizing a sample of the largest 192 metropolitan regions in the country, we first used a quantitative approach to identify those regions with above-median performance in terms of both economic-growth and social-equity indicators and conducted regression-style analysis to explore the demographic, political, and economic determinants behind these patterns. We then identified a set of seven regions for more in-depth case-study research in order to help identify the more subtle and detailed processes, policies, and institutional arrangements that might help explain more equitable growth (or its absence) in our metropolitan settings.

The research provides insights into both the why and the how of achieving growth with equity. On the why side—what factors explain superior performance on both growth and equity—some of our findings square with previous work in the field, while others represent both a challenge to current thinking and a reason for further research. For example, the case-study work suggests that jurisdictional fragmentation is bad for a region's economic and social health, a point previously made by urban scholar and former Albuquerque Mayor David Rusk (2001, 2003). But there are a series of other factors that emerge in both our statistical and our qualitative work: the stabilizing effect of the public sector; the generally positive impact of de-concentrating poverty; the growth-enhancing but equity-reducing impacts of having a large immigrant population; and the important role of an influential minority middle class, which we argue contributes both to a political interest in prosperity and continuing attention to fairness.

But the case studies also suggest a factor that is a bit harder to quantify precisely: the importance of efforts to create a diverse epistemic community. By this we mean conscious efforts to develop a shared understanding of the region among diverse constituencies, which seems to make a difference for blending the imperatives of equity and growth. Formally, epistemic communities are defined as like-minded networks of professionals whose authoritative claim to consensual knowledge provides them with a unique source of power in decision-making processes (Adler and Haas 1992; Haas 1992). We suggest that when such collective knowledge includes not just the "usual suspects" of urban-growth coalitions but a broader constellation of community interests and perspectives, it seems to make a difference in regional trajectories. In the various case studies, we find that creating a regional consciousness about the problems of poverty and their impacts on growth potential tends to focus attention; jurisdictional ties can help (because suburbs, for example, that are annexed realize more quickly that they cannot escape the drag on regional growth from high levels of poverty), but this can be pushed along by intentional leadership programs and other strategies for collaborative governance.

The Role of Diverse Epistemic Communities

Generating a commitment to both growth and equity in a region necessarily involves a wide diversity of people and interests. Of course, when divergent constituencies come together to determine strategies for regional development, it frequently results in conflict, not collaboration. At the root of the conflict are often not just differences in ideology or political position but more fundamental chasms in understandings of how change is made, what processes are important, and who should be involved. In essence, the conflict is rooted in people having different information and valuing differing knowledge in shaping their positions.

By taking this view, we do not mean to underrate the importance of ideology or partisanship. Business leaders often are deeply committed to an economic worldview in which labor unions slow growth, regulation is an impediment, and fairness is an afterthought to be taken up in one's charitable spare time. In contrast, community and labor leaders may be steeped in a framework where the economy is a site of exploitation, protection against insecurity is essential, and economic growth is someone else's concerns. Conflicts can deepen when political entrepreneurs jump into the stew, seeking to advance their own partisan interests by fueling divisions in the pursuit of short-term gain—something done by activists on both sides of the aisle.

Nor do we have a simple view that collaboration is a solution to all our problems. We understand that we can be read that way: In a very effective sympathetic critique of our work and that of others, Lester and Reckhow (2012) suggest that regional progress on equity, particularly in light of generally weak metropolitan governance structures, should really be seen as advancing through a series of policy skirmishes between various actors. This is also the underlying perspective of Amy Dean and David Reynolds (2009), who argue that more inclusive growth will come only through the strengthening of central labor councils and the emergence of community-labor coalitions.

But we do not think that our notion is free of conflict; in fact, what we are suggesting is that there are ways to locate conflict at a "table" where the basic facts will be undisputed even as policies and strategies are under debate. And we come to this not because of an a priori belief but, rather, because of a process of discovery in our research effort.

Indeed, this notion emerged as we looked at a set of case studies that were actually chosen using an entirely quantitative approach. We then went into the field hoping to uncover a set of key structural factors that might be moved for better outcomes; what we found instead was that in our more successful case-study regions there had been some process or organization that brought people from widely different constituencies together and helped them overcome differing perspectives and knowledge bases. This did not mean that conflict disappeared. Rather, regional leaders seemed to have an appreciation for and acceptance of a wide range of diverse perspectives and a sense that, while they may not necessarily agree with those other viewpoints, those viewpoints were based on valid knowledge and that the future of the region in some way involved accommodating the diversity of priorities and perspectives.

We will admit to being initially confused by the role of political and governance process; we both tend to lean to economic explanations, so the idea that people just talking actually made a difference was comforting in one sense (ideas do matter!) and discomforting in another (how do you name and measure this element?). We eventually came to describe what we were seeing as the construction of *diverse epistemic communities*. Haas (1992) describes an epistemic community as a group of people who have:

(1) a shared set of normative and principled beliefs, which provide a value-based rationale for the social action of community members; (2) shared causal beliefs, which are derived from their analysis of practices leading or

contributing to a central set of problems in their domain and which then
serve as the basis for elucidating the multiple linkages between possible
policy actions and desired outcomes; (3) shared notions of validity; that
is, intersubjective, internally defined criteria for weighing and validating
knowledge in the domain of their expertise; and (4) a common policy enterprise; that is, a set of common practices associated with a set of problems
to which their professional competence is directed, presumably out of the
conviction that human welfare will be enhanced as a consequence. (Haas
1992, p. 3)

How do epistemic communities form? Haas argues that the major dynamics are
centered on uncertainty, interpretation, and institutionalization. Conditions of
uncertainty exist when actors must make decisions without adequate information
or knowledge about the context of their decisions, or when they are unable to accurately predict the outcomes of different courses of action. This can lead them
to seek out other sources of information and knowledge. Since outcomes depend
on the actions of multiple different actors, and choices will be shaped by others'
choices, there also is a process of collective interpretation of these new forms of
information and knowledge, including efforts to further estimate possible consequences of different actions.

These processes of interaction often are institutionalized when the need for
collective interpretation and knowledge generation results in the need for repeated
interactions over extended periods of time. One variant of the model suggests that
hybrid groupings wind up pulling together both experts and laypeople, reducing
the privileged position of one and incorporating the real-world insights of the other
(Irwin and Michael 2003; Chilvers 2008). Ultimately, the generation of epistemic
communities helps people to develop a common language and cognitive frames that
allow them to communicate effectively and share knowledge (Hakanson 2005). Finally, it is important to recognize that, while the notion of epistemic communities is
linked with some kind of common policy enterprise, these enterprises are not limited to formal legislative or policy processes. As Adler and Haas (1992, p. 374) put
it, "the policy ideas of epistemic communities generally evolve independently, rather
than under the direct influence of government sources of authority."

Conversation and Community

The processes by which such epistemic communities are formed in any region, how they develop their policy agendas, and how they articulate with governmental structures are complex. Furthermore, the specific outcomes of such
epistemic communities undoubtedly will be shaped by the character and diversity
of perspectives of people involved in these processes. Fully understanding such

processes would require substantially more in-depth research than we were able to conduct in this project. But we did find some intriguing evidence of the formation of diverse epistemic community formation in the activities of particular organizations and policy processes in several of the regions we studied.

In Nashville, for example, Leadership Nashville deliberately selects participants who represent the diversity of races, religions, ages, political persuasions, and geographic location of residents of the Nashville region. Over a yearlong process, the organization brings leaders from these various constituencies together to talk about a wide range of issues and processes shaping the region. The goal is not to solve these problems but simply to build channels of communication between various leaders and to develop a common understanding of issues facing the region. Each year a new set of leaders is selected, but interaction with previous cohorts occurs through the activities organized for each year's cohort as well as through collective alumni events.

At the time we visited, Leadership Nashville had been operating for thirty-three years and more than twelve hundred people had gone through the program, with more than 80 percent still living in Nashville. While Leadership Nashville makes a point of not taking stands on public issues, and thus the organization itself does not serve as a forum for developing specific solutions to regional problems, the discussions that occur during the program and between participants and alumni create new policy ideas that may be realized through other venues. Furthermore, alumni interact with one another in multiple other regional forums and organizations, and their experience in Leadership Nashville undoubtedly helps facilitate communication and knowledge sharing in those other forums as well.

The Jacksonville Community Council Inc. (JCCI) is another example that has played a prominent role in building cross-constituency communities. Since 1975 JCCI has brought together diverse constituencies to address a broad range of issues: everything from teenage pregnancy to mass transit to air quality to racial relations to incentives for economic development.[15] Again, JCCI has a very deliberate process for selecting a diverse group of people to be part of its "study committees," who then meet weekly during a six- to nine-month process to gain a deeper understanding of the issue under consideration and recommend solutions. The process is driven by consensus, thus requiring detailed discussions to help reconcile differing interpretations of information and finding solutions that, if not equally supported by all participants, are at least acceptable to all involved. Again, this process occurs outside of formal policy channels or governmental authority, involving citizen representatives and not elected officials. We would argue that another factor that has prompted cohesion here is the fact that Jacksonville is one of the few American cities that have consolidated their city and county governments.

In Kansas City, another metropolitan area with positive metrics in achieving equity and growth, we did not uncover any similar organization that played an explicit role in building communication and conceptual understandings across multiple constituencies. In fact, several key informants described the undue influence on regional policy making of a few key private-sector business and labor leaders; at the time of our visit, the African American female president of the Greater Kansas City Central Labor Council, Bridgette Williams, had just been appointed to the board of directors of the Greater Kansas City Chamber of Commerce. But in the absence of a JCCI or Leadership Nashville-type organization, the Mid-America Regional Council (MARC) played an important role in building a collaborative regional epistemic community, a role not always played by a metropolitan planning organization.

MARC is quite unusual in the range of regional issues it addresses. Most metropolitan planning organizations (MPOs) deal only with transportation planning, as required by federal transportation policy. A few exemplary MPOs link transportation planning with land-use planning in an effort to limit sprawl and improve the urban form. MARC, in contrast, has a large number of departments and programs, including early-childhood education and services for the aging, public safety and emergency services, environmental programs and community development, a health care initiative and, until 2012, even a department of international affairs.

In 2000 MARC initiated a regional indicators project—very similar to the type of indicators work that JCCI has done as well—and this was followed quickly by a prominent Citistates report and Brookings study on the region (Brookings Institution 2002; Johnson and Peirce 2002). All of these publications, and the processes they involved, help develop a common understanding of the problems and future fate of Kansas City as being rooted in regional dynamics and regional solutions. The Citistates report seemed to have been influential. Originally published in the newspaper—as most Citistates reports are—it ensured that the findings were shared in a broad community of civic leaders, not just within certain academic or policy circles. And it is striking that Kansas City and MARC are the recipients of one of HUD's Sustainable Community Initiatives grants and that the collaborative team they have put together includes business leaders, city and regional planners, and community organizers from the People Improving Communities through Organizing (PICO) National Network.

We also found interesting gaps in the places that had done less well at achieving growth with equity. Denver, for example, had been able to achieve remarkable consensus on tying together the region with a light-rail system, but there were fights about community benefits agreements and a weak voice for labor, a pattern consistent with the area's up-and-down economic pattern. Sacramento had actually launched an award-winning Blueprint planning process through its Council of Governments in the 2000s, but it did not lift up equity till late in the process. That decision was illustrated both by who was at the table and by the indicators on the distribution of opportunities as well.

Cleveland was the most fragmented of our regions, and it also was the worst performer. (Indeed, it was included because it was an in-state contrast to Columbus, an Ohio city where the power to annex had helped to produce less division between city and suburb.) On the other hand, the Cleveland metro region had initiated the Fund for Our Economic Future, an innovative effort that came together in 2003 (and more formally in 2004) as local philanthropies realized that the need to restore economic competitiveness in northeast Ohio was fundamental to their shared charitable missions. Of course, in keeping with Cleveland traditions of disconnection, the biggest funder eventually pulled out, although the fund continues to operate at a more modest level.

There were great variances in other factors in the case studies, but it is this qualitative feature that intrigued us. And we have begun to notice that this notion of an epistemic community plays out in other arenas as well. For example, in a study of the relative receptivity of regions to new immigrants, Pastor and Mollenkopf (2012) find that a more cohesive regional business class can play an important role. Henton, Melville, and Walesh (2003, 1997) argue that this sort of collaboration by what they call "civic entrepreneurs" is critical to economic growth. The question in this volume is what this broad framework regarding knowledge communities might mean for the specific field of workforce development.

Workforce Development and Just Growth

While workforce intermediaries were not a particular focus of our research on *just growth*, they did emerge in several of the case studies as a key ingredient in the regional mix. This was true in Jacksonville, where the local community college system evidenced particular flexibility and sensitivity to local industry needs, and in Kansas City, where the workforce-development system had become deeply integrated into hiring and training programs of major regional employers. We discuss these efforts briefly below, then turn to two more general issues: What makes for a good workforce intermediary in this changing economy, and what is the role of workforce intermediaries in prompting the sort of regional conversations that lead to the creation of shared concerns and strategies?

What Works So People Can Work?

Given the evident ability of our just-growth regions to link prosperity and inclusion, we were curious about the set of institutions—workforce intermediaries—that might be most effective at making that link real to ordinary worker and employers.

What we found to some extent confirmed what is familiar to those who have either labored in or studied this field: It is key that workforce developers have a dual focus, resolving the needs of both businesses and job seekers. Since most workforce-development initiatives have emerged from a history of focusing on job seekers, it is building ties with the private sector that has been most challenging.

In Jacksonville, WorkSource, the regional workforce investment board, was described as working "hand in glove" with the private sector.[16] Its collaborations also include the community college system; the president of the Florida Community College at Jacksonville (FCCJ) serves on the board of the chamber of commerce. Moreover, FCCJ is vigilant about insuring that its degree programs match up with industry needs, annually reviewing its degree offerings, funding labor-market research to that end, and including forty-seven industry-based standing advisory committees to provide advice in the curriculum-development process. As a result, between 2001 and 2008, FCCJ deactivated 188 existing degrees that were not geared toward meeting current labor-market needs and activated 156 new degrees. Better yet, while about 20 percent of degrees granted by the institution in 2001 were in high-wage, high-skill occupations, the figure climbed to 60 percent by 2008.[17]

The Jacksonville Chamber of Commerce (through the Cornerstone Economic Development Partnership), WorkSource, and FCCJ also have been working in secondary schools to develop Career Academies—schools within high schools that offer focused technical skills in particular industries.[18] Academies operate through small learning communities that combine rigorous academics with career-specific skills meant to match up with the region's industries, including health care, information technology, finance, and aviation. Since being launched in 2001, the region has developed more than forty Career Academies in which nearly eight thousand high school students participate each year (CREDP 2010).

Workforce-development programs in the Kansas City region also are exemplary, producing effective programming that helps meet the skilled workforce training needs of business. One example of workforce innovation in the region was the creation in 1994 of the Business and Technology Center through an initiative of the region's Metropolitan Community Colleges. The center was formed as an economic- and workforce-development arm, to provide consulting, development, and training for Kansas City–area businesses and organizations. In 2002 the center expanded its facilities, nearly tripling in size, and became a full college, the Business & Technology Campus (BTC). BTC has developed strong partnerships with prominent area employers, including Harley-Davidson, Honeywell, Sprint, Ford Motor Company, and others. The partnership with Harley-Davidson, for example, had resulted, at the time of our interview, in an eleven-year relationship of contract training in which Harley-Davidson donated custom machinery to make the BTC machine-tools shop state-of-the-art, and counted on BTC not only to provide training but also to handle job applications and other employment assessments (e.g., team-building skills and basic math and reading abilities) to the point that reportedly all new hires at Harley-Davidson were coming directly from BTC training programs.[19]

The development of a self-sustaining call center by BTC in collaboration with regional businesses is another example that shows the ability of the region to adapt for new growth with an eye for inclusivity. In the 1990s the project was developed to both fill a gap in industry—as a major location for call centers, there was a shortage of customer-service representatives in the region—and provide jobs for economically and educationally disadvantaged individuals (Ream et al. 2001). AT&T, Lucent Technologies, Gateway, Sprint, DST, Citibank, and the Missouri departments of Workforce Development and Elementary and Secondary Education contributed equipment and funding for the state-of-the-art call-center training facility at the BTC. Training dollars were provided by the private, independent Full Employment Council (for welfare participants) and the Missouri Department of Elementary and Secondary Education. Workers with barriers to employment were sent by Project Refocus and the Kansas Private Industry Council, with both organizations contributing funds as well. With such a network of participants and stakeholders, the Call Center Training Program at the BTC became well-known and received awards, including the 1999 American Association of Community Colleges/U.S. Department of Labor Workforce Development Award and the Vision 2000 Model of Excellence Award (Ream et al. 2001).

Kansas City also has paid attention to training for manufacturing and was one of thirteen regions in 2005 to receive a first-generation grant from the Department of Labor's Workforce Innovation in Regional Economic Development program. Meanwhile, Project Prepare is a pre-apprenticeship program to draw more minorities and women into construction work that is a joint effort of the Full Employment Council, Kansas City-area unions and contractors, the Kansas City AFL-CIO, and the city.[20] This attention to growth and equity is of a piece with the larger findings offered earlier.

Workforce Intermediation for a New Economy

What does all this mean for the current era? We see several implications that we might call technical: the need to better forecast employment and employer needs, the imperative of wedding the goals of creating jobs and decreasing inequality, and the necessity of building flexibility into workforce systems. But we think the biggest and most important implication may be what initially seems to be the vaguest: the need for workforce developers to see themselves as creating a conversation about the future.

On the technical front, forecasting employment needs is crucial but, we acknowledge, difficult. The economy seems to have been turned upside down by the financial crises and consequent restructuring; once solid sectors, such as construction, only now are limping back to duty even as areas, like manufacturing, that were once thought long gone are staging a modest resurgence. Getting data-analytic systems in place, particularly to avoid having all regions decide that "meds and eds" are for them, will be crucial (Cowell, Gainsborough, and Lowe 2013). Intermediaries need to have both their own capacities to generate research and reliable partners with which to work.

It also is important to provide a better ranking of which strategies will generate job growth and which strategies will actually address underlying inequalities. Jacksonville sought to attract employers, but it made an early decision to confine its attraction efforts to companies paying at least 15 percent above the state's average wage (Benner and Pastor 2012, p. 95). In Los Angeles, the labor-affiliated Los Angeles Alliance for a New Economy has taken an approach more rooted in upgrading jobs that are currently in the region or slated to expand. Assisting this new focus should be the emerging research suggesting that this is better for sustainable economic growth over time, a finding that provides some cover for being selective, even in more difficult times.

A third key technical element is building flexibility into workforce systems. It is often said that "change is a constant" is the new normal, but that's not quite right; change is, in fact, accelerating. Given this, we have to understand the role of workforce intermediaries as going beyond their widely understood contributions to economic growth and job access, particularly for disadvantaged populations. It will be increasingly important that intermediaries are prepared to continually retrain incumbent workers as well as those moving in and out of employment paths as they shift jobs and even careers. In the future, success will not be defined as successful placement per se but, rather, as creating the sort of skills and platforms that will keep workers moving at the speed of the economy.

But adding to the tasks ahead will be a more conscious recognition of the role of the workforce developer as civic leader and convener. This will require a set of discursive and organizing skills as the underlying task is to create a conversation about the future that will lead to a shared understanding—in other words, an epistemic community. This means that the quality of the conversations and the depth of relationships between actors will be metrics that should be included with more standard measures, such as the number of jobs created/retained, wage rates secured, and disadvantaged workers hired—not because these other data are not important but because the only way to get there sustainably is to promote conversation as well as competition.

Grappling with new economic realities requires a new set of tables, and workforce intermediaries can play this role. The NOVA employment and training agency in Silicon Valley, for example, has been exemplary in its ability to link knowledge generation with collaboration partnership development. NOVA invests substantially in detailed analysis of labor-market trends—seven major regional industry studies in 2011 alone, for example—informed by available government data, customized surveys, and in-depth qualitative interviews. These studies become resources for employers in the industries as much as for job seekers and training providers, helping to furnish the common base of knowledge for developing coordinated workforce strategies.

The celebrated Project QUEST in San Antonio also illustrates the importance of this combination of knowledge generation and convening role. The focus there is on in-depth occupational analysis in a smaller number of targeted industries. This occupational analysis—helping to identify the factors driving change and how best to respond—has cemented relationships with targeted area employers and in some cases contributed to employers' restructuring positions to make them more attractive to area workers. With deep roots in poor neighborhoods, training partnerships with multiple campuses of the Alamo Community College District, and a diverse set of funding relationships, Project QUEST helps stitch together a collaborative response to area economic and workforce challenges. Perhaps not coincidentally, San Antonio also emerges as a just-growth region in our quantitative analysis.

Philanthropic organizations can play an important role in the process of convening the diversity of actors required for collaborative knowledge generation. SkillWorks in Boston, discussed in Chapter 7 in this book, provides one of the most well-developed examples. Launched in 2003 with initial funding from the Boston Foundation and a number of other regional foundations, along with support from the City of Boston, the initiative combines public-policy advocacy and capacity building with the support of workforce partnerships in specific industries. This has served as a focus point for unions, employers, community organizations, foundations, and government to come together to understand and address economic and workforce challenges in the region. And it was an important inspiration and model for the National Fund for Workforce Solutions (mentioned below and highlighted in Dyer et al., Chapter 5, and Popovich, Chapter 12). While we believe that the challenge of measuring and valuing knowledge sharing as highly as formal job placement remains, the flexibility afforded through foundation-funded initiatives can be important in providing the institutional infrastructure necessary for such collaborative knowledge sharing to happen.

Indeed, we note with approval the emphasis on collaborative approaches to workforce intermediaries in the evaluation reports of the National Fund for Workforce Solutions. Highly effective partnerships in the initiative were more likely to be employer-led and involve more employers, including having multiple employer "champions" who contributed financially to the training, along with joint labor-management partnerships. They were more likely to include both job-seeker and incumbent-worker training, and many had forged relationship with community colleges in their training work (Baran et al. 2012).

Project QUEST's work also highlights, though, one of the more difficult challenges of being an effective regional convener as a workforce-development intermediary, namely the special challenges of working with disadvantaged workers. The barriers of soft-skill shortfalls, transit dependence, and language access all are much easier to overcome with a single employer who gains a buy-in with the employee in question. Project QUEST demonstrates that it is possible to maintain a focus on disadvantaged workers while focusing on a limited number of whole sectors. But this challenge becomes even more substantial when trying to work across an entire regional economy. Clearly one way would be to combine regional economic analysis of growth poles with a particular emphasis on those sectors with career ladders and opportunities for less-advantaged residents. But deep engagement with private-sector leaders also may require focus on sectors of primarily high-skilled workers and more restricted points of entry. Understanding how regions are successfully able to navigate these tensions remains an area of our continued research.

Working Regionally, Thinking Nationally

The nation stands at an economic and political crossroads. We have been through the most dramatic downturn since the Great Depression, the sharpest rise in inequality since the Roaring Twenties, and what seems to be the sharpest ideological and party disputes in modern times. All these crises, we have suggested, are connected: The rise in inequality damaged growth and polarized politics, low growth has exacerbated these tensions by restricting resources, and political fragmentation has made it challenging to settle on a strategy that will work to recover both our jobs and our hopes.

So why raise these national issues in a chapter on regional workforce development, and why think that regional workforce efforts have anything to contribute to the national debate? Part of the reason is the increasing understanding of the importance of metropolitan regions to the overall future of the U.S. economy, as well as our attempts to address lived inequality (Brookings Institution 2010;

Pastor, Lester, and Scoggins 2009). Regions are in some sense "the factories of the twenty-first-century economy," in part because we believe that workers will understand that a one-company or one-career work life is unlikely and so will increasingly choose where to live and then navigate across multiple jobs in that locale (Benner 2002).

But metropolitan regions may be the hope for more democratic discourse in the twenty-first century as well. The disconnection at the national level may be profound, but local actors are realizing that they need to collaborate across municipal boundaries and that the way they bridge the discursive gap at the metropolitan level could better inform national conversations about America's future. As we have noted, our research on regions that better marry equity and growth over the long haul was initially driven by regression analysis, and our case-selection process was quantitative in nature; we asked who was doing better on both measures and then went to find out why. We thus were unprepared for what seemed like a nearly anthropological finding in the field: Where equity and growth come together, it is partly because a mind-set has changed in a way that allows regional actors to agree on a basic understanding of regional challenges and issues even as they may disagree on the particulars of solutions.

This is clearly a needed direction to resolve the political paralysis gripping Washington, and regional workforce-development initiatives fit it, because they actually have to play this bridging role all the time. Firms generally want available workers with training costs that are offset on others to the extent possible, along with compensation packages as low as are feasible and no special costs that might be incurred by taking on less advantaged, skilled, or prepared workers. Employees want higher wages, of course, while labor unions want more control over the training and work processes, even as community groups attempt to provide a leg up to those who often face discrimination in the hiring process. Out of this conflict is expected to come a "win-win," and it is the role of the workforce developer to find the sweet spot the market may miss and use this to make all the actors feel that a solution has been found.

To do this, workforce developers and regional workforce collaboratives have to think about how the needs of many can be crafted into a shared plan for regional development. Identifying growth sectors and building career ladders still is central to workforce development, but practitioners increasingly need to promote and sustain conversations among key actors so that they can better understand the metro region's economic conditions and future. As such, they have a discursive and organizing role in building a more resilient, flexible, and inclusive region.

This broader perspective about the common good is exactly what is missing in the national debate, and it can and should be modeled up from this regional work. Of course, saying it *should* happen is easy; envisioning *how* it might happen is more complex. Economic life may be increasingly occurring at a regional level, but ultimately we need to address the broad trends of slow growth and widening gaps that affect all of America's regions.

The dialogue that is needed to deal with our multi-dimensional crisis is unlikely to be led by formal institutions of government, where the incentives for partisan grandstanding and a "50 percent plus 1" framework for constructing "thin" coalitions seem to hold sway. But it's not just polarized politics and a creaky structure of governance that stand in the way: we are unlikely to make progress as long as key actors gaze warily at each other across an epistemic chasm. Growing together will require knowing together, and researchers as well as workforce developers will need to think more consciously about how information about our economic conditions can be used to stir a more productive, collaborative and strategic conversation about our national future.

Notes

1. At least according to the criteria developed by the National Bureau of Economic Research's Business Cycle Dating Committee that determine such things. http://www.nber.org/cycles.html.
2. http://www.nelp.org/index.php/content/content_about_us/tracking_the_recovery_after_the_great_recession.
3. Quoted in Lowrey (2013).
4. The Center for Economic and Policy Research estimated that, when measured against population growth and labor-force participation rates, the jobs deficit in 2013 was more than eight million, and that the gap would be unlikely to be filled in the next decade. See http://www.cepr.net/index.php/blogs/cepr-blog/back-to-full-employment.
5. Source: U.S. Bureau of Economic Analysis annualized quarterly GDP growth rates.
6. For updated data, see http://elsa.berkeley.edu/~saez/atkinson-piketty-saezJEL10.pdf.
7. http://stateofworkingamerica.org/chart/swa-wages-table-4-2-average-hourly-pay-inequality.
8. Ibid.
9. http://stateofworkingamerica.org/chart/swa-wages-table-4-14-hourly-wages-education.
10. http://www.pollingreport.com/CongJob1.htm.
11. In fact, when asked if they have a higher opinion of Congress or a series of unpleasant or disliked things, voters said they had a higher opinion of root canals, NFL replacement refs, political pundits, used-car salesmen, and even cockroaches, head lice, and colonoscopies than they did of Congress. http://www.politicusa.com/congress-popular-lice-popular-meth-labs-lindsey-lohan.html.
12. http://www.naa.org/Trends-and-Numbers/Readership/Age-and-Gender.aspx.
13. http://www.pewforum.org/Politics-and-Elections/Little-Voter-Discomfort-with-Romney%E2%80%99s-Mormon-Religion.aspx.

14. http://newspolls.org/articles/19604.
15. A full list of more than thirty years of reports and studies conducted through JCCI's broad consultative process is available at http://www.jcci.org/projects/projectreports. aspx#!library/c6o2.
16. Interview, July 21, 2008, with Jerry Mallot, executive vice president, Jacksonville Chamber of Commerce, by C. Benner and R. Ramirez.
17. Interview, July 23, 2008, with Jim Simpson, associate vice president for workforce development at FCCJ, by C. Benner and R. Ramirez.
18. http://www.careeracademies.net (accessed March 20, 2011).
19. Interview, July 2, 2008, with Gary Sage, executive director of economic and resource development, business and technology, Metropolitan Community College, by C. Benner and R. Ramirez.
20. http://www.thepowerpartners.com/training.

Bibliography

Adler, E., and P. Haas. 1992. "Epistemic Communities, World Order and the Creation of a Reflective Research Program." *International Organization* 46(1): 367–390.

Atkinson, A.B., T. Piketty, and E. Saez. 2011. "Top Incomes in the Long Run of History." *Journal of Economic Literature* 49(1): 3–71. doi:10.1257/jel.49.1.3.

Autor, D. H., L. F. Katz, and M. S. Kearney. 2006. "The Polarization of the U.S. Labor Market." *American Economic Review* 96(2): 189–194. doi:10.1257/000282806777212620.

Baran, B., S. Michon, S. Teegarden, L. Giordono, and K. Lodewick. 2012. *National Fund Principles: Collaborative and Partnership Achievements, Fourth Annual National Evaluation Report*. Boston: National Fund for Workforce Solutions. http://www.nfwsolutions.org/ sites/nfwsolutions.org/files/Fidelity%20Report%2010%2017%2012.pdf.

Benner, C. 2002. *Work in the New Economy: Flexible Labor Markets in Silicon Valley*. Oxford, UK, and Malden, MA: Blackwell.

———— and M. Pastor. 2012. *Just Growth: Inclusion and Prosperity in America's Metropolitan Regions*. New York: Routledge.

Bishop, B., and R. G. Cushing. 2008. *The Big Sort: Why the Clustering of Like-Minded America Is Tearing Us Apart*. Houghton Mifflin Harcourt.

Bogliacino, F., and M. Vivarelli. 2010. *The Job Creation Effect of R&D Expenditures*. SSRN Scholarly Paper No. ID 1549204. Rochester, NY: Social Science Research Network. http://papers.ssrn.com/abstract=1549204.

Brookings Institution. (2002). Growth in the Heartland: Challenges and Opportunities for Missouri. Washington, DC: Brookings Institution. Retrieved from http://www. brookings.edu/reports/2002/12metropolitanpolicy_program.aspx.

————. 2010. *State of Metropolitan America: On the Front Lines of Demographic Transformation*. Washington, DC: Brookings Institution. http://www.brookings.edu/metro/ stateofmetroamerica.aspx.

Brynjolfsson, E., and A. McAfee. 2011. *Race Against the Machine: How the Digital Revolution Is Accelerating Innovation, Driving Productivity, and Irreversibly Transforming Employment and the Economy*. Cambridge, MA: Digital Frontier Press.

Chilvers, J. (2008). Environmental Risk, Uncertainty and Participation: Mapping an Emergent Epistemic Community. Environment & Planning A, 40, 2990–3008.

Chinni, D., and J. Gimpel. 2011. *Our Patchwork Nation: The Surprising Truth About the "Real" America*. New York: Penguin.

Cowell, M., J. Gainsborough, and K. Lowe. 2013. *Homogenized Diversity: Economic Visions in the Great Recession*. Building Resilient Regions Working Paper. MacArthur Foundation Network on Building Resilient Regions, University of California, Berkeley. http://brr.berkeley.edu/wp-content/uploads/2013/05/Cowell-et-al..pdf.

Dean, A., and D. B. Reynolds. 2009. *A New New Deal: How Regional Activism Will Reshape the American Labor Movement*. Ithaca, NY: ILR Press.

Eberts, R., G. Erickcek, and J. Kleinhenz. 2006. *Dashboard Indicators for the Northeast Ohio Economy: Prepared for the Fund for Our Economic Future, Working Paper 06-05*. Cleveland: Federal Reserve Bank of Cleveland. http://www.clevelandfed.org/Research/Workpaper/2006/wp06-05.pdf.

Frank, R. H. 2012. *The Darwin Economy: Liberty, Competition, and the Common Good [New in Paper]*. Princeton University Press.

Haas, P. 1992. "Introduction: Epistemic Communities and International Policy Coordination." *International Organization* 46(1): 1–35.

Henton, D., J. G. Melville, and K. A. Walesh. 2003. *Civic Revolutionaries: Igniting the Passion for Change in America's Communities*. John Wiley & Sons.

———. 1997. *Grassroots Leaders for a New Economy: How Civic Entrepreneurs Are Building Prosperous Communities*. San Francisco: Jossey-Bass.

Irwin, A., & Michael, M. (2003). Science, Social Theory & Public Knowledge. Philadelphia, PA: McGraw-Hill International.

Johnson, C. W., & Peirce, N. R. (2002). Many Communities, One Region. (four-Part Series). Kansas City Star, Jan. 6, 13, 20, 27, 2002.

Kneebone, E., C. Nadeau, and A. Berube. 2011. *The Re-Emergence of Concentrated Poverty: Metropolitan Trends in the 2000s*. Washington, DC: Brookings Institution. http://www.brookings.edu/~/media/research/files/papers/2011/11/03%20poverty%20kneebone%20nadeau%20berube/1103_poverty_kneebone_nadeau_berube.

Lester, T. W., and S. Reckhow. 2012. "Network Governance and Regional Equity: Shared Agendas or Problematic Partners?" *Planning Theory*. doi:10.1177/1473095212455189.

Lowrey, A. 2013. "The Low Politics of Low Growth." *New York Times*. January 12. http://www.nytimes.com/2013/01/13/sunday-review/the-low-politics-of-economic-growth.html?ref=annielowrey&_r=0.

Mann, C. L. 2012. *Information Technology Intensity, Diffusion, and Job Creation*. Boston: Brandeis University. http://www.brandeis.edu/departments/economics/RePEc/brd/doc/Brandeis_WP46.pdf.

Mann, T. E., and N. J. Ornstein. 2012. *It's Even Worse Than It Looks: How the American Constitutional System Collided with the New Politics of Extremism*. Basic Books.

McCarty, N., K. T. Poole, and H. Rosenthal. 2006. *Polarized America: The Dance of Ideology and Unequal Riches*. Cambridge, MA: MIT Press.

Mortensen, D. T., and C. A. Pissarides. 1998. "Technological Progress, Job Creation, and Job Destruction." *Review of Economic Dynamics* 1(4): 733–753. doi:10.1006/redy.1998.0030

Owen, D. 2012. "Media Consolidation, Fragmentation and Selective Exposure in the USA." In *The SAGE Handbook of Political Communication*, edited by H.A. Semetko and M. Scammell. SAGE Publications.

Pariser, E. 2011. *The Filter Bubble: How the New Personalized Web Is Changing What We Read and How We Think*. New York: Penguin.

Pastor, M. 2006. "Cohesion and Competitiveness: Business Leadership for Regional Growth and Social Equity." In *Competitive Cities in the Global Economy*, pp. 393–406. OECD Publishing. http://www.oecd-ilibrary.org/urban-rural-and-regional-development/competitive-cities-in-the-global-economy/cohesion-and-competitiveness-business-leadership-for-regional-growth-and-social-equity_9789264027091-16-en.

———— and C. Benner. 2008. "Been Down So Long: Weak Market Cities and Regional Equity." In *Retooling for Growth: Building a 21st Century Economy in America's Older Industrial Areas*, edited by R.M. McGahey and J.S. Vey. Washington, DC: Brookings Institution Press.

————, T.W.Lester, and J. Scoggins. 2009. "Why Regions? Why Now? Who Cares?" *Journal of Urban Affairs* 31(3): 269–296. doi:10.1111/j.1467-9906.2009.00460.x.

———— and J. Mollenkopf. 2012. "Struggling Over Strangers or Receiving with Resilience? The Metropolitics of Immigrant Incorporation." In *Urban and Regional Policy and Its Effects, Vol. 4: Building Resilient Regions*, edited by N. Pindus, M. Wier, H. Wial, and H. Wolman. Washington, DC: Brookings Institution Press.

Reardon, S., and K. Bischoff. 2011. "Growth in the Residential Segregation of Families by Income, 1970–2009." American Communities Project of Brown University. www.s4.brown.edu/us2010/Data/Report/report111111.pdf.

Ream, J. W., Wagner, B. G., & Knorr, R. C. (2001). Welfare to work: Solutions or snake oil? New Directions for Community Colleges, 2001(116), 61.

Rusk, D. 2001. *Inside Game/Outside Game: Winning Strategies for Saving Urban America*. Washington DC: Brookings Institution Press.

————. 2003. *Cities without Suburbs: A Census 2000 Update*. Woodrow Wilson Center Press.

Stiglitz, J. E. 2012. *The Price of Inequality: How Today's Divided Society Endangers Our Future*. W.W. Norton.

Treuhaft, S., A. G. Blackwell, and M. Pastor. 2011. *America's Tomorrow: Equity Is the Superior Growth Model*. Oakland, CA: PolicyLink.

Uslaner, E. 2012. *Income Inequality in the United States Fuels Pessimism and Threatens Social Cohesion*. Washington, DC: Center for American Progress. http://www.americanprogress.org/wp-content/uploads/2012/12/Uslaner.pdf.

Voith, R. 1998. "Do Suburbs Need Cities?" *Journal of Regional Science* 38(3): 445–464. doi:10.1111/0022-4146.00102.

19

Conclusion

Maureen Conway and Robert P. Giloth

Our initial aspiration for this edited collection was to update *Workforce Intermediaries for the Twenty-first Century*, published in 2004. That book grew out of the American Assembly convening in 2003 to design more effective approaches for supporting and growing workforce or sector intermediaries and partnerships throughout the country. It included multiple perspectives on the intermediary role and how it could be better supported by public policy, philanthropy, and business. The Assembly suggested ways to expand the impact of sector intermediaries and partnerships, explored the relevance of sector strategies for lower-skilled workers, and discussed the relationship between sector partnerships and the public workforce system. The Assembly gave impetus to the formation of the National Fund for Workforce Solutions (NFWS), the Sector Skills Academy, the rigorous study of three sectoral employment programs conducted by Public/Private Ventures (P/PV), and other efforts to strengthen and further sector-based workforce partnerships.

This book, however, came to have a broader purpose. While focused largely on the past ten years, it recounts the central storyline of sector-based workforce development going back several decades (see Conway, Chapter 3). In so doing, it highlights issues related to job quality and economic development that are part of sector strategies. And it sketches the elements of the "ecological system" of the multifaceted sector workforce field.

The book raises two big questions for sector workforce development: First, how can the sector field continue to grow and adapt to new economic realities, navigate competing and complementary workforce approaches, attract and sustain workforce-related philanthropy, and negotiate today's challenging political environment? In particular, how can the sector workforce field sustain itself when neither business nor government sees the provision of sustained funding as its role? The ideas of sectoral workforce development have been positively received by both, with business leaders supportive of the idea that workforce efforts should be aligned to business needs, and a number of large federal grant-making initiatives including principles of sector practice. But financial support of sector initiatives from business has rarely been substantial, and episodic federal grants often lead to starts and stops of initiatives rather than sustained efforts. A sustainable funding model that is supportive of the best in sector practice remains elusive for the field. Second, what role, if any, does the sector workforce field play in relationship to the growing number of low-wage jobs and the unwillingness of many employers to improve job quality? Although chapter authors offer important perspectives on these two big challenges, these questions remain salient for the field going forward.

In this concluding chapter, we hope to accomplish three things. We want to celebrate what has been accomplished in building the sector-based workforce-development field, especially in the past decade. We also want to summarize and focus the challenges for the sector workforce field raised in the book. We hope this beginning list of critical challenges will serve to galvanize additional reflection and action. Finally, we want to call attention to the economic, political, and social policy trends that give us optimism about the potential for a next generation of sector-based workforce development.

Major Accomplishments of the Sector Workforce Field

The sector approach to workforce development has been widely accepted as a leading set of ideas and practices about how to deliver value for employers and job seekers and workers, the human-capital skills needed by firms to be competitive, and the skills required for career advancement. An infrastructure and set of promising practices are advancing sector strategies with a focus on policy, financing mechanisms, technical assistance, leadership development, evaluation, and communities of practice. Hundreds of workforce sector partnerships serve hundreds of thousands of workers and job seekers; the public sector has invested significant resources at local, state, and federal levels in sector workforce approaches; philanthropy has invested hundreds of millions of dollars in sector strategies over the last ten years; tens of thousands of employers have engaged in sector partnerships; and many states have adopted a sector framework for workforce development.

Two critical successes for the sector field in the 2000s were the completion of the P/PV sector study and the formation of the NFWS (see King, Chapter 11; and Dyer et al., Chapter 5). Another critical factor in promoting the adoption of the sector approach was the National Governors Association (NGA) State Sector Academy, which contributed to over half of all states supporting the approach during the past decade. Although strong non-experimental evaluations confirmed the positive impacts of sector partnerships, P/PV's randomized-control trial of three partnerships provided more rigorous evidence for their efficacy.

For its part, the NFWS provided a venture capital pool that catalyzed local funder collaboratives. Workforce and sector partnerships require "glue" money to develop collaboration among firms and educational partners, prepare and support employment pipelines, and cultivate multiple funding streams. This is the most difficult type of support to raise, and it is generally not available through public funding streams. But without these funds, sector partnerships cannot spread and expand. Many states, prominently including Pennsylvania, Washington, Massachusetts, and Michigan, supported industry-partnership programs as well as specific sector training. Federal discretionary workforce investments also supported such investments, and NFWS received federal Social Innovation Fund investments, an achievement made possible by the P/PV evaluation.

The sector approach for improving job quality also expanded in the 2000s. Cooperative Home Care Associates in the Bronx now employs more than two thousand workers, and its policy and training affiliate, the Paraprofessional Healthcare Institute (PHI), has expanded from the New York base to play a major role in crafting and advocating federal and state policies to support home health workers, focusing on wages, benefits, and career opportunities. In addition, PHI leverages its enterprise-based experience in New York and Philadelphia to work with long-term care and home health employers in several states, shaping business models and workforce-training strategies to create better jobs and improve care. More recently, the Restaurant Opportunities Centers United (ROC) has used advocacy and enterprise development to make the case for better wages and benefits in the hospitality industry (see Jayaraman, Chapter 10). Both of these sector efforts are leading actors in a larger movement on behalf of low-wage workers.

In sum, a dedicated group of practitioners, policy makers, and philanthropic investors has created a sector workforce field that contributes to regional economic competitiveness while helping workers and job seekers obtain family-supporting careers. The job is not done, but there is much to celebrate.

Nine Challenges for the Sector Workforce Field

Progress over the past decade has made sector-based workforce development a central feature of the workforce and education landscape, no longer the novel approach advocated by a few nonprofit entrepreneurs and their partners. Yet it would be misleading to conclude that all is well with the sector workforce field. The chapters in this book have identified an array of critical challenges that require attention if the sector field is to continue expanding and achieving results.

No Big Policy Win

No overarching federal policy has adopted sector-based workforce development as a key framework or component. States have moved in this direction, but many cut back investments as their budgets shrank in the economic downturn. And in addition to economic challenges, state investments can be difficult to maintain when administrations change, often leading to more instability in funding streams. Federal legislative attempts have failed or stalled, such as the Sectors Act (see Van Kleunen, Chapter 16), and budget pressures have reduced regular and flexible public funding for workforce development. Funding reductions have been partially offset by discretionary funds, which have favored sectorlike training. While discretionary funding has been helpful, its episodic nature often creates challenges for building durable relationships among industry, education providers, and other stakeholders.

Where Are the Business Champions?

The American Assembly of 2003 called for business to take the lead in supporting the spread of sector-based workforce intermediaries and partnerships. At the time, the values to business seemed clear, given the looming skills gap and skill shortages. From the vantage of ten years, recognizing the impact of the Great Recession, this hope for business leadership has floundered at best, at least at the national level. Businesses have increased engagement in regions and with local sector efforts, but they are only now becoming more of a national voice through coalitions like Business Leaders United. National business associations like the National Association of Manufacturers and the Business Roundtable issue reports documenting the skills problem but are not galvanizing a national business movement around skills and sector-based workforce development. At most, these efforts encourage business leaders to advocate for federal funding of workforce development, but business leaders often have more pressing issues to address at the federal level, such as taxes and regulation, and do not prioritize investments in building a skilled workforce.

It's difficult to imagine a major reworking of the workforce landscape without deep business engagement. It remains a question, however, as to how to generate true business engagement. Certainly one needs to keep in mind the tremendous heterogeneity of businesses; the needs of small firms are different from those of large firms, and the needs of retail health care employers are different from those of manufacturers. The goal of business engagement also may need to be examined. Should we be focused on organizing business to move a policy agenda or to address their own practices and methods for investing in their workforce? Does the answer to this question vary by industry or by firm size or by region? One step to address these questions has been CareerSTAT (see Dedrick, Chapter 4), an approach to measuring the return on investment for training of frontline health care workers that has had some success encouraging health care employers, largely hospitals in major metropolitan areas, to reconsider their own practices for investment in their workforce. But we need more ideas for deepening employer engagement and identifying new ways that business leaders can serve as champions for workforce development. The question remains at to whether it is reasonable to engage business leaders at a national level and, if so, what will it take to accomplish that?

Faulty Sustainable-Funding Assumptions

Sector practitioners and investors believed that demonstrating positive impacts and showing how replication could occur would be enough to attract more permanent business and public-sector investment. This assumption may have been overly optimistic from the outset, but it has certainly not become a reality, although there have been some successes (see Watson, Chapter 17). The sector field needs to rethink its business model for expansion and sustainability, perhaps seeking more sustainable state resources or stronger across-the-board incentives for businesses to invest in low-skilled workers.

The field also needs to consider how to balance two institutional objectives: (1) the need for more-permanent specialized education and training capacity for specific sectors and occupations and (2) the need for sector-partnership nimbleness to switch sectors or occupations when labor-market demand is low. Both are needed. Moreover, are there ways in which sectoral workforce programs can be more tightly linked to economic development and improved job-quality standards? Are new innovations in enterprise creation and support for entrepreneurship needed to stimulate demand in a sector or demonstrate new models? As this rethinking occurs, the sector field needs philanthropy to remain engaged and support innovations and ideas for addressing some of the difficult questions that the field now faces. While new models and other priorities are competing for foundation resources, the goals of sector strategies remain in sync with the mission of many foundations, and the slow rate of job creation, reduced labor-force participation, and declines in family income and economic mobility have kept the issues of jobs and skills in the forefront in philanthropy. The investment and leadership of philanthropy will be crucial to building on what has been learned over the past decade and advancing new opportunity for economically vulnerable groups. The strength of the sector field and infrastructure may falter without continued investment by philanthropy.

Dilution of Partnerships into Programs

Along with some dedicated and serious efforts to implement sector workforce approaches, we have seen some mediocre attempts. It's relatively easy to use secondary data to show employer demand, incorporate off-the-shelf training models, and rely on referral relationships rather than serious partnerships. This type of dilution happens in many fields, so it is no surprise to see it in the sector workforce field. Programs are easier to implement when there are no agreed-on, evidence-based standards. In the long run, the adoption of "best practices in the air" will translate into skepticism about the sector approach as less-than-optimal results are produced. This raises questions for the sector workforce field: What level of employer engagement do we really need to get grounded in business reality? Do we really have to work for "systems change" while also working to achieve individual-level results? Which activities need to be sustained over time, and which can be episodic in response to the ebbs and flows of real-time labor-market needs? What does all this imply for the staff and organizational capabilities needed to implement a sector strategy and manage its complexity? Finally, what group of stakeholders is responsible for the "fidelity" of workforce sector partnerships, and what is the right framework to determine "fidelity" for the sector approach?

Sector Infrastructure Stress

Diminished philanthropic support, fragmented efforts, and evolving institutional leadership have produced challenges for the sector workforce field even as it has grown and become more widely adopted. Some of this change is for the better. But now more than ever we need to seed and support sectoral workforce leadership, emphasize increased fidelity to the sector model while supporting new variations, and mobilize renewed momentum for building the sector field. While a strength in the evolution of the sector field over two decades was its relatively unplanned, entrepreneurial, networked approach, perhaps now more than ever we need more directive field planning for the future. As a part of this effort, raising up the high aspirations and necessary ingredients of the sector approach will reinforce the need for continued investment.

Need for Continued Evidence Building

Gathering evidence for effective interventions is not a one-time affair and does not always move forward in a linear fashion. Evidence building for sector workforce partnerships has been a circuitous thirty-year journey, now even more complicated by the range of initiatives that share some of the components of sector strategies. While the P/PV sector study of the mid-2000s provided breakthrough evidence, it is certainly not the last sector workforce evaluation. And there is no doubt, as the sector approach becomes more widely adopted, that evaluations will show a mix of results for a variety of reasons, including poor implementation and immature efforts, lack of fidelity, mismatch of interventions and populations, inability to provide treatment for the treatment group, and the short duration of evaluation studies. Further, evaluation results are often interpreted in a binary fashion—either "it" works or not. Given the complexity of a sectoral workforce approach, this interpretation of evaluation findings misses significant learning opportunities that could inform future work.

In addition, while evaluation methodologies are well accepted for looking at individual impacts, there are no accepted approaches for looking at systems-change efforts that attempt to take sector workforce partnership to scale. Nor is there an accepted "gold standard" approach to assessing business outcomes or contributions to economic-development goals. Progress has been made in addressing business outcomes, but often the results are shared within the context of an initiative and may seem anecdotal to those looking across the field of practice. For systems change, the methodologies will look very different from standard approaches to measuring individual-participant outcomes, and greater conversation with the research and evaluation community is needed to consider how to effectively assess and communicate progress in this area. Finally, many believe that there is interplay between these three areas of activity, yet most evaluation work addresses either worker outcomes or business outcomes but not both, and even less commonly are systems change outcomes included. The sector field should be more forthright in defining the types of evidence needed to determine more clearly "what works" and to achieve policy goals.

Competing and Complementary Approaches

The last decade has seen the proliferation of "bridge" and "career pathways" programs that have generated instructional innovation and helped to align educational offerings with industry needs, primarily within community colleges and partner institutions (see Ganzglass et al., Chapter 14). These efforts integrate basic-skills training with technical training in new ways. The evidence to date shows that obtaining one-year post-secondary education or an industry certificate can boost incomes. Bridge programs operate largely within community colleges and adult-education programs and are often part of a broader effort to boost community college graduation. Key federal agencies have agreed to emphasize integrative efforts like career pathways in their investments. While career pathways could easily fit within or contain a sector workforce strategy, they frequently operate without deep engagement of employers, focus on graduation rather than employment, and may experience the retention and graduation challenges that characterize many community colleges.

A related, complementary approach, career academies within the K-12 public education system, also have the potential for informing sector workforce development and serving as a pipeline to more advanced training and education.

Inside/Outside Tensions

A perennial challenge is the accusation that the sector workforce field has ignored the public workforce system or deliberately built a parallel system. This is a bit of a red herring, because the U.S. workforce system is made up of many components, including the Workforce Investment Act (WIA), Temporary Assistance for Needy Families, adult-education programs, community colleges, food stamp employment and training efforts, transportation programs, and affordable-housing efforts. Sector partnerships can serve to reform a system by integrating these funding streams and connecting them to expanding industry sectors and viable employment opportunities for workers and job seekers. In many cases, mainstream workforce institutions and funding streams have become key partners in the sector workforce field, and WIA discretionary funds have been used to support sectoral partnerships.

In many communities, sector partnerships and the public workforce systems have found productive ways to work together, but it also remains the case that assigning credit for partnerships and results can be contentious and can inhibit cooperation. Particularly in this era of extremely tight resources, we need a fresh conversation about how different parts of the workforce field can work together more productively to advance the sector approach in concert with the workforce-development system. In doing so, we should fashion a bold vision for the public workforce system of the future.

Growth of Low-Wage Jobs

A growing portion of new jobs require few skills and pay low wages. This pattern of low-wage job generation has grown worse coming out of the last few recessions and is projected to continue (see Osterman, Chapter 2). Some have depicted our economy as an hourglass in shape, with many high- and low-wage jobs but fewer in the middle. Others contend that the hourglass overstates the demise of "middle-skills" jobs when impending retirements and cyclical factors are considered. A key question for the sector field is whether a deep understanding of industries provides unique insights into how to improve all jobs, especially in low-wage sectors. In the 1990s, job improvement was a part of sector strategies, especially in home health care. Today hospitality has become an additional focus for this approach, and other organizations are focusing on the growing retail sector. Of course, the job-quality challenge raises controversial questions about labor organizing and policy advocacy focused on such things as the minimum wage, paid sick days, and health insurance. Workforce training cannot change the quality of jobs per se, but deep sector engagement has led to real changes in wages, career ladders, and business work environments. Further, sector workforce training has the potential to demonstrate why firms should invest in employees because of saved costs and higher productivity. The rise of low-wage work challenges the sector field more than ever to deepen engagement in sectors and develop strategies that go beyond pre-employment training and embrace public and private policy change. At the same time, changes in demand also challenge the field to revise estimates of how much "middle-skills" training is needed at a particular time and within a particular labor market to avoid the familiar trap of training for jobs that do not exist.

Eight Positive Trends for Building the Sector Field

Addressing these critical challenges will occur amid new opportunities for the sector workforce field. Some of these new opportunities are the continuation of trends that reinforced the rise of the sector field in the first place; others represent new directions and may bring in new partners and advocates. These are the kinds of opportunities for which the sector field has to be prepared to offer its advice and leadership. At the same time, ignoring the underlying challenges for the field discussed above would be a grave mistake. A solid infrastructure is a key factor for expanding the sector workforce field.

Fifteen to Twenty Million Middle-Skill Jobs

Looming shortages of skilled workers for jobs requiring so-called middle skills have served as a core justification for sector strategies since the 1990s. In 2001 the Aspen Institute released a report on these projected shortages. The report was the culmination of work by a prominent group of leaders that included Democrats and Republicans, business and labor leaders, and prominent representatives from academia, think tanks, community organizations, and the media. This report served as an intellectual framework for The American Assembly of 2003 that advocated for policies that explicitly supported workforce and sector intermediaries.[1] A variety of publications signaled the coming skill-gap crisis in 2010 as baby boomer retirements change the face of the labor market. The Great Recession has slowed this trend, but projections now show that the economy will need to fill fifteen to twenty million jobs that require some college by 2020. Shortages in some parts of the health care sector continued throughout the recession, although this varied substantially across regions, and the implementation of the Affordable Care Act will certainly shape workforce demand as new skills are needed. Post-recession skill gaps are also likely to emerge in a variety of skilled trades occupations in manufacturing, energy, transportation, and construction. Sector partnerships will be one of the answers to address this economic priority.

Adoption of Sector Job-Quality Policies

Policy changes can directly affect the quality of jobs and the success of the workforce. But they are often not recognized as policy wins for the sector field as a whole, since they often affect workers in only one sector, and these changes do not typically ease the funding constraints many sectoral workforce programs face. For example, early in the 2000s, Massachusetts offered a model for a different type of policy framework. The Extended Care Career Ladder Initiative (ECCLI) was part of a broader policy initiative that sought to improve the quality of nursing home care. ECCLI provided resources to improve training of frontline caregivers but also tied success in training to wage increases for those workers. Recently, at the federal level, PHI and other advocates have won the right for home care workers to be covered by minimum-wage and overtime protections. Previously home care agencies were able to claim the "companionship exemption" to the Fair Labor Standards Act and were therefore exempt from minimum-wage and overtime requirements. Relatedly, organizations in several cities that focus on the building trades and infrastructure investments have won agreements that tie major infrastructure and commercial revitalization projects to skills training and access to jobs for local residents. Through the use of policy vehicles like community-benefits agreements and first-source hiring agreements, such cities as Los Angeles, Milwaukee, and Washington, D.C., have shaped policy decisions about contracting and public investment in ways that direct investment toward building the skills of local residents and connecting them to opportunities. These types of policy changes can be critically important "systems changes" that improve job quality; they should be recognized and counted even as the struggle for operational funding continues.

Cradle-to-Career Movement

There is a growing movement in the United States to align education funding to support the most effective interventions promoting educational progress from "cradle to career," a pipeline to success that starts at infancy (or event with support to pregnant women) and extends to post-secondary attainment and career development in the workforce. Key actors in this movement include STRIVE, Promise Neighborhoods, and the Campaign for Grade-Level Reading. There is also more attention to early-childhood investments and community college attainment. New focus on disconnected or "opportunity" youth, those who are not in school or in the workforce, represents an attempt to get young people back in the pipeline to economic success. Many of these efforts build upon a "collective impact" approach to bring together key stakeholders and investors to achieve a few agreed-on breakthrough results. Less attention, overall, is focused on the career and workplace-learning dimensions of such pipelines, and this is where sector partnerships and the National Fund for Workforce Solutions could play an important role and contribute to a larger effort at promoting economic mobility and opportunity. These connections would also enable workforce partnerships to better understand how to align and complement public-education objectives and outcomes, potentially opening up new collaborations and investments.

Regional Economic Development

The tepid economic recovery has inspired renewed interest in regional economic development. Chief among these efforts is the Brookings Institution's Global Cities Initiative, launching in four to six cities, which focuses on increasing exports, economic innovation, reducing carbon emissions, and economic inclusion to create opportunities for minorities and women. Another set of economic-development initiatives focuses on the so-called Legacy Cities, like Detroit, that are shrinking (or "right-sizing"), as well as jump-starting new economic efforts. A recent study of the Baltimore region identified sectors that have the potential to grow and create more middle-skill jobs: manufacturing, technology, biotechnology, and logistics. Somewhere near the top of the list of key priorities in all these economic-development initiatives is an emphasis on skill building to serve new and renewing industries. New economic-development efforts by groups like Living Cities and Emerald Cities reinforce this interest in combining regional and sector economic development with sector workforce strategies. And recognition that regional equity contributes to future economic prosperity underscores the civic value of sector funding collaboratives and partnerships.

Bipartisan Advocacy for Skills Development and Business Engagement

A bipartisan interest in the American skills gap goes back at least to the 1980s with seminal national reports on education and the adult workforce. Similar bipartisan reports were published in the 2000s. Today conservative writers have expressed interest in European apprenticeship models and in vocational schools or career academies, non-college approaches to help low-skilled young adults get a foothold in the economy and move ahead. Bipartisan interest also has surfaced in the reinvigorated focus on youth employment over the past several years. And, even though many efforts to advance sector policies at the federal level have failed or stalled, there has been bipartisan interest in working more closely with firms and sectors. The question becomes how to create more of a bipartisan effort to develop a concerted "skills" agenda for business and the country in the context of apparently modest business interest at the moment and political stalemate at the national level. Benner and Pastor (Chapter 18), in their discussion of "epistemic communities," suggest that building authentic regional conversations about the economy and well-being can increase common action. We should pay more attention to the social capital built through sector partnerships and workforce funding collaboratives.

Renewed Interest in Apprenticeships

Apprenticeships are a time-honored "earn and learn" model supported financially by employers that design step-by-step career ladders and use on-the-job mentoring and skill building. In the United States, they are most prominent in the building trades, especially the unionized sector, but they have wider adoption in northern European countries like Germany. In the United States, the apprentice system is perhaps the largest unrecognized part of the workforce-development landscape and is growing in several ways. A common workforce sector partnership is the pre-apprenticeship that gets people ready for apprenticeships. These programs work primarily in the construction field, since that industry has the greatest use of formal apprenticeship training. Only now are these "bridgelike" efforts deepening their relationships with formal apprenticeships and doing more to support apprenticeship completion and success. There is also movement to expand the use of apprenticeships in other sectors, like health care and manufacturing. New advocates for apprenticeships argue that this approach is more relevant for many low-income and/or low-skilled workers than the dream of post-secondary education. Most low-income workers find it unaffordable to cut back on work in order to pursue post-secondary degrees, and long work hours often interfere with student success at the post-secondary level. Apprenticeship addresses this challenge by combining work and learning. In addition, apprenticeship offers applied-learning opportunities and often integrates academic and technical training, although most apprenticeships require a high school degree or equivalent and relevant math skills. The academic rigor of an apprenticeship should not be underestimated, and indeed there has been renewed interest in articulating apprenticeships within post-secondary institutions for college credit and potential degrees.

To date, spreading the apprenticeship approach presents a stubborn challenge in the U.S. context. Apprenticeship programs receive minimal national attention as part of the workforce system, despite their self-funding, deep employer engagement, and career outcomes. Moreover, it has proven difficult to expand the approach to other sectors, even with recent experimentation by states and regions. More could be done to expand apprenticeships, and policy makers should consider how to offer incentives to employers to work with local institutions to expand apprenticeship opportunities. Local colleges and secondary schools have played roles in preparing students for apprenticeship and certifying and articulating apprenticeship learning to credentials and degrees so that apprenticeship learning is not only immediately valuable to industry but also offers a foundation for further skills development and advancement. Local nonprofits and workforce agencies have also played important roles in supporting individuals to prepare for and access apprenticeship opportunities, and particularly in opening these opportunities to women and minority workers, who may face barriers in accessing these opportunities. Policy makers should consider support and incentives for these organizations to work with employers on the design and implementation of apprenticeship opportunities in order to develop expanded and accessible apprenticeship opportunities.

Scale and Philanthropy

Philanthropy is again concerned about a nonprofit landscape filled with "boutique" efforts that affect relatively low numbers of participants and seldom lead to systems change. Today that concern has evolved into identifying and supporting viable scaling approaches for our most promising investments. In general, this is a good idea, because it asks program designers and innovators to think about scale at the outset, not just down the line. At the same time, scale involves more than replicating specific programs; it's about systems change and adoption, policy advocacy, and building fields or industries to serve as seedbeds and infrastructures for continued expansion. The sector workforce field is a great example of scaling in all these ways, although with different levels of success. It offers many lessons about how to replicate successfully, how to build a dynamic field, and how to plan for the next generation. Several federal Social Innovation Fund (SIF) grants have recognized the sector field's achievements and provided funding for further expansion. The danger is that it may give a sense that the scaling job is done. Every metropolitan area and rural region should have multiple sector partnerships; we're a long way from that goal. The sector field could also be much more influential in telling the story of what it really takes to change systems and workforce practices to achieve its vision of scale.

Recognition of Declining Economic Mobility

While this trend does not sound all that positive, recognition of a problem helps challenge assumptions and brings new ideas to the fore. In this case, there has been a growing recognition both in the field and among the general public that economic mobility is low, and many working people are not achieving a family-supporting income. Recognizing this challenge has spurred the development of ideas for new business models that can offer opportunity for both successful businesses and good jobs. For example, the recent attention to Benefit Corporations—businesses that meet standards of social and environmental performance, accountability, and transparency—is a trend to watch. BCorps, as they are sometimes called, are evaluated on four areas, one of which is management of the workforce, including worker compensation, benefits, training, and ownership opportunities. Similarly, a renewed interest in worker cooperatives and employee stock-option plans indicates innovation in the area of not only improving workers' skills but also improving their stake in economic growth and business competitiveness. For the sector field, the opportunity to connect in a deep way to these new ideas about business formation can help the sector field truly engage with the demand side of the labor market.

An Agenda for the Next Generation of Sector Workforce Efforts

A sector workforce field or industry is in place today with interrelated parts that together are helping practices and policies expand and move forward. We believe that the sector field is at an inflection point in its development, however, and requires coordinated reflection, agenda setting, and investment if it is to continue its growth trajectory, deliver results for employers and workers and job seekers, and meet the challenges of the decades ahead. While the field has not relied on strategic plans to grow in the past, we think a change of approach is needed. In this spirit, we offer five suggestions for next steps. We hope that each will lead to a specific set of recommendations and action plans.

Convene Inside Conversations

The sector field needs to engage in focused and coordinated conversations about its present and future. Topics should include many of the issues discussed throughout this book and in this conclusion: engaging employers, strengthening policy, funding assumptions, developing standards for the model, evaluations, infrastructure, and investment. If nothing else, the field should envision the role of sector partnerships in addressing upcoming skill shortages as well as persistent job-quality challenges. A core set of the philanthropic and public-sector funders might set up a special pre-meeting at an upcoming workforce gathering. A sponsoring group for these conversations might commission a white paper on the future of the sector workforce field that picks up many of the themes recounted in this book, as well as other ideas and observations from practitioners and policy makers, so that we can have a robust conversation. A key question for the groups will be how we translate these suggestions and next steps into action. One critical next step will be engaging the public sector, education, workforce, economic development, infrastructure, and human services in a productive conversation about the role of sector strategies in overall workforce-development policy and practice.

Conduct the Next Generation of Research

In the past decade, research on the outcomes of individual participants of sector initiatives has generated compelling results. But this research also leaves a number of unanswered questions. An important question has to do with career trajectories. One of the challenges of even the best research on outcomes for participants in sector initiatives is the relatively short follow-up period. Many initiatives get individuals to better jobs but may not get them all the way to a family-sustaining income. Do individuals' earnings climb with experience, or do they remain relatively stable, or do they decline as the effect of their participation wanes? Can other kinds of services influence the likelihood of career advancement? These questions about career trajectories are critical, given the goal of helping more individuals earn a family-sustaining livelihood. And now is a good time to be thinking about them as state and federal agencies are considering how to build databases that can connect education, employment, and other information so that these questions can be addressed in a more cost-effective manner. We applaud these efforts and believe that the resulting research will offer great value to the field.

Another critical question has to do with the cost of these initiatives. Resources are scarce, and funders are rightly asking what they should expect to invest in order to achieve the outcomes they would like to see. One must acknowledge, however, that addressing this question is complicated. Looking at how one funding stream is spent or even the costs incurred by one organization often will not capture the full cost picture, since sector initiatives often are implemented in partnership with other agencies. In addition, the level of effort needed to achieve a particular outcome may change over time, given changing economic conditions and policy decisions. More research is needed to illuminate this cost picture and to set expectations about the level and type of resources needed to implement a quality sector initiative. The question of costs has received too little attention over the past decade and is too often reduced to a simplistic understanding of the cost per participant that is embedded within one funding stream. A more sophisticated understanding of the drivers of costs is needed to support an understanding of resource allocation needed for success.

Two other key research areas are in the areas of business outcomes and systems change. These needs have been previously discussed, but it is important for an outline of ongoing research needs to include them. Work has been done to assess value to business (see Conway, Chapter 3, and Dedrick, Chapter 4), but this work needs to be synthesized, expanded on, and, critically important, effectively communicated to the broad group of local-initiative leaders, public and philanthropic investors, businesses, and other stakeholders in sector strategies. Similarly, understanding the dynamic relationship between the sector strategy and the "ecosystem" of policy, industry mix, infrastructure, and other ingredients in the local economy is critical to choices about which strategies to employ in different environments and how to organize resources and efforts toward accomplishing the goals of the sector initiative. Again, some work in this arena has begun, but gaps remain, and a need for synthesis and communication in formats that are accessible to the diverse array of sector stakeholders is critical to maximizing the value of next-generation research investments.

Highlight Synergies with Career Pathways

Sector strategies identify in-demand jobs and the skills required for career advancement. Career pathways combine basic and technical skills with wraparound services that lead to certifications and stackable credentials with meaning in the labor market. We need an analysis of how these two strategies complement each other today and how they could be better aligned in the future. There is nothing wrong with using multiple strategies—with some focused inside education systems and some working more with business—but missing opportunities for synergy is a mistake in the current economic, financing, and policy environments. This exploration will also help to clarify the relationship between sector strategies and various community college reform efforts with relevance for employers and low-skilled workers. Already there are productive coalitions that bring these advocates and investors together. We should try to get more specific about how to work together.

Build Allies outside the Sector Field

Another strategic conversation is needed for a better understanding of organizations, coalitions, and movements that intersect with the sector field or could intersect under the right conditions. Again, we've mentioned many of these groups—Emerald Cities, Living Cities, Brooking's Global Cities, Legacy Cities, STRIVE, Promise Neighborhoods, and Choice Neighborhoods. The emerging bipartisan interest in skills and vocational education requires a special exploration, including stakeholders who want to expand apprenticeships. In this vein, the renewed focus on disconnected or opportunity youth who are out of school and out of work offers another intersecting set of interests and strategies. Two generation approaches to poverty and opportunity may also provide a receptive audience for learning about sector strategies. Regional equity strategies as well may include sector partnerships as a key part of a broader strategy of creating livable and competitive regions. Again, we need to start with mapping these opportunities and finding common points as well as clear differences in approach. Mapping opportunities could lead to another set of strategic cross-field conversations.

Focus on Improving Low-Wage Jobs

A key question for the sector field is whether it will re-establish relevance for the growing movement to improve the quality of low-wage jobs. While the "making good jobs from bad jobs" strategy was originally a part of the sector framework of the 1990s, many of the organizations focused on job quality have developed new networks as the sector workforce field has intensified its focus on skills and education and expanded to include a wide range of education partners. At this time, a basic question is how relevant sector training is to this process of transforming low-wage jobs and improving wages, benefits, and employer practices. There is certainly a role for training, as demonstrated by Cooperative Home Care Associates and ROC. But training for jobs that continue to leave workers with economically unstable lives is a lose-lose investment. The training does not lead to better economic outcomes for workers and families, nor does it lead to better business outcomes, since trained workers may nonetheless leave the job, and even while they remain after training, the instability in their lives can leave workers distracted by pressing life needs, limiting their ability to effectively use new skills on the job.[2] If the sector strategy in these situations does not also address questions of business models and business practices related to job quality and to business success, then the strategy is unlikely to improve business or worker outcomes. In general, sector partnerships can and should decide what kinds of firms to work with in terms of job quality and which ones to turn away unless they make changes in wages and benefits that translate into improved job retention and career advancement. But the sector field faces a dilemma similar to that faced by community development corporations in the past, when they chose to be community organizers as well as developers of projects. Many times advocacy and development and implementation just do not go together and may produce more conflict than progress. The sector field needs to have this discussion.

A Comparative Story

Workforce Intermediaries for the Twenty-first Century includes a chapter by Christopher Walker and John Foster-Bey that recounts lessons from community development with relevance for the emerging field of sector-based workforce partnerships.[3] That chapter focused on the utility and effectiveness of a national venture fund, the National Community Development Initiative (now Living Cities), as a financial mechanism for expanding and strengthening the community-development field. This community-development model inspired the formation of the National Fund for Workforce Solutions, and, as a consequence, we have seen added growth in the sector field. It is worth reflecting again, at the close of this book, on community development as a guidepost for what to anticipate next.

Community development offers an instructive story for sector-based workforce development, although there are many differences. We provide only a high-level interpretation of this rich history. Community development corporations (CDCs) emerged in the 1960s from philanthropic and War on Poverty investments and grew dramatically in subsequent decades. CDCs were seen as critical entrepreneurial structures for disinvested neighborhoods and communities that could plan and implement an array of physical, economic, and human development growth strategies. How broadly or deeply CDCs should invest has been a matter of debate over the decades; as a practice, there has been great variation in how comprehensively they have invested in their communities. In the 1980s and 1990s CDCs became highly focused on housing production as new financial incentives became available. In the 2000s many CDCs refocused on other aspects of community development and community building as they realized that housing alone was not enough to build healthy communities. The neighborhood or place focus of CDCs even came into question as many social-equity challenges came to be seen as shaped by regional systems like housing, transportation, and economic development.

Community development stakeholders built an industry infrastructure with many components. Two major intermediaries, the Local Initiatives Support Corporation and the Enterprise Foundation, emerged in the 1970s and 1980s to provide funding, technical assistance, and policy advocacy. Community development funders also supported leadership and human-capital investments, state and national associations, local funder collaboratives, federal and state policy advocacy, and the national funding collaborative, NCDI, formed in the 1990s. And Community Development Financial Institutions (CDFI) grew up to support CDCs and carry on their work on a broader geographic scale.

Today, however, many experts agree that community development plays many different roles and that the field has not charted a clear vision for moving forward. There are too many CDCs, many of which were ultimately low-performing and non-sustainable as housing producers or developers. There are also a number of highly effective regional housing developers, many of which have lost their community connections. What exists today is a vibrant field of diverse community-based developers doing lots of different things under a variety of names and banners. Some now focus on community planning; others have returned to their community-organizing roots. Still others represent a new generation of partnerships with a focus on economic opportunity and integrating human-capital development.

Why conclude a book about sector-based workforce development with a reflection on community development? One lesson of the community development story is that success does not guarantee future viability. That is, growth in numbers and a community development infrastructure do not guarantee sustainability. Nothing should be taken for granted as fields of practice develop and mature. What is inevitable is that environments change and investors and policy makers adjust their investment strategies to address new challenges. Lack of sufficient public messaging and advocacy about the important role of CDCs and community development made it difficult to sustain community development investments in tough economic times.

A second lesson for the sector field is the need to embrace distributed decision making as a field. Like sector initiatives, CDCs have lacked precise, agreed-on definitions and standards of performance for CDCs. This encouraged a great deal of creative adaptation and variation as community development grew but made future field-building and policy efforts more challenging. What is needed in both fields is a way to assess quality operations without removing decision making about strategy and resource allocation from local operators, who need to respond to emerging needs and changing conditions.

Finally, building a field of practice around the piece of the strategy that attracts large public investment may lead to the creation of a toolkit that is inadequate for addressing a broader array of community-building challenges. In the case of CDCs, the success in developing public policies that unleashed significant resources for housing led the field to focus narrowly on the issue of housing rather than broadly on the issue of community development. Similarly, the availability of resources to support sector-based training, through the federal Perkins loan program, the WIA, Pell grants, and other funding streams, encourages a focus on training programs and credentials and less on building broad and deep industry relationships, creating opportunities for practical work experience, highlighting business leaders with exceptional human-resource practices, and other activities that could enhance the ability of the sector initiative to open economic opportunity to low-income individuals.

Conclusion

Building the sector workforce field over the past thirty years has been a remarkable journey. Sector practitioners are social entrepreneurs who saw the potential for advancing social equity by working closely with business in their local economies. They stuck with their new approach because it showed promise, not because of any specific policy incentive or programmatic funding category. And they found unlikely allies in the business community, philanthropy, and the public sector who saw the need to seed different approaches to get better results. More broadly, the sector field represented a turn of the poverty-alleviation field from consumption or rights strategies to the pragmatic goal of finding niches in the economy to create win-wins for workers or job seekers and businesses. And yet, as the economy has shifted and business profits rise while wages remain flat, it is clear that the niches in which sector strategies can find traction have become narrower, and new and creative thinking will be needed to address today's challenges.

Sector strategies have succeeded at some things that represent profound changes for the workforce-development field. These strategies analyze specific multi-employer demand, learn deeply about the real-time, human-capital needs of industries, train for jobs that exist as defined by business, focus on career-building skills and training, create connections and networks for workers and job seekers, integrate funding streams, and, advocate for better, more efficient public and private policies. Importantly, sector strategies also take the perspective of the worker or potential worker and identify and address systemic barriers that inhibit workers and employers from coming together productively. These barriers may range from hiring practices among employers that exclude some potentially qualified workers, to resource constraints that prevent workers from fully participating in an education opportunity, to transportation policies that make it difficult for workers to get to jobs. This ability to understand the perspective of both the worker and the employer is key to a sector entrepreneur's being able to intervene and find leverage points to create "systems change" that creates opportunity for individuals beyond those directly touched by the initiative.

In many respects, sector partnerships fundamentally involve community organizing of industry and education/community partners for a common set of dual-customer results. And that's the rub. Sector partnerships require flexible funding on a reliable long-term basis to organize industries and partnerships in order to achieve these kinds of results. Resources of this kind are not part of normal public funding formulas for employment and training programs. Yet these resources are the bedrock upon which sector partnerships can flourish, not as one-off training programs but as durable, entrepreneurial capacities of regional economies. Future visions for regional workforce and economic development boards should embrace this challenge.

The sector field was built by many stakeholders over the years but inspired by pathbreaking social entrepreneurs and promising dual-customer results. A sector field containing many voices and capacities now exists, and this industry has propelled further adoption of the sector approach in practice and policy. This book has sought to document this progress, share valuable lessons, chart future directions, and challenge the field to do more and do better. At this economic moment, with rising inequality and tepid economic growth, with businesses looking for skilled workers and many workers unable to find family-supporting careers, with ever-growing economic division and divided politics, the vision of sector work—a vision that brings mutual success for business and workers, that supports families and rebuilds communities—could not be more important. We hope this book stimulates a vibrant set of field-building conversations and investments that will galvanize commitment to build the next generation of sector workforce development. We hope that sector leaders will see their vital importance to their communities and redouble their efforts. We hope that public and philanthropic leaders will recognize the contributions of the sector field to date, and the tremendous potential for this work to engage leaders across America in rebuilding communities and generating shared prosperity.

Notes

1. *Grow Faster Together, or Grow Slowly Apart: How Will America Work in the 21st Century?* Aspen Institute Domestic Strategy Group, David Ellwood, director, 2001. http://www.aspenwsi.org/wordpress/wp-content/uploads/GrowFast.pdf.

2. For a discussion of the impact of poverty on cognitive power and workforce performance, among other issues, see Sendhil Mullainathan and Eldar Shafir, *Scarcity: Why Having Too Little Means So Much* (New York: Times Books, Henry Holt and Company, 2013).

3. Christopher Walker and John Foster-Bey, "Community Development Intermediation and Its Lessons for the Workforce Field," in *Workforce Intermediaries for the Twenty-First Century*, Robert P. Giloth, ed., published in association with the American Assembly (Philadelphia: Temple University Press, 2004).

Appendix

ABOUT THE SPONSORS

About The Aspen Institute

Based in Washington, D.C, the Aspen Institute is an educational and policy studies organization that works to foster leadership based on enduring values and
provide a nonpartisan venue for dealing with critical issues. The Institute's primary home for workforce research and dialogue is the Economic Opportunities
Program (EOP), which identifies and promotes strategies to better the range of
economic opportunities available to low-income Americans. EOP has more than
two decades of work documenting economic advancement strategies in the areas
of workforce development, U.S.-based microenterprise development, and asset
building. Defining and documenting the field of sectoral workforce development
has been an area of focus for EOP since the 1990s, an effort that led to the establishment of EOP's Workforce Strategies Initiative (AspenWSI). Founded by
Maureen Conway, AspenWSI works to identify, evaluate, and promote promising practices and policies that improve access to quality training and open av-
enues to better employment for low-income Americans. For more than a decade,
AspenWSI has helped shape America's workforce development strategies and
practices to enhance outcomes that enable low-income individuals to successfully complete training programs and access quality jobs, and is often credited
as a thought leader in the area of sector strategies for workforce development.

About The Annie E. Casey Foundation

The Annie E. Casey Foundation is a private philanthropy that creates a brighter future for the nation's children by developing solutions to strengthen families, build
paths to economic opportunity and transform struggling communities into safer
and healthier places to live, work and grow. For more than two decades, Casey has
promoted family economic success through a combination of jobs and career development, work supports, and financial coaching and asset-building opportunities. Working closely with business, integrating services and systems, using data to
guide performance improvements, and advocating sensible policies have defined
the core of Casey investments with a diversity of nonprofit partners and public
agencies. Casey has focused these investments on improving economic opportunities for young families, especially those disconnected from work and education.

About The American Assembly

The American Assembly was founded by Dwight D. Eisenhower at Columbia University in 1950 as a national, nonpartisan, public affairs forum. It illuminates issues of national policy through commissioning research, sponsoring meetings, and publishing books, reports and other literature. The Assembly seeks to stimulate discussion and evoke independent conclusions on matters of vital public interest.

AUTHOR BIOGRAPHIES

Chris Benner is an associate professor of Community and Regional Development and chair of the Geography Graduate Group at the University of California, Davis. His research explores the relationships between technological change, regional development, and the structure of economic opportunity, focusing on regional labor markets and the transformation of work and employment patterns. His applied policy work focuses on workforce-development policy; the structure, dynamics, and evaluation of workforce intermediaries; and strategies for promoting regional equity. His recent book, co-authored with Manuel Pastor, *Just Growth: Inclusion and Prosperity in America's Metropolitan Regions*, helps uncover the subtle and detailed processes, policies, and institutional arrangement that might help explain how certain regions around the country have been able to consistently link prosperity and inclusion. He received his Ph.D. in city and regional planning from the University of California, Berkeley.

Earl Buford's career includes seventeen years of experience in workforce development, diversity initiatives, and executive leadership. As president and CEO of the Wisconsin Regional Training Partnership/BIG STEP, Buford has developed strong partnerships with national and statewide businesses, labor unions, government agencies, and nonprofit organizations to develop high-road workforce and economic development efforts. Under Buford's leadership, WRTP/BIG STEP initiated the Center of Excellence, a central clearinghouse for the recruitment, assessment, preparation, and placement of qualified candidates into the construction, utility, and manufacturing labor pools. In the spring of 2004 Buford served on Tom Barrett's mayoral transition team in Milwaukee. Buford also received the 2005 Educator of the Year award from the Daily Reporter and is a past winner of the Wisconsin Apprenticeship Advisory Council Affirmative Action Award, AGC of America Training Craft Award, Marquette University High School Merit Award, and Milwaukee Area Technical College Partner Award. Buford holds a B.A. from the University of Wisconsin–Milwaukee.

Maureen Conway is vice president of the Aspen Institute, executive director of the Economic Opportunities Program (EOP) and director of the Workforce Strategies Initiative (WSI). Conway has led workforce research at the Aspen Institute since 1999. As WSI director, she leads a team of researchers and consultants in a variety of initiatives to identify and advance strategies that help low-income Americans gain ground in today's labor market. Under her guidance, WSI has grown and expanded the range of its activities to support the field of sectoral employment development. Her vision has led WSI to take on new initiatives that mirror the growth and expansion of the sector approach nationally, including projects that seek to assess the value of sector work to business partners, to shed light on the ways in which sector programs support constituents in their struggles to overcome a range of personal and systemic barriers, to create a framework for and document approaches to systems change, to understand the potential for greater collaboration among community colleges and community-based organizations, and much more. Her previous experience includes consulting work on issues of social exclusion and community development practice for the Organization for Economic Cooperation and Development in Paris and work for the U.S. Peace Corps, where she advised on the design, management, and monitoring and evaluation of the organization's economic-development programs in Eastern Europe and the former Soviet Union. Conway is the author of numerous publications on industry-specific workforce development, including case studies, policy briefs, and research reports. She also has presented findings from her research at various national and regional conferences. Conway holds an M.B.A. from Columbia University, a master's degree in regional planning from the University of North Carolina, and a B.A. in economics and mathematics from Holy Cross College.

Fred Dedrick is the executive director of the National Fund for Workforce Solutions, a public/private initiative investing in the career advancement of low-wage workers by addressing the skill needs of employers. The National Fund supports regional workforce funder collaboratives throughout the United States that organize and develop sectoral industry partnerships. Previously Dedrick served as Pennsylvania's deputy secretary for workforce development, in which capacity he was responsible for overseeing the Commonwealth's workforce-development programs. He was a key leader in developing Pennsylvania's nationally recognized Industry Partnership initiative, aimed at creating employer/worker consortia in the state's targeted industry clusters. Prior to becoming deputy secretary, Dedrick was executive director of the Pennsylvania Workforce Investment Board, where he organized the Pennsylvania Center for Health Careers, designed the state's first Performance Management Plan for workforce programs, and developed the High Performance Standards for local workforce investment boards. Earlier in his career, Dedrick was director of workforce development for the Reinvestment Fund (TRF), where he served as president of the Regional Workforce Partnership. Prior to joining TRF, he was director of economic development for Greater Philadelphia First, a regional business leadership organization. Dedrick has a bachelor's degree from the University of Notre Dame and an M.P.A. from Princeton University's Woodrow Wilson School.

Laura Dresser is associate director of the Center on Wisconsin Strategy. A labor economist and expert on low-wage work and workforce-development systems, she has both written about ways to build stronger labor-market systems and worked extensively with labor, business, and community leaders in building them. Dresser has written widely on race and gender inequality and labor-market reform. She is most recently co-editor of *The Gloves-Off Economy: Workplace Standards at the Bottom of America's Labor Market*. She has a master of social work degree and a Ph.D. from the University of Michigan and a bachelor's degree from Rice University.

Barbara Dyer is president and CEO of the Hitachi Foundation, Corporate Social Responsibility advisor and member of the Hitachi Chief Executives group, and senior lecturer at MIT's Sloan School of Management. The Hitachi Foundation, established in 1985, is an expression of Hitachi's commitment to global corporate citizenship. Dyer has shaped the foundation's focus on the role of business in society with an emphasis at the intersection of people and profit. Under her leadership the foundation has been an influential force in the corporate social responsibility field and has been instrumental in shaping two major national collaborative philanthropic initiatives: Jobs to Careers, with the Robert Wood Johnson Foundation and the United States Department of Labor; and the National Fund for Workforce Solutions, initially with the Ford and Annie E. Casey foundations. Dyer is a trustee of Clark University and has served as a member the American University School of Public Affairs Dean's Advisory Council. She serves as a member of the Points of Light/Hands-On Network Corporate Advisory Council, was a member of the Council on Foundations Corporate Committee, and was an inaugural member of the More for Mission Leadership Committee. Dyer had an extensive career in public policy as co-founder of the National Academy of Public Administration's Alliance for Redesigning Government, deputy executive director/director of research with the National Governors Association's Council of Governors' Policy Advisors, special assistant to the Secretary of the United States Department of the Interior, and deputy executive director of the Western Regional Office of the Council of State Governments.

Denise G. Fairchild is the inaugural president of Emerald Cities Collaborative (ECC), a national nonprofit organization based in Washington, D.C., with affiliates in major urban centers across the United States. She was recruited in 2010 to launch ECC, a coalition of labor, business, and community-based organizations organized to accelerate the growth and distributive benefits of the emerging green economy. Fairchild has dedicated more than thirty years to strengthening housing, jobs, businesses, and economic opportunities for low-income residents and communities of color, domestically and internationally. In 1995 she founded and directed the Community and Economic Development Department at Los Angeles Trade-Technical College, as well as an affiliated nonprofit community development research and technical assistance organization, CDTech. She helped launch the Regional Economic Development Institute, an initiative of Los Angeles Trade-Technical College to provide inner-city residents with career and technical education for high-growth, high-demand jobs in the Los Angeles region, with a focus on the green economy. From 1989 to 1994 Fairchild directed the Los Angeles office of the Local Initiatives Support Corporation and is credited with raising more than $100 million in equity, grants, and loans for community-based housing and commercial development projects and, generally, with building the nonprofit housing and community development industry in the Los Angeles region. Her civic and political appointments have included the California Commission on Regionalism, the California Economic Strategy Panel, the California Local Economic Development Association, the Urban Land Institute National Inner City Advisor, the Coalition for Women's Economic Development, and the Los Angeles Environmental Quality Board. She also served as Mayor Antonio Villaraigosa's special advisor for South Los Angeles investments.

Marcie W. M. Foster is a policy analyst for Workforce Development in the Center for Postsecondary and Economic Success within the Center for Law and Social Policy (CLASP). Her work is focused on analyzing and advocating for federal higher-education policies that help underprepared and low-income adults and youth access and succeed in college. Foster also advocates for federal adult-education policies that help low-skilled learners prepare for career and economic success and provides technical assistance to states designing career-pathway and bridge programs for low-skilled adults. In addition to her role at CLASP, she is a member of the Board of Directors and chair of the public-policy committee of the National Coalition for Literacy and a member of the National Board of Advisors for the Goodling Institute for Research in Family Literacy. Prior to joining CLASP, she worked at GMMB, where she provided strategic communications support to a variety of organizations in higher education, environmental issues, and public health. She also served as an intern at the Center for Economic and Policy Research, where she conducted research for a three-year project to improve the availability of work supports for low-income families. Foster graduated from the University of Virginia with a bachelor's degree in American politics and earned a master of public policy degree from George Mason University. She was awarded a 2012–2013 fellowship with the Bryce Harlow Foundation for excellence in federal advocacy.

Evelyn Ganzglass is a senior fellow at the Center for Law and Social Policy's (CLASP) national and state advocacy and technical-assistance efforts related to post-secondary and adult education and workforce investment policy. Under her leadership, CLASP created its Center for Postsecondary and Economic Success to advocate for better policies, more investment, and heightened political will to increase the number of low-income adults and disadvantaged youth who earn post-secondary credentials. Much of her career has been devoted to strengthening alignment and collaboration across education and workforce-development delivery systems, and her recent work has focused on career pathways and competency-based credentials. She widely publishes and presents on these topics. Prior to joining CLASP, she directed the Global Workforce in Transition project, a U.S. Agency for International Development global initiative to help developing and transition countries respond to changing economic needs. Before that, Ganzglass worked for the National Governors Association (NGA) for more than twenty years. From 1991 to 2002 she directed employment and social-services policy studies at the NGA Center for Best Practices, where she led the association's research and technical-assistance activities focused on promoting effective state practices and policy innovation related to workforce development, youth development, social services, welfare reform, criminal justice, and performance management. Ganzglass started her career at the U.S. Department of Labor and served as a Peace Corps volunteer in Somalia.

Robert P. Giloth is vice president of the Center for Community and Economic Opportunity at the Annie E. Casey Foundation, a private philanthropy dedicated to developing solutions to build a brighter future for kids, families and communities in the United States. He is responsible for planning and integrating economic opportunity and place-based investments, including the foundation's workforce-development agenda. Prior to joining the foundation in December 1993, Giloth managed community development corporations in Baltimore and Chicago and was deputy commissioner of Economic Development under Chicago mayor Harold Washington. He has a Ph.D. in city and regional planning from Cornell University. He has edited *Jobs and Economic Development: Strategies and Practice; Workforce Intermediaries for the Twenty-First Century; Workforce Development Politics: Civic Capacity and Performance; Economic Development in American Cities: The Pursuit of an Equity Agenda*; and *Mistakes to Success: Learning and Adapting When Things Go Wrong*. He has also written *Nonprofit Leadership: Life Lessons from an Enterprising Practitioner*.

Matt Helmer joined the Aspen Institute's Workforce Strategies Initiative (AspenWSI) in 2009. He manages and assists the AspenWSI team with a variety of projects conducting quantitative and qualitative research, planning site visits, conducting focus groups, writing research publications and program profiles, and facilitating meetings and webinars. Matt has helped with planning and coordinating high-profile roundtable discussions as part of the Reinventing Low-Wage Work and Working in America conversation series. He has conducted quantitative analysis of students' education and employment outcomes for nonprofit–community college partnerships and examined the challenges adult learners face on today's community college campus as part of the Courses to Employment project. Matt has assisted Goodwill Industries International with assessing the impact of Goodwill–community college partnerships and helped facilitate a national learning community through the Goodwill C4 project. With funding from the Annie E. Casey Foundation, Matt has been deeply involved in looking at the construction sector, including the role pre-apprenticeship programs play in the industry and the challenges construction apprentices experience on the job and in the classroom. He also manages and facilitates meetings for the Sector Skills Academy and the Greater Seattle Sector Skills Academy, yearlong fellowship programs for workforce-development leaders. Prior to joining Aspen, Matt worked in Seattle with Neighborhood House, a community-based organization that collaborated with the Seattle Jobs Initiative and Airport Jobs to help low-income individuals obtain employment. Matt has a master's degree in public administration from the Daniel J. Evans School of Public Affairs at the University of Washington and a master's degree in Teaching English to Speakers of Other Languages. He has worked in the ESL and special-education fields for a number of years, leading several large curriculum-development projects and serving as a teacher and teacher trainer. Matt served as a Senior English Language Fellow at the University of Damascus in Syria on a U.S. State Department grant, has instructed visiting scholars from Afghanistan in research and academic writing skills, and worked as a Peace Corps volunteer in the Kingdom of Tonga.

Saru Jayaraman is the co-founder and co-director of the Restaurant Opportunities Centers United (ROC) and Director of the Food Labor Research Center at University of California, Berkeley. After 9/11, together with displaced World Trade Center workers, she co-founded ROC in New York, which has organized restaurant workers to win workplace-justice campaigns, conduct research and policy work, partner with responsible restaurants, and launch cooperatively owned restaurants. ROC now has ten thousand members in twenty-six cities nationwide. The story of her and her co-founder's work founding ROC has been chronicled in the book *The Accidental American*. Jayaraman co-edited *The New Urban Immigrant Workforce* (M.E. Sharpe, 2005). She is a graduate of Yale Law School and the Harvard Kennedy School of Government. She was profiled in the "Public Lives" section of *The New York Times* in 2005, and was named one of Crain's "40 Under 40" in 2008 and one of *New York Magazine*'s "Influentials" of New York City in 2006. She authored *Behind the Kitchen Door* (Cornell University Press, 2013), a national best seller, and has made several national television appearances.

Patricia Jenny is acting vice president for grants and program director, Community Development and Environment, managing environment and workforce-development grants programs, at the New York Community Trust, New York City's community foundation. The environment program includes a national focus, supporting efforts across the country to address climate change, environmental health, and habitat protection. Its New York City environment grants target urban environmental issues, including solid waste management, development of open space and parks, waterfront and brownfield reclamation, and air pollutants and other toxins. Jenny leads a regional funders' collaborative promoting sustainable transportation policies and transportation-oriented development in the metropolitan area. She also manages grant making on citywide employment issues, as well as a philanthropic collaborative focused on improving the system of workforce services for New York City job seekers. From 1993 to 2001 Jenny served as the director of the Neighborhood Strategies Project, a multi-year effort to expand economic opportunities for residents of Washington Heights, Mott Haven in the Bronx, and Williamsburg in Brooklyn. Jenny also served as a senior program officer at the Trust from 1983 to 1992, responsible for the Community Development and Environment grant programs. Prior to that, she worked as a consultant in community-development public policy in California and Washington, D.C. She holds a master's in regional planning from the University of North Carolina, Chapel Hill, and a bachelor's degree in history from Brown University. Jenny serves on the board of the Environmental Grantmakers Association and Health and Environmental Funders Network, is a director emeritus of Cause Effective in New York City, and was a founding board member of the Montclair Economic Development Corporation in New Jersey.

Richard Kazis is senior vice president of Jobs for the Future (JFF), where he leads its policy and advocacy initiatives. Since he joined JFF in the early 1990s, his areas of focus have included state and institutional strategies for improving outcomes for low-income community college students; policies to promote low-wage worker advancement; state policies to promote college and career readiness for struggling students; the emerging role of labor-market intermediaries in workforce development; and school-to-career models and policy. His recent publications include *Stepping Up for Community Colleges* (Boston Foundation, 2013), *Design Principles for a Performance-Based Funding System* (JFF, 2012), and *Community College Performance and Regional Recovery: Strategies for State Action* (Brookings Institution, 2011). Kazis has taught at an alternative high school for returning dropouts. He has also helped organize fast-food workers, supervised a Neighborhood Youth Corps program, managed a cooperative urban food production wholesaler, supported labor-environmental jobs coalitions, and studied experiential learning for new immigrants in Israel. He serves on the board of the Institute for College Access and Success. Kazis is a graduate of Harvard College and the Massachusetts Institute of Technology.

Christopher T. King directs the Ray Marshall Center for the Study of Human Resources and is a lecturer at the University of Texas at Austin's Lyndon B. Johnson School of Public Affairs. He is a labor economist with decades of experience conducting policy and program analysis, designing programs, evaluating impacts, and measuring the benefits and costs of education, employment, and training interventions. In early 2012 the Aspen Institute selected him as one of twenty leaders in its inaugural class of Ascend Fellows, working on two-generation antipoverty strategies. He is co-directing a team analyzing the implementation and impacts of a sectoral jobs strategy for the parents of Tulsa Head Start/Early Head Start children, working with a multidisciplinary team from Northwestern, Columbia, and New York universities. King was assistant professor of economics at the University of Utah (1973–1976), an economist with the U.S. Secretary of Labor (1976–1980), and director of Research, Demonstration, and Evaluation for job training in Texas (1983–1985). He has a B.A. in economics from the University of Texas at Austin and an M.A. and Ph.D. in economics from Michigan State University.

Marianne Krismer is the national director of the Health Professions Pathway Consortium at Cincinnati State Technical and Community College. Krismer's career at Cincinnati State spans more than thirty-five years, serving as faculty, program chair, associate dean, and dean in the health and public safety professions. She is now directing a $19.6 million Department of Labor Trade Assistance Act Community College Career Training (TAACCCT) Grant for nine community colleges in five states, with a focus on transforming health-education pathways to employment in health care. Krismer has been a community leader and innovator in health and public safety education. She is one of the founders of the Health Careers Collaborative of Greater Cincinnati, a college-access program for entry-level health care workers moving into nursing and allied health careers. She has led efforts to secure several governmental and private grants to support education and access for "at promise" students. Her most recent accomplishments include implementation of the Bridge to Employment Program, sponsored by the Johnson and Johnson Foundation, and acquisition and oversight of three Department of Labor grants in excess of $26 million. These funds have resulted in improvements in the health care workforce for the greater Cincinnati community. Krismer has been a guest speaker for such groups as the Conference Board in New York City, the American National Standards Institute, and the Workforce Council in Seattle. She is a registered dietitian and earned her Ph.D. in education from the University of Cincinnati in 2005.

Loh-Sze Leung is the executive director of SkillWorks: Partners for a Productive Workforce, a $25 million public-private investment partnership that helps residents of greater Boston move to family-sustaining jobs and helps employers find and retain skilled employees. Since 2005 she has led the initiative's implementation and expansion. She has also helped SkillWorks gain national recognition for its work to strengthen workforce systems and investments in Massachusetts, including its leadership role in securing more than $60 million in increased state investments in job training and adult education. Prior to SkillWorks, Leung was the Assistant Executive Director of the Los Angeles Youth Opportunity Movement, a federally funded youth development and employment program, and Development Manager for the Los Angeles Regional Foodbank. Leung serves on the Massachusetts Governor's Advisory Council on Refugees and Immigrants; the National Fund for Workforce Solutions' Partners Council; the Boston Private Industry Council's workforce-development committee; the advisory board of the Massachusetts Workforce Competitiveness Trust Fund; the National Skills Coalition's leadership council; and the board of the Brookline Community Foundation. She is a graduate of Harvard-Radcliffe College and the UCLA School of Public Affairs.

Sheila Maguire has almost thirty years of experience in the workforce-development field. Upon coming to the United States in 1984, Maguire worked for Essex County College, which served downtown Newark, N.J., where she placed dislocated workers, welfare recipients, people returning from prison, and young adults in employment. While there, Maguire pioneered the development of sector-specific certificate programs that combined credit and noncredit courses providing skills for both immediate employment and the start of a college career. For thirteen years Maguire served as a senior staff person at Public/Private Ventures (P/PV), where she created training curriculum for frontline job-development staff, developed and implemented technical-assistance projects to help New York City non-profits and public-sector workforce agencies develop evidence-based approaches to workforce development, oversaw the development of an innovative approach to benchmarking performance in the workforce-development field, and served on the evaluation team for an impact study of three sector employment programs. While at P/PV, Maguire also led an initiative to launch social purpose staffing agencies in the Gulf Coast and managed a process evaluation of the California Community Colleges' effort to develop Career Advancement Academies. Maguire has been offering consulting services since March 2012. Her clients include the Aspen Institute's Workforce Strategies Initiative, the Training, Inc. National Association, the Southwest Center for Economic Integrity, the CUNY Graduate Center's Labor Market Information Services, and JobsFirstNYC. Before coming to the United States, Maguire volunteered in community-development projects on the Isle of Dogs in London, the Abruzzi region of Italy, and communities in Maharashtra and Calcutta, India. Maguire serves on the board of the National Skills Coalition, as an advisor to the New York City Labor Market Information Service, and as an ambassador for her hometown of Coventry in the United Kingdom. She has written or co-authored various publications. She holds a bachelor's degree in adult learning from the Gallatin Division at New York University and a master's in organizational development from American University.

Abigail Newcomer is an associate director at Arabella Advisors, a firm that helps philanthropists and investors achieve greater good with their resources. She is responsible for providing strategy, evaluation, and program implementation consulting services to a variety of philanthropic clients. Prior to joining Arabella, Newcomer served as a policy analyst on the workforce-development team at the Center for Law and Social Policy. Her work focused on coordination among public income and work-supports programs and improving federal and state policies to help nontraditional and low-income college students access the financial supports they need to complete degrees and credentials. Newcomer also managed Benefits Access for College Completion, an initiative to assist community colleges in connecting students to resources to finance their education. Her prior professional experience includes working for state- and city-level elected officials and managing a statewide financial-literacy program in Massachusetts. In this role, she led an effort to train volunteers and community organization staff to provide sound financial information to those disconnected from the economic mainstream. Newcomer holds a master of public policy degree from the University of Michigan, a graduate certificate in women in politics and public policy from the University of Massachusetts, and a bachelor's degree in sociology from Bates College. She also volunteers as a tax preparer in her community.

Paul Osterman is the NTU professor of Human Resources and Management at the M.I.T. Sloan School of Management. His most recent books include *Economy in Society* (MIT Press, 2013), *Good Jobs America: Making Work Better for Everyone* (Russell Sage, 2011), *The Truth About Middle Managers: Who They Are, How They Work, Why They Matter* (Harvard Business School Press, 2008), and *Gathering Power: The Future of Progressive Politics in America* (Beacon Press, 2003). He has written numerous academic journal articles and policy issue papers on such topics as the organization of work within firms, labor-market policy, and economic development. Osterman has been a senior administrator of job-training programs for the Commonwealth of Massachusetts and consulted widely for firms, government agencies, foundations, community groups, and public interest organizations. He received his Ph.D. in economics from M.I.T.

Manuel Pastor is srofessor of Sociology and American Studies and Ethnicity at the University of Southern California. Director of USC's Program for Environmental and Regional Equity and co-director of USC's Center for the Study of Immigrant Integration, he holds an economics Ph.D. from the University of Massachusetts, Amherst. His most recent book, co-authored with Chris Benner, *Just Growth: Inclusion and Prosperity in America's Metropolitan Regions* (Routledge, 2012), argues that growth and equity can and should be linked, offering a new path for a U.S. economy seeking to recover from economic crisis and distributional distress. Recent other books include *Uncommon Common Ground: Race and America's Future* (W.W. Norton, 2010; co-authored with Angela Glover Blackwell and Stewart Kwoh) and *This Could Be the Start of Something Big: How Social Movements for Regional Equity Are Transforming Metropolitan America* (Cornell University Press, 2009; co-authored with Chris Benner and Martha Matsuoka).

Mark Popovich is a senior program officer at the Hitachi Foundation. He participated in the initial discussions that culminated in the launch of the National Fund for Workforce Solutions and served on the Investor's Committee and the Evaluation Subcommittee through 2012. He also helped spearhead the Jobs to Careers: Transforming the Frontlines of Health Care Initiative with the Robert Wood Johnson Foundation. Popovich works with a Hitachi Foundation team to discover and spread adoption of employer practices that generate high returns for the businesses and earnings gains and career advancement for lower-wage workers. Before entering the philanthropic sector more than a decade ago, he had a long career in public policy research and development, technical assistance, and leadership development across a wide range of issues and focused primarily on state governments and governors.

Marlene Seltzer has served as president and CEO of Jobs for the Future (JFF) since 2004. With the goal of helping more Americans obtain the skills they need to succeed in today's economy, JFF has grown since its founding in 1984 to become one of the nation's leading research and policy development organizations focused on education and workforce strategies. A nationally recognized thought leader, Seltzer is a frequent consultant and speaker on systemic reforms in secondary and post-secondary education and the ability of the labor market to serve low-income workers and employers, as well as local and state economies. Her commentaries and other writings help the nation think in new ways about policy and program delivery at all levels of government. Before joining JFF in 1996, Seltzer held a number of prominent positions in nonprofit management, government, and the workforce-development field. From 1987 to 1989 she was commissioner of the Massachusetts Department of Employment and Training, after serving as deputy commissioner for four years. She administered the Commonwealth's $1 billion federal- and state-funded employment and training programs, including ET Choices, a $40 million comprehensive state welfare-to-work effort. As president of Seltzer Associates, a for-profit consulting firm, she provided policy development assistance to the U.S. Department of Labor on its workforce-development initiatives. She also served as co-founder and president of Employment Resources, Inc., a nonprofit, community-based workforce-development organization. Seltzer serves on the board of the Rural Policy Research Institute, which provides unbiased analysis and information on the challenges, needs, and opportunities facing rural America. She holds a bachelor's degree in urban economics and American history from American University, a master's degree in labor economics from Northeastern University, and a certificate from the Harvard University Employment and Training Institute.

Andy Van Kleunen is executive director of the National Skills Coalition, which he founded in 1998 in collaboration with leaders from the workforce-development and philanthropic communities. He has led the coalition to become a nationally recognized voice on behalf of its member stakeholders—business leaders, labor leaders, community colleges, community-based organizations, and leaders from the public workforce system—who have come together to advocate for an America that grows its economy by investing in its people. He is a recognized expert on state and federal workforce policy issues and is regularly invited to advise Congress, the federal government, and state agencies. He is also the author of numerous pieces in the areas of workforce policy, health care policy, and urban community development. Prior to founding the coalition, Van Kleunen was Director of Workforce Policy for the national Paraprofessional Healthcare Institute, where he worked with employers, unions, and client advocates to improve job quality and training for low-wage workers within the nation's long-term care sector. He spent more than fourteen years in community organizing and development efforts within several of New York City's low-income and working-class neighborhoods. He holds a master's degree in urban sociology from the Graduate Faculty at the New School for Social Research, and a bachelor's degree in political science and honors studies from Villanova University.

Orson Watson is a Boston-based philanthropic advisor specializing in economic and workforce development. He is the current advisor for Community Revitalization Programs at the Garfield Foundation and is on the board of the Funders Network for Smart Growth and Livable Communities. From 1999 to 2002 Watson was Vice President for Research and Strategy at Initiative for a Competitive Inner City (ICIC) where he was instrumental in the design and implementation of the *Pioneering Workforce Practices of Inner City Companies: Enhancing the Skills and Income Capacity of the Working Poor* study. He also managed the Partnership for Employee-Employer Responsive Systems, a Ford Foundation–sponsored peer network investigating the demand-side role of labor-market intermediaries, and was a discussion leader of the 102nd American Assembly on *Advancing Workers, Business and Economic Growth*. Prior to joining ICIC, Watson was a Fellow at the Batten Center for Entrepreneurial Leadership at the Darden School of Business Administration and worked for the Multilateral Investment Guarantee Agency, the Overseas Private Investment Corporation, and Marsh and McLennan in Saudi Arabia. A native of New York City, Orson holds an A.B. from Vassar College, and an M.A. and Ph.D. in international political economy from the University of Virginia.

ACRONYMS

(ABE)	Adult Basic Education
(ACA)	Affordable Care Act
(AQCP)	Alliance for Quality Career Pathways
(ARRA)	American Recovery and Reinvestment Act
(ASTD)	American Society for Training and Development
(ASCE)	American Society of Civil Engineers
(AUR)	Apprenticeship Utilization Requirement
(ABC)	Associated Builders and Contractors
(BACC)	Benefits Access for College Completion
(BACH)	The Baltimore Alliance for Careers in Healthcare
(BTC)	Business and Technology Campus
(BLU)	Business Leaders United
(CEO)	Center for Economic Opportunity
(CET)	Center for Employment Training
(COE)	Center of Excellence for Skilled Trades and Industries
(COWS)	Center on Wisconsin Strategy
(CHOW)	COLORS Hospitality Opportunities for Workers
(CBA)	Community Benefits Agreements
(CDC)	Community Development Corporations
(CDD)	Community Development Department
(CWA)	Community Workforce Agreements
(CBO)	Community-based organizations
(CHCA)	Cooperative Home Care Associates
(CNC)	Computer Numerical Control
(CSW)	Corporation for a Skilled Workforce
(C2E)	Courses 2 Employment
(CORI)	Criminal Offender Record Information
(ETPL)	Eligible Training Providers List
(ECC)	Emerald Cities Collaborative
(ECCLI)	Extended Care Career Ladder Initiative
(ESOL)	English for Speakers of Other Languages
(ELMS)	Entry-level manufacturing skills training package
(FPI)	Fiscal Policy Institute
(FCCJ)	Florida Community College at Jacksonville

(FTCC)	Forsyth Technical Community College
(GAO)	Government Accountability Office
(GCHC)	Greater Cincinnati Health Council
(GCWN)	Greater Cincinnati Workforce Network
(GROW)	Growing Regional Opportunity for the Workforce
(HCC)	Health Careers Collaborative
(HELP)	Health Education Labor and Pensions
(HPOG)	Health Professions Opportunity Grant
(HGJTI)	High Growth Job Training Initiative
(I-BEST)	Integrated Basic Education Skills Training
(ICCB)	Illinois Community College Board
(ITA)	Individual Training Accounts
(IAF)	Industrial Areas Foundation
(IP)	Industry Partnerships
(ISP)	Industry Skills Panel
(IT)	Information technology
(ISIS)	Innovative Strategies for Increasing Self-Sufficiency
(IHI)	Institute for Healthcare Improvement
(IRR)	Internal rate of return
(JCCI)	Jacksonville Community Council, Inc.
(JOTF)	Job Opportunities Task Force
(JTPA)	Job Training Partnership Act
(JFF)	Jobs for the Future
(JATC)	Joint apprenticeship and training committee
(KCTCS)	Kentucky Community & Technical College System
(KCC)	Kingsborough Community College
(LISC)	Local Initiatives Support Corporation
(LARCA)	Los Angeles Reconnections Career Academy
(MPO)	Metropolitan planning organizations
(MARC)	Mid-America Regional Council
(MJI)	Milwaukee Jobs Initiative
(MACED)	Mountain Association for Community Economic Development
(MC3)	Multi-Craft Core Curriculum
(NEWWS)	National Evaluation of Welfare-to-Work Strategies

(NFWS) National Fund for Workforce Solutions

(NGA) National Governors Association

(NNSP) National Network of Sector Partners

(NRA) National Restaurant Association

(NSC) National Skills Coalition

(NYACH) New York Alliance for Careers in Healthcare

(NYCETC) New York City Employment and Training Coalition

(NYCLMIS) New York City Labor Market Information Service

(NYSBS) NYC Department of Small Business Services

(OECD) Organzation for Economic Cooperation and Development

(OJT) On-the-job training

(OICs) Opportunity Industrial Centers

(PHI) Paraprofessional Healthcare Institute

(PCW) Partners for a Competitive Workforce

(PICO) People Improving Communities through Organizing

(PLA) Prior Learning Assessment

(PIC) Private Industry Council

(PLA) Project Labor Agreement

(PACE) Property Assessed Clean Energy

(P/PV) Public/Private Ventures

(RISE) Regional Industry Skills Education

(RTI) Related technical instruction

(RFP) Request for Proposal

(ROC) Restaurant Opportunities Centers United

(ROI) Return-on-investment

(SAA) State Apprenticeship Agencies

(SAWDC) Southwest Alabama Workforce Development Council

(SECTORS) Strengthening Employee Clusters to Organize Regional Success

(SEIS) Sectoral Employment Impact Study

(SEIU) Service Employees International Union

(SIF) Social Innovation Fund

(SNAP-ET) Supplemental Nutrition Assistance Program/Employment and Training

(SSP) Sector Strategies Practicum

(TANF) Temporary Assistance for Needy Families

(TAACCCT) The Trade Adjustment Assistance Community College and Career Training

(DOL) U.S. Department of Labor

(OA) U.S. Department of Labor's Office of Apprenticeship

(ETA) U.S. Department of Labor Employment and Training Administration

(VIDA) Valley Initiative for Development and Advancement

(WRTP) Wisconsin Regional Training Partnership

(WCTF) Workforce Competitiveness Trust Fund

(WIF) Workforce Innovation Fund

(WIRED) Workforce Innovation in Regional Economic Development

(WIA) Workforce Investment Act

(WIBs) Workforce Investment Boards

(WPTI) Workforce Professional Training Institute

(WSG) Workforce Solutions Group

Index

Made in the USA
Monee, IL
05 March 2021